DATE DUE

HIGHSMITH #45231

D1295366

THE DAMNATION OF HAROLD FREDERIC

The Damnation *of* Harold Frederic

His Lives and Works

Bridget Bennett

Syracuse University Press

First Edition 1997
97 98 99 00 01 02   1 2 3 4 5 6

Permission to quote from the following sources is gratefully acknowledged: Harold Frederic Edition, Department of English, University of Nebraska, Lincoln; *The Correspondence of Harold Frederic*, edited by George E. Fortenberry, Stanton Garner, and Robert H. Woodward, University of Nebraska Press, copyright © 1977 by the University of Nebraska Press; Stephen and Cora Crane Papers, Rare Book and Manuscript Library, Columbia University. Finally, I am especially grateful to the staff of the Library of Congress who were tireless with their time and assistance during my research of this book.

Library of Congress Cataloging-in-Publication Data
Bennett, Bridget.
The damnation of Harold Frederic : his lives and works / Bridget
Bennett.—1st ed.
p. cm.
Includes bibliographical references and index.
ISBN 0-8156-0390-8 (alk. paper)
1. Frederic, Harold, 1856–1898.   2. Authors, American—19th
century—Biography.   I. Title.
PS1708.B46   1996
813'.4—dc20
[B]   96-32953

For Duncan and Josephine Bennett . . .
and, inevitably, for Sanju Velani, too

BRIDGET BENNETT is a lecturer in the Department of English and Comparative Literary Studies at the University of Warwick, England, and editor of *Ripples of Dissent: Women's Stories of Marriage from the 1890s.*

Such conflicts and clashings between two hostile inner selves have a part in the personal history of each of us.

—HAROLD FREDERIC

Contents

Illustrations

Acknowledgments

Acknowledgements require tact, space, and a good memory. So many people have contributed to this book in such a variety of ways that I cannot acknowledge my debts as fully or as graciously as I might. I owe a great deal to a good many and I certainly shall not forget, but I will keep my thanks here brief, and alphabetical.

Sincere thanks then to Philip Bean; to Duncan and to Josephine Bennett and to the rest of my family, for everything; to Frank Bergmann, for perceptive reading and sound advice; to Bob Bergstrom, for letting me camp out in his office for a week while I ransacked the files of the Harold Frederic Edition, and to his colleagues in the English Department at the University of Nebraska, Lincoln, who made me so welcome; to Mike Bott, of the University of Reading Library, for scouring through the Chatto and Windus archives in record time; to Patty Burchard, of the Utica College Library; to Lucy Dale; to Hugh Haughton; to Robin Hood; to Norm Hostetler, who first invited me to Nebraska and made the visit so easy and worthwhile; to David Howard I owe particular thanks for first introducing me to Frederic, thank you; to Stanton Garner; to Sally Green, who read very early drafts and gave very wise advice; to the dextrous and patient Emma James; to Hermione Lee, who read it all more times than most and was enthusiastic and perceptive in equal measure, thank you; to John Lucas, who read an earlier version and (wisely) counseled irreverence; to Cynthia Maude-Gembler; to Robert Myers; to Douglas Preston of the Oneida Historical Society, who spent a whole afternoon answering questions and filling in gaps, with no advance warning; to Jo Poole; to Fiona Shaw, for advice and friendship; to Joanne Shattock; to Sanju Velani (where should I begin—or end?); to Reverend and Mrs. Vonberg of The Vicarage, Kenley, for tea and the guided tour. I should also particularly like to thank my colleagues at Warwick, past and present, who have helped and encouraged me throughout the last few years, especially Liz Cameron; Richard Canning (for the book); Kate Chedgzoy; Mike Davies; Helen Dennis; Gill Frith; Ed Gallafent (thanks for the books, too); Anne Janowitz; Peter Larkin; John Stokes, who read the lot and offered invaluable suggestions;

Jeremy Treglown; Helen Taylor; and Sue Wiseman. The students who take my turn-of-the-century option deserve a special mention for weekly doses of enthusiasm that helped immeasurably in the final stages of this work.

Thanks, too, must go to the staff of the libraries I have worked in: the British Library, both in London (particularly Elizabeth James) and in the distribution center, Boston Spa; the Brotherton Library at Leeds University; Colindale Newspaper Library; the Rare Book and Manuscript Library at the Butler Library, Columbia University; the Library of Congress; the New York Public Library; the New York State Library; the University of Warwick Library; the J.B. Morrell Library at the University of York. I would particularly like to thank the staff of the data entry unit in the Computer Services Department at the University of Warwick, both for technical expertise and for therapy, who rescanned the entire book twice after my computer decided that it no longer liked it. This book could not have been written without financial assistance from a number of institutions. I would like to thank the Leavis Fund at the English Department, University of York; the British Academy; and the Research and Innovations Fund at the University of Warwick for generous grants.

Notes on Texts

Seth's Brother's Wife: A Tale of Northern New York (1887).
January 1887. Begins run in *Scribner's Magazine*.
1887. Published by Charles Scribner's Sons, New York, and Chatto and
  Windus, London.

In the Valley (1890).
September 1889. Begins run in *Scribner's Magazine*.
1890. Published by Charles Scribner's Sons, New York, and William Heinemann, London.

The Lawton Girl (1890).
October 1889. Frederic receives letter from Harper and Brothers regret-
  ting that they cannot serialize the novel in *Harper's Magazine*.
1890. Published by Charles Scribner's Sons, New York, and Chatto and
  Windus, London.

*The Young Emperor William II of Germany: A Study of Character Development on
  a Throne* (1891).
June 1890. Begins run in *New York Times* as "An Empire's Young Chief."
1891. Published by G. P. Putnam's Sons, New York, and T. Fisher Unwin,
  London.

The New Exodus: A Story of Israel in Russia (1892).
September 1891. Begins run in *New York Times* as "An Indictment of Russia."
1892. Published by G. P. Putnam's Sons, New York, and William Heinemann, London.

The Return of The O'Mahony (1892).
April 1892. Begins run in *New York Ledger.*
1892. Published by Robert Bonner's Sons, New York.
1893. Published by William Heinemann, London.

"The Copperhead" (1893).

July 1893. Begins run in *Scribner's Magazine.*

1893. Published by Charles Scribner's Sons, New York.

1894. Published with "My Aunt Susan," "The Eve of the Fourth," and "The War Widow" in *The Copperhead and Other Stories of the North During the Civil War* by William Heinemann, London.

"Marsena" (1894).

April 1894. Begins run in *New York Times.*

1894. Published with "My Aunt Susan," "The Eve of the Fourth," and "The War Widow" in *Marsena and Other Stories of the Wartime* by Charles Scribner's Sons, New York.

Mrs. Albert Grundy: Observations in Philistia (1896).

February 1892. Begins run in *National Observer* as "Observations in Philistia."

April 1896. Published by John Lane, London, and The Merriam Co., New York, as *Mrs. Albert Grundy: Observations in Philistia.*

The Damnation of Theron Ware or Illumination (1896).

June 1895. Charles Scribner's Sons cable Frederic to say that serialization of the novel is impossible.

July 1895. Frederic offers *The Damnation of Theron Ware* to Stone and Kimball. Letters are exchanged between Frederic and both publishing houses until December. Charles Scribner's Sons agree to allow Stone and Kimball to take the book off their hands. Frederic prevaricates about the title of the novel, and eventually the American and English editions are published under different titles.

1896. *The Damnation of Theron Ware* published by Stone and Kimball, Chicago.

1896. *Illumination* published by William Heinemann, London.

March Hares, by "George Forth" (1896).

1896. Published by D. Appleton, New York, and John Lane, London.

March 1897. Charles Scribner's Sons publish a "Uniform Edition" of all that they have published. Frederic contributes a Preface to the work, published in a volume of Civil War Stories called *In the Sixties,* which contains "The Copperhead," "Marsena," "The Eve of the Fourth," and "My Aunt Susan."

1898. Lothrop Publishing Co., Boston, publish *The Deserter and Other Stories: A Book of Two Wars,* which contains "The Deserter," "A Day in the Wilderness," "How Dickon Came by His Name," and "Where Avon into Severn Flows."

Gloria Mundi (1898).
January 1898. Begins run in *Cosmopolitan*.
1898. Published by Stone, Chicago, and William Heinemann, London.

The Market-Place (1899).
December 1898. Begins run in *Saturday Evening Post*.
February 1899. Begins run in *West-End*.
1899. Published by Frederick Stokes, New York, and William Heinemann, London.

Chronology

19 August 1856. Born Harold Henry Frederick, Utica, New York.

23 February 1858. Death of his father, Henry De Motte Frederick.

1860. Marriage of his mother, Frances Ramsdell Frederick, with William De Motte. One child, Helen De Motte, born in 1866.

1861–71. Education in Utica.

1871–75. Miscellaneous jobs in Utica and Boston, notably in photographic studios.

1875. Employed by the *Utica Herald* as proofreader from late summer until September. Employed by the *Utica Daily Observer* as proofreader from December.

1876. Begins publishing short stories in journals and newspapers.

10 October 1877. Marries Grace Williams. Four surviving children born.

May 1880. Editor of *Utica Daily Observer*. Resigns 1 August 1882.

4 September 1882. Editor *Albany Evening Journal*. Resigns 15 March 1884.

ca. 26 April 1884. London Correspondent for the *New York Times*. Position held until death.

11 June. Leaves for England, planning to return shortly as a successful novelist. He visits the United States on three occasions only, in 1886, 1888, and 1890.

21–26 July 1884. Makes his name with an extended piece of journalism on the cholera epidemic in the South of France. *September*. One of his early stories, "Brother Sebastian's Friendship," appears in book form.

26 October 1887. Frederic's first novel, *Seth's Brother's Wife*, is published in New York after serialization in *Scribner's Magazine*. Published in London in November.

ca. 1889. Probably meets Kate Lyon, and begins to live with her in 1891. Three children born to them.

April 1898. Falls ill, and in the late summer has a stroke. Dies on 19 October 1898.

October to December 1898. Investigation of Frederic's death and trial of Kate Lyon and Athalie Mills. Both acquitted of manslaughter.

THE DAMNATION OF HAROLD FREDERIC

Introduction

The Quest for Harold Frederic

Harold Frederic's "Preface to a Uniform Edition" (1897), the only introduction that he wrote to his work, opens with a passage that dwells upon the act of composition itself. He engages with his own writing predicament in a characteristically robust manner. His are not the measured tones of private anguish, but the strident self-possession and humor of a man accustomed to acting out his life in the public eye. He is decidedly self-confident, yet wry. The first paragraph ranges through a jovial, masculine, and somewhat patronizing aside about women's clothes, the prelude to a description of writing within a predatory and market-based literary world, to a poorly disguised admission of reluctance. This is recognizably Frederic: breezy, off-hand, overbearing, forthright, engagingly unaffected. He writes,

> In nothing else under the latter-day sun—not even in the mysterious department of woman's attire—has Fashion been more variable, or more eccentric in its variations, than in the matter of prefaces. The eternal Revolution of letters devours its own children so rapidly that for the hardiest of them ten years counts as a generation; each succeeding decade has whims of its own about prefaces. Now it has been the rule to make them long and didactic, and now brief and with a twist towards flippancy. Upon occasion it has been thought desirable to throw upon the introductory formula the responsibility of explaining everything that was to follow in the book, and again, nothing has seemed further from the proper function of a preface than elucidation of any sort. Sometimes the prevalent mode has discouraged prefaces altogether—and thus it happens that the present author, doomed to be doing in England at least something of what the English do, has never before chanced to write one. (Frederic Misc. 1977, 1.)

It is characteristic that even in this self-consciously authorial piece, Frederic's character should impress itself so fully, as it does in all his varied writings. Whatever he wrote, whether it was stories or novels, letters to publishers or newspaper colleagues, or his extensive journalistic writing, the finished product is unmistakably shaped. One of the great pleasures of reading Frederic is the vivid sense of his presence looming amongst the commas and the apostrophes: one detects him in every word. It is as though Frederic could not, even if he had wanted to, subsume his vital sense of self. Never a man guilty of overt repression, he seems to unburden himself with joyful lack of restraint. This makes for a tone which, though not necessarily confessional, seems to be allusive and uninhibited, allowing for a wide range of expression. All these statements need qualification. For Frederic the act of openness was a method of concealment. He was adept both at the art of fantasy and at self-promotion, telling compelling stories of an invented farmhood childhood to whatever audience he could. The stories were just that though: invention, exaggeration. Frederic took pleasure both in the varied dramas that he created and in theatrical recitation. Because of his capacity and aptitude for invention he has left a confusing legacy for those who are interested in establishing the facts of his life.

Establishing the parameters of probability has been one of the problems with which I have had to deal when researching and writing this book. Frederic's diffidence with the form and content of any introductory piece is an apt paradigm for my own writing dilemma. The problem of writing itself is not one simply of literary fashions, as Frederic well realized. My difficulties include that of establishing basic facts. One superficial paradox that confronted me as I began researching Frederic was the question of how such a voluble writer could have been silenced through neglect. The question can be answered by reference to Frederic's early death and to the circumstances of it, to his debts to his publishers, and to the literary market without doubt. He was just beginning to experience literary success in the last four years of his life, yet although he was an established novelist, he could not rely upon good sales. Still, it is difficult not to feel some bafflement when the man of booming voice and boisterous paragraph is set against the unfamiliar name "Harold Frederic" that he has become. The gap between the life and the posthumous reputation formed one of the puzzles for this book. More pragmatic problems have been the difficulties in locating primary materials, let alone secondary texts, and in obtaining reliable biographical detail.

There are tantalizing gaps in Frederic's biography. Only the sketchiest outlines are known of his friendships and the daily routine of his life. Although the dates of the main events of his life are known, they are restricted: birth, school, jobs, marriage, death. Very little information survives of many of its most important events. One frustrating absence is the tiny amount of available fact regarding his wife, Grace Frederic, and his lover, Kate Lyon. These two "invisible" women, to use Claire Tomalin's phrase, shared Frederic between them from about 1890 onward, forming a reluctant *menage à trois*. That Grace Frederic was hostile to Kate Lyon and bitter toward Frederic can be inferred from her initial refusal to grant him a divorce, and from the fact that she finally took the initiative and sued for divorce as he lay dying in the house that he shared with Kate Lyon. Little more can securely be said of her. As for Lyon, we cannot even be certain when or where she met him. Although this makes for an unsatisfactory picture of the two women, it does so still more for Frederic.

Although little is known of his daily life, still less is known of his reading habits, or the contents of his library, which might have made the task of researching his literary interests easier. It is certain that he had a library both in the house shared with Grace Frederic, and in that shared with Kate Lyon. His will specifically mentions books that were kept in London at Grace Frederic's house. His publishers sometimes sent him books that were on their lists, and from odd comments made in his letters some inference of his reading can be made. The few book reviews that he wrote and the literary news that he regularly appended to his cable letters to the *New York Times* give additional information.[1] All this is erratic and unsystematic: but it is all there is to work with. The earliest critical writing on Frederic was often unreliable too, especially in biographical detail. The pattern began in the obituary notices: Frederic's name might be spelled incorrectly, or the title of a novel confused. Some newspapers even misstated his place of death. Many gave false information about his life, something that he was not averse to himself. Without realizing the implications of his actions, Frederic had pioneered a tradition of misrepresentation when he invented stories about his boyhood.[2] Researching this book has been, in part, a voyage of discovery through obscure and poorly charted territory.

1. The spelling of the title of the paper alternated during the time Frederic was associated with it. At one point the title was hyphenated. I have followed the convention of leaving the title unhyphenated throughout.

2. The critic most responsible for the long-term misreading of Frederic is usually held to have been Vernon Louis Parrington. In a piece of work left unfinished upon his death he described Frederic as a bitter realist who hated rural America and spent his writing life revenging himself upon it. See Briggs 1969, 4. Carey McWilliams's 1933 article "Harold Frederic: A Country Boy of Genius" continued the tradition of misinformation. Austin Briggs, a more recent admirer of Frederic, has accused McWilliams of composing a biography from Frederic's fiction, and then reading the fiction in the light of the invented biography. Although it is tempting to infer biography from fiction, it is also inadvisable. The work of Parrington and McWilliams has been widely debated, but it has had a lamentable effect upon Frederic's reputation. Entries in dictionaries of American writers have often been inaccurate or dismissive. Frederic would be described as having written one, perhaps two, interesting novels, making him barely worth a mention in American literary history. There has been a grudging recognition that Frederic was a figure of some interest, but that was undoubtedly reluctant. No published biography of Frederic exists. The major pioneering study was Paul Haines's 1945 doctoral dissertation "Harold Frederic." But the Harold Frederic Edition was calling this "outdated" as long ago as 1977. Still, the study is of interest to any serious student of Frederic. Haines's research included exclusive interviews with Frederic's friends and family,

Disclosing Frederic

I first encountered Harold Frederic, as do many of his readers, through *The Damnation of Theron Ware*. Fascinated by the novel, I was surprised to read of his prolific fiction writing and tried to obtain more of it. Frustrated by its unavailability, I began to scour for clues through literary histories and dictionaries. What I encountered was the inaccuracy and contradiction I have described. As far as his personal life was concerned, what I read seemed, often, prejudiced and euphemistic.[3] Grounds for further interpretation and disclosure of Frederic seemed strong. One aspect of his history that interested me was his careful creation of a public persona. The irony of his situation struck me forcefully. His life was a series of attempted escapes—from obscurity in small-town America, from newspaper journalism, from an unsatisfactory marriage. In one sense he failed manifestly, and the measure of his failure is encoded within the newspaper reports of his death. He had set himself up as an example of successful escape but on his death—a victim, the newspapers argued, of Christian Science—he was presented as a slave to delusion and folly. Escape appeared as unworthy escapade: ultimately he had trapped himself. Still harsher was the final result of years of fruitless attempts to get out of journalism. The man who had struggled with a newspaper career had become prime "copy." His name was kept vivid through newspaper stories of his death, but the emphasis was on the lurid details of his life and death, not on the literary work by which he hoped to earn fame. The story of his death and its aftermath was one of the few that he could not tell about himself, but it was the most sensational of all and in some ways the most revealing. It is the story with which I will begin and end.

Much early writing on Frederic enlisted him to a cause, to naturalism or realism. Attempts to appropriate his writing are uneasy. He resists easy definition, and though self-avowedly a believer in Howellsian realism, he warned W. D. Howells in a letter of 11 December 1890 that it "by no means follows that I see all things as you do, or that the work I am going to do

---

and his work has been widely used by writers on Frederic. It remains a vital source of information, and I have drawn on it for biographical details. Much of the information that Haines included has since appeared elsewhere, often without acknowledgment. My work acknowledges wherever he is the original source of facts and details.

3. Though there are certainly numerous inaccuracies and difficulties there is also a body of invaluable work that I have relied upon. These include Garner 1972; Garner and O'Donnell 1969; O'Donnell, Garner, and Woodward 1975; O'Donnell 1969; Polk 1979; Woodward 1960, 1968, and 1982; Woodward and Garner 1968. *The Frederic Herald*, which was edited by Thomas F. O'Donnell with a combination of humor and fanaticism, is an invaluable and eccentric resource. It appeared three times a year in a newspaper format from April 1967 to January 1970. Other significant pieces of criticism have been cited elsewhere in this book and are acknowledged in the list of works cited.

will wholly please you" (Frederic Misc. 1977, 269–70).[4] He was right: Howells was not pleased by Frederic's Revolutionary novel *In the Valley*— the historical novel was not a form that a Howellsian should adopt. Still, Frederic would give whole-hearted allegiance to no one but himself. His hesitation and independence are also found in his reaction to other literary manifestos. In detail, his method is that of a realist: he is concerned with verisimilitude of accent, locale, history, and his desire for accuracy is reflected within the careful preliminary notes for his fiction. He is familiar with the precepts of naturalism, and many of its ideas are reflected obliquely in the pages of his fiction. He did not find in naturalism, or in realism, a suitable vehicle for his ideas. He took what he wanted from them and discarded the rest. What was left, as the most important influence upon his fiction, was his newspaper training. The legacy of Frederic's journalism is embodied in his fiction. He learned how to research and observe in detail, to pursue a story and make it concise, readable, and informative. He developed the dubious talent, common at that moment in American journalism, of the "cut and paste" method of lifting material from other newspapers. Although he only published one known piece of plagiarism under his own name, an early newspaper article, he would often rely closely on other people's writing for information that he put into his novels. It could not be called plagiarism, but it could certainly be traced to his early newspaper days. He had to acquire the ability to work to tight deadlines. All of these skills shaped his novel writing, but the most important influence that journalism had upon fiction was in teaching him how to translate his own experiences into the context of the public arena and the written word. In this matter he was both supremely able and willing.

It would be naïve and misleading to argue that his fiction was a form of autobiography in any simple sense. The act of writing the real into the imagined necessarily involved invention, as well as renegotiation of facts. What is unquestionable is that Frederic made extensive use of his own experience and that, often, models or partial models for his fiction can easily be traced. One reason for this was his desire for accuracy. The connections between fiction and biography are close. Yet, just as his fictional names for an imagined landscape are often disguised or are partial anagrams, the translation from real to imagined is not straightforward. Since even Frederic's avowedly autobiographical stories are invention, it is unwise to look for, still less to hope to find, unmediated autobiography in fiction. Frederic was deeply divided and left a difficult and confusing legacy. He calculatedly invented himself in the late nineteenth century with such skill and deliberation that it is tempting simply to accept his own version of himself. My task in this book has been to invent him all over again.

4. Interestingly, Stephen Crane made a similar claim with an equally idiosyncratic twist to it. See Benfey 1993, 10.

Frederic's Lives

Fears of Oblivion: The Construction of Fiction

On 17 August 1898 Harold Frederic started, and completed, one of his final pieces of writing. Though, of necessity, it was a dictated text, he added his name to it, affirming authorship. The tremors in his usually exquisite signature are articulate testimony to the fact that the document, his will, was produced at considerable personal cost: he was dying, indeed, he had only two months to live. The contents of the will show that it was a costlier document still. It was a potent symbol of the double life he had led for many years, a final, formal division of himself. The American copyrights of his works and his American property were to go to "my very dearly beloved and faithful Kate Lyon and to her children" while the effects of 101 Brook Green, London, and his English copyrights were to go to "Mrs. Frederic and my daughter Ruth in general trust for themselves and my other children now residing or generally residing with them." Ruth Frederic, his oldest child, was to have a piano, an earlier gift that was formalized here. She was to choose any books that she wanted from 101 Brook Green for herself or that "she may consider of use in the education of her sister and brothers." The other books were to be moved to Homefield, in Kenley, Surrey. These two houses contained and represented the two families of Harold Frederic. He lived in Kenley during the week with his lover, Kate Lyon, and usually spent weekends with Grace Frederic, his wife, in Brook Green. How he negotiated these parallel lives and moved between his parallel wives must remain to some degree a matter of speculation. Only fragmentary evidence of the way in which Frederic conducted his private lives has remained.

His tone matches the coldly formal legalistic wording of the document. He offers no apologies or explanations for his life, though the gravity of his situation must have been clear to him. He seems indifferent to his seven children, with the exception of his oldest child, Ruth. In financial terms his bequests meant little. He had borrowed against his royalty accounts, partly to help friends who were continually in need of money, and partly to prevent his two families from becoming destitute. Clearly, the significance of this text lies in the life that it reveals, even tangentially, rather than in the material bequests that it makes. This life was exposed more dramatically in international press coverage of the inquest and court case that followed his death, in which Kate Lyon and another woman, a Christian Science healer called Athalie Mills, were accused of his manslaughter.

His death caused an international sensation. He was seen as the latest "victim" of Christian Science, Mary Baker Eddy's cult that would later be treated with ambivalence by Mark Twain in his book *Christian Science* (1907).[1] More sensationally still, it was questioned whether Frederic was a true believer or whether the ministrations of a healer had been forced upon him. Rumors circulated that his death might be more accurately described as suicide, turning the affair into a representative death of the 1890s.[2] Years of overwork and the strain of supporting two families (born, it was whispered, to two different women without the sanctification of death or divorce to separate the unions) had finally caught up with him. Salacious gossips were gratified, and an accompanying flurry of press interest in faith healing followed his death. Writing to his brother almost a year after Frederic's death, his friend and fellow expatriate Stephen Crane notes robustly,

> The rumpus about H continues. As I have told you he had enemies. He did not kill himself and if his ladylove [sic] killed him she picked out one of those roundabout Sherlock Doyle ways of doing it. It is simply too easy to call a man you don't like a suicide. Mrs. Frederic loved H. maybe. She has taken precious little trouble to put him right with people since May. Neither do I much like Mr. [Henry] James' manner. He professed to be er, er, er much attached to H. and now he has shut up like a clam. Do you not think that men like Robert [Barr] and me who were close to H and knew how sane he was should take some trouble to shut this thing up and off? (Crane to William Howe Crane, 10 August [1899], Crane 1988, 2:496).

The newspapers relished the idea of a macabre struggle between the sexually and medically unorthodox wishes of Kate Lyon and those of his legitimate family, represented by Ruth Frederic. Grace Frederic was dying of cancer, and Ruth's presence as representative of the claims of legitimacy provided great copy for the press. The two sides were presented in terms of a struggle: the youth and innocence of Frederic's daughter versus the

---

1. After Frederic's death some friends claimed that he had planned to write a similar account of Christian Science. Whether this is true or not must remain speculation, as must arguments about the nature of Frederic's belief.
2. See chap. 5.

age and experience of Frederic's lover—respectability against a Bohemian disregard for social mores. The *Daily Graphic*'s illustrations of the two women capture this vividly. Kate Lyon is depicted as a villainous, possibly murderous, scowling creature, wearing a dark, masculine outfit and glasses that hide her eyes but emphasize a pair of pinched eyebrows. The iconography is clear. Denatured by her illicit passion, she neglects her dying lover by refusing him medical treatment, denying her responsibility and thus condemning him to death. In contrast, Ruth Frederic is clear-faced and serene, resolute yet unthreatening. A face of sorrow, but not a challenging face. The antifemale tone of a hostile press was common to much newspaper coverage of Frederic's death. The case developed into an international scandal uniting adultery, illegitimacy, bankruptcy, and a manslaughter trial. Ironically, it was more gripping than any story that Frederic might have invented and was more likely to secure better sales. When the public furor had died down, his reputation had died with it. The debts with which his publishers were left did not predispose them toward his work, although one fine posthumous novel, *The Market-Place,* temporarily kept him from the oblivion he had always feared before his works gradually went out of broad circulation. Despite this obscurity, his personality remained vivid to his friends and acquaintances, and vignettes and anecdotes about him are scattered throughout many memoirs.

The revelations that his death had prompted continued as Ruth Frederic was forced to write begging letters to his friends and colleagues, a correspondence that revealed the degree of her emotional desperation as well as her financial exigency.[3] Supporters of Grace Frederic took out a public subscription letter to collect funds for her and her children, and Kate Lyon's friend Cora Crane, the lover of Stephen Crane, wrote private letters to individuals she hoped would be sympathetic to Kate Lyon and her children or "little barbarians" as Henry James fondly called them. In the case of illegitimacy a public appeal would have been out of the question. The all-male committee for the public fund for Grace Frederic included Henry James; J. M. Barrie; A. Conan Doyle; Henry Beerbohm Tree; Arthur Wing Pinero; James McNeill Whistler; Henry Irving; W. E. Henley; George Bernard Shaw; as well as several prominent politicians. Contributors to this fund included all of these men, and also H. G. Wells; Mrs. Humphry Ward; George Gissing; Rudyard Kipling; William Archer; and numerous others. The list was compiled in order of sums donated: it was headed by the name of Sir Charles Dilke, and one notable detail is that several women contributed funds too. Some people even gave money to both funds, though it is clear that Cora Crane, working alone and privately

3. Some of these letters are in the Ernest L. Oppenheim Papers in the New York Public Library.

with the weight of public opinion against her, had a difficult job obtaining money.[4] Julia Field-King, one of the leading Christian Scientists in Britain, sent money to her collection, together with a letter arguing that Kate Lyon was not, in her opinion, a true believer. Robert McClure sent money; Sir Alfred Milner, having given £10 to the public fund, said he had little to give for Kate Lyon though offered something; Arthur Wing Pinero contributed generously to both funds as did Henry James; George Bernard Shaw contributed £5; and a number of others contributed, though some declined to do so and were outraged at being approached. Joseph Conrad neatly summarized the views of many when he wrote to Cora Crane on 28 October 1898 telling her that, "My admiration of your courageous conduct exists side by side with an utter disapproval of those whom you in your own extremity befriend. They invoke the name of faith and they've dragged its substance pretty well through the mud. It may be only folly —of course—unutterable *folly*. But it looks worse. The only Christian in sight in this whole affair is you, my dear Mrs Crane—exercising that rarest of the Creed's virtues: that of Christianity" (Stephen and Cora Crane Papers).

The double life that had been acted out, if not discreetly, then at least with some degree of privacy, was ruthlessly opened up to the public gaze. Although certain areas of Frederic's life were scrutinized and gossiped about, this publicity further obscured the details of other aspects of his life as though nothing could be of as much interest as the scandalous finale to his career. In this respect Frederic's story seems very much one of the 1890s: a brilliant short career followed by an ignominious fall. Although it may be true that in some lives such a death may deservedly eclipse the life itself, in the life of Frederic this is not the case. Yet for many his death was the single most interesting fact about him. If a reductive assessment of his history was one unfortunate inheritance of his premature death, one that affected his posthumous reputation more than it did his family, the same cannot be said of another direct effect of it. The traumatic events that followed his death so shook his children that the only three who could be traced and then persuaded to discuss him in the 1950s and 1960s, Barry Forman, Harold Frederic, and Ruth Frederic (Keen), had clearly not been able to overcome them, and though their memories of details were often faulty, they had forgotten nothing of the horror of publicity. Their letters are marked by ellipses; sudden flurries of memory; omissions and negations; and occasional retractions. They seemed to have spent their own lives living down the life of their father and keeping their relation to him

---

4. One remarkable letter, to Alice Creelman, written on 30 December 1898, is a response to a vitriolic letter she received from her after she wrote requesting a contribution. For an account of the life of Cora Crane see Gilkes 1962.

hidden.[5] In contrast, he had spent his life courting publicity, displaying himself and his achievements for all to see in the hope that his name would remain vivid for years to come.

The fantasy of earning or of in some way achieving lasting fame was always with him. It is clearly traceable as early as 1883, when as an ambitious young newspaper editor and short story writer, Frederic contributed a short preface to a posthumous collection of the works of a young Utica poet, "Vandyke-Brown." Marc Cook (the poet's real name) had recently died of tuberculosis in his twenty-ninth year. Frederic's preface is both memorial and celebration, "Worse than the terrors of dissolution itself is the fear that death may bring forgetfulness. The oldest graven records of the race are barriers raised to stop this dread oblivion,—at once a protest against the effacing march of generations and a plea for posterity's attention, pitiful in its very helplessness. 'Let his name be forgotten,' was the sternest and most merciless form of ancient condemnation" (Cook 1883,v.). Underlying his sympathetic and sensitive picture of Cook is horror at the possibility that he might be experiencing a premonition of his own fate. Might he meet death before securing his reputation and so go forgotten to his grave? If so, then death would have its "final triumph." He would fight against this all his life.

The short life of Harold Henry Frederick began on 19 August 1856, in Utica, upper New York State. He was born into the "dread oblivion" that he so feared. When he died on 19 October 1898, in Kenley, he had become the novelist, critic, and journalist Harold Frederic. It was an accomplished transformation, though not a lasting one. His reputation would vanish with the waning century. Frederic was always ambitious, inheriting his intense self-belief from his mother, who, he said, "had very tender and ambitious notions of the kind of son she desired to have" (Sherard 1897, 534).[6] His high opinion of his mother was not disinterested. A character in one of his novels comments that there is "nothing clearer in natural law" than the

---

5. One daughter, Helen Forman, would say nothing and would not cooperate with her brother Barry when he requested information. Ruth was reticent at first, but once she began discussing her father she became far more open. Both she and her brother Harold (children of Grace and Harold Frederic) began to send pieces of either poetry or prose along with their letters to Hoyt Franchere, as if to prove that the creative gift had not perished with their father. This correspondence is in the files of the Harold Frederic Edition.

6. Paul Haines warns that Sherard is not "always convincingly accurate," so, following Haines, I have specifically noted everything drawn from Sherard's interview with Frederic, a conversation piece published a year after Frederic's success with *The Damnation of Theron Ware* (Haines 1945, 7).

fact that "sons inherit from their mothers" (Frederic Novels 1890a, 34).[7] His profuse compliments to his mother were, to some degree, self-glorification. The power of their joint resolve propelled him, motivating him to levels of endeavor that culminated in a series of strokes, and finally death at the age of only forty-two. Yet he enjoyed the challenge of emerging from obscurity into fame, once writing to his friend Charles Sherlock that "I never work so well as when I have impossible tasks jammed upon me" (Frederic Misc. 1977, 489, n.d.). The task of escaping from small-town Utica and becoming internationally famous certainly seemed "impossible." His intense belief in the sustaining power of his own physical strength led him to overestimate his own capacities. His friends were concerned that he took his health for granted—"He was not afraid of labour. It would have been better for him if he had a little wholesome fear of it. Like most men of great physical strength, he overtaxed himself. He was careless of consequences in everything except writing" (Warren 1898, 19). By his early death he thwarted the ambitious projects that had propelled him through his life.

Frederic was an opinionated and egotistical man. Once, praising his own work to Charles Miller, the editor of the *New York Times*, he wrote that though his high estimation of his own work was "not precisely modest" it was "everlastingly true" (27 March 1886, Frederic Misc. 1977, 104). It makes an appropriate epitaph—the quality of Frederic's journalism enables it to survive despite neglect, much like his opinion of himself. Some thought that Frederic's egotism had surprising and mysterious charm. It was boyish and ingenuous, the boasting of a man favored both by considerable natural talent and by circumstance.[8] He was famously outspoken, "you never had to guess at Frederic's opinion of anything in the heavens above or on the earth beneath. He would give his opinion without hesitation and multiply it by two" (Warren 1898, 19). Like Theron Ware, one of his troubled protagonists, he was fascinated by the workings of his own mind.[9] It was a mind that was split by contradictory impulses. The desire for

---

7. "I know of only two cases in all history where an able man had a father superior in brain and energy to the mother—Martin Luther and the present King of Prussia."

8. William H. Rideing wrote that "What would have offended in another became mysteriously charming in him. He made egotism pleasant by hypnotizing us into his own point of view, and his glory became ours." (Rideing 1909, 397).

9. In a letter of 9 May 1883 to Benjamin B. Blood, Frederic writes "I have treated you with this introspective analysis, because I have come to take a quite impersonal interest in studying myself, and my notes may be not without interest to you." (Frederic Misc. 1977, 16). This is a somewhat extraordinary and egotistical claim. The theme emerges in *The Damnation of Theron Ware* too: "Theron Ware was extremely interested in the mechanism of his own brain, and followed its workings with a lively curiosity" (Frederic Novels 1986, 38.)

achievement, and the belief that he was capable of important work, were continually undermined by self-doubt. He could be enormously and irritatingly self-assured, yet curiously anxious. These conflicting emotions fueled his boasts, which ranged from picturesque descriptions of an invented farmyard youth to bombastic claims about his past and future achievements. He even claimed that he could have been president of the United States if he chose to do so, an echo of which emerges, in *The Market-Place,* in the megalomaniac Joel Thorpe's desire to rule England.[10] Frederic was clearly afraid of seeming marginal. He believed that his birthplace of upstate New York had been neglected by historians and that he could remedy that omission while making a name for himself as a chronicler of the region. His identification with his state was so strong that he was afraid of, as it were, inheriting neglect. At a personal level he ensured that this was impossible by his domineering and vivid presence. He was noisy, boisterous, anecdotal, argumentative, witty. Above all, he was memorable. The forgotten and the marginalized are given prominent roles in his writing—Russian Jews, the civilian population during the American Civil War, the Irish peasantry—but he was determined to be neither forgotten nor marginalized.

At some point in his early years Harold Henry Frederick had dropped the *k* from his name, with a self-conscious desire for distinction. Although he might, like Ford Madox Hueffer (who became Ford Madox Ford), have wanted to de-Teutonize his name, it is more likely that like Hilda Doolittle (who preferred "H. D.") or Oscar Fingal O'Flahertie Wills Wilde (who dropped his cumbersome full name hoping to be known simply as " 'The Wilde' " or even " 'The Oscar' ") he wanted both to be idiosyncratic and to play an active part in his own creation through the act of naming. Frederic also toyed with the name "Henri": "Harold Frederick" was prosaic, but "Harold Frederic" or even "Henri Frederic" had potential. (Ellmann 1987, 16; Haines 1945, 7).[11] Individualism of this sort characterized his life. In the forty-two years between his birth and death his most vivid creation, in one sense his most convincing piece of fiction, was "Harold Frederic" the novelist, journalist, and expatriate *bon viveur.* This character emerges in fragmentary form and in various guises throughout his fictional

10. "When he told us how he had made Grover Cleveland President of the United States, we had to believe him, and when he declared that if he chose he could be President himself, it did not seem in the least ridiculous" (Rideing 1909, 397).

11. In *The Market-Place* Joel Thorpe renames himself "Stormont Thorpe" and his nephew and niece change their names from Dabney to "D'Aubigny" as part of a process of gentrification, to their mother's consternation. She tells them, "Everybody can call themselves whatever they please; its no affair of mine. You and your sister spell your father's name in a way to suit yourselves; I never interfered, did I? You have your own ideas and your own tastes. They are quite beyond me, but they're all right for you" (*The Market-Place,* 175).

Cartoon caricature of Harold Frederic.
Reproduced from *Bookman* (New York), III (July 1896).

work, glimpsed sometimes as a knowing youngster and elsewhere in a variety of adult forms.

Frank Harris wrote that Frederic's vigor and charm emerged in only a diluted form in his work. It impressed itself most fully firsthand. In an obituary of Frederic in the *Saturday Review,* which Harris edited, he lamented that "there is not in one of his books a vestige of that divine humour that used to set the table on a roar" (Harris 1898b, 528).[12] Even if we allow for exaggeration and a self-conscious and dated style, this still suggests one aspect of Frederic. A similar point is often made of Oscar

12. Since Harris was a notorious liar it is always as well to treat his claims with some skepticism. This statement is often corroborated elsewhere, however.

Wilde, who, self-avowedly put his genius into his life. Like Wilde, Frederic had considerable conversational abilities, and both men took roaring tables in their stride. Wilde's wit was more poised than that of Frederic, and in one recorded meeting Wilde's urbanity savaged Frederic's studied charm with a cool and practiced pounce.[13] Another shared characteristic was that, like Wilde, one of Frederic's favored topics of conversation was himself. In this preoccupation he was less single-minded than Wilde although he could use extreme measures to capture and captivate an audience. When recounting a story that particularly interested him, the tale,

> would be related in merciless detail while the minutes passed into hours, and the reluctant audience thought of missed trains and neglected appointments. But Frederic, the fury of the anecdotalist being upon him, would block the doorway with his towering bulk, and suffer no man to go till he had fashioned the last link of the long chain, till he had elaborated his theme with a Rabelaisian minuteness of detail. But it was not always thus: he was a master also of the short American story that leaves you with a gasp at the audacity of its abrupt last sentence. ("By an Old Friend" 1898, 571–72.)[14]

Again, there is an element of willfulness in this description of Frederic (which appeared only ten days after his death). Yet it has a circular function: it is a neat anecdote about anecdotalism, and it suggests a dual element of Harold Frederic, for in it he has mastered two types of narrative, the long, detailed story as well as the short, thrilling one. For Frederic, "storytelling" had a similar double aspect: it might mean recounting a tale, and it could also suggest constructing a fiction. Frederic's carelessness with facts has contributed to what Paul Haines, the pioneering biographer of Frederic, calls "The Frederic Myth," which makes him an impoverished and underschooled farmboy who hated New York State (Haines 1945, 2). Frederic willingly contributed to an aspect of this "myth" by exaggerating the rural aspect of his youth. Warnings of his culpability appeared within days of his death. In an appreciation of Frederic, his friend and fellow-journalist Clement Shorter cautions against accepting Frederic's own version of his early years. Frederic, he says, was a "most remarkable conversationalist" (he compares him with Johnson, as Richard Ellmann

13. "Oscar Wilde was at this pleasant breakfast, and fairly scintillated with wit. [!] The host was talking to a radiant blonde, and Oscar Wilde asked Mrs. T. P. if she wasn't jealous? She said 'No—T. P. doesn't know a pretty woman when he sees one.' Harold Frederic said, 'I beg to differ—what about yourself?' Mrs. T. P. answered, 'Oh, I was an accident.' 'Rather,' said Oscar Wilde, 'a catastrophe!' " ([Elizabeth Paschal] O'Connor 1910, 238). This compliment was even more barbed than it seems: the marriage was always somewhat uneasy.

14. See *Mrs. Albert Grundy: Observations in Philistia*, 17–19, for an example of one of his stories.

does Wilde), and men would visit certain London clubs for the sake of hearing him speak, "C.K.S." 1898, 4).[15] His undoubted skill had its drawbacks, especially for the prospective biographer.

Like many great storytellers Frederic's priority was the story itself. In this he participates in an established tradition: Wilde and his mother both "enjoyed improving upon reality," Ford Madox Ford was notorious for it, and (later) Ernest Hemingway's boasts of both his physical and sexual prowess would become legendary (Ellmann 1987, xiv).[16] In 1842 Charles Dickens had suggested that Americans would be well advised to love the Ideal rather more than they regarded the Real (Dickens 1985, 227). Frederic had learned by his suggestion, idealizing reality in his reminiscences, and Wilde had never needed such a suggestion. He was no American! Hemingway was addicted to it. Accuracy was often secondary to Frederic, and the imaginative retelling of reality was less the deliberate appropriation of falsehood than the desire for a different sort of truth. He might give his listeners what he thought they wanted to hear, or perhaps what he thought they ought to hear. Macaulay is said to have sacrificed truth for epigram. Frederic, compared after his death with Macaulay, "talked with such a reckless bluntness that everything in his early biography may be accepted with some hesitation" ("C.K.S." 1898, 4).[17] Shorter's reservations are atypical. Many of Frederic's friends accepted his anecdotes at face value: they heard what they wanted to hear. Some, no doubt, provided their own embellishments, inventing what they did not hear. Some years before Frederic's death, Stephen Crane had remarked upon the vividness of Frederic's storytelling. His first impression of Frederic was of him in anecdotal mode, surrounded by a group of intent faces at one of the London clubs, an image that is frequently invoked. Frederic's distortion of his own childhood causes difficulties not least because his life is poorly

15. For example, "he kept us alert with a fund of anecdote, of reminiscence, of Johnsonian incisiveness, which one sighs to think is never more to brighten our lives" and "His bluntness and roughness are counted in Dr Johnson and others for independence, and Frederic was essentially a man of remarkable independence." For a comparison of Wilde and Johnson see Ellmann 1987, xiv.

16. Anthony Burgess writes of Hemingway that, "the habit of lying, or romancing, about his outdoor prowess began when he was not quite five. He told his grandfather Hall that he had stopped a runaway horse singlehanded. The old man said that with an imagination like that he would end up either famous or in jail" (Burgess 1979, 9). Alan Judd writes of Ford Madox Ford that "in this as in others of his tales, Ford's eye is on the right effect, not the right fact. It is as if he were writing a novel. It is not that he did not see the difference between the truth and what he said but that he chose on the basis of effect, as a novelist would" (Judd 1990, 61).

17. Louise Imogen Guiney compares Frederic with Macaulay and calls him a very "American" voice: "In his indignations, there was a fine Niagara freshet of words, which the late Mr. Macaulay could barely hope to rival" (Guiney 1899, 601).

documented and his remarks form a crucial part of his biography. When the stories are taken up and retold by another inventive voice, that of a friend or memoir writer, they become more suspect and more interesting too. They invite retelling, but need careful supervision. Frederic presents his childhood as part Twainian idyll and part Alger myth, and it does resemble both of these.

Frederic gradually became convinced by the character that he had constructed for himself, though he was aware of the drawbacks of self-preoccupation. At the start of *Gloria Mundi* Christian Tower tells Frances Bailey that "It is only natural . . . that one should try to think as well as possible of oneself." When she retorts that he thinks about himself "a good deal," he replies, "It is my fault—my failing. I know it only too well" (*Gloria Mundi*, 10). Yet as the novel progresses it is clear that he continues in his self-absorption. The novel appeared at the end of Frederic's life, and by then he must have realized that, like Theron Ware, he had become something of a "bore." Anecdotes that amused or interested audiences when he first arrived in England gradually lost their charm as they staled with repetition. Hosts could dread the moment at which Frederic began his routine. What was once picturesque and piquant became a social liability. As years progressed and he realized that interest in his stories was waning, Frederic began to remember the past in a different and more striking light. His American youth was a long way off, and as another great anecdotalist, Mark Twain, records in his autobiography, events can be experienced differently as time passes: "When I was younger I could remember anything, whether it had happened or not; but my faculties are decaying now and soon I shall be so I cannot remember any but the things that never happened. It is sad to go to pieces like this but we all have to do it" (Twain 1960, 3).[18]

Frederic's fictionalizing became habitual: he invented fictions to amuse his companions, wrote them to support his families, and told fictions to account for an unconventional domestic life. There is no real Harold Frederic to be found in the web of these enmeshing fictions, and it would be foolish to search for one, more so to expect to find one. He is all that he claims to be, and none of it too. His fantasies and lies are as much of him as if they were true—indeed more so. While piecing together evidence of Frederic's knowable history, his invented autobiography is haunting. It will not be dismissed and nor should it be. Facts need to be established, and some can be, but whoever or whatever Frederic was belongs both to

---

18. In act 2 of *The Importance of Being Earnest* (1895) Miss Prism tells Cecily that "Memory . . . is the diary that we all carry about with us." Cecily replies, "Yes, but it usually chronicles the things that have never happened, and couldn't possibly have happened. I believe that memory is responsible for nearly all the three-volume novels that Mudie sends us" (Wilde 1992, 49).

the facts and to the shadowy recesses of his invention. Despite Frederic's openness, his childhood is not to be found in the versions that he rehearsed in his clubs surrounded by an audience of British men at once credulous and incredulous. His interpretation of his life protects reality: his history resists and teases. His apparent lack of inhibition is a form of censorship. Even when he seems most exposed, he is evasive: he goes to pieces.

His extant correspondence is not large and is fragmentary. Transactions with publishers or the *New York Times* predominate. Frederic put this down to the demands of his job: to a fellow journalist, Aaron Watson, Frederic once wrote that "We do not belong to a letter-writing trade" (12 December 1887, Frederic Misc. 1977, 198). No letters have been found of the correspondence between Frederic and his mother, and the only surviving letter from his mother (written to Frederic's editor at the *New York Times* after Frederic's death) is full of great liveliness.[19]

Compiling a version of Frederic's life story from minimal and questionable sources requires arbitration between his fictitious autobiographical statements and the fictionalized reality of much of his writing. Any account of Frederic's life must work through the obscuring details of his early life and negotiate among his enticing falsehoods, informed guesswork, and inaccuracies. His life in London must be pieced together from fragmentary sources—letters, memoirs, the minimalist notes in his surviving appointment diaries, odd invitations, and newspaper reports. The sources for biography are eclectic and unsatisfactory. Frederic is filtered through the observations of others, presented incompletely in the context of their memories. From this assortment of sources he emerges as a vivid and brilliant public figure but little is revealed of a private self that was not on display. It may be that he was always on display. Inevitably the personality presented is one perceived chiefly through anecdote and incident, and though pertinent and often funny or memorable, these form a more prominent part of Frederic's biography than is desirable. They capture Freder-

19. She writes on 27 October 1898, "I must say to you in the beginning that I am Harold Frederic's mother and have read the Newspaper accounts of him with a great deal of interest —but there are some things published which are not true with regard to Harold's childhood. . . . [N]ow what I have written you is plain unvarnished truth—if you would like to know what manner of woman I am I refer you to The Boston Excelsior Company where I sell excelsior or have for the last two years—It is very aggravating to spend as much care and money in rearing a son and having it go all over the country that he was almost a pauper if you could modify any of the statements you would confer a favor to the Family. . . . If this letter is verbose kindly excuse." (Harold Frederic Papers) "Excelsior" is the name for wood chippings or shavings, which are used for stuffing furniture or mattresses, and for packing. No letters either to or from his mother appear in the *Correspondence*, and there are none in the *Harold Frederic Papers* from Frederic to her.

ic's public image, celebrating the persona that he so capably presented to the world, but contributing little to an understanding of his movement between a private world and a public persona.

Frederic's willingness to embrace a history that was not his own suggests a desire for drama and a lingering dissatisfaction with the more prosaic reality of his childhood—an ordinary boyhood in a small American town. Less solemnly, his imaginative retelling of his early years (a carefully constructed and frequently rehearsed fiction) is a light-hearted version of Edward Albee's "humiliate the host." Frederic's stories of early hardship are part of an elaborate American confidence trick played by American expatriates upon their credulous English hosts. Such deceptions were popular among Americans abroad.[20] Frederic's enjoyment of minor deceptions is suggested by a delighted letter to a friend in Utica describing an act of American whimsy prompted by snow in London:

> As the horses are all perfectly flat-shod, traffic was practically impossible. . . . The theatres were almost empty those nights, owing to the impossibility of getting about. Minnie Palmer, who was then playing in the Strand Theatre, got a splendid advertisement by writing to all the papers, deploring the sufferings of the poor horses which were tumbling on their heads every-

20. This was a two-way process. Deceptions also were popular with Englishmen on the "other side." Peter Conrad describes the way in which Auden "dressed down" for New York (Conrad 1980, 219). Joaquin Miller was fond of the game, smoking three cigars at once "as we do it in the States." (Briggs 1969, 8). Miller had long cultivated his studied and extraordinary appearance, surprising the American novelist Gertrude Atherton after London had recovered from the effect of his visit. She writes, "I didn't wonder that he had made a sensation in London, for the English like the Americans to be as different from themselves as possible. He wore a black broadcloth suit, the trousers tucked into boots—with high heels—that reached almost to his waist. His shirt had no collar but his neck was encircled by a lace scarf. On his head was a sombrero . . . his long hair, touching his shoulders, was gray on top, and ended in a series of stiff 'rat tails' that were dyed a bright orange. . . . It was my first experience with a genius; and no lion I have ever met has roared so accommodatingly" (Atherton 1932, 113). Stephen Crane played up to his audience, acting the part of "an almost fabulous Billy the Kid" together with a provocatively phallic gun to Ford Madox Ford, though he also presented himself as "a Bowery boy of the most hideous type" to the fastidious Henry James. Ford describes his antics: "Then he wore—I dare say to shock me—cowboy breeches and no coat, and all the time he was talking he wagged in his hand an immense thing that he called a gun and we should call a revolver. From time to time he would attempt to slay with the bead-sight of this Colt such flies as settled on the table, and a good deal of his conversation would be taken up with fantastic boasts about what can be done with these lethal instruments." (Crane 1968, 154). Crane himself claimed to be exasperated by British responses to stories of American life lamenting that, "They [the British] will believe anything wild or impossible you tell them . . . and then if you say your brother has a bathtub in his house they—ever so politely—call you a perjured falsifier of facts." (Berryman 1950, 199). Gelett Burgess, whom Frederic knew in the latter part of his residence in England also writes farcically about the subject (Burgess 1898, 399).

where, and blaming the Londoners for not putting rubber overshoes on their horses' feet—a practice which she averred was universal in America. Drolly enough, nobody contradicted this assertion, and the London papers were all fooled by it. (Frederic to John B. Howe, ca. 16 December 1886, Frederic Misc. 1977, 147)

Frederic enjoyed being his own "splendid advertisement." At first he was delighted by his ability to fool the British and enjoyed playing the part of the American outsider with privileged insights into both British and American life. In his early days in London he signed himself "An American in London" in articles that appeared in the *Pall Mall Gazette.* In later years Frederic became more frustrated by the apparent willfulness of British ignorance, ridiculing it in *Mrs. Albert Grundy: Observations in Philistia.* Mr. Hump (a young literary type whose sloping shoulders make him resemble a wine bottle) expounds upon American customs to Mrs. Grundy's suburban household. Americans were often forced to survive on nothing but "fried salt pork" for many months of the year—owing to the scarcity of meat (Frederic Misc. 1896a 16).[21] Later, on the evidence of an equally ignorant British man, he says that "it is an extremely rare experience to meet an adult American who has not been divorced at least once." Mrs. Grundy replies, "I suppose the trouble arises from their all living in hotels—having no home life whatever" (Ibid., 19–20).[22] One can detect Frederic's wry irony here: at this point he was living with two women in two separate homes with no possibility of divorce from his wife, Grace Frederic. Frederic explained his open ridicule by writing, in self-justification, to his friend W. E. Henley, the editor of the *National Observer,* which was printing the series, "You get so much satisfaction out of baiting Brother Jonathan, that you oughtn't to begrudge him a slap back once in a while" (13 March 1892, Frederic Misc. 1977, 310).

This chapter covers Frederic's early life in detail, for his American years played a vital part in his fiction writing. His imagination was fired by the human history and the topology of New York State. He had a rare genuine passion for his birthplace, although he was not blind to the political and economic corruption of the region. His life in London is more difficult to capture adequately. A series of vignettes are used to suggest a shielded

21. Charles Dickens had noted, while in Boston, that a visitor "is certain to see, at every dinner, an unusual amount of poultry on the table; and at every supper, at least two mighty bowls of hot stewed oysters, in any one of which a half-grown Duke of Clarence might be smothered easily." (Dickens 1985, 54).

22. Henry James was also keen to repudiate such misconceptions. Daisy Miller says to Winterbourne, "That English lady, in the cars . . . Miss Featherstone—asked me if we didn't all live in hotels in America. I told her I had never been in so many hotels in my life as since I came to Europe. I have never seen so many—it's nothing but hotels" (James 1984, 160).

private life and a public facade that operated as a mask. This approach is unsatisfactory yet unavoidable, though it is preferable to a reductive list of friendships, visits, and holidays. Frederic died in his forty-third year, having exchanged the Mohawk Valley for the Caterham Valley, the Deerfield Hills for the North Downs.

A Utica Boyhood: "Where the Mohawk Gently Glides"

Utica, Frederic's birthplace, is in the central Leatherstocking region of northern New York, an area that James Fenimore Cooper chronicled. Utica is in the valley of the Mohawk River, close to the Deerfield Hills. This location made it a valuable route through northern New York, and a local song celebrates the river, "Sweet is the vale where the Mohawk gently glides / On its clear running way to the sea" (Frederic to Edward L. Burlingame, 2 September 1887, Frederic Misc. 1977, 180).[23] The city is served by a canal system, and the New York Central Railway follows the course of the valley. Today it is skirted by the New York State Thruway, compounding its status as a place to visit but not to stay. For all his eulogizing of the region, this was certainly Frederic's attitude to it as well.

The Mohawk flows east to join the Hudson just north of Albany, the state capital. The Hudson then flows south to New York, its course forming the eastern boundary for the Catskills where Rip Van Winkle spent twenty years asleep. Frederic spent most of his first twenty-six years in Utica before moving, via Albany, to London. He may have found, like Rip, that his memories of his birthplace did not match a rapidly changing community.[24] In his fiction Frederic would use his memories of the towns and villages of upper New York State to create a fictional domain that closely resembled the area. Oneida County became "Dearborn County," a touching memorial to his birthplace. The area was the site for some of the most significant

23. Frederic thought of incorporating the song into the title of what would become *In the Valley* and calling it "Where the Mohawk Gently Glides."

24. Rip finds his return bewildering: "The very village had altered—it was larger and more populous. There were rows of houses which he had never seen before, and those which had been his familiar haunts had disappeared. Strange names were over the doors—strange faces at the windows—every thing was strange" (Irving 1983, 778). Jessica Lawton's return to Thessaly suggests a similar disorientation: "The street up and down which she glanced was in a sense familiar to her, for she had been born and reared on a hillside road not far away, and until her eighteenth year had beheld no finer or more important place than this Thessaly, which once had seemed so big and grand, and now, despite the obvious march of 'improvement', looked so dwarfed and countrified in its overlarge, misfitting coat of snow. . . . Among all who passed, Jessica caught sight of no accustomed face. In a way, indeed, they were all familiar enough—they were types, in feature and voice and dress and manner, of the people among whom her earlier life had been spent—but she knew none of them, and was at once glad of this and very melancholy" (Frederic Novels 1890b, 7–9).

battles of the Revolution, as Rip would discover when he woke up. Frederic was excited about its history from an early age. It was to be a rich source of inspiration for him, awakening him to the dangers of tyrannical oppressors. Many of its earliest settlers had fled from political and religious persecution in Europe and were exiled peoples who had themselves displaced the Native Americans, an act that still has repercussions today. At the time of Frederic's birth there was still a strong Germanic influence in Utica; Frederic was brought up in the German quarter of the town. Utica had something of the racial mix of Frederic's fictional Octavius, but just as Utica is an incomplete anagram of Octavius, the analogy between the fictional and real places is only partial. The older Dutch and German settlers mixed with the newest immigrants, many of whom were Irish and Italians—"Eyetalians" as Loren Pierce calls them in *The Damnation of Theron Ware.* Pierce complained that the "place is jest overrun with Irish," but Frederic would celebrate the Irish in his fiction and journalism.[25]

Little is known of Frederic's father or of his paternal grandparents. His paternal grandfather, Henry Frederick, was one of four coopers in Utica. He and his wife Mathilda De Motte (who exists only as a name) had three sons, William, George, and Henry De Motte Frederick—the father of Harold Frederic. William was a cooper, George a shoemaker or cordwainer, and Henry (the youngest) was a chair-finisher. Frederic's maternal grandmother, Lucretia Newland Ramsdell, was a strong and resourceful woman who could, like Frederic, be self-willed and obstinate. Her character emerges in glimpses: refusing to have her photograph taken because it meant preening herself for the camera; wearing a voluminous apron (hook and line in pocket for impromptu fishing with her grandson); and in old age carrying her great-grandchildren, two at a time, on her shoulders (Haines 1945, 10–11). She undoubtedly inspired Frederic's love of fishing (which plays a part in *Seth's Brother's Wife* and "The Editor and the School-Ma'am"—Frederic was a keen and opinionated fisherman throughout his life), though her influence on his passion for photography remains uncertain.

She bequeathed to her grandson a rich oral history, passing on stories that she herself had heard as a child. Her father had been a soldier in the Revolution, and her husband's father, Moses Ramsdale (the name is

---

25. Frederic claimed that "I traded candy with a boy for old copies of the *Gartenlaube,* for I knew German as a boy, having been brought up in the German quarter of the town of Utica" (Sherard 1897, 538, and see also 538). For a detailed account of the immigration history of Utica, see Pula 1994. Guiney suggests that Frederic probably forgot most of his childhood German and never learned another language (Guiney 1899, 601). In *Gloria Mundi* the protagonist Christian Tower, a former language tutor calls language acquisition "the cheapest and most trivial of acquirements, if it stands alone, or if it is not put to high uses" (Frederic Novels 1898, 9).

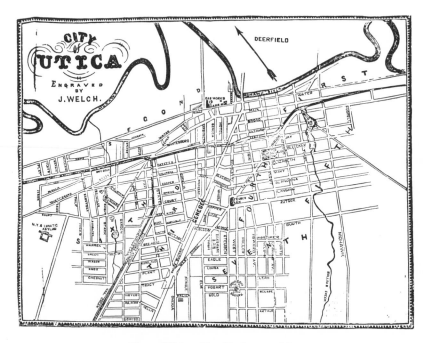

Map of Utica, New York, ca. 1860.

spelled variously), had been a drummer-boy in the Fourth Regiment of the New York infantry. As an adult he had the reputation of being the strongest man in the Mohawk Valley. Frederic inherited this strength: a large number of anecdotes comment upon it. Lucretia Ramsdell's evocations of the family's past and of the history of the Mohawk Valley itself provided an important awakening for Frederic, who was later to exploit the fictional possibilities of her stories. In some ways it was she who gave him a voice.

Both sides of Frederic's family had lived in the Mohawk Valley for generations. Henry De Motte Frederick was descended on one side from eight generations of Dutch colonial settlers, and on the other from a Palatine German family. His Dutch ancestors were industrious pioneers, but his German ancestors had a more vivid and active history. Two of them were captured (one by the French and one by the Mohawks) in raids upon the Mohawk Valley. One fought with Nicholas Herkimer, the Dutch general, at the Battle of Oriskany in 1777. Frederic would later record the events that culminated in Oriskany in the historical novel *In the Valley*, always his favorite of his novels. His mother came from a family with its own dramatic revolutionary past. In his "Preface to a Uniform Edition." Frederic acknowledges his imaginative debt to both sides of the family: "All four of my great-grandfathers had borne arms in the Revolutionary War, and one of them indeed somewhat indefinitely expanded this record by fighting on both sides" (Frederic Misc. 1977, 2).

Frederic's earliest memories were of being told his grandmother's exciting stories: "At the age of six it was her task to beat linen upon the stones of a brook running through the Valley farm upon which she was reared, and the deep-hole close beside where she worked was the spot in which the owner of the farm had lain hidden in the alders, immersed to his chin, for two days and nights while Brant's Indians were looking for him. Thus, by a single remove I came myself into contact with the men who held Tryon county against the King, and my boyish head was full of them." [26] Her stories were full of historical and heroic potential. Yet it was often the juxtaposition of the ordinary (Lucretia Ramsdell washing linen) and the extraordinary (the farm owner's ingenious escape from the Mohawks) that fascinated Frederic. He was interested in the potential that real—domestic or routine—life had for fiction.

Lucretia Ramsdell had married a blacksmith and was widowed at an unknown date, though it was before 1850. Little is known of her husband —or indeed of any of the men in Frederic's family. Like Frederic's father, Lucretia Ramsdell's husband is remembered for a particular physical characteristic: his great strength was inherited from his own father and passed down to his grandson Harold. Ramsdell was the "bugging" champion of Herkimer County. "Bugging" is wrestling in which the participants grip each other around the thorax while trying to endure the pressure of the opponent's grip. Ramsdell was a ferocious fighter. In a friendly match with Joseph Baxter (the father-in-law of his eldest daughter) he crushed three of Baxter's ribs (Haines 1945, 8).[27] The men in Frederic's family might be described as the strong, silent types. Frederic was to inherit the physical strength of the men and the loquacity of the women—a potent combination.[28]

Henry Frederick died when his son Harold was an infant. A significant number of Frederic's male protagonists (especially the boy-narrators of the

26. Haines suggests that his family associated this story with the War of 1812 (Haines 1945, 11). For Frederic's fondness of similar stories, see Frederic to editor *Daily Chronicle*, 13 January 1893, Frederic Misc. 1977, 329.)

27. Haines claims that he "died within the year," though it is not clear whether this was from injuries sustained in the fight.

28. Arthur Warren put Frederic's success at proposing him for membership of a dining club down to Frederic's burly strength. The club's first rule was that "if a member proposing a candidate were not set upon and beaten under the table he could consider his candidate elected. . . . I have always attributed his escape to his physical prowess. There was only one man among the Ghouls who could have stood up to him—Conan Doyle—and he was absent on the night of my election" (Warren 1898, 19).

Civil War stories) are orphans or fatherless. If Frederic felt the absence as loss he was adept at hiding it in his public pronouncements. Still, throughout his life he would seek surrogates: men, often older than himself, whom he could idealize. His own paternal feeling was minimal, and his description of his father in an interview a year before his own death suggests no obvious sense of longing: "I have no recollection of him, but from what I was always told he was very popular with all who knew him. It appears he was a very little man, and was always spoken of as little" (Sherard 1898, 532).[29] The recurrence of the adjective "little" is telling. The memory of Frederic's father was dwarfed by the strong relationship that Frederic developed with his mother, Frances Grace Ramsdell. Frederic spoke of his mother in reverential terms, and throughout his fiction strong female figures—Celia Madden, Sister Soulsby, Frances Bailey, Louisa Thorpe, Aunt Susan—play active and dominant roles. His mother was the strongest influence in his early life, along with his maternal grandmother, Lucretia Ramsdell.

The mental resilience of Frederic's mother earned her the nickname "Frank," and Frederic would use this name for an independent businesswoman in *Gloria Mundi*. When she married Henry Frederick in about 1850, she was living with her mother in the boarding house that they ran together at 44 Elizabeth Street, Utica. The newlyweds lived with Frances's mother at first, just as Frederic and his wife, Grace Williams, would live with his mother in their turn.

At some point in the next two years Henry Frederick set out on an adventure with his brother-in-law John Baxter. He had been bitten by the gold-prospecting bug and like the absent father in "My Aunt Susan" he went west to make his fortune in California. He returned to Utica in 1853 with enough money to move into a large, timbered house, 324 South Street, in which Harold Henry (Harry to his family and in cemetery records) was born on 19 August 1856.[30] The house, a large, gabled, structure, still stands in one of the oldest parts of Utica. In recent times, a stucco addition to the front of the building has provided room for both a gift shop, and at another point a beautician's. The building is now sadly decayed, and the area has become seedy and rather ominous.

In 1855 poor health forced Henry Frederick to abandon his regular trade of chair finishing. He began work as a freight conductor on the New York Central Railway. Much of the cargo on that railway line was human, and it was heading west, to the frontier. The work kept him away from the

29. The letters held in the Harold Frederic Edition poignantly suggest Frederic's inadequacies as a parent.

30. The family's movements can be traced in the Utica City Directories of the period, which also give useful information (via advertisements and so on) of the commercial and economic activites of the town, and (via family names) of origins and ancestry of the inhabitants.

Birthplace of Harold Frederic, Utica, New York.
Note addition to the front of the house.

pungent shellac fumes that were ruining his health. The job had its own dangers, though. On 23 February 1858, his train was derailed near Amsterdam, New York. Frederick returned to his wife and eighteen-month-old son in a plain wooden coffin, an event symbolically recreated in the return of the unknown soldier in Frederic's Civil War story, "The War Widow."

Frederic's mother, characteristically, got on with the daily routine. Soon after her husband's death she joined her mother in the vest-making business. The boarding-house business had been given up some time earlier and the new business was one of the many which she would turn to in the next few years. This prompted Frederic to say at a later date, "My mother is a most remarkable woman," he says, with stress and emphasis, and with an indescribable ring in his voice; "in force, and courage, and initiative, I have never seen a woman like her. If she were ruined to-day, although she is now nearly seventy years of age, she would turn to work again, to typewriting or to shorthand, or to some business, as readily as you would turn to a new brand of cigarettes." (Sherard 1897, 531–32).[31]

---

31. It is an unfortunate phrase. Many smokers are very loyal to their brand.

Frederic dedicated his first novel to his mother.[32] By 1860 when she married William H. De Motte (a machinist and a cousin of Frederic's father) her dowry was over four thousand dollars. Frederic later cited this proudly as an instance of her capability: he seemed increasingly to respect her solvency, as his own financial insecurity increased. She was like the mother in "The Eve of the Fourth"—unimpressed by ostentation and fixed in her notion that "Wilful [sic] waste makes woful [sic] want" (Frederic Short. 1966, 307).[33] It was an adage her son was incapable of accepting as a personal creed, though he appreciated it in her. Continually and woefully wasteful, he was often in want. In his fullest comment upon her he compares her, in her ability to support her family, to "a very Roman matron," continuing, "I often think . . . of what Napoleon said of his mother: 'I owe everything that I have done to my mother:' I understand the feeling" (Sherard 1897, 534). Yet Ruth Frederic, who lived with her paternal grandmother after Grace Frederic's death, was less generous toward her and portrays her as being bullying, grasping, and harsh, and without business acumen. Writing on 26 March 1935 she called her "a domineering and meddlesome woman, of strong will and bias," and "a source of unhappiness and discomfort to practically everyone she came in close contact with." She told her correspondent, Paul Haines, of "the classic of the coffin she kept in the front piazza, ready for her husband's death! One can judge of the quality and extent of her sensibilities from that!" Finally, and somewhat oddly, she adds that "she had many good points" suggesting that she was unwilling to dismiss her grandmother altogether (Harold Frederic Edition).

At about this time Lucretia Ramsdell moved into the roomy house in South Street. In 1867 William and Frances De Motte had their only child, a daughter, Helen, who died in Denver in 1887. Little is known of Frederic's feelings for his half-sister, but he and Kate Lyon named their oldest child Helen. Family life was uneventful and unpretentious Frederic's mother and grandmother remained strong influences on the young Frederic. His stepfather, William De Motte, was a quiet, hard-working character. He often found himself with uncongenial tasks—washing the dog against both their wills—but he joked with Frances about his submissiveness, proud of, or possibly simply awed by, the resourceful woman whom he had married. Frances's voice was so penetrating that Frederic's eldest daughter, Ruth,

32. Haines shared Frederic's admiration, telling with relish a story of how she coped with a fire that destroyed one of her businesses: "This courage appears in an episode of her late sixties: awaking one night to see her excelsior factory in flames, uninsured, she brusquely ordered her condolers to their beds, went back to bed herself, and in the morning made arrangements to start the business afresh" (Haines 1945, 10).

33. In order to avoid confusion, the stories from this edition will be referred to simply by page reference, like Frederic's other writing.

later said that he "remembered the exceeding harshness of his mother's voice" until his death. Frederic not only remembered it—he inherited it (Haines 1945, 10). His voice, a friend said, was like the siren of an ocean-going ship. So his early youth was associated with female voices: with his grandmother's stories and with the memorable sound of his mother's speech—and her more mellifluous singing.

William and Frances De Motte started a wood and milk business which she managed. When one interviewer asked him how he researched farm life for *Seth's Brother's Wife* he replied, "Bless you man! I was brought up on or near a farm. I spent my boyhood in getting out of bed at five in the morning to look after the cattle, and until I was fourteen I drove a milk-wagon as a 'side issue' in my agricultural duties" ("How the Popular Harold Frederic Works," 1896, 397). He expanded upon this in conversations with his friends, explaining that he hated having to go to school in clothes that smelled of cows and milk because he was teased by his class-mates.[34] Frederic's "farming" youth had nothing of the quality of Hamlin Garland's childhood in the harsh Midwest, in which his mother was "imprisoned in a small dark cabin on the enormous sunburned, treeless plain, with no expectation of ever living anywhere else" (Garland 1962, ix). Garland's worn-out wives and embittered farmers are quite different from the genial and inefficient Lemuel Fairchild and Mose Whipple of *Seth's Brother's Wife* and "The Deserter." Frederic's "agricultural duties" did not interfere with his education and compel him to a life of hopeless toil like Garland's tragic Grant McLane, nor to the emptiness of frontier life captured so poignantly in Willa Cather's story, "A Wagner Matinee." His life in Utica was a sort of existence that Garland's young men and women dreamed of. Yet he learned about the brutal side of farm life; as a young reporter on the *Utica Daily Observer* he wrote of the madness, the suicide, the dreaded black moss that destroyed farms, and also the cunning of the rural murderer (Haines 1945, 44–51). In "The Copperhead" he describes the failure of the hoped-for "rural millennium," writing, "Farmer's wives continued to break down and die under the strain, or to be drafted off to the lunatic asylums; the farmers kept on hanging themselves in their barns, or flying off westward before the locust-like cloud of mortgages; the boys and girls turned their steps townward in an ever-increasing host. The millennium never came at all" (Frederic Short. 1966, 9).

All of this is used in his writing (he writes knowingly of sowing corn in

---

34. "Occasionally, when detained on his 'route,' he would appear at school clad in his rough, milk-soiled garments, a circumstance, he used to say, that did not enhance his popularity with his fellow-pupils" ("Harold Frederic Dead" 1898, 7). The article contains several inaccuracies, notably, that Frederic died in "Henley-on-the-Thames," an error that has been taken up and repeated elsewhere, even confusing one of Frederic's sons in later life.

"The Deserter" and amusingly on a newspaperman who advised farmers to feed their chickens on rock salt in *Seth's Brother's Wife*), but it formed no direct part of his own childhood though it was a part of his experience as a young journalist. In later years he liked to exaggerate the rural aspect of his childhood, and as Stephen Crane recalled in 1898 (in a piece of journalism that doubled as private thanks to Frederic for his championing of *The Red Badge of Courage* [1895] in the *New York Times*) Frederic's stories of his early agricultural duties were well known:

> He pitilessly describes the gray shine of the dawn that makes the snow appear the hue of lead, and, moreover, his boyish pain at the task of throwing the stiff harness over the sleepy horse, and then the long and circuitous sledding among the customers of the milk route. There is no pretense in these accounts; many self-made men portray their early hardships in a spirit of purest vanity. "And now look!" But there is none of this in Frederic. He simply feels a most absorbed interest in that part of his career which makes him so closely acquainted with the voluminous life of rural America. (Crane 1898, 358) [35]

Certainly Frederic was "closely acquainted" with rural America—*Seth's Brother's Wife* portrays many aspects of farm life brilliantly—and he was appreciative of novels that dealt with farm life. In 1891 he was to write to Hamlin Garland, praising *Main-Traveled Roads* (1891), "things of that big sort do something more than make an impression; they seem to make over and remodel the mind itself, so that it shall be fit for the new impact" (Frederic to Hamlin Garland, 30 December 1891 Frederic Misc. 1977, 296). Several of the boy-narrators of his Civil War stories live on farms. In his public version of his farmyard youth, he partly models himself along the lines of his boy-narrators and partly models his narrators on himself. He is an amalgam of the narrator of "The Copperhead," working on Abner Beech's farm, Harvey Semple, and Job Parshall of "The Deserter," who plunges his freezing hands into brewer's grain after washing the cows' udders, a trick told with a familiarity that suggests firsthand acquaintance. This was the stuff of the stories that Crane admired, but it also betrayed Frederic's real knowledge of farm lore. Perhaps with geographical and temporal distance from the Mohawk Valley, his childhood did seem rural. Compared with the great European capitals which he was to visit, Utica was a curiously old-fashioned and remote spot, perhaps just as Europe had once seemed. Yet Utica had a population of around twenty thousand when he was a boy, and had "three daily newspapers, twenty three churches,

---

35. Frederic's review, "Stephen Crane's Triumph," appeared in the *New York Times* on 26 January 1896, 22. In it he writes that he "remembered the title [of *The Red Badge of Courage*] languidly from self-protection" having been first recommended the book by "a person whose literary admirations serve me generally as warnings [of] what to avoid." Thomas Beer identifies this "person" as Henry James, though Beer is, notoriously, not fully reliable (Beer 1924, 152).

eight banks and a progressive school system" (Eisenstadt 1968, 6B).[36] On the basis of these figures, it is interesting to speculate what Frederic might have made of frontier life.

Frederic's family were religious people and they were also keen Democrats.[37] Politics were keenly discussed in the family home with a vividness and passion that suggests they were central to their lives. Frederic's mother dressed him in a Kossuth hat and Garibaldi jacket, clothes that reflected her strong political sympathies.[38] The household were keen supporters of the Deerfield politician Horatio Seymour, even after he was denounced as a Copperhead.[39] Frances De Motte kept her only son away from neighborhood children, wanting him to grow up with greater aspirations than those of the other youngsters of his age.

Frederic was a lonely child who carried the residuum of his childhood solitariness with him into adulthood: "In a face somewhat immobile, his eyes had the look which often survives a shy and stubborn childhood" (Guiney 1899, 601). One refuge from loneliness was, he claimed (possibly truthfully, certainly unoriginally), the written word, although the family

36. Haines says that the population in 1870 was thirty thousand (Haines 1945, 2). Utica may have been provincial, but it was not rural in the way that Frederic suggests.

37. William De Motte was a Presbyterian, and his new wife, though a Methodist, sang in a Presbyterian choir. Harold was a member of the Junior Order of Rechabites, a temperance group. His paternal grandmother, Mathilde De Motte, was the first child baptized by Francis Asbury, the first Methodist bishop of America. In April 1873 Bishop Jesse Truesdell Peck and his wife were to stay at the South Street house for the New York Annual Conference of Methodists. The pair were the great uncle and aunt of Stephen Crane, who would later become Frederic's good friend. Crane once said of his uncle, "Upon my mother's side, everybody as soon as he could walk, became a Methodist clergyman—of the old ambling-nag, saddle-bag, exhorting kind. My uncle, Jesse T. Peck, D.D., L.L.D., was a bishop in the Methodist Church." (Crane to John Northern Hilliard, 2 January [1896], Crane 1968, 94). It is likely that Frederic was present when the Bishop read out the list of new appointments, a scene that may have inspired the opening chapter of *The Damnation of Theron Ware*. One of Frederic's cousins identified the description of the house in which the fictional Bishop was staying as "Aunt Frank's house" (O'Donnell 1968, 5). O'Donnell located an 1899 edition of *The Damnation of Theron Ware* in which a number of comments have been penciled into the margins. The writer, probably Frederic's first cousin, John Baxter, makes a range of observations that connect fictional names with their "real" counterparts.

38. Kossuth hats had a great vogue following Louis Kossuth's extensive lecture tour of the country in "the most impressive exile ever known," as Howells describes it. Howells also wore one, after being moved by the "wonderful English" and personal beauty and picturesqueness of the Hungarian. Years later Whistler would mock Wilde for wearing "the combined costumes of Kossuth and Mr. Mantalini!" (Howells 1975, 57–58; Whistler 1953, 243).

39. Seymour had been Governor of New York from 1852–54, and again from 1863–65. In 1868 he was the Democrat's nominee for president against Grant, and though he lost, he would remain an idol to Frederic throughout his boyhood. In 1886 Frederic wrote of his fervent hope to write Seymour's biography, and in 1890 he dedicated *In the Valley* to him. When he wrote *The Damnation of Theron Ware* he would model Dr. Ledsmar's house on Seymour's Deerfield home (Frederic Misc. 1977, 100 and 267).

collection of books was limited. He was forced into an inventive use of whatever materials were available. Like so many other childhood experiences, his account of learning the alphabet would become a useful anecdote in his club. He also used it as a "candid" piece of autobiography, and as material for a short story. His journalistic training had taught him to make good use of copy. Like the boy-narrator of "My Aunt Susan," he claimed to have learned his letters from a soapbox in which the wood was kept. His autobiographical and fictional accounts of his early learning are almost identical. The autobiographical statement is more directly colloquial: "[I] learned to read by studying the tradesmen's signboards. . . . I had learned my letters from the label on an old soap-box which held the firewood at home" (Sherard 1897, 534). The fictionalized version is more self-conscious: "I had learned my letters from the old maroon plush label on the Babbitt's soap box which held the wood behind the stove, and expanded this knowledge by a study of street signs" (Frederic Short. 1966, 330.)

His earliest encounters with books were not with imaginative literature, but with social and political history, and with his grandmother's religious books. His grandmother's stories compensated for the dryness of his early reading and took on some of their vividness from comparison with their less gripping competitors. After Frederic's death, stories of his precocity and ingenuity abounded. Shortly after his death a Utica newspaper recounted (possibly even invented) a Tom Sawyer-like anecdote. Frederic's stepfather had told him to saw up some wood and left him to it. "When it was time for the work to be finished, his stepfather found Harry seated on a part of the wood pile reading a novel. He had engaged a man to saw the wood and the excuse he made was that it was easier to hire a man to do the work than to do it himself" ("Death of Harold Frederic" 1898c, 3.) The four books that he particularly remembered were Horace Walpole's *Life and Letters of George III* (whom Frederic regarded as a tyrant), a biography of Ulrich Zwinglius, a Swiss religious reformer, Hale's *History of the USA* and "the book which made the deepest impression on me," Prosper Mérimée's *History of Peter the Cruel*, which he read in translation. All these nonfiction works seem somewhat serious reading matter for a young boy, but he did encounter some lighter material that made a lasting impression.

At some point in his early years, though possibly not until 1873, he was to come across the work of the French collaborators Émile Erckmann and Louis-Alexandre Chatrian.[40] Frederic was to claim them, along with

40. O'Donnell and Franchere write that the Erckmann-Chatrian novels were available in the School District Library (O'Donnell and Franchere 1961, 28). Frederic told Robert Sherard that he had first purchased the novels (though not that he had first read them) when he lived in Boston (Sherard 1897, 536). The writers were popular in Europe and the United States: on 12 September 1875 Vincent Van Gogh wrote to his brother Theodore recommending the novels (Cabanne 1975, 15). Some years later, a reviewer compared Crane's *The Red Badge of Courage* with "some of the Erckmann-Chatrian novels" (Weatherford 1973, 104).

Nathaniel Hawthorne, as his literary parents, for they influenced his ideas about writing at a time when he was most susceptible to influence. In a (somewhat tawdry) tribute to the French collaborators, Frederic bought all of their works and had "each book bound in white vellum as an individual token of my literary indebtedness to them" (Sherard 1897, 534).[41] Among his earliest attempts at fiction were imitations of Erckmann-Chatrian. Much later he was to dismiss his early fictional writings as "pretty bad," though at the time he was characteristically optimistic about both their quality and the chances of their success (Sherard 1897, 537). Between 1873 and 1875 he bought a large number of books, spending much of his spare time and money in bookshops in Boston, though his specific interests are unknown. When lack of money forced him, as he claimed, to sell his collection of books in 1875 at a fraction of their price, he refused to part with those by Erckmann-Chatrian.

Frederic's education spans about nine years, from about 1862 to 1871. He left school shortly before his fifteenth birthday.[42] Frederic had the educational experience of most young Uticans, and school may have taught him, as Mark Twain was taught (informally), to chew tobacco, as well as harsher lessons (Henry Adams bitterly remembered his schooldays as "time thrown away.") (Twain 1960, 12; Adams 1973, 38).

From 1871 to 1875, when he joined the *Utica Morning Herald* as a proofreader, only a fragmentary picture of his life exists.[43] After graduating from school he took a variety of jobs, working at a confectionery until he lost the job through eating the nuts that he was supposed to crack, an early manifestation of a lifelong interest in food. His next jobs stimulated another long-term interest: photography. Until 1875 he was to work at a series of different photographic studios learning every aspect of photography. At first he worked at the studio of L. C. Mundy, but he soon became dissatisfied with his dull chores and moved to another studio.[44] At his next

41. See also "Preface to a Uniform Edition" (Frederic Misc. 1977, 5).

42. He attended Public School No. 12 on Seymour Avenue, very close to his home, and then the South Street Intermediate School. In 1869 he moved to the Advanced School at Utica, which had about 430 pupils, mainly girls.

43. Odd details give an impression of his interests. In August 1872 he joined the Adjutant Bacon Corps of Cadets, named after a dead local hero—like the fictional De Witt C. Hemingway Fire Zouaves of "The Eve of the Fourth." The Corps practiced elaborate formal maneuvers, sometimes blindfolded to improve their precision. This was the closest that Frederic ever got to the life of a soldier.

44. Later he would revenge himself on his erstwhile employer by revealing trade secrets to the current chore-boy. Mundy demanded $135 from his apprentice, Carl Frey, but Frederic told Frey "To hell with the old man—I'll teach you" (Haines 1945, 15). He would always be impatient with ungenerous conduct. At his new job Frederic revealed an indolent and fanciful side to his character. He first ruined a stack of expensive paper through daydreaming, and then a series of prints by falling asleep while they turned black. He lost his job despite his stepfather's pleading on his behalf—no doubt another unwelcome task given to De Motte by his forceful wife.

job at another studio (they seem to have proliferated in Utica) he learned an innocent form of deception—how to "beautify the image" (Haines 1945, 15). He acted as an aesthetic censor, removing signs of age and unsightliness from the faces of his subjects. This deception influenced the development of his fiction. His earliest writing, which was often melodramatic and sentimental, could be called "beautified." Later he learned that the blemishes on human faces were more interesting and revealing than an unreal image, and produced memorably unbeautified figures. Yet like Marsena Pulford of his eponymous Civil War story, even at this age Frederic had a secret wish: he hoped to become an artist, perhaps a painter. Marsena, a failed artist, turns to photography when he finds that his art is "no good." He hates photography "like pizen" (Frederic Short. 1966, 189). (Frederic would adopt the long hair and flowing frock coat of Marsena on his return from Boston in 1875.)

At this stage in his life Frederic did not know whether his art would be any good, but he was keen to find out. He had already shown himself to be a capable caricaturist, capturing his teacher so well (in colored chalks on the schoolyard) that she made him scrub away his work (Haines 1945, 13–14). It would not be the last time that his work would annoy its subject. After Frederic's, death, his friend Clement Shorter would write that Frederic's cables to the *New York Times* were "excessively irritating to many of us" because his "very Bohemian instincts made him somewhat antagonistic to many of our social institutions" ("C.K.S." 1898, 4). This criticism was not caricature, although it became so in *Observations in Philistia, The Return of The O'Mahony,* and *March Hares,* in which the adult Frederic did with words what he had done as a boy with colored chalk.[45] He always had a keen visual sense. He was three when John Brown was hanged, and later claimed that he could remember the pictures of the hanging "perfectly" (Sherard 1897, 534).[46] In his preliterate years it had been pictures that had caught

45. While in Utica though, his caricaturing was more pictographic. Frederic played a clever practical joke on the Cadets combining his photographic and artistic skills to make a collage: "In 1873 Harold made a set of pen and ink caricatures of the Cadets, using snapshots for the heads and adding bodies in comic postures: the commander rides a hobby horse, one cranks a hand-organ, another grins from a cradle. Harold himself stands with a palette and sign-painter's brush beside an easel, and he signed the page 'Frederic,' a more comely spelling of the name" (Haines 1945, 16). This is his first known use of the name with which he is associated. He had been drawing in earnest for about five years at this time. When he was about twelve he had taken one of his drawings to the local portrait painter. The photographer's helper, George Pflanz, liked both picture and artist, and they became firm friends, rowing together on the river, talking art and politics, eating and sketching together. Frederic was serious about his art, although it was not always itself serious, and spent one summer camping in the woods in the company of a collection of artist's materials as well as an ancient pistol.

46. It seems unlikely. It may be that he remembered the incident through the pictures that he collected of it. In the same interview he estimated that his collection of newspaper pictures totaled over twelve thousand.

his imagination, and he contemplated becoming a professional illustrator and retained a strong interest in the illustrations for his own novels long after he had given up the idea of being an artist. He designed the covers of the Heinemann editions of *The Damnation of Theron Ware* and *Gloria Mundi* himself. Art would always remain a passionate hobby; but it was in journalism that Frederic would make a name for himself as one of the great foreign correspondents by making journalism itself into an art form.

Boston, and In the Valley Once More

In 1873 Frederic left Utica for Boston. He later romanticized this move, telling an interviewer that he "ran away from home to Boston, where . . . [he] had a friend" (Sherard 1897, 536). Who this friend was remains unknown. Economic depression and frustration with his provincial home town certainly prompted the move.[47] One of his greatest joys, he later claimed, was to buy himself a cigar on Saturday nights, and go to a local billiard hall. Making sure that he was out of the draught so that the cigar would burn well, he would sit watching people. The premeditation of this elaborate ritual is immensely appealing. Saturday nights at the billiard hall would later prove to be admirable training for his journalist's eye.[48] While in Boston he continued with his photographic career, working in the photographic studio of Allen and Rowell in Winter Street. Although his wages were initially low, he soon prospered: "He not only retouched all of the negatives for Allen and Rowell, but did a large amount of similar work for other firms in the surrounding towns. For a while his earnings ranged from $30 to $90 a week, 'an extraordinary income for a lad of his age' " ("Harold Frederic Dead" 1898, 7). These wages (if not exaggerated) were certainly high: Frederic's weekly wage for the *New York Times* was $80 from 1884 until the end of his life. He later used his photographic experiences to force a comparison between American and British work practices. In 1886 he was in East Anglia trying to persuade the employees of a studio to

47. This episode of his life had nothing of the quality of W. D. Howells's journey to his New England Mecca or Hamlin Garland's later move there. Howells's recollections of his first visit to Boston and Cambridge glow with the reflected light of the New England luminaries whose homes he visited. Although meetings could occasionally be disappointing (Howells's meeting with Hawthorne was a disaster), the pleasure that he received from firsthand acquaintance with his literary heroes overflows into the nostalgic and overlaudatory accounts of them. Years later Frederic would pay a similar visit to Howells, a distinguished Boston resident by this time, and would write telling him that "I shall carry away to London no other recollection of my visit equal in value to the memory of my call upon you" (Frederic to W. D. Howells, 11 December 1890, Frederic Misc. 1977, 269) Later still, one of Frederic's sons by Grace Frederic would run away from the home he shared with his paternal grandmother, he would never return.

48. Haines questions this anecdote on specific historical grounds, yet what is interesting about it is the care in which Frederic constructs himself through it.

photograph a document, and turned an account of failure into a very funny open letter to an American colleague (Frederic to John B. Howe ca. 16 December 1886, Frederic Misc. 1977, 144–46). Frederic later referred to this period in Boston as the happiest in his life. He was young and unmarried; he was living in a big city. The dominant women in his family were left far behind him, and though he was not the country boy that he would have his listeners believe, perhaps for the first time he was made acutely aware of his ingenuousness. What passed for sophistication in Utica took on a rural aspect in Boston.[49]

He claims that in 1875 his eyesight deteriorated significantly—whether this was due to too many visits to the billiard hall or to too much work remains unknown. He either lost or gave up his job, sold his prized books for a fraction of their value, and returned to Utica. Returning home meant a loss of liberation, but his mother and stepfather welcomed him. His short-lived rebellion over, he settled into a short period of rest in which his half-sister read to him while his eyesight recovered. In the summer of 1875 he started his first job in journalism, as a proofreader for the *Utica Morning Herald* at twelve dollars a week. Either his eyestrain had been temporary, or, like the famous and false announcement of Mark Twain's death, it was greatly exaggerated.

Between 1875 and 1884 Frederic's career took on the dimensions of a Horatio Alger story. Night work for a morning paper affected his health, so leaving his job, he moved to the *Utica Daily Observer,* an afternoon paper. He began reading proofs there in December 1875 and by May 1880 he had become editor of the paper at the age of twenty-three. His wages increased to twenty-four dollars a week. Something of the charge of that time is captured in "The Editor and the Schoolma'am." Like Alexander Waring, the protagonist of the story, Frederic was contemplating marriage. On 10 October 1877, two months after his twenty-first birthday, Frederic married Grace Williams, a quiet Utica girl. Frederic was never open about his married life, and since little of his personal correspondence has survived, she exists in snippets, silenced and overshadowed by her garrulous husband. What can be established is that her life was to be lonely and unhappy and the marriage increasingly unsatisfactory to both partners.[50]

---

49. He may have had the discomfort of hearing young urban dwellers shout " 'Hop-pick —ers!' " after him (for to them if he was not from the city, then he must be a rustic) and, like Seth Fairchild, been aware of the cardinal rule that hotel porters were all brigands waiting to rob unsuspecting strangers. Like Theron Ware, he may have found that unaccustomed sight of a "swarm" of people running for trains may have made him question whether there was a fire. Why else would they run?

50. Many of the details of the couple's early married life are fictionalized in *The Damnation of Theron Ware,* though the resemblance between life and work is in no way exact. They were married at the deathbed of Grace's mother, and after a short stay at the South Street home

That the first years of their marriage were happy is suggested by a letter describing himself as he was in 1879 as "a poor devil of a reporter, with $12 a week, a young girl wife and a baby daughter—and happy as a lord." Four years after that the Edenic, idyllic nature of his life had changed. His innocence had gone, and "there are ashes inside the apple," "I know better than they are worth knowing a host of eminent political humbugs and sharpers; I get five or six times as much money; I do not eat or sleep as well and drink better; I am unhappy. . . . Surely it is all vanity and emptiness" (Frederic to Benjamin P. Blood, 9 May 1883, Frederic Misc. 1977, 16). The couple were to have six children, but only four survived infancy. Ruth (named after her maternal grandmother) was born in 1878. The following year a second daughter, Ruby, was born, but she died in infancy. Another child, also called Ruby, was born in 1880, and Harold Jr., in 1885 (dying two years later). Hereward was born in 1887, and a second Harold Jr. in 1889.

In 1877 or 1879 Frederic made an important—and lifelong—friendship. This friendship would stimulate the love of Ireland and the Irish, which would be vital to his life. Edward Aloysius Terry, an Irish-American priest, had come to America with his family when he was five. In June 1876 he had moved to Utica as parish priest of St. John's, the large Catholic Church that still stands close both to Frederic's birthplace in South Street and to the building that housed the *Utica Daily Observer.* Frederic's friendship with Terry began at an important, formative time. Terry, older by some years (he was born in 1842), provided companionship and intellectual stimulation, and Frederic acknowledged his debt to him by using him as a model for Father Forbes in *The Damnation of Theron Ware* and by dedicating *The Lawton Girl* to him. (If Grace Frederick felt that his third novel would more appropriately have been dedicated to her, she was powerless to do anything about it. By 1890 the marriage had broken down irreparably.)

Terry was an intelligent and open-minded theologian and was committed to pastoral work. He quickly endeared himself to his parishioners. Frederic welcomed the opportunity to understand, through Terry, the alien social group that the local Protestants alternately ignored and abused. Patrick Mullany (Brother Azarius of the Cross), a close friend of both

---

they moved, in May 1878, to 58 Mary Street. Frederic's mother later recounted, in a letter to Charles Miller of 27 October 1898, that like Theron and Alice, who found themselves eight hundred dollars in debt after a year of marriage, the young couple "did not make it a success at keeping house," and returned to the capable management of her own household at South Street (Harold Frederic Papers). It was not an auspicious start to married life and was the beginning of a pattern of financial difficulty that increased the strain on both partners and would continue throughout Frederic's life.

men, had discovered, while at school near Utica, that "many of his fellow citizens thought that it was a disgrace to be Irish and a crime to be Catholic"—a sentiment captured in the first few chapters of *The Damnation of Theron Ware* (Frederic Misc. 1977, 507).[51] Frederic was fascinated by Terry's love of Ireland, his knowledge of its history and culture, and his sympathetic concern with the political and economic condition of the country and its people. He was equally captivated by Terry's eloquent explanation of Catholic dogma—between 1868 and 1875 Terry had occupied the chairs of Dogmatic Theology and Sacred Scripture at Mount Saint Mary's Seminary, Emmitsburg, Maryland.[52] Frederic realized that the Catholic Church had a powerful hold upon its members: no matter how badly Catholics behaved, they remained Catholics. They could not drop out of the Church. The parishioners might take the pledge and become "Pioneers," as they are still called, or they might drink as they pleased but— saints and sinners alike—they were still Catholic. As Dr. Ledsmar says, "There's no bottom to the Catholic Church. Everything that's in, stays in. . . . [T]hey all have a right here, the professional burglar every whit as much as the speckless saint. The only stipulation is that they oughtn't to come under false pretences: the burglar is in honor bound not to pass himself off to his priest as the saint" (Frederic Novels 1986, 75–76).

Frederic enjoyed this seemingly liberal arrangement that appeared to be so much more frank and human than the narrowness of the Methodism he had encountered. He had become an enthusiastic fan of the Catholic priest and of his flock and might have said, with Theron, "I am in love with your sinners" (Frederic Novels 1986, 237). He was drawn to dramatic statements. (Later, having visited Ireland for the first time, he told the

51. Gertrude Atherton confirms this distrust of Catholics in her autobiography, "Roman Catholics were candidates for hell fire. While I was there an extremely pretty girl moved to Lexington with her family, but she was a Papist and Society would as readily have admitted a rattlesnake to its sacred preserve. My aunt pointed her out to me in a hushed whisper" (Atherton 1932, 39).

52. Like Father Forbes, Terry organized outings and events for his parishioners. These could have enormous dimensions. One picnic had an attendance of twenty-five hundred people. They were taken to the picnic spot by forty-six hired railway carriages, and on their return to Utica were given the sort of welcome usually reserved for important politicians (Haines 1945, 67). Frederic is thought to have accompanied them on at least one of these expeditions to Trenton Falls, a spot he knew well from sketching expeditions (Haines 1945, 37). He may, like Theron, have been amazed and perhaps a little shocked at the informality and lack of decorum of the event. While the Protestant leaders of the local Y.M.C.A. congratulated themselves on discouraging vice (one said, "I have knelt by the side of sixty men who have signed the pledge and given their heart to Jesus"), Terry's picnics were indulgent—even shocking—affairs by comparison (Haines 1945, 60). Beer was freely available and spirits were high: just as in *The Damnation of Theron Ware*, both beer and petticoats were frothy and clearly visible.

Utica Irish that "I came back an Irishman."[53]) He was attracted to the dignity and history of Catholic ritual and to the Irish Catholics that he met through Terry, but he probably never considered conversion. Catholicism meant Father Terry—he embodied the finer aspects of the religion—and Terry saw no need to evangelize. He left that to the Protestants. This friendship enabled Frederic to move between worlds and to begin to enact a parallel life, away from his wife and from the beliefs he had been brought up with. In September 1880 Terry was transferred to St. Ann's Parish Church in Albany, to the dismay and anger of many of his parishioners.[54] The two men kept in close contact with each other, and when Frederic was offered the editorship of the Republican *Albany Evening Journal* in 1882, he lodged with Terry for a time, leaving his young family in Utica, another suggestion of the strain that had already emerged in his marriage and of the division of his lives. Frederic remained on close terms with Terry throughout his life despite seeing him seldom after 1884, and after Frederic's death Terry contributed to the upkeep of Grace Frederic and their children.

In Albany, Frederic became a member of the Fort Orange Club, where local Democrats met and argued politics, and he soon threw himself into the political life of the State Capital. He met the governor of New York, Grover Cleveland, and his "enthusiastic admiration" for the future president "repeatedly cropped out in the supposedly Republican editorials of the *Evening Journal* like veins of gold in a cold quartz ledge" (Nevins 1932, 133).[55] Yet the way in which all this friendship may have developed was abruptly challenged when Frederic resigned from the paper over a matter

53. "I confess that when I went over [to England] it was with the common idea that there was a great deal in England's position. Then I went to Ireland and saw, not the show places which tourists see, with their mock-Irish pretense, their swarms of beggars, and their odious trading upon their rags and dirt, but that real Ireland where rogues put the law on honest men, and only the crows and the constabulary get enough to eat—and I came back an Irishman" (Haines 1945, 142).

54. Several local priests, envious of his personal popularity and angry with his liberalism, had requested that the bishop move him. A number of his parishioners complained to the bishop (against Terry's will) and begged the prospective candidate to refuse his appointment. Terry told them, "Ah, bless ye, ye meant well. But now I'm going anyway. Ye've all turned protestants. There is no disputing the authority of the Church. Ye meant well, but ye've broke my heart" (Haines 1945, 69). Tolerant—indeed good-humored—to the last, Terry saw through the petty jealousies that had led to his transfer, and his last sermon to his parishioners was a call to acceptance entitled "Catholic Obedience."

55. Terry was also friendly with Cleveland, and when Frederic visited the United States in 1886, Cleveland canceled a cabinet meeting in order to introduce Terry and Frederic to his new wife. Other men with whom Frederic established firm friendships included Edgar Kelsey Apgar, Daniel Scott Lamont, Cleveland's secretary in his first administration and secretary of war and close advisor to the president in the second administration, and Thomas MacDonald Waller, consul general in London in Cleveland's first administration.

of political principle, in March 1884 (see chapter 3). The easy intimacy of regular meeting was replaced by the formality of the written word. For, around 26 April 1884, Frederic accepted the post of London correspondent to the *New York Times*. He had been offered other newspaper editorships, but had decided to accept a job that would leave him time for writing fiction. He planned to lead a split life as a journalist moonlighting as a novelist until the time that he could live from writing fiction. Frederic and his family sailed to England in *The Queen* on 11 June 1884.

London

In his racy autobiography, Frederic's friend Frank Harris writes of his experience of arriving in London after years of travel, with the enormous expectancy of ambitious youth,

> London in the early 'eighties; London after years of solitary study and grim, relentless effort; London when you are twenty-eight and have already won a place in its life; London when your mantelpiece has ten times as many invitations as you can accept, and there are two or three pretty girls that attract you; London when everyone you meet is courteous-kind [sic] and people of importance are beginning to speak about you; London with the foretaste of success in your mouth while your eyes are open wide to its myriad novelties and wonders . . . who could give even an idea of its varied delights? (Harris 1958, 183).

Henry Adams, James Fenimore Cooper, Nathaniel Hawthorne, Margaret Fuller, Henry James, and Harriet Beecher Stowe were all Americans who left vivid testimony to their first impression of England. Unfortunately, Frederic's existing correspondence does not record his feelings as he landed in England in June 1884, in his twenty-eighth year, although the following year he wrote (probably to Terry) comparing Paris and London, in terms that Harris would have enjoyed but that seem like curious ones to use in addressing a Catholic priest:

> I can think of no better simile to describe my meaning than that of two girls —one of whom shall be beautiful with sparkling black eyes and red, laughing lips, gay in mood and ready of jest; while the other is only good looking, with gray, quiet eyes and a soft voice. To see them, a man will prefer the former; to meet them for an hour, again he will prefer her, but when he comes to know them, and learns on the one hand how superficial, selfish, mean in spirit this beauty is, and on the other hand what fine reality of mind and nature there is under the serious air of the other, then if he be a wise man his preference will shift—and now I have told you why I like London better than I do Paris. (Frederic to Edward A. Terry, [?] August 1885, Frederic Misc. 1977, 66–67).

What is certain is that he left New York only after he had prepared himself for every aspect of transatlantic life. Before he sailed, he went to see the newspaper editor Edward Mitchell, who had been to Europe twice: "His main anxiety was about the etiquette of the steamship, not at all about his press functions after landing. He wanted to know how much he would be expected to fee the table steward, the room steward, the bath steward, and so on; and the inexpert advice he received was noted carefully in his memorandum-book" (Mitchell 1924, 279–80). This seems an extraordinary reversal of priorities. Frederic's anxieties were not about his work but about his lack of sophistication. His work would speak for itself, he felt, but his appearance and manners needed nurturing. Mitchell, whose memoirs reveal him to be something of a snob, expresses supersensitivity toward Frederic's provincialism: "He wore a long green overcoat that made him look like a cucumber and was uncouth and awkward" (Mitchell 1924, 280). The comparison was appropriate—Frederic was large and greenly naïve despite his two years in the state capital. He no doubt thought that he was rather swagger in the coat. He had shown a tendency toward sartorial individualism early in his life, when he returned from Boston in clothes designed to suggest that he was an artist. He was outdistancing his Utica peers—even at this early age—and it was this that would later contribute to the breakdown of his marriage. In England he would act the part of the bluff Yankee. He would wear a soft shirt rather than a stiff one, for starched shirts, he said, implied servitude to fashion and to propriety. In London he would champion the United States loudly and aggressively. He would assert his right to a voice in London, dominating drawing-room conversations. By the time of his death he had gained a reputation as a clubman, a connoisseur of food and drink, a singer of college songs and (like Mark Twain) black spirituals, a *siffleur* of rare quality, like O. Henry's tramp, Whistling Dick, and a world expert on philately. These accomplishments, and indeed their variety and veering between aestheticism and antidecadence, were not necessarily intended to surprise his British contemporaries, but surprised they were.

When Frederic arrived in England in 1884 he rapidly became engrossed by the necessity of making contacts in a country where "news and favors are strictly social things" (Frederic to Charles R. Miller, 21 February 1885, Frederic Misc. 1977, 45). He had a talent for using social situations to his advantage, and with extraordinary rapidity he established friendships with a range of politicians, journalists, writers, and artists. He had carried a personal endorsement with him from Grover Cleveland, and when Cleveland became president the document helped his smooth passage through the social hierarchies of London: "Mr. Harold Frederic until recently was a resident of the city of Albany where I have enjoyed his acquaintance and friendship. His ability and success as a journalist are conceded; and I am much pleased to have the opportunity of testifying to his rare attainments, as well as to his qualities of heart and mind, that have made him my friend, [and] gained for him an enviable place in the esti[mation] of the entire community" (Grover Cleveland to Frederic, 6 June 1884, Frederic 1977, 21). It materially assisted his entry into the National Liberal Club, and also the Savage Club, a Bohemian association of actors, writers, artists, and journalists, which became virtually his base until he resigned in 1887. In the fourteen years that he lived in London, Frederic led an active and eclectic social life. It had nothing of the epic quality of Henry James's innumerable dinner engagements, which Frederic knew about and affected to despise.[56]

Frederic was quick to recognize the value of making acquaintances and friendships work for him, despite the fact that he had little time for "Society." He might visit the political salon of Lady Jeune at which politicians and literary figures mingled and exchanged pleasantries or unpleasantries, dine at one of his clubs—or visit the Reform Club, the Carlton, or the St. Stephen's Club. As he became more familiar with London life he began to entertain at his own home or at the Savage Club. His range of friends and acquaintances was large and diverse, encompassing journalists, politicians, government officials, literary figures, miscellaneous Americans (for he had a talent for picking them up), and theatrical impresarios, actors, and actresses.[57]

He was always happy to meet fellow Americans in London and was generous with both time and money. One American with whom he would form a close friendship was Stephen Crane. Frederic had warmly reviewed Crane's *The Red Badge of Courage* (1895) for the *New York Times*. Crane wrote in a letter to Ripley Hitchcock on 2 February 1896, that he was "very much delighted" with the review, and when he came to England the two people that he wanted to meet were Frederic and Joseph Conrad (Crane 1968, 110). Within a few days of arriving in England the young man who had already met and impressed Hamlin Garland and W. D. Howells was taken around London by Frederic. Frederic's boisterous enthusiasm for

56. According to Beer, he called James "an effeminate old donkey who lives with a herd of other donkeys . . . and insisted on being treated as if he were the Pope. He has licked dust from the floor of every third rate hostess in England" (Beer 1924, 151–52). This is standard exaggeration, possibly masking envy or certainly disquiet. As ever, Beer's attributions must be treated with caution.

57. For an exaggerated account of gluttony at the Cafe Royal, see Harris 1931, 248–49. He was a member of the Ghouls, a club that dined monthly at Roma's restaurant in High Holburn, presided over by Frederic, who bullied the Ghouls good-humoredly. Members included W. E. Henley, the editor of the *National Observer,* J. M. Barrie, A. Conan Doyle, Bernard Partridge—the *Punch* cartoonist—and Arthur Warren, a journalist. He might breakfast at T. P. O'Connor's, where he exchanged wit with Oscar Wilde, lunch with Bernard Shaw and Frank Harris, or dine with the artists Joseph and Elizabeth Pennell.

Homefield, Kenley—now The Vicarage, Valley Road.

expatriate Americans may have threatened to overwhelm Crane on occasion, but Crane enjoyed Frederic's frank generosity and unambiguous Americanness and was glad of his compatriot's presence. Frederic attended a Savoy lunch given for Crane by Richard Harding Davis, the distinguished war correspondent, and the following day he traveled to Dover with Crane to see him off on a trip to Paris. When the Cranes returned to England they settled at Ravensbrook, Oxted. The house was close to Homefield in Kenley, where Frederic had been living on a part-time basis, and the Cranes were soon acquainted with a literary group of near-neighbors who included Ford Madox Ford, Robert Barr, George Gissing, and H. G. Wells.[58] The Cranes and Frederic and Kate Lyon regularly visited each other.

On 19 August 1897, the Cranes had a carriage accident on their way to Kenley to celebrate Frederic's birthday. They arrived covered in blood and were at once taken in by Kate Lyon and Frederic. After recuperating with them, the Cranes, Lyon, and Frederic all traveled together to Ireland for three weeks to a house loaned to Frederic by a wealthy female admirer. Yet by the following year, the suggestion of a similar holiday caused an explo-

58. See Milne 1980. Frederic continued his sharp criticisms of his friends, saying of Wells, "H. G.'s idea of utopia is a world of nickel-plated push-buttons and no trees." This recalls Theron's difficulties with the doorbell at the Catholic pastorate (Haines 1945, 216).

sion of anger from the volatile younger man. The two men had already argued over Crane's story "The Monster" (Frederic had suggested that he throw it away), and Frederic's invitation to Ahakista, the Irish house, triggered a violence that had been building up for some time.[59] Frederic wrote a sad and contrite letter to Cora Crane, and although the two men were reconciled, and the holiday plans revived, Crane left England for Cuba shortly before the start of the holiday and Cora Crane went to Ireland without him. Frederic was recovering from the first attack of the ill health that would cause his death later in the year, and Crane wrote to Henry Sanford Bennett in April, "Sorry not to have seen you. I have raised the wind and sail tomorrow Nothing I can do for Harold. Barr will look after him" (Beer 1924, 177).

Frederic and Crane would never meet again, though apparently later in the year Crane, ill and hallucinating, would imagine that he saw Frederic standing over him wearing a fur coat. Before this he had discovered, bitterly, that Frederic's warning of the viciousness of literary gossip was not idle. In a letter to Robert Barr, Crane laments that "Now I owe Harold an apology for laughing when he said they would tear me in pieces the minute my back was turned. Hi, Harold! I apologize! Did you know me for a morphine eater? A man who has known me ten years tells me that all my books are written while I am drenched with morphine. The joke is on me" (Crane to Robert Barr, 20 May 1898, Frederic Misc. 1977, 472).[60]

Within five months of this letter, Frederic was dead, and the gossip-mongers rejoiced. Less than two years later Crane himself died. On 8 June 1900, three days after Crane's death, Robert Barr described a séance that he and Crane had once held:

> Stephen died at three in the morning, the same sinister hour which carried away our friend Frederic nineteen months before. At midnight, in Crane's fourteenth-century house in Sussex [Brede Place], we two tried to lure back the ghost of Frederic into that house of ghosts, and to our company, thinking that if reappearing were ever possible so strenuous a man as Harold would somehow shoulder his way past the guards, but he made no sign. I wonder if the less insistent Stephen will suggest some ingenious method by which the two can pass the barrier. I can imagine Harold cursing on the other side, and welcoming the more subtle assistance of his finely fibred friend. (Weatherford 1973, 317)

59. In her biography of Cora Crane, Lillian Gilkes has suggested that Crane's reaction was partially caused by his guilt at his well-documented "illegitimate" relationship with Cora, and of the parallels that the Frederic/Lyon relationship suggested to him. The house in Ireland "became a blazing issue, a symbol of Bohemian laxity" to him. This is not a very convincing argument (Gilkes 1962, 134–35).

60. Berryman gives further examples of Crane's experience of gossip (Berryman 1950, 233–34).

Barr, who calls himself the last of the Three Musketeers, suggests the contrasts between Frederic and Crane. Frederic was burly, powerful, and prone to irascibility. Crane was physically more slight, though athletically built, boyish, clever, and persistent. Since the two men lived so close to each other and saw each other so regularly, and since their friendship was abruptly terminated by Frederic's death, there is no epistolary testament to their relationship (unlike, say, that of Twain and Howells, Wharton and James, or Wells and Gissing). The friendship of these men of letters, as they (unaptly) might be called, was mainly conducted verbally. This probably suited both men. Crane's unwillingness or inability to indulge in written literary criticism (a reluctance that verged on overt anti-intellectualism) was a trait partially shared by Frederic, though Frederic could be an acute book-reviewer.[61]

Home: "A Double Household"

In a letter written about a decade after his return from Boston Frederic refers obliquely to a "woman much older than myself" whom he knew "very intimately" in Boston. Nothing is known of this woman, except that she was bookish, and that he was sufficiently interested in her to read a book because she particularly liked it (Frederic to Benjamin P. Blood, 9 May 1883, Frederic Misc. 1977, 15). The tone of Frederic's reference to her implies, and is intended to imply, that they shared more than a passion for books. Perhaps it was in Boston that Frederic began his forays into the world of sexual experience.[62]

When Frederic first arrived in England he established a friendly relationship with the journalist and social reformer W. T. Stead that was not to last long. Stead soon clashed with Frederic over the sexual scandal surrounding Frederic's friend, the Liberal M. P. Sir Charles Dilke, and the friendship rapidly disintegrated into an undignified public wrangle in which the two men attacked each other in print. Frederic apparently made two anonymous contributions to Stead's "Maiden Tribute"[63] case, a campaign to raise

---

61. Frederic has been castigated for offering Crane bad literary advice—to throw away "The Monster" and to write *Active Service* (1899), and for providing Crane a model, in the form of *The Return of The O'Mahony*, for Crane's own Irish picaresque, *The O'Ruddy* (1903).

62. It is even possible that he first met Kate Lyon in Boston. See Myers 1995, 92–93.

63. For details of Frederic's support of Dilke, see the index in *The Correspondence of Harold Frederic*. Frederic attacked Stead in "An Indictment of Russia" as well as in the *Welsh Review*. Haines identifies him, an identification that has been generally accepted by Frederic scholars. Although Haines does not give his source for the attribution, the claim was certainly made to him in a letter of 30 September 1935 from Edwin H. Stout, who first prefaces his claim with a note that his memory is not what it was. Yet he sounds certain of his information despite this disclaimer. For further accounts of the "Maiden Tribute" case, see Walkowitz 1994, 81–134, and Schults 1972, 128–68.

Harold Frederic at an unknown age.

the age of consent and stop the "sale" of young girls. He signed them "A Saunterer in the Labyrinth" and "An Altered Man." One made the impossible claim (presumably to hide his identity) that he had been sauntering in the labyrinth for twenty years (impossible, that is, unless he was extraordinarily sexually precocious). In the first article the Saunterer warns the *Pall Mall Gazette* against its own "Bumbledom" in relation to prostitution, and offers a defense of "the public women of London": "I have never frequented the kind of houses which the Commission visited, but in the quieter callings of the region which I know, I never found the women other than kindly and gentle, and by no means addicted either to heavy drinking or obscene conversation" (Frederic Misc. 1885d, 22).

These comments on "the labyrinth" indicate a relatively liberal and humane attitude toward sex. Prostitutes (either actual, would-be, or reformed) figure in three of Frederic's novels: Jessica Lawton is a former prostitute who is forced onto the streets after being abandoned by her lover; Vestalia Peaussier considers prostitution as an escape from destitution; and Christian Tower finds that the sight of the prostitutes at the Empire Theater moves him to exclaim in sorrow at the fate of his "sisters."[64] Frederic probably had personal experience of the prostitutes of the Empire Theater, for he took at least one of his visitors—a Utican—to the Empire, where he introduced him to a woman who he thought might be a congenial companion (Haines 1945, 182). In a comment that reflects interestingly on his later relationship with Kate Lyon, he suggests that "affectionate and lasting concubinage" may occur more frequently in the future: "Concubinage is apt to turn into marriage if the woman behaves well. . . . After that, London suburban life is very merciful. Nobody has any history there, and for the new couple the past is buried" (Frederic Misc. 1885f, 11). Frederic was to underestimate the power of the past and the viciousness of London suburban life. On his early death his life with Kate Lyon would be dragged up in newspapers in Britain and in the United States, and London suburban life would show that its mercy is only assured at the price of extreme discretion or, possibly, death.

When Frederic had first arrived in England he was keen to establish a congenial home for his young wife and family. His early correspondence with his *New York Times* editor, Charles Miller, contains frequent references to his wife and his growing family, usually in the context of general domestic gossip. Yet difficulties emerged early: on 14 July 1884 he writes to Charles Miller that "Mrs. F. is ill, and both little girls are in the throes of whooping cough, but I have just leased a fine house in Bayswater [12 Pembridge Crescent], where I think they will recover health and spirits" (Frederic Misc. 1977, 25).[65] Although Grace Frederic appears to have recovered both for a time, she had frequent relapses. Frederic's letters to Miller are punctuated by references to her: to loneliness caused by lack of companionship, to unspecified illnesses, and to depression caused by the death of their first son.[66] The Frederics made several visits to the Continent in the years between 1884 and 1889, partially, at least, for the requirements of mental as well as physical well-being. Grace comes across, in Frederic's

64. "These are my sisters—my unhappy and dishonoured sisters, scorned and scornful—oh yes, they are all my sisters!" (Frederic Novels 1898, 186). For a further account of contemporary debates about the Empire and indecency, see Stokes 1989, 53–93 and Davis, in Foulkes 1992, 111–31.

65. Initially the Frederics shared their house with Edmund Moffat, at that time the United States Agricultural Agent in Europe.

66. See, for example, Frederic to Charles R. Miller, 1 November 1884, Frederic Misc. 1977, 33.

letters, as a solitary and subdued figure: the ghost of his Utica past personified in a woman who was never at home in England.

They lived in several different houses in London, their moves necessi-
tated by cost, or by the demands of Frederic's work.[67] Around 1895 they
moved once again, to Old House, Dunsany Road, in Brook Green. He had
a well-stocked garden where he could potter (it was usually attended to by
Ruth) and a greenhouse that he stocked with rare plants. The last home
they would share as a family was in Bedford Square. Within the next two
or three years Frederic began a relationship with Kate Lyon that would
split his domestic life in two and divide his friends.[68] Frederic would spend
weekends with Grace and her children, but weekdays would be spent with
Kate Lyon and the three children who were born to the couple. Frederic
had a study in each of his homes: part workplace, part refuge. Even after
he had established a household at Kenley with Kate Lyon he retained a
study at Grace's house. He also used his clubs as a haven, often working
and eating there, and created a private domestic space for himself. His
household was divided, not just between his two families, but between the
domestic world that they inhabited and the man's world—the club life—
that he so enjoyed. Clubs also functioned as neutral territory in which he
could meet his daughter Ruth. One of the symptoms of his deteriorating
relationship with his wife was his companionship with Ruth, which was
based on comradely more than paternal interest. Ruth gradually replaced
Grace Frederic as Frederic's formal companion on public occasions.[69]

67. After hints about extravagance from Charles Miller, they moved from Bayswater, on 1
December 1885, to 8 Osnaburgh Terrace, Regent's Park. In 1887 the family moved again, to
39 Bedford Square. The house was ideally situated for Frederic, for it was near to the British
Museum at which he was a frequent visitor, to his clubs, to his office, and to the bustle of
London life. In 1892 Grace and the children moved to Claremont Gardens in Surbiton.

68. Guiney writes that "By an attitude and conduct which can have no defenders among
those who knew the facts, Harold Frederic put in abeyance the love and allegiance of half his
friends" (Guiney 1899, 602).

69. She was often his theater or dinner partner. Sometimes, if he was busy, she would go
to attend a play in his place and her opinion became the basis of his report to the *New York
Times*. The pair would go for walking trips in the countryside, perhaps taking several days
over the walk and staying overnight somewhere. They had a shared sense of mischief. Once,
on a train journey, a priggish English couple came into their carriage. Frederic reached into
his pocket and took out two cigars, keeping one himself and offering the other to his daughter. Ruth took it, lit it, and smoked it—all straightfaced—while the English couple sputtered.
Haines tells of an occasion when Frederic played a practical joke on a man who had patroniz-
ingly offered him an expensive cigar: " 'Do you know,' said Frederic, 'when I was in Cuba a
chemist told me that the architecture of a cigar was more important than the brand. Let me
give you his explanation.' Then with his penknife Frederic slit the cigar, sliced and dissected
it, all the while delivering an extemporized lecture, full of sounding terms. 'You see, I'm
right. Notice those yellow lines of oxide of silicate—very essential to blandness of flavor.' . . .
Frederic, when he had reduced the cigar to shreds, took one of his own cheaper brand and
lighted it." (Haines 1945, 181).

When Frederic returned to the United States in 1888 it was his eldest daughter, not his wife, who accompanied him to comfort Frances De Motte after the deaths of Harold Frederic Jr. and Frederic's half-sister, Helen Gilmore. When Frederic died Ruth was at his side with Kate Lyon. She accepted Frederic's domestic situation with dignity, which she maintained in the genteel and tragic begging letters she was forced to write after his death.[70]

In Frederic's surviving correspondence, references to his wife decreased as time went on. It was in 1889 (or 1890 at the latest) that he had met the woman in whose home Ruth became a reluctant guest for the last two months of Frederic's life. Ruth believed that he had sacrificed everything for Kate, but others—including George Gissing—believed that Kate had saved him from drinking himself to death. Gissing eloquently echoes what many of the couple's friends thought of her. Writing to Cora Crane on 2 January 1899 he offers a staunch defense of Lyon: "I feel that everyone who has read with understanding and pleasure any of Frederic's recent work owes to her a vast debt of gratitude, that but for his true companion, his real wife, this work would never have been done. . . . [S]he saved him and enabled him to do admirable things" (Stephen Crane Collection).[71]

Like Frederic's stepfather, Kate Lyon came from Oswego, in upper New York State. She was probably born in 1856, the same year as Frederic himself. Tradition has it that the couple met either at the British Museum, or possibly when Frederic lived in Boston as a young man. Other elements of their relationship are purported, by their son Barry Forman, to have been incorporated into the fantastical novel *March Hares*.[72] Under oath, Kate testified at the manslaughter trial that took place after Frederic's death that she had first met Harold and Grace Frederic at their house in Bedford Square. It is unlikely that such a religious woman would have lied under those circumstances, yet without further evidence it is impossible to be certain of the exact details of their first meeting.

At some point in their relationship, probably in 1889 or 1890, after several months of intense pressure from Frederic, Kate agreed to live with him at Furnival's Inn, London—where Dickens had begun his married life. At first Kate would be as invisible to others as Dickens's lover Ellen Ternan was to his adoring readership. At this time only Frederic's closest

70. One particularly moving letter is in the Oppenheim Collection in the New York Public Library.

71. See also Gissing 1978, 510, diary entry for 1 January 1899: "At lunch-time came [John Scott] Stokes. He made it clear that Kate Lyon is an admirable woman, who saved Frederic from sheer drinking and has enabled him to do all his work."

72. "I do honestly beleieve that 'March Hares' was a truthful record of meeting [sic] between my father and mother, in the library of the British Museum, but of course, this again is dependent on a memory which sometimes plays tricks" (Harold Frederic Edition, Forman to Hoyt Franchere, 17 August 1960).

Harold Frederic at an unknown age.

friends knew about his relationship with Kate, and many of them were unhappy with the situation. In 1893 the couple moved to Homefield in the village of Kenley, Surrey. Here Kate was known as "Mrs. Frederic," a name that outraged some of Frederic's acquaintances who had met a quite different "Mrs. Frederic" a short time earlier. Initially they were secretive about their relationship, but by 1895 Frederic was more open about his second family. Nevertheless, he remained sensitive to the difficulties of his situation. On 20 February 1895 he wrote to his main English publisher, William Heinemann, referring to the Homefield address as "the address which isn't mentioned to the *hoi polloi*" and marking the letter "personal"

(Frederic Misc. 1977, 390). On 1 March he wrote to the editor of *Black and White* magazine saying, "This address of mine relates to an intimately personal phase of my life which isn't talked about. I do all my work here, and never see anybody about me whom I don't wholly like" (Frederic Misc. 1977, 392).

His unwillingness to talk about this relationship is understandable: and it is significant that it is one of the only aspects of his life on which he was silent. Although he had friends who cohabited (sometimes openly) with their lovers, his relationship with Kate Lyon was complicated by the existence of his legitimate family, who were entirely dependent on him. His cohabitation with Kate was not a political statement but an awkward compromise. Earlier, Grace Frederic had refused him a divorce—which he wanted on the grounds of incompatibility. During his final illness, believing that she had been abandoned by Ruth Frederic, she changed her mind, and a divorce writ was served through the open window of Homefield. This may have been calculatedly vindictive, but it is more likely that it was the despairing action of a wretched woman. It is very possible that she wished to secure a settlement for her children, realizing the severity of her own illness.[73] Frederic was not told of her action, and his friends believed that the shock would have killed him. Yet it is difficult to understand why he should have been shocked; a divorce was what he claimed to want. Was it because his passive wife had finally taken the initiative and challenged her domineering husband, or was it because he had hoped for a quiet legal case and by her actions she proved that she would not let him go without exposing his double life publicly? Without further evidence, either explanation is speculative, though both are likely. Frederic must have been aware of the public sympathy for the wives of Bret Harte and Oscar Wilde, both effectively abandoned by their husbands. No matter how much he scorned conventional morality, he wanted to avoid a messy confrontation if he could.[74]

Frederic's increasing awareness that he would never again live in the United States was no longer related just to financial exigency, but to the social constraints of his double life. It seems certain that this awareness must have added to the periodic depression that he suffered in the 1890s. He began to lead a highly complicated existence, spending time with both families, and supporting both financially: as R. W. Stallman puts it: "Kate endorsed what Grace endured: a double household" (Stallman 1968, 301). The situation cannot have been easy for any of the participants. It

73. See also Myers 1995, 156–57, for a similar interpretation of the case.

74. He was an enthusiastic and public supporter of two friends, Sir Charles Dilke and Sir Charles Russell, in their brushes with Victorian morality. See indexed references to Dilke and to Russell in Frederic Misc. 1977, and see Harris 1958, 178–80, on Dilke.

may have been most difficult for Grace Frederic, the quiet and lonely woman who had been first eclipsed and then rejected by her ambitious husband.

In 1892 a child, Helen, was born to Kate and Frederic. In 1893 a second daughter, Heloise, was born, her name an apt choice for the offspring of a love that was to have disastrous consequences. In February 1894 a son, Barry, was born, named after John Barry, an Irish nationalist and industrialist. Stephen and Cora Crane considered formally adopting Barry after Frederic's death, but the children moved back to the United States with their mother in 1901 or 1902.[75] A letter written to Cora Crane after Frederic's death suggests that at Homefield Frederic and Kate achieved a rare harmony, but one that was constantly under threat. On 21 January 1899 Linn Boyd Porter wrote:

> I need not tell you that I found at Kenley a marvel, a miracle—the happiest home, it seems to me, I ever saw, and yet to my mind, even then—one with an awful thunder-cloud hanging over it. I was obliged to tell Mr. Frederic that I did not see how he could contemplate the possibilities without fear. The children—*such* children—had they been mine I could never have closed my eyes in slumber. It was soon after being there that I wrote these lines in "Out of Wedlock":—
>
> There is no motherhood outside of wedlock that can be tolerated in a civilised country—none that may not bring to its possessor a terrible load of ignominy and suffering. I could not get that family out of my mind. Nothing was wanting but compliance with the form that men have made—and here would be a Paradise. Without it, any moment might plunge them into an Inferno.
>
> Harold told me that for the first time in years he was now free of evil. He said that his mind was calm, his conscience clear. His marital relations were pure, his children growing up in an atmosphere of love. (Stephen and Cora Crane Collection)

The expansive language of this extract continues throughout the letter. The writer was clearly inspired by the example of Frederic's relationship with Lyon: but Paradise necessarily suggested Paradise Lost. Despite his idealization of the relationship—the miraculous happiness, angelic children, the purity of the couple's sexual relationship, and the redemption of the fallen sinner—his firm belief was that "civilised" society could not sustain a relationship that ran counter to "the form that men had made."

75. The files of the Harold Frederic Edition contain letters from several of Frederic's children to Hoyt C. Franchere and Paul Haines, as well as correspondence between Kate Lyon and publishers that detail copyright payments to her.

Frederic honored his financial responsibility to both his families to the best of his ability, but he did it in the only way that he knew. With Jurgis in Upton Sinclair's *The Jungle* (1906) and Boxer in *Animal Farm* (1945) he might have said "I will work harder" It was a pathetic and self-defeating resolution. Faced with the strain of supporting two families, Frederic buried himself in his work in a desperate attempt to maintain both of them. This continual strain had inevitable consequences. From spring until early summer 1898 he was constantly ill. In March he began to lose weight rapidly, and a dose of what he believed to be food poisoning in early summer resulted in what was probably a minor stroke. He recovered his health to some extent, but when Ruth Frederic met him at the National Liberal Club in mid-July she was alarmed by his ill health.[76] On 12 August his health deteriorated further, and the following day he had a severe stroke in the bathroom at Homefield. He became very anxious to see a doctor, and on 14 August Lottie Sayer (Lyon's "ladies' help") was sent to call an American neighbor and friend, Dr. Nathan Ellington Boyd. This delay suggests that Frederic was either too ill or too stubborn to call a doctor, or that he was willing to allow Lyon to try a "mind cure"—earlier she had "cured" rheumatic pains. Frederic was under medical supervision for the first month of his illness, but he paid so little attention to the advice of his doctors and battled against it so remorselessly that his strength gradually ebbed.

Kate Lyon talked Christian Science with or to Frederic, Boyd tried vainly to get him to agree to a restricted diet, and Frederic raged, hating illness and finding his helplessness unendurable. At the coroner's inquest and subsequent trial, several witnesses testified to his contempt for the medical profession—an attitude that emerges throughout his fiction—but they agreed that he abused everybody.[77] This led to playful badinage among the lawyers: one questioned whether he had abused the legal profession and another butted in that Frederic had not heard that particular lawyer's method of cross-examination.

Thrown into a panic by the stroke that had paralyzed half of his body and face, he had wanted a doctor's reassurance, but he openly told Boyd that he would not follow his advice. Lyon continued to press Frederic to

76. The details of Frederic's illness and death have been compiled from the newspaper reports of his death. These have all been included in the bibliography. See also Weintraub 1979; Bigsby 1968; and Andrews 1982.

77. An undated letter that Frederic wrote suggests his distrust of conventional medicine: "Dear Dr./ My wife would be greatly obliged if you could manage to call during the forenoon tomorrow, and lance her tooth. Precisely how she got it I don't know, but she seems to have a great opinion of you—which nothing I could say could shake" (Frederic to ?, n.d, Frederic Misc. 1977, 486). Also see Frederic Short. 1966, 339-"do you think the doctors kill people *every* time?"

adopt Christian Science, and on 16 August she sent two telegrams to Athalie Goodman Mills, a healer. The first was the subject of close scrutiny at the inquest and trial: "Victory! Send someone to stay immediately— must be strong and wise—not Mrs. Boyd's healer—send at once—terribly urgent.—FREDERIC." Dr. Boyd's wife had been treated for hayfever on two occasions by a Christian Science healer, a curious coincidence. Boyd later testified that this would not have materially affected Frederic's attitude toward him: though he did not believe in the powers of Christian Science healing, he wished to humor his wife. It suggests a degree of marital mistrust that would have amused Frederic. Athalie Mills, a Christian Science healer, arrived in Kenley with her musician husband. Athalie Mills was a stylish dresser with a dark complexion, "piercing" eyes, and a "generally striking presence." Her testimony at the inquest was electrifying. She was witty, sharp, and formidable.[78] She had a bedside consultation with Frederic telling him that her healing could be effective only if he abandoned medical treatment. Frederic announced that he wanted her to leave his room, and Lyon had to ask her to go—but his reluctance was only temporary. Frederic would later assure his daughter that Mrs. Mills was making a special case of him: he could have the ministrations of both a doctor and a healer. Despite this dispensation he asked her not to tell Kate Lyon that he was wearing a belladonna plaster on his leg, and conversation about Christian Science stopped whenever Kate came into the room. Dr. Boyd remonstrated with Mrs. Mills at Kenley railway station, traveling to London with her in the hope of persuading her to stop attending Frederic. Two types of treatment are possible under Christian Science, "absent" and "present" treatment. Healers claim that both are equally efficacious. Boyd suggested that she continue "absent" treatment as a compromise. Asked to define "absent" treatment, he would later explain that he did not fully understand it, but that the practitioner was absent—which he thought "very desirable."

On 17 August Frederic demanded the presence of a solicitor friend, and dictated his will despite Kate Lyon's reluctance. The solicitor persuaded her that this would pacify Frederic, but she remained insistent that Grace Frederic should inherit Frederic's estate, threatening to tear the

---

78. One such exchange was:

The Coroner—What has to be done to be a 'Christian Scientist'?

Witness—To be good. To obey the laws of God.—Anything else, I hope we all do that? Anything else?

—To know the truth and love it.

—Anything else?

—That keeps you pretty busy.

Asked why she charged a fee, she replied, "Is the servant not worthy of his hire?" ("Mr. Harold Frederic's Death" 1898, 3).

will up if he did not acquiesce. Dr. Hubert Montague Murray, lecturer in pathology at Charing Cross Hospital, appeared on the same day, the seventeenth, at the request of Dr. Boyd. He diagnosed Frederic as suffering from paralysis and an "affection of the heart." Frederic's conversation was occasionally irrational, but he remained characteristically willful and obstinate. He refused to recognize the seriousness of his position: in the following weeks he would not rest in bed and insisted on smoking cigars and drinking spirits and beer, and on taking long and unauthorized carriage rides in the country. Stephen Crane's Greek servant, Adonai Ptolemy, testified that these journeys might culminate in a visit to a hotel where he would eat beef and drink ale or champagne. The lawyers were amazed at this, so astonished at Frederic's recklessness that they disbelieved the testimony. Ptolemy was asked whether he knew the difference between Munich beer and champagne. His reply suggests ingenuousness or lurking wit. He said that of course he did—he used to open bottles for Mr. Frederic! Frederic struggled against his failing physical strength, prompting Ruth to write later that "It probably never dawned upon him until he lay dying—that at last he was face to face with something that was stronger than he" (Ruth Frederic (Keen) to Hoyt Franchere, 4 August 1960, Harold Frederic Edition).

Impatient with his doctors' orders of a light diet (which they all agreed was essential to his recovery), Frederic told Dr. Murray pointedly, "Doctor . . . I have an intellectual contempt for milk," recalling Wilde's banter at his first trial.[79] Dr. Boyd appointed male nurses to attend Frederic, and he quickly christened them the "mamelukes." They were dismissed after a short time—told that their patient did not want them in his room. They irritated Kate Lyon and Frederic alike: Frederic hated having his food, drink, and cigars rationed. After one of them had physically prevented him from smoking a cheroot, she was furious. Frederic constantly requested whiskey, which the nurses refused him, and he swore continually (a lifetime's habit)—but the nurses were used to it. They failed to break his indomitable spirit even when one, following a doctor's advice, allowed Frederic to fall over when he tried to get out of bed. When he lifted his patient up and suggested that he return to bed Frederic told him that he would go downstairs even if he had to slide down the banisters. On 19 August, Frederic's forty-second birthday, Dr. Boyd returned, but Frederic had a violent quarrel with him and refused to see him again. Although the cause of the dispute remains unclear, Boyd had probably tried to shock Frederic into accepting medical treatment. Frederic's response suggests

79. See Hyde 1962, 129. " 'Do you drink champagne yourself?' 'Yes. Iced champagne is a favourite drink of mine—strongly against my doctor's order.' 'Never mind your doctor's orders, sir!' Carson rapped out. 'I never do,' Wilde answered sweetly."

fright and obstinacy. He told Boyd that doctors were killing him but Christian Science could cure him within two days. Boyd wrote to Lyon warning her that if Frederic died, she would probably be tried for manslaughter. She wrote back requesting that he stop attending Frederic.

A Dr. Brown of Kenley began visiting at this point—probably on 23 August. Brown found Frederic impossible to manage. Warned by Boyd's experience, he quickly realized that his difficult patient required humoring. Although he wished to forbid alcohol altogether, he made a compromise arrangement: Frederic was to have a small whiskey water twice a day and a bottle of beer at night. Frederic was infuriated by his helplessness, and his outbreaks of apoplectic rage constantly threatened his health. When Brown mentioned the "mamelukes" Frederic became so angry that Brown tactfully changed the subject. In desperation Brown called in a specialist on 28 August. Dr. Freyberger echoed the advice of the other doctors: Frederic was very ill and required careful treatment and diet. Frederic was undaunted by this diagnosis, telling him, "You order what you like and I'll take what I like." At Frederic's request Ruth Frederic was sent for. She would remain at Homefield until Frederic's death, though she made occasional trips from the house—once going to the theater, and bringing Frederic sausages from London. Freyberger warned that he might have another stroke that would paralyze or kill him. Although Frederic rallied a week later, on a subsequent visit Freyberger found him lying on damp grass in the garden in a state of fever. Frederic assured him that the temperature caused by this ill-advised behavior was solely due to wearing warm underclothes. Like the other doctors, Freyberger was reduced to threats and cajoling. He warned Kate that the damage to Frederic's brain and heart was irreparable, but that his life could be prolonged if he followed the advice of his doctors. Freyberger was convinced that Frederic was not in his right mind and that he was being unduly influenced by Kate Lyon—he claimed at one point that she formulated his thought for him. Frederic was ironic about Freyberger's own mental powers—he told Cora Crane that the doctor had thought so much about his rheumatism that he had thought it into his leg. Frederic told Freyberger that the Christian Scientists had assured him that they could not cure him while he was being attended by doctors. This contradicts his assertion to Ruth Frederic that he was a special case, though it suggests that he had lost whatever tolerance he had for the medical profession (as, later, he would with Christian Science). His doctors stopped attending him on 20 September, to be recalled to his deathbed a month later.

Over the next month Athalie Mills visited Homefield and sat in Frederic's room reading to herself from the Bible and from Mary Baker Eddy's *Science and Health With a Key to the Scriptures* (1875). Frederic was as irritated with Mrs. Mills as he had been with his doctors. His acceptance of Christian

Science suggests desperation. He was not a Christian Scientist although he was interested in the successful cures that it claimed for itself. His mother had been a great believer in the power of the mind (positive thinking), and Frederic had inherited a belief that mental attitude could influence the physical state of the body. He enjoyed disputing with Mrs. Mills, once triumphantly proving that she had misquoted from the Bible, but in retrospect it seems a hollow victory. Lyon, who was distraught, virtually lived in his room, weeping at his bedside. Her affection for him and devotion to him were unquestionable, though a key question at the manslaughter trial was whether she had exercised undue influence on a helpless man. John Scott Stokes, his last assistant, collected material for his cables, read the proofs of *Gloria Mundi* to him, and also read him Twain to divert him from the work that he refused to give up. At a reception at the Savage Club years later, Twain would express pleasure that his work had helped Frederic in his final days, and disappointment that they had never met (Twain 1910, 386).

On 17 October Cora Crane called at the house and was so horrified at Frederic's condition that she personally called the doctors in once more. Kate Lyon was still unwilling to see them return but did not stop her from cabling. Frederic found speech difficult, but when he heard that the doctors were returning he smiled and waved a handkerchief to Ruth, a sign of surrender, perhaps, or a victory wave. Ruth sent a telegram to a friend which echoes Kate's earlier telegram: "Victory! Doctors in. Please tell at old house." Brown and Freyberger were called against Athalie Mills's wishes—Frederic was in a state of "chemicalization" she said, a stage that all Christian Science patients went through. At the trial this was dismissed as nonsense. She swiftly left the house, enabling her to claim truthfully that Frederic had not died under her care. Frederic was now fluctuating between sanity and delusion. He was convinced that he was going to be taken to an asylum and that there was a cart at the door with two men waiting for him. Freyberger saw at a glance that he was dying and reminded Frederic that he had promised to recall him if his condition deteriorated. Frederic turned to Lyon and said, "I never said that this Christian Science would do a ——— bit of good, and this ——— woman Mills bores the head off my shoulders." Evidently he had his sane moments. At some unspecified date Frederic had written to John Scott Stokes giving advice on the death of an unknown friend: "You say your poet friend is gone with half his work undone, and there is nothing more you yourself can do. My dear fellow, I am no preacher, but I will buffet you to-night with a text all of my own. You can make your dead friend live once more by finding out what he would have wished and then doing it. Many of the tears shed on the graves of today dry all too soon. What lives and does not perish is the act of the man who stands over his dead friend against all comers and

The trial: Kate Lyon and Athalie Mills in court.

assailants, for the defenseless dead too often have a bad time of it" (Frederic to John S. Stokes, n.d., Frederic Misc. 1977, 487).

The letter was prophetic: on 19 October, in the early hours of the morning, Harold Frederic finally gave up struggling against life and became one of the "defenseless dead." The name was more appropriate to him than most: he was a man who had made many enemies in his lifetime. He was cremated at Woking Cemetery on Monday, 24 October. Stokes formally identified the body and found that Frederic's face looked youthful and at peace. Mourners included J. M. Barrie, William Heinemann, Brandon Thomas, and Joseph Lawrence. Grace Frederic attended the service, but Kate Lyon stayed away.

The first hint of a scandal that would receive extensive press coverage appeared almost immediately. On 21 October the *New York Times* announced the forthcoming cremation. A line adds that he had "been in the hands of Christian Scientists." This was the start of a sustained campaign against Christian Science—"the protean monster" or "this wretched delu-

The trial: the protagonists in court.

sion," as it was dubbed. Over the next two months the Frederic case was covered in detail by the *New York Times,* and the paper published letters denouncing faith healing and stories about Christian Science healers whose patients had died while under their care. The paper's tone was seldom neutral and was sometimes outraged, sometimes scoffing. The case was also covered in England, for another sect, the "Peculiar People," was acquiring a similar notoriety. The Frederic case had captured the public imagination: Canon Eyeton preached a sermon against Christian Science in Westminster Abbey. Later he would donate money to Grace and her children.

The Coroner's inquest was followed by a manslaughter trial in which Kate Lyon and Athalie Mills were charged with "being concerned together in feloniously killing and slaying one Harold Frederic, by neglecting to supply him with proper medical attendance." The two were eventually acquitted owing to lack of evidence, but only after a highly publicized ordeal that lasted almost two months. Frederic's life with Kate Lyon had divided his friends and cut him off from the Mohawk Valley. Self-publicizing in his lifetime, the circumstances of his death ensured him a degree of notoriety which would have bemused and saddened him. Both of his families were exposed to hardships that he had desperately tried to keep them from. On 27 October his mother, who had outlived her children and two husbands, wrote a lively and anguished letter to Frederic's editor at the *New York Times* correcting the paper's version of Frederic's early life. She wrote, "It is very aggravating to spend as much care and money in rearing a son and have it go over the country that he was almost a pauper if you could modify any of the statements you would confer a favour to the Family. . . . If this letter is verbose kindly excuse." (Frances Motte Frederic to Charles R. Miller, 27 October 1898, Harold Frederic Papers. [Punctuation hers]) What she wrote, she told Charles Miller, was "plain unvarnished truth." Her letter falls so far short of the truth that it must be questioned how much she knew of her son's life until it filled the newspapers for the next two months. The truth was anything but "plain" or "unvarnished."

⟨2⟩

The American Context

Influence

Frederic's Civil War stories are, in a broad sense, autobiographical accounts of his boyhood during one of the most significant chapters of American life. Like Twain, Frederic always sought to represent his childhood as being in some ways archetypal. He presented himself as a product of values and attitudes formed in a new republic, locating himself firmly within particular moments and a specific geography. He was always keenly aware of the influences of both time and place, articulating them in his fiction and nonfiction writing and even combining the two. One instance of this is in one of his most ambitious, though not (in any sense) his most successful, sustained writing projects, in which he traced the history of Kate Lyon's ancestors, the O'Mahonys, and wrote a series of fictionalized accounts of O'Mahony folklore throughout the ages basing stories around locations specifically associated with the family.[1] The stories themselves are not particularly striking: what is interesting is the meticulous care with which he researched them, and also the desire behind such research.

This relentless search for origins, his own as well as others, implies an obsessive desire to find a place, and an inevitably connected sense of displacement, too. This is a regular theme in his letters after 1884, the year in which he moved to London. Yet it is clear that, outwardly at least, he thrived in England: he rapidly adapted to London life and went out of his way to represent himself publicly as a London-based writer perfectly able to span two geographies. Despite his continual reiteration of his origins, what is immediately striking about him is his flexibility and adaptability, his ability to evolve continually to suit changing conditions. In his Civil War stories he writes about childhood loneliness, but he also writes of fellowship with other boys—of swimming in bore-holes in the river, playing with fireworks, fighting—of boyish pleasures. Here, and also in anecdotes and correspondence, he concentrates upon immediacy, activity, and sensa-

---

1. See chap. 4.

59

tion. The stories are about engaging with a world that is full of challenge, and they celebrate this engagement. What are notably absent, both in Frederic's recollections of his boyhood and Twain's reminiscences, are descriptions of childhood reading. In the case of Twain the influence of an oral tradition has been well-documented and has become something of a critical commonplace; it may be that in Frederic's case it has not yet been fully taken into account.[2] Frederic certainly had a passion for reading from an early age, and his mother admired and encouraged it. Had he lived longer it is virtually certain that he would have written memoirs of some sort, as so many of the period did, possibly even an autobiography. He enjoyed his own history enough to share it with others through anecdotes, and he would undoubtedly have wanted to leave a permanent record of his life. As it is, however, he left no clear account of the early reading that influenced his later writing, unlike two near contemporaries with quite different backgrounds, Henry Adams and W. D. Howells. Without an autobiographical account to turn to it may be useful to "read" Frederic tangentially, through the writings of contemporaries, and with and against them.[3] His invocation of displacement can be used as a tool to elicit details of his life from other sources. By using other narratives of origin and influence as frames, and by filtering or displacing him, it may be possible to make Frederic emerge from the protective shell of his fantasies.

In *The Education of Henry Adams* (1907), Adams describes himself as a child of the eighteenth century, born into an eighteenth-century Boston. He and "troglodytic" Boston were both "cut apart" by the advent of three harbingers of the nineteenth century: the Boston-Albany railroad opening up the country; the Cunard steamers first sailing into the bay; and the nomination of Henry Clay and James K. Polk for the presidency. Adams writes of himself, "This was in May, 1844; he was six years old; his new world was ready for use, and only fragments of the old met his eyes" (Adams 1973, 5). These "fragments" included the contents of his father's library, which was largely comprised of the works of eighteenth-century historians. The young Adams turned to these when he found that the style of more modern writers, Dickens and Thackeray, did not suit "tastes founded on Pope and Dr. Johnson." His father read James Russell Lowell's *Biglow Papers* (published serially and collected in 1848 and 1869) and the speeches of Horace Mann aloud to his children. He read Longfellow and Tennyson when they published new works. Yet his son turned to the preceding century, rejecting even Wordsworth in favor of Pope and Gray, who

2. Of course this should not be taken to suggest that the oral tradition was the only significant influence on Twain.

3. For a further account of the reading habits of American children, see Avery 1994.

were easier, he said, to read (Adams 1973, 35–36). Later, having been sent off to school, his ideas on literature altered.[4] He retained the eighteenth-century idea that books were "the source of life" (as opposed to nine-teenth-century realism's idea of life being the source of books), but his tastes became more modern. He read British writers, "Thackeray, Dickens, Bulwer, Tennyson, Macaulay, Carlyle, and the rest," but spent his most enjoyable moments escaping in historical romance, "lying on a musty heap of Congressional Documents in the old farmhouse at Quincy, reading 'Quentin Durward,' 'Ivanhoe,' and 'The Talisman,' and raiding the garden at intervals for peaches and pears" (Adams 1973, 39). The image is a highly charged one: the young boy reveling in European historical ro-mance from a bed made of the dull, decaying words of American political life.

Adams's European inheritance is in no way unusual—similar catalogues of reading are common (though of course he had exceptional access to books because of his family position)—nor is his taste for Scott. Scott was widely read in the United States: Twain, for example, was famously acerbic regarding his pernicious effects upon the self-image of the American South. In "On Historical Novels Past and Present" (1898) Frederic claimed to have read all of Scott by the age of eighteen:

> At the age of eighteen, or thereabouts, I had read Sir Walter Scott's novels so often and so thoroughly that there seemed nothing left in them for me. I had sucked them dry, and I turned away to other things, never doubting, however, that the wizard of the North was the greatest of novel-writers. To this conviction I remained constant for a long time; it lost definiteness in my mind, no doubt, as years went on, but it continued to be a rule for me that nobody could ever touch Scott. At last, when I was perhaps twenty-five, chance set me to reading him again—and to my amazement it was a difficult task. . . . With much sadness, but no self-distrust, I concluded that Sir Walter had been a vastly over-rated man. It was plain that he could be no hero to thoughtful and enlightened citizens of mature years, and I fancy that I said so in print. We are so very old at twenty-five! ("On Historical Novels Past and Present" 1898, 330)

Frederic's account of reading Scott suggests an active engagement and a mind determined to fill itself from all available sources. It does not neces-sarily describe a discriminating intellect, but one which is keen and full of life, certainly one full of bombast ("no self-distrust"). As a boy and young man Frederic read whatever was available to him, and this, doubtless, had limits.

---

4. This was not thanks to his teachers: his attitude toward them was unswerving, defining the schoolmaster as "a man employed to tell lies to little boys" (Adams 1973, 9).

W. D. Howells's account of the reading habits of the inhabitants of Midwestern Columbus suggests a shared interest in European writing as well as a shift in taste toward American writing. The older members of the community read the classics, the younger preferring Thackeray; George Eliot, Hawthorne, Reade, De Quincey, Tennyson, Browning, Emerson, and Longfellow. Howells had found literary life in Columbus restricted and restrictive. When Emerson told him that it was a shame that the editors of a Cincinnati magazine looked to the East for articles, Howells replied that there were not enough writers in the West "to write that magazine full in Ohio" (Howells 1968, 57). Writing in 1895, Howells could refer to the "refluent wave of authorship" from West to East, but in the 1860s the situation was different (Howells 1968, 98). Westerners looked East for their literary opinions: to New England or to Europe. This was not a healthy situation for writers or readers. Edmund Wilson compares the neglect experienced by both Frederic's Civil War stories and Henry Fuller's stories of Chicago life in terms of their failure to capture the reading public's interest. American readers were accustomed to literature that had some association with New England. Writing of Frederic, Wilson notes, "the cultural poverty of the upstate milieu that produced him may have had something to do . . . with the little attention they [the Civil War stories] attracted. . . . People in Frederic's period loved to read about New England —which was richer in history and better established. We had fed to us in school in the early nineteen-hundreds Longfellow, *Thanatopsis,* and Oliver Wendell Holmes. People in my mother's generation liked to read Mary E. Wilkins Freeman. I had had to find Walt Whitman for myself, my curiosity aroused by the many parodies" (Wilson 1972, 95).[5]

Howells recognized an element of the cultural poverty of his own Midwest inheritance when he described arriving in New England and discovering "a more complex civilisation than I had yet known." He was bewildered to discover the social significance of the family and of family names, though through reading Thackeray he had realized their importance in England. His life had been spent in a new land, a region where "men were just beginning ancestors," and he had previously thought that it was only in colonial Virginia that the family was taken seriously "where it furnished a joke for the rest of the nation" (Howells 1968, 20). Although

5. Wilson's charge no longer has quite the same edge as it may have had when he first made it. Feminist scholars are actively engaged with rereadings of women writers such as Wilkins Freeman, producing readings that liberate her from the cloying label of gentility which Wilson implicitly conjures up. New generations of women like to read her too, though perhaps not with the same impulse as that of Wilson's mother. Two of her stories have, for instance, been included in a recent collection of lesbian short fiction (See Koppelman 1994).

Frederic never experienced an awakening of this sort, for the idea of family had long been important in New York State, Utica lacked the cultural polish of larger towns. Frederic was determined to interest readers in the rich, though unwritten, history of his region; indeed, he was determined to write it. It is not surprising that the first novel Frederic worked on with sustained attention, a work that eventually became his second published novel, *In the Valley,* was largely modeled on Scott.[6]

Given this interest in the raw material that New York State offered to Frederic, a nonliterary background might be seen to be an advantage. In his weekly letter for the *Chicago American* on 24 August 1901, Frank Norris tells an anecdote about a young American from a small city in Pennsylvania who wrote an original first novel at the age of twenty-two. He went to New York where he fell in with a crowd of "third-raters" who flattered him and persuaded him to write a second, imitative novel. It was an abject failure. Rejected by his crowd of early admirers, he returned home and became a law clerk, his chance of literary success finished. Norris turns this tale of corrupted innocence (a story, he says, based on actual events) into a warning of the perniciousness of literary sets and of writing for others. The novelist should, he believed, write from her or his experience, should draw upon what is most familiar. This echoes Howells's infamous injunction on the smiling aspects of American life and was taken up by many American writers of the late nineteenth century. A similar theme underlies Henry Blake Fuller's story "The Downfall of Abner Joyce," in which the protagonist rejects his early radical rural writing as he falls in with a literary set. He adopts a more temperate reconciliatory tone, writing about the possibilities of the city rather than the harshness of rural living. By the end of the story Abner has destroyed even the half-hearted idealism of the people that he used to despise, as well as compromising himself. He is doubly culpable. Both young writers have unwisely allowed themselves to be influenced by undesirables; indeed, it might be argued that by implication both are the victims of confidence tricksters of a particular sort.

Norris and Fuller are both engaged in producing manifestos for American literary production (specifically fiction), and both warn explicitly against servile imitation, or the dangers of influence. Yet by locating these discussions within the familiar motif of the young innocent in a dangerous metropolis, they avail themselves of a huge body of literature that is specifically about urban danger, and most particularly about that posed by the confidence trickster. Within these discourses "influence" is a key word,

---

6. It might also be that his earliest interest in the possibilities of writing about Jewish figures—for example, in "The Jew's Christmas" (1882)—came from Scott.

encompassing a host of meanings.[7] Both Norris and Fuller are interested in the possibility of fine writing emerging in an unencumbered form—in a sense, direct from the earth itself without the belittling effect of a precious literary set and their hypocrisies. In an extended sense both speculate upon the prospects of the future of an American production that is independent from Europe. Norris writes that "This sort of thing happens oftener than you would suppose in little out of the way communities, where a boy will begin to write before he has, one may almost say, begun to read, and where there are no 'literary' people to bother him and sidetrack him" (Norris 1964, 31).

Utica in the 1870s was similar to the Pennsylvania small city of the fictitious writer's childhood, and the young Frederic, attempting to capture the life of upstate New York, was, "one may almost say," writing before he could read, or at least before he had begun to read broadly or in depth. Reading was a significant part of his childhood, but the range of writing available to him was more restricted than that in which either Adams or Howells were able to browse. Frederic may have encountered the lovingly described collection of books from "The Copperhead" either at his own home, or in that of a friend of the family. The young narrator of the story writes that Abner Beech's books were far more vivid than his experiences in the classroom: "I can recall the very form of the type in the farmer's books." These were mainly concerned with American history and politics and included "most imposing of all, a whole long row of big calf-bound volumes of the *Congressional Globe,* which carried the minutiae of politics at Washington back into the forties" (Frederic Short. 1966, 5). If this description is based on actual recollection, it is certain that Frederic would not have been allowed to loll on these treasures reading Scott.

Utica had a relatively substantial library to which Frederic had access, and he certainly read newspapers and magazines keenly.[8] So in his earliest days, he read whatever was available—religious books, historical works,

---

7. The word also fits into discourses of mesmerism and is used specifically in terms of an individual's control or sway over another, usually mediated through the trance. It is within this sort of catalogue of authority that the word was used against Kate Lyon after Frederic's death. It played a key part in the prosecution of Oscar Wilde when it came to represent both his relation and that of his works to his reading public. In this respect it fits into debates concerning the censorship of literature. To give another example, Edith Wharton invokes "influence" repeatedly in her 1912 novel *The Reef,* which deals with the catastrophic outcome of a short affair, and accords it multiple possibilities that range across social, sexual, class, gender and race dimensions.

8. Later he became a careful collector of reviews of his writing, which he pasted into a "Mark Twain Scrap Book." Although most of his collection has not been traced, and may not have survived, a substantial collection of reviews of *The Lawton Girl* exists in the Utica College Library. The collection reveals that he subscribed to Romeike and Curtice's Press Cutting Agency. Patty Burchard kindly gave me details of this collection and made it available to me.

and political writings rather than novels; newspapers and magazines rather than poetry—and developed an abstract sense of the significance of events and ideas rather than a keen aesthetic sense of the way in which words might be made to work together to produce literature. This was what would influence Frederic most in his writing life, and it was this knowledge that he carried with him to Boston in 1873, where he began to collect and read books in earnest and started to develop his own ideas about literature. It was at this point that he appears to have embarked upon more substantial and systematic reading of literature.

Once he returned to Utica from Boston, his early newspaper criticism provides a clearer insight of what he was reading and how he responded to it. As early as 1878 Frederic was writing letters to actors and actresses from his desk at the *Utica Daily Observer* signing himself "Amusement Ed. Observer" (Frederic to Augustin Daly [?] 1878, Frederic Misc. 1977, 10). By 1879 his title became more sonorous and abbreviated. He became "Lit. Ed. Obs.," though he may have been principal book reviewer for the paper's book review column for some years before this.[9] Frederic writes about established European and American writers, mainly men: Charles Reade, Anthony Trollope, Erckmann-Chatrian, Émile Zola, Edward Eggleston, W. D. Howells, Mark Twain. He also writes about the less famous, mainly women: Julia Kavanagh, Alice Perry, Constance Fenimore Woolson.

His critical writing veers from the appreciative to the caustic. Writing on 11 June 1877 of Charles Reade's active social conscience and the sharp tone of his writing, he says, "If he sees a wrong he rasps it." One year later, by 10 June 1878, he is dismissive of an anonymous novel, *Justine's Lovers:* "The writer's name is withheld presumably for the reason that the boarding school at which she is a pupil objects to its publication. The style is that of a child of twelve, but the dialogue betrays maturer experience—say of seventeen years" (Woodward 1968, 8 and 11). Frederic's own experience was not very much greater at this point (the novel is actually by John William De Forest), but he was already adept at posing authoritatively, at turning out material rapidly, and at playing a part with skill. His preoccupations include the pirating of literature and the past and future of American writing, and these would remain keen interests. He is uneasy, though, with original judgments. His tone is often polished and assured, yet it seems that he may well have taken his earliest opinions from elsewhere, appropriating them as his own. In a piece that appeared on 16 December 1878 he discusses the "Great American Novel," which he subtitles (with awkward syntax) "that stupendous and awesome myth of prophecy, for the appearance of which so many eyes have grown blurred in watching" (Woodward

---

9. Robert Woodward has collected a number of the column's early reviews together, providing an invaluable insight into what Frederic was reading at the time.

1968, 12). Arguing that it is not yet time for such a piece of writing, he uses mixed metaphors of farming and building to explain the blossoming and harvesting of the great European writers within the structure of European writing. He namedrops with audacious aplomb, citing "the tales of Geoffrey Chaucer, the quaint Nieblungen Lied [sic], the Chronicles of Froissart, the Mabinogion, and the Romance verses." He invokes Fielding and Smollett, "acrid Dean Swift and poor Dick Steele," Dickens, Thackeray, Scott, Hugo, Rousseau, Balzac, Rabelais, and finally "Reade and Black, Heyse and Auerbach, Cherbuliez and Daudet, George Eliot and George Sand." This erratic compendium has little logic or cohesion. It reads like a random concoction of names put together in order to impress, and it seems highly unlikely that Frederic cram-read all of those writers and works during his stay in Boston, and doubtful that he read them before he left Utica.[10]

When Frederic poses as an authority on world literature the strain is obvious. He struggles with the unfamiliar names of writers whose works he had probably never read. Yet when he admires Trollope's "series of studies of English folk-life," as he did on 17 August 1880, or Eggleston's description of "the political campaign, of the revival, and of village manners and customs," as he did on 16 December 1878, all of which are important in his own novels, his tone is genuine and unmannered (Woodward 1968, 21 and 12). His intense personal feeling for the local and the rural is self-evident. Although his attempts to impress are remarkably unimpressive, his quieter moments are revealing. Again what stands out in Frederic's criticism are his mimicry and adaptability, the very qualities that Norris and Fuller warn about, though in Frederic's case they served him well.

Frederic's formal education was short, and he always admired those who, like himself, were self-made. The success story was an aspect of the American fable exploited in popular fiction by scores of writers. Frederic praised Howells's *The Rise of Silas Lapham* (1885): for him it meant, as he told Howells himself on 5 May 1885, "the scrutiny of a master turned for almost the first time upon . . . the most distinctive phase of American folk-life" (Frederic Misc. 1977, 58). The reiterated interest in "folk-life" suggests that both Trollope and, later, Howells, were important models for him.[11] Like those two writers Frederic would also transpose the real into

---

10. The descriptions of Swift and Steele might come directly from Thackeray's *The History of Henry Esmond* (1852), in which the two writers both make appearances and are described in similar terms. Frederic hoped that his own *In the Valley* would be an American *Henry Esmond* (Frederic to John B. Howe, 27 February 1886, Frederic Misc. 1977, 100–101.)

11. Both men introduce characters from early novels into later ones, something that Frederic would imitate (though more tentatively). Both use real issues and events as background for their novels. One brief example is Trollope's use of the Earl of Guilford's abuse of church privilege as material for *The Warden* (1855), deliberately misspelling "Guilford" as "Guildford" throughout.

the fictional, often for the sake of authenticity, but also because as a jour-nalist he knew a good story when he heard one. One striking example of his use of a catchy story is his transposition of the remarkable Irish-American publisher Sam McClure's story of his boyhood as a model for the early youth of Reuben Tracy.[12] It was this sort of success story that Frederic appreciated, because it was both archetypal and mythic, but also because it had a personal relevance to him. It suggested that his own lack of formal learning need not be a disadvantage. Despite his ordinary boyhood, he hoped to be an extraordinary writer, a successful novelist.

The American Literary Marketplace

Expansion

In the nineteenth century the prospective novelist aimed not simply at an extended piece of fiction but at an Olympian challenge—that of writing the Great American Novel.[13] This novel was to be the product of a new republic celebrating its own traditions and its separation from Europe. The novel would attract an American audience within an independent and established national market for literature, and within an international mar-ket. Within these terms it would be an American product. Frederic hoped that his Revolutionary novel *In the Valley* would be a characteristically Amer-ican epic and whimsically wrote that he would like every adult American male to read the novel—his imagination was expansive (see chapter 4). His fantasy for the novel, and allied hopes for his career as a novelist, were possible only within the context of a growing market for American literature. In *American Romanticism and the Marketplace* (1985), Michael Gil-more argues that between about 1832 and 1860 "Literature itself became an article of commerce . . . as improvements in manufacture, distribution, and promotion helped to create a national audience for letters. (Gilmore 1985, 1.) He chooses these dates (the year Emerson left the ministry and the year of the publication of Hawthorne's final romance, *The Marble Faun*) as the important markers in the transformation that took place in the American economy. The origins of this change took place some time ear-lier: though Gilmore argues that a market economy had fully emerged by the end of the Civil War, it might be argued that it was only in 1891, when the International Copyright Agreement afforded protection to authors, that the literary marketplace was fully operational.

---

12. Frederic had met McClure in England in March 1887, and the two great talkers had indulged in a marathon conversation. Frederic's own early life bears a slight resemblance to that of McClure (the fathers of both men were accidentally killed when their sons were very young). For another example of translation from fact to fiction see Hirsch 1984.

13. For an extended discussion of this phenomenon see Spencer 1957. Although the work is now dated it is an extremely well researched and wide-ranging piece of documentation.

Gilmore describes the transformation of American economy from its agrarian beginnings in largely self-sufficient units in which mutually beneficial exchanges were the commonest transactions into an industrialized market-based urban society in which money-based exchanges predominated. The expansion of the economy had been inhibited by the lack of adequate transportation systems, by the inadequacy of investment capital, and by labor shortages. The transport system was opened up after 1815 as land routes were improved, and as transport costs dropped owing to the construction of canals and railroads. This expansion was financed by income from exports and from credit as well as credit from the growing number of state banks. Bank notes predominated as the means of exchange. A massive population increase, owing to both high birth and immigration rates, formed a large base of labor for the market. From 1820 to 1860 the population expanded from approximately 10 million to almost 32 million. The rate of expansion of the cities surpassed even that of the population. In the same period there was an 800 percent increase in the number of Americans living in cities; the number of banks and the value of circulating banknotes increased five times (Gilmore 1985, 1–4.) Equally fantastic figures are repeatedly cited by other writers on this period. In his book *American Fiction 1865–1940* (1987), Brian Lee writes that in the 1860s the populations of Saint Louis and Philadelphia each increased by one hundred thousand and Chicago's by almost two hundred thousand. He also writes that "In eighteen of the twenty-eight cities over 100,000 in 1890, foreign-born adults preponderated, and New York at this time had twice as many Jews as Warsaw, twice as many Irish as Dublin, and as many Germans as Hamburg" (Lee 1987, 4).

The growth of the cities and the concomitant problems of poverty, overcrowding, violence, and disease, were captured in uncompromising fiction, usually realist or naturalist, which centered upon city life, notably Stephen Crane's *Maggie: A Girl of the Streets* (1893), Frank Norris's *McTeague* (1899), Theodore Dreiser's *Sister Carrie* (1900), and Upton Sinclair's *The Jungle* (1906). These were novels of New York, San Francisco, Chicago, and Philadelphia, about immigrants, prostitutes, industry, struggle, and hardship, and if they owed a debt to naturalism and realism, they also drew enormously from the possibilities offered by New Journalism. Realism and reportage were close cousins. Muckraking exposés such as Jacob Riis's *How the Other Half Lives* (1890) explored new urban realities.[14] In metropolises represented in this fiction and in nonfictional journalism spectatorship, commercialism, social and sexual hierarchies and differences, strikes, social and sexual, class and gender unrest were all mingled. Urban dialects and the mixed voices of the metropolis were also registered. As the cities

14. For a fine and concise introduction to muckraking, see Fitzpatrick 1994.

expanded, so did the transport system. Railroads appeared, opening up the countryside and transforming the landscape and making their way into literature, most ominously in Frank Norris's *The Octopus* (1901), but also, of course, in other American novels of the period.[15] By 1860 their extent totaled thirty thousand miles of track.

In *"Friction with the Market": Henry James and the Profession of Authorship* (1986), Michael Anesko argues that a key word in nineteenth-century book trades, both in America and Britain is "expansion." Marcia Jacobson, in her book *Henry James and the Mass Market* (1983), argues that the mass market for American books began to emerge in the 1880s and 1890s (Jacobson 1983, 4).[16] Although Gilmore suggests that a mass market developed earlier, by about 1850, both he and Jacobson agree on the factors that made the transformation possible. Between 1820 and the end of the century production and distribution of books changed with the introduction of woodpulp paper, cheap cloth covers, and high-speed printing. Books could be printed in large editions at cheap prices and be distributed by the railroads that opened up the country. By 1850 more than 90 percent of adult whites could read and write and "the United States boasted the largest literate public in history" (Gilmore 1985, 4).

As the audience for books changed, so did the control writers had over their works. Within this context of previously unthought-of social and economic change writers were coming to terms with a changing literary marketplace. In the early days of literary production in America it was common practice for writers to hire publishers, paying them a percentage of profits. Writer and readers often came from similar backgrounds and had shared interests, and the expense of manufacturing and distributing books limited their audience and sales. By the 1890s bookselling had become an important and profitable trade with a large reading public. Cheap reprints flooded the market. English books began to be published in one volume, and the English lending libraries were gradually weakened as the three-volume books that they had relied on were gradually replaced by cheaper single volumes. The death of the triple-decker novel, butt of much bitter humor, marked a significant phase in the development of the novel. A mass market did not simply rely on book publications, however. The new readership, which cut across boundaries of class, was available to the producers of magazines and newspapers that flourished in this period.

---

15. Both *Sister Carrie* and *The Jungle* open with train journeys into a city.

16. Michael Anesko writes that "The volume of book production in the United States not only showed a constant absolute increase throughout the century, but outran population growth as well. In the 1830's American publishers issued about 1000 new titles annually; by the 1870s [sic] the number had grown to 3000; and at the beginning of the twentieth century 6000 new books were coming from the presses every year" (Anesko 1986, 34).

Women were increasingly a significant force both as readers and as arbiters of taste.

The Movement for an International Copyright Law

Copyright was one of the most keenly discussed issues within late-nineteenth-century writing and publishing circles. The absence of an international copyright agreement between England and the United States had a significant effect on the international book trade, and some understanding of the maneuvers that culminated in the 1891 International Copyright Agreement is an integral part of any account of the context within which writers' works were written and received. Copyright issues are especially germane to a study of Harold Frederic because of his involvement in the 1887 "*Locrine* incident." In an elaborate journalistic stunt he cabled the whole of Swinburne's *Locrine* to the *New York Times* without Swinburne's knowledge (see below and chapter 3).

The debate preceding the formulation of the 1891 International Copyright Agreement continued throughout the nineteenth century. Authors and publishers argued their respective positions privately and publicly. Their interests were sometimes shared and could be opposed. The demand for some sort of copyright protection was intimately related to a transformation of the practice of writing and to the increasing commodifying of art. The development of a healthy literary marketplace could be fully successful only if authors' works were adequately protected, and the Great American Novel, if it were to appear, could be nurtured in a national market that would encourage it and make it widely available to an American audience. It was within this context that the debate for an international copyright agreement progressed. The precursor to, and model for, all copyright laws was the 1710 Statute of Anne. This protected authors' copyright for a fixed period of twenty-eight years. In 1790 the United States passed a similar copyright law, again with the twenty-eight-year protection. As the nineteenth century progressed several countries developed copyright laws that protected the works of nationals. It was increasingly felt that owing to technological advances in book production and distribution, authors required protection on an international level. In 1852 France had extended copyright laws to cover all authors regardless of nationality. In 1887 the Berne Convention, comprised of fourteen member states, agreed to provide protection for the nationals of these member states. The copyright laws of the United States, which was not a party to the convention, had developed along slightly different lines. It was only in 1891 that the United States was finally to develop an international copyright law after long debate.

Prior to the Chace Act of 1891, all major countries except the United

States had signed the Berne Convention. Americans were still arguing over the Hawley Bill, which favored the Berne Convention, and the Chace Bill, which was more protectionist in character. The Chace Bill was supported by, among others, Mark Twain and Grover Cleveland (who was then president). Certain stringent requirements had to be met if copyright were to be obtained for both American and British editions of a book: "Under British law the 'world premiere,' so to speak, must be the British edition. The necessary sequence therefore—in say the 1880s—was (1) deposit of title-page in Washington; (2) publication of book in Britain; (3) American publication, and deposit of copies within ten days; (4) deposit in the British Museum within a month of (2); with (5) optional registration at Stationers' Hall at any time after (2) if the British publisher sought to maintain his rights in the courts" (Nowell-Smith 1968, 65).[17]

Frederic had shown an active interest in copyright from about 1886 onward. Copyright had personal significance: Frederic was careful to ensure simultaneous publication of his novels by his English and American publishers in order to safeguard his work from piracy. His interest in copyright was initially encouraged by an anticopyright letter to the *New York Times* on 23 January 1886, and was deepened when the forthcoming publication of his first novel made copyright into a personal issue (Frederic Misc. 1977, 97–98). As early as 11 February 1886, Frederic had written to his editor, Charles Miller, enclosing the proofs of a "very bright pamphlet" that he assured Miller would reach him "four or five days" before the other American papers. The pamphlet, written by Robert Pearsall Smith, was *International Copyright Protected Copyright With Free-Trade Competition*. Frederic suggested that the paper could make a "mighty good special article" of it (Frederic Misc. 1977, 97). The *New York Times* had wisely taken the early precaution of protecting themselves from pirating: Frederic's superiors had copyrighted his regular newspaper columns in 1886, appending his initials to them. Later his full name would appear by his regular cable letters.

The publishers of Frederic's first novel were acutely aware of the problems caused by the absence of a legally binding copyright agreement. Andrew Chatto, the English publisher of *Seth's Brother's Wife*, was keen to avoid pirating of his authors' works, and the American publisher of the novel, Charles Scribner, was the treasurer of the American Publishers' Copyright League, revived in November 1887. The novel suffered poor sales because of excessive competition within the price range of one dollar owing to the large number of cheap pirated books in the market. The Publishers' Copyright League worked in tandem with the Authors' Copy-

17. See Nowell-Smith 1968, 64–68, for an account of the situation in the United States up to, and shortly after, 1891.

right League. The latter held benefit readings on 28 and 29 November 1887 in New York's Chickering Hall. Mark Twain, Edward Eggleston, W. D. Howells, and James Russell Lowell were among those who attended, and the *New York Times* gave the event significant coverage in an editorial, also printing the whole of Lowell's address to the meeting. Despite the League's attempts at securing copyright legislation, the Chace Bill was unsuccessful when it was reintroduced to Congress on 12 December. The campaign continued however.

W. D. Howells was, quite properly, a leading figure in the copyright campaign. He was, without doubt, a leading literary figure of late nineteenth-century America. His correspondence with Mark Twain reveals both men's long-term interest in the campaign. Howells recalled that he first saw Twain in the white suit that he made famous at the authors' hearing before the Congressional Committee on Copyright in Washington in 1906. Between what Edwin Cady calls Howells's first "significant article," published in 1860, and his last article of 1920 (which remained incomplete upon his death), his critical work appeared in sixty-four periodicals and nineteen newspapers. In his working life he may have published as many as two million words of criticism and reviews, as well as being a prolific writer of fiction. (Howells 1973, 1). Howells made and unmade reputations through his endorsements or criticisms of writers: his word, as Frank Norris shows in his fictional representation of an influential literary figure in "A Lost Story," was a defining one within late-nineteenth-century American literary criticism. The trajectory of his career was to have a significant impact upon the direction taken by late-nineteenth-century American writing.

Some years earlier, in 1879, Mark Twain and an American publisher, Frank Bliss, had together sufficiently confused the accepted sequence of depositing and then publishing a book to exasperate Andrew Chatto, who was trying to arrange simultaneous publication of *A Tramp Abroad* (1880). In May 1879 an irritated Twain, who should share substantial blame for the chaos of this attempt at Anglo-American cooperation, wrote, "Dam [sic] business of *all* sorts!—that's my only religious creed" (Welland 1978, 103.) One of the damnable areas of this complex issue was the status of the Canadian market, which led to difficulties in defining and defending the American market prior to 1891. In 1880 Twain wrote to Howells telling him that unless the currently proposed copyright treaty protected authors against Canadian piracy, "there is not a single argument in favor of international copyright which a rational American Senate could entertain for a moment." Twain gave an interesting alternative view to the American authors' position regarding international copyright. Telling Howells that his views have "mightily changed," he explained that so much good English literature was available at such low prices that they make "a pack-

age of water closet paper seem an 'edition de luxe' in comparison." He
continued:

> A generation of this sort of thing ought to make this the most intelligent &
> best-read nation in the world. International copyright must becloud the
> sun & bring on the former darkness and dime-novel reading. . . . Interna-
> tional copyright would benefit a few English authors, & a lot of American
> publishers, & be a profound detriment to 20,000,000 Americans; it would
> benefit a dozen American authors a few dollars a year, and there an end. The
> real advantages all go to English authors & American publishers.
> And even if the treaty *will* kill Canadian piracy, & thus save me an average
> of $5,000 a year, I'm down on it anyway—& I'd like cussed well to write an
> article opposing the treaty. Dern England! Such is my sentiments. (Twain
> and Howells 1960, 1:335–36)

Twain's changing and complex attitude toward copyright, though too
detailed to examine here, demonstrates the wealth of perspectives on the
argument. One forceful American argument in favor of the pre-1891 situation was that Americans had access to famous works of literature at a
fraction of the price that English readers paid for the same works. Yet
Twain, American through and through, recognized the importance of de-
veloping and protecting American literature and turning away from English models. Despite the inconsistency of his outbursts, he was an ardent
supporter of the campaign for international copyright. He was in the fortunate position of having a sympathetic and honest English publisher (Andrew Chatto) who helped him secure copyright for his books. In 1882
Twain wrote, "I comfort myself that while the rest of our tribe are growling
over international copyright, I am the recipient of a most gaudy English
income, from three books which cannot be pirated" (Welland 1978, 129).
The purported gaudiness of his English income suggests his discomfort
when confronted with the demands of both his writing and its position
within the marketplace: his desire to write as he wanted to and his need to
sell significantly.

Twain had previously been in the position of having his work pirated
both by American publishers and by an English publisher, John Camden
Hotten. Publishers like Hotten drew down the wrath of writers who could
be scathing about them—even about their last hours: Swinburne's remark
on Hotten's death is wonderfully malicious: "When I heard he had died
after a surfeit of pork chops, I observed that this was a serious argument
against my friend Sir Richard Burton's view of cannibalism as a wholesome
and natural method of diet" (Welland 1976, 28).

There are no records of any remarks by Swinburne on Frederic, or on
the *New York Times*.

The Literary Center

Until the 1880s Boston and Cambridge were together recognized as America's literary center. Boston was, in Hamlin Garland's phrase, the "literary autocrat of the nation" (Garland 1960, 115). In the 1880s Boston's literary preeminence went into decline as a new group of writers challenged its right to dominate the literary output of America. In "Literary Centers," the tenth in Garland's *Crumbling Idols* (1894), a collection of polemical essays, Garland confidently pronounces that "the literary supremacy of the East is passing away." New York is the new literary center of the United States, he writes, and its supremacy is as undeniably "complete" as its commercial domination. For a short time it had seemed that Boston's loss would be New York's gain, but it would soon become clear that the days of a single, dominating, literary center were over. Competing cities from all over the West and South pressed their claims to literary status: "The process," as Garland puts it, "is one of decentralization, together with one of unification." He predicts that the "shadow" of Chicago "already menaces" New York (the World's Columbian Exposition had taken place in Chicago the previous year) and that it was only a matter of time before a new literature, genuinely democratic, will emerge from the West and the South (Garland 1960, 114–18). The process is traced as one of an intellectual coming-of-age.

The celebrated writers of "American literature," with a few exceptions (notably Cooper, Poe, and Irving), had been of New England origin. American literature had been New England literature, dominated by English traditions. Now, accompanying new clamors for an idiosyncratic national literature, writers sought to break New England's hold on American writing, and with it establish independence from Europe. Young writers with Slavonic, Teutonic, Scandinavian, and Jewish backgrounds, among others, particularly African Americans, were being recognized, and are still being recognized, as an exciting force in American writing.[18] But other significant challenges were the threats New York posed to Boston and the animosity New Yorkers felt toward New England, with its Anglo-European inheritance. This traditional hostility was shared by Frederic, who rebukes the "Boston talkers" in *In the Valley:* "I could not foresee how we were to be

18. Many contemporary scholars are currently engaged in debates that explicitly raise issues of heterogeneity in terms both of writers of this period and of their works, challenging categories such as realism and naturalism and rediscovering writers against whom it is necessary to interrogate assumptions about American literature and the canon at the turn of the century. This is exceedingly welcome work. See, for example, the range of writers whose works are debated in Ammons and White-Parks 1994, who include Charles Chesnutt, Paul Lawrence Dunbar, Mourning Dove, Sui Sin Far, Frances E. W. Harper, María Cristina Mena, Alexander Posey, Zitkala-Ša, and Onoto Watanna.

snowed under by the Yankees in our own State, and, what is worse, accept our subjugation without a protest—so that to-day the New York schoolboy supposes Fisher Ames, or any other of a dozen Boston talkers, to have been a greater man than Philip Schuyler" (Frederic Novels 1890a, 123).

By 19 January 1902, when Frank Norris wrote "New York as a Literary Center," the decentralizing that Garland predicted was becoming a reality. Never again would Boston be the nation's "literary autocrat" (Norris 1964, 36–40). Democratic America wanted neither autocrats nor dictators. Three days later, in "An American School of Fiction? A Denial," which appeared in the *Boston Evening Transcript,* Norris argues that there had not yet been a distinctively American school of fiction. Lowell, Longfellow, Holmes, Whittier, and Hawthorne were not American writers but writers of New England, "[a]nd New England," he solemnly intones, "is not America." He dismisses other writers, all male, for a variety of reasons. Cooper's novels emerge from Bulwer, Byron, and Walter Scott. Poe does not rank as a novelist, and Bret Harte "abandoned the field [of short stories] with hardly more than a mere surface-scratching." Continuing in a tone of criticism alternately characterized by machismo and philistinism, he argues that James might have written with more vigor and decision had he remained in the United States. Twain, "American to the core," is a humorist rather than a novelist. Howells alone of the "larger names" has the "broadest vision" of the American writers, "at once a New Englander and a New Yorker, an Easterner and—in the Eastern sense—a Westerner" (Norris 1964, 108–9). For Norris it seemed that Howells could best act as a representative American of his time, not just in terms of his writing, his chosen themes and modes of representation, but in his personal history, too.

The reputation of Howells, an Ohio-born son of a Swedenborgian family, has now been largely eclipsed by those writers he so generously supported and championed. In his early career his realist novels and philosophy were attacked for their openness that verged, it was argued, on immorality: the publication of *The Rise of Silas Lapham* was greeted by howls of prurient disapproval that recall the later response to *Maggie: A Girl of the Streets* or *Sister Carrie.*[19] Later, his reputation suffered a curious reversal, and in old age he found himself accused of prudishness, of sentimentality, and of cloying genteelness. Younger writers, who saw Howells's careful negotiation between propriety and candidness as a sign of servile decorum, thought of him as a sort of literary old maid. Yet his career was an inspiration to many writers—a model by which they could, and often did, judge

19. See Cady's dismissive comment that "Here, as in many places, the evidence mounts that those who insist that Howells was invincibly genteel may themselves be invincibly unread" (Howells 1973, 256).

their own achievements. In recent years he has found a staunch and eloquent defender, Edwin Cady, who has argued that his reticence was not equivalent to prudery and that he was certainly no "sentimental Pollyanna" (Howells 1973, 4). When Harold Frederic arrived in Boston in 1873, keen to find a job during an acute economic depression, Howells's long literary career was already taking shape. Howells had himself visited Boston and Cambridge in 1860, a "passionate pilgrim from the West" as he later wrote (purposely turning James's phrase into an American pilgrimage), visiting "his holy land at Boston" by an appropriately modern form of transportation, "by way of the Grand Trunk Railway from Quebec to Portland" (Howells 1968, 16). Howells's opportunity for widespread fame had been assisted by the patronage of established New England writers who recommended that he should write the campaign biography of Lincoln, *Lives and Speeches of Abraham Lincoln and Hannibal Hamlin* (1860). The biography had earned him a consulship, and he became a diplomat for a time, just as Irving, Hawthorne, and Lowell had before him, and other literary figures would later. (Frederic saw a consular post as a way out of journalism, petitioning Grover Cleveland in the hope of obtaining the consular position that Hawthorne had once held.) When he returned from Venice, Howells could not find work in Ohio and wrote occasional articles for New York papers, demonstrating the fluidity of the profession of authorship. On New Year's Eve 1865 he renewed his acquaintance with the New England publisher James Fields. Their farewell to each other was an exchange that, given its consequences, takes on a quasi-Masonic significance: "At the end Fields said, mockingly, 'Don't despise Boston!' and I answered, as we shook hands, 'Few are worthy to live in Boston'" (Howells 1968, 96–97). The verbal exchange was shortly followed by a contractual one: Howells was offered a job on the prestigious *Atlantic Monthly*. True to form, he swiftly negotiated a 25 percent increase in the proffered weekly salary, and took the job. Evidently Fields thought that Howells was one of the worthy few. On 1 March 1866, he started work. He would prosper intellectually (and financially) in the congenial and sophisticated cultural climate of New England as he could never do in the raw air of the Midwest.

Through living in Boston and showing a keen and supportive interest in young writers, Howells formed a personal link between the older writers and the literary center, and the newer generation that was replacing them. He had been drawn toward Boston by the lure of its glittering reputation, like one of his protégés, the young Hamlin Garland. He had been acquainted with figures who represented America's literary establishment such as Emerson, Hawthorne, Holmes, Longfellow, and Lowell. During the time he was a resident an extraordinary number of vivid new talents were also collected in or around that city: Brooks and Henry Adams; Alice,

Henry, and William James; Charles Sanders Peirce; John Fiske; and in a wider geographical circle, Mark Twain; Richard Watson Gilder; Bret Harte; and Charles Dudley Warner. Charlotte Perkins Gilman was born in Hartford, Connecticut, in 1860; Emily Dickinson was living quietly in Amherst; and Mary Baker Eddy would soon make herself famous through Christian Science, and this would prove fatal to Frederic. Some years later, in 1894, Howells wrote, "I suppose there is no question but our literary center was then [in 1860] in Boston, wherever it is, or is not, at present" (Howells 1968, 14).

On 6 October 1885, Howells signed a remunerative contract with Harper and Brothers, the start of the "Editor's Study," his regular column in *Harper's New Monthly Magazine*. Aware of the rumors circulating about his imminent departure from Boston to New York, Howells chose an Author's Club dinner in his honor as the occasion to make a public statement denying that he was in the process of permanently leaving Boston. Thomas Bailey Aldrich added a bantering note to the proceedings by reading out a semiserious note, "Come back to Boston and all will be forgiven" (Cady 1958, 1–4). The jocularity did not dispel the real fears that Howells's longstanding cultural exchange with New England had ended, or was nearing its end. This was a critical moment in Boston's history: the "passionate pilgrim" had rejected the "holy land." Boston's literary supremacy was finally over.

Howells's ambivalence about his move is expressed in *A Hazard of New Fortunes* (1890). Basil March (Howells's alter ego) moves to New York and establishes a new fortnightly literary magazine, aptly named "Every Other Week." At one point he remarks, "I always feel a little proud of hailing from Boston; my pleasure in the place mounts the farther I get away from it" (Howells 1976, 23). For Howells, "expatriation" meant appreciation, as it has for generations of American writers, including Frederic.[20] Yet for some the passing of Boston as the literary center marked a significant change in the tenor of American life. Years later Garland would call New York "a mart and not a capital, in literature as well as in other things." Boston suggested a purity that New York, rocked by scandals of financial and political corruption, lacked.[21] Howells enjoyed a story about Oliver Wendell Holmes (the epitome of the Brahminical patrician and creator of

20. Mrs. March is openly hostile to New York: "I could go West with you, or into a new country—anywhere; but I don't like New York; I never did; it disheartens and distracts me; I can't find myself in it; I shouldn't know how to shop" (Howells 1976, 28).

21. In *Crumbling Idols* Garland writes that "Boston artists go one by one to New York. Literary men find their market growing there, and dying out in Boston" (Garland 1960, 149). The *New York Times* had, in a sustained campaign, exposed the corruption of the Tammany ring in the 1870s.

the most famous Boston autocrat). Holmes had a theory that the higher the civilization, the more minuscule the quantities involved in exchange: "The ideal, he said, was a civilization in which you could buy two cents worth of beef, and a divergence from this standard was towards barbarism" (Howells 1968, 128). Although Howells was canny himself in matters of money, this was a result of prudence rather than greed. He appreciated Holmes's witty alliance between an exact apportionment of supply and demand, though it is surprising that the democratic Howells did not quibble over the elitism of Holmes's principle, which favored finicky over healthy appetites. Howells's own ideal was to live in an intelligent, cultured, democratic society, and he celebrated Bret Harte's Western appreciation of the civilized and creative inhabitants of Cambridge: "Why, you couldn't stand on your front porch and fire off your revolver without bringing down a two-volumer" (Howells 1968, 245). Howells's enjoyment of the genteel literary establishment of Boston and Cambridge separated him from many of the new young writers who wrote within the crowded metropolises of late-nineteenth-century America. One distinctive marker between Howells and some younger writers was in their respective treatment of sexuality.[22]

The question of the censorship of literature, clearly related to the issue of what is a proper subject for literature, was one of the pressing issues that contemporary writers had to encounter. Frederic's response to the question was characteristically unstraightforward and is closely connected with the vicissitudes of his relationships with Grace Frederic and Kate Lyon. As he confronted the ethical dilemmas of his double life with the two, he reassessed his attitude toward the hypocrisy and double standards inherent in sexual relationships. Although no sexual puritan, he undoubtedly believed in a double standard of behavior for men and for women. He does not seem to have been a champion of equal rights for the sexes.

Censorship

Oscar Wilde, during questioning in his first trial, made the memorable comment that "In writing a play or a book, I am concerned entirely with literature—that is, with art. I aim not at doing good or evil, but in trying to make a thing that will have some quality of beauty" (Hyde 1962, 108). In making an unequivocal distinction between art and morality at the very outset of his examination by Edward Carson, Wilde was preparing the way for one of his most brilliant and energetic defenses of literature. Part of

---

22. Frederic was convinced that Howells had hated *The Damnation of Theron Ware*, possibly believing that Howells would disapprove of the degree of openness in his treatment of sexuality. Part of this anxiety was owing, however, to his desire for approval from the influential critic.

the Marquis of Queensberry's plea of justification against Wilde in the libel trial of 3 April 1895 was that *The Picture of Dorian Gray* (1890) was a covert description of "the relations, intimacies, and passions" of homosexuals (Hyde 1962, 102). The libel trial, and the two trials that followed it, centered on more than questions of public morality. They were crucially concerned with the effect that works of literature had upon the actions of individuals. Could an "immoral" work result in, or even cause, acts of immorality by those who came into contact with it? That is to say, could influence be quantified? Wilde thought not, reiterating the position expressed in *The Picture of Dorian Gray* that "There is no such thing as a moral or immoral book. Books are well written or badly written." (Hyde 1962, 109). Wilde's opinion on this matter, and, notoriously, on others, was not generally held. At the time of his trial his name was removed from posters advertising *An Ideal Husband* and *The Importance of Being Earnest* (both produced in 1895 and published in 1899), both enjoying great success in London (Ellmann 1987, 430). Yet even this act of censorship was not extreme enough. Soon the runs were condemned to death—abandoned because of a hostile public—and Wilde received two years hard labor.

Among the most important of the censors in Britain were the circulating libraries. In 1885, the year after Frederic moved to London and ten years before Wilde's encounter with a censorious Establishment, the Irish novelist George Moore wrote an attack on Mudie's library. The title of this piece, "Literature at Nurse; or, Circulating Morals," is a witty allusion to the power of the circulating libraries, whose audience was mainly young women. Moore argues that the virility of the novel is being stifled by the motherliness of the librarian: "Instead of being allowed to fight, with and amid, the thoughts and aspirations of men, literature is now rocked to an ignoble rest in the motherly arms of the librarian. . . . Mudie is the law we labour after; the suffrage of young women we are supposed to gain: the paradise of the English novelist is in the school-room: he is read there or nowhere" (Thomas 1969, 470). Moore uses an interesting and confused mixture of images to express his horror at the circulating libraries' emasculation of literature. Mudie is the mother and nursemaid, guardian of morality and protecting jailer of the slumbering form of literature. Mudie usurps the writer's position as a mother (a producer who brings forth the novel after much hard labor). The word "suffrage" is a triple pun on "suffrage," "sufferance," and "suffering": literature suffers by seeking the support or votes of young women; the only suffrage that such young women seek is to be allowed to read titillating sentimental literature, an ignoble ambition. The word "labour" also doubles, suggesting both the labor of birth and economic labor. (This stresses Mudie's stranglehold on the market.) The motherly rocking is transformed into infanticide:

mothering becomes smothering. Moore adds "Let us renounce the effort to reconcile those two irreconcilable things—art and young girls."[23]

Much nineteenth-century writing had already, or would, renounce the effort to reconcile the irreconcilable. Louisa May Alcott's *Little Women* (1868) had great appeal as a conduct manual for young girls and continues to have a hold on the public imagination. As such, it was hugely popular. The book was part of the childhood reading of the heroine of Ellen Glasgow's *The Sheltered Life* (1932), a novel that centers on conduct and its consequences. Popular novels like *Little Women* brought substantial financial rewards to their authors. Many popular novelists, like the reading public that Moore complains of (as Hawthorne had, famously, done at an earlier date), were women—Frances Hodgson Burnett, Marie Corelli, "Ouida," "Iota," Sarah Grand, and the immensely successful Mrs. E.D.E.N. Southworth. In Moore's account of censorship the market becomes a battlefield in which male novelists and feminized librarians (and perhaps female social reform activists) confront one another about and over male literary productivity. Yet one of the most interesting battles between censored and censoring in the 1890s was concerned with the New Woman fiction, and male antagonists would often become allies as they opposed and condemned the innovations and outspokenness of women who, literally, "did."[24]

Frederic participates in Moore's satire on censorship, writing a version of Mrs. Grundy in *Observations in Philistia*. (The original Mrs. Grundy was an imaginary figure in Thomas Morton's play *Speed the Plough* (1798). She became an arbiter of moral actions—"What will Mrs. Grundy say?") Grundyism was often attacked as the voice of dull moral conservatism, and the figure of Mrs. Grundy, later personified as the Victorian matron (often

23. Several years before Moore's attack, Thomas Hardy (who would abandon writing novels after the critical response to *Jude the Obscure*) contrived a complex play between art and the young girl in *A Pair of Blue Eyes* (1873). Elfride Swancourt, the heroine of the novel, writes a historical novel, *The Court of King Arthur's Castle. A Romance of Lyonesse*, and finds herself torn between Henry "Knight," a hostile reviewer, and Stephen Smith, one of Knight's protégés. Knight first attracts Elfride's attention by his review (brilliantly deflated by Elfride's stepmother, who turns a sneering reference to *Ivanhoe* into a complimentary comparison with Scott). Knight and Smith compete for Elfride's heart through two very different kinds of writing. Elfride reads the vigorous and attacking review on the same day as she receives a love letter from Smith. The success of Knight's rivalry with Smith is assured when Elfride falls asleep that night, in love with Smith, but thinking about the unknown reviewer. The young girl reader/writer chooses the sturdy intellect of Knight over the sentimental love of Smith when given a choice between the two. Eventually she marries an aristocrat and dies after a miscarriage, a premature labor that suggests her early thwarted career as a writer.

24. Although Frederic said little on the subect of New Women fiction, it is clear that he disapproved of much of it. See, for example, Frederic to editor, *Daily Chronicle*, 5 October 1894, Frederic Misc. 1977, 383–84.

specifically as the British social purity campaigner Laura Ormiston Chant), came in for ridicule and abuse.[25] She was, however, defended by an unlikely figure. In *Tono-Bungay* (1909) H. G. Wells liberates Mrs. Grundy from a reputation that had lasted over one hundred years, and suggests that it is Mr. Grundy, a middle-aged man, who is responsible for society's inhibitions and guilt:

> "Did I tell you, Ponderevo, of a wonderful discovery I've made?" Ewart began presently.
> "No," I said, "what is it?"
> "There's no Mrs. Grundy."
> "No?"
> "No! Practically not. I've just thought all that business out. She's merely an instrument, Ponderevo. She's borne the blame. Grundy's a man. Grundy unmasked. Rather lean and out of sorts. Early middle age. With bunch black whiskers and a worried eye. Been good so far, and it's fretting him! . . . She's a much maligned person, Ponderevo—a rake at heart. . . . Grundy sins. Oh yes, he's a hypocrite. Sneaks round a corner and sins ugly. It's Grundy and his dark corners that make vice, vice! We artists—we have no vices" (Wells 1972, 142–44).[26]

In Frederic's satirical collection *Observations in Philistia* Mrs. Grundy plays a more traditional role, though she is not treated harshly by him. She is horrified by Hardy's *Tess of the D'Urbervilles* (1891) (a novel that had a long struggle against the censors), locking it away from her daughters and returning it to Mudie's with a note expressing her outrage that it should be sent into a Christian home. Meanwhile, her daughters read a scandalous and sensational popular novel, presumably a piece of New Woman fiction, simply on account of the publicity surrounding its female author. Frederic's satire is somewhat heavy-handed: Mrs. Grundy calls the popular novel the talk of her friends, "many of them people, too, whom you would not suspect of any literary tastes whatsoever" and who think it "an exposition of those Christian principles which make our England what it is" (Frederic Misc. 1896a, 5–11).

Ten years after Moore's attack on Mudie's, Frank Norris continued the offensive in a robust discussion of the magazine short story. In "The Decline of the Magazine Short Story" he cleverly reversed moralists' attacks on literature and claimed that the victims were readers not authors (or literature itself). He wrote a piece of pointed criticism of the "professional

---

25. See, for example, Walkowitz 1994, 129, and Beckson 1992, 119–20 and 121–28, for details of Mrs. Chant's activities.

26. This extract is a very small portion of the discussion of Grundyism and censorship, which extends from 142 to 147.

magazinists" who flooded the literary magazines with hackneyed plots and unoriginal stories. He argued that editors liked the stories because they were "safe" and continued, "They are safe, it is true, safe as a grave yard, decorous as a church, as devoid of immorality as an epitaph. They have not the vigor or decisiveness to offend the most invertebrate taste. They adorn the center table. They do not 'call a blush to the cheek of the young.' They can be placed—Oh crowning virtue, Oh supreme encomium —they can be 'safely' placed in the hands of any young girl the country over. It is the 'young girl' and the family center table that determine the standard of the American short story" (Norris 1964, 28).[27] Within the context of Norris's other writings it is clear that one of his anxieties was that the quality of American fiction (as product within the literary marketplace) would be undermined by such censorship.

The attack on this literary censorship raged at the end of the century. On one side were general diatribes on the morality of writing and of writers symbolized by a series of events that included the trials and imprisonment of Oscar Wilde, the 1880s Vizetelly trials for obscene libel (Henry Richard Vizetelly was imprisoned for publishing translations of a number of French writers, including Zola), and the English publication of Max Nordau's *Degeneration* (1895). On the other were eloquent defenses, including Wilde's responses to hostile examination at his trials, Howells's ridicule of *Degeneration,* and his defense of Zola.[28]

27. See also Edward Carpenter (to whom Frederic refers in *Gloria Mundi*) on this question: "The British drawing-room of the last century was a center from which many paralysing influences radiated. Here the British matron, surrounded by her virginal daughters, sat enthroned. The men—husbands, brothers, sons, and their friends—were to all appearances inferior creatures. They took their cue from the ladies, and studied only the convenience of the latter. They effaced themselves, and deliberately talked a kind of nonsense which was called conversation. They wore clothing of a subdued and dark hue, which served as a foil to the feminine glory; they sat on the more uncomfortable chairs, and were careful to take their tea and their tea-cake after the others. It was touching" (Tsuzuki 1980, 1). Also see, for example, Henry James, who, in "The Art of Fiction" (1884) writes that "To what degree a purpose in a work of art is a source of corruption I shall not attempt to inquire; the one that seems to me least dangerous is the purpose of making a perfect work. As for our novel, I may say lastly on this score that as we find it in England to-day it strikes me as addressed in a large degree to 'young people', and that this in itself constitutes a presumption that it will be rather shy. There are certain things which it is generally agreed not to discuss, not even to mention, before young people. That is very well, but the absence of discussion is not a symptom of the moral passion" (James 1981, 66).

28. See Howells 1973, 217–24 and also the indexed references. Frederic may have had a personal interest in Hardy's struggle against the censors. One anecdote tells of a meeting of the two men at one of the functions of an unidentified hostess at whose home politicians, writers, actors, and barristers were purportedly shown the war-club of the Native American Chief, Sitting Bull. Swinging the weapon in the air, Hardy exclaimed, "How much I should like to have that in my hand when I encounter the critic who calls 'Jude the Obscure' 'Jude

Censorship had a profound influence on Frederic's work. His instincts were against it: he hated the petty tyranny that secrecy could cause. Several images reinforce this: Frederic revealing the trade secrets of photography to a young apprentice to stop his boss exploiting the boy; his conversational frankness; his refusal to be cowed by sartorial censorship; his attacks on the fettered press of Russia and Spain; his lamentable inability to appreciate fully the necessity of prudence in his personal relationships: his intolerance of secrecy and of censorship increased with age, as did his need for it. In his early writings Frederic was not a radical critic, and his criticism for the *Utica Daily Observer* suggests an acute sense of the hyperconventionality of much of his small-town readership. In a review of Zola's *L'Assommoir* (1877), his desire to negotiate between his readers' sensibilities and those of more liberal critics results in some funny underhand satire on Utica reading habits. So on 12 May 1879 he writes that the novel is held to be a "temperance story": "But we owe it to our readers who are also readers of T. S. Arthur, and the admirers of TEN NIGHTS IN A BAR-ROOM, to warn them that it is not their type of a temperance book, and that they will not like it" (Woodward 1972, 15). He admires the "photographic realism . . . which out-Balzacs Balzac in minutiae" (and, he says, makes the novel especially useful for the language student!). Although concerned about seeming prudish, he accuses Zola of pandering to the "lowest cravings of a debased reading public." It would seem that here he is implying code of self-censorship, indeed, such a code seems to have regulated his writing up until 1896 and *The Damnation of Theron Ware*. He was careful to avoid offending propriety in his early work—he depended on magazine serialization of his novels for extra income. When he came to write *The Lawton Girl* he ended the novel by the death of Jessica Lawton, a reformed prostitute and single parent, "she who had not deserved or intended at all to die," but admitted in 1897 that "I see now more clearly than anyone else that it was a false and cowardly thing to do" (Frederic 1977, 4–5). His realization was assisted by the existence of his three children by Kate Lyon. If Jessica Lawton had to die in order not to offend his reading public, what sacrifice was required of Kate Lyon?

Later, especially in *March Hares* and *The Damnation of Theron Ware*, Frederic's treatment of sexual relationships is more daring. Theron's late-night visit to Celia Madden's rooms was, in 1896, indiscreet, to say the least. Yet

---

the Obscene'!" The critic, a woman, was sitting next to Hardy at the time. This resulted in a good deal of nervous giggles. The furious response to *Jude the Obscure* (1895) contributed to Hardy's decision not to write another novel. Famously, R. L. Stevenson burned the first version of *The Strange Case of Dr. Jekyll and Mr. Hyde* after his wife's objections to it. See Veeder, "The Texts in Question" and "Collated Fractions of Manuscript Drafts" in Veeder and Hirsch 1988, 3–56.

though Frederic's development enabled him to be more suggestive about his belief that sex is a driving force behind all human activity, he was anxious that this was treated with intelligence and care. He deplored much of the New Woman fiction, which he regarded as being indecent in its treatment of sex and sexuality, and wrote *Gloria Mundi* with what appears to be a genuine desire to state the case for women's independence in such a way that it would attract a serious readership, not one simply eager for, as he saw it, cheap titillation. Yet it is equally apparent that he is not acting without self-interest and that, like many of the seemingly liberal men who supported women's emancipation, he wanted it on his own terms. Educated, independent women would be worthy companions for men, including himself. He felt that he could write a novel that dealt with issues of marriage, of challenges to established norms of relationships, and of the possibilities for women in the 1890s better than women could.

One striking act of censorship suggests how far it was a significant feature of the time in which Frederic was writing. In autumn 1897 he signed agreements with William Heinemann and Frederick A. Stokes Company to undertake the English and American publication of *The Market-Place*. He promised to deliver a completed manuscript to Stokes on 1 September 1898 and to Heinemann on 12 October 1898. He worked steadily on the novel for the next few months, and when he returned from Ireland in May, he probably delivered a package of work to be typed for him. By summer 1898 he had certainly started making handwritten corrections to the typescript, but after his stroke on 12 August, he relied on John Scott Stokes to assist him in corrections and alterations. Frederic's relations with William Heinemann were relaxed. The two were old friends, and Frederic was motivated to complete the typescript of the novel by his need for advance royalties. Negotiations with his latest American publisher were more formal, however. The September deadline passed, and Frederic retained the final two chapters of the novel. Hearing of Frederic's ill-health, Frederick Stokes (no relation to John Scott Stokes) began to contemplate arranging for a conclusion to be written for the novel. He sold the serial rights of the novel to William George Jordan of the *Saturday Evening Post:* careful placing of the novel was bound to increase sales figures. The two agreed to use the same typescript to set copy, and Jordan decided to add a short chapter "with as much care as if Mr. Frederic had himself written it" to take the place of the missing chapters. Shortly after this transaction Frederick Stokes received the missing chapters in unrevised form, but on Frederic's death on 19 October the publishers were able to treat the novel as they wished. Although Heinemann and Stokes did not take advantage of this latitude, Jordan acted "cavalierly," bowdlerizing freely.

Yet Jordan's influence was not as pernicious as that of George Horace Lorimer, who replaced him as editor of the magazine:

While Jordan embellished and refined, Lorimer abbreviated the novel by excision; both editors bowdlerized, deleting or abbreviating references to liquor and impious and sexually suggestive words. . . . But the most radical change to the serial introduced by Lorimer, "a devout worshipper of the free enterprise system," was the deletion of the last two chapters, which terminated the novel (at the end of chapter twenty-five) with Thorpe's claim that he had become a better man rather than with the suggestion that he is a threat to society and a potential murderer. (Frederic Novels 1981, 372, [ed. comment]).

Quite apart from reversing the entire intention of the novel, Lorimer added a final decorative touch. From 4 February on, installments were headed by an art nouveau drawing of "a woman, a money sack, and a laurel wreath." This has a grim aptness, and its iconography suggests Frederic's position, torn between his two families, his two careers, his need for money, and his desire for literary fame. Frederic would have been horrified that what amounted to his final earthly statement should have been tampered with in such a vulgar way.

⤳ 3 ⤳

The Journalist

The American "Paper-Stainer"

On 11 May 1892 Harold Frederic wrote to an Utica Irish friend, John Howe, congratulating him on his recent appointment as editor of the *Rochester Herald.* He told him, "I hope you get time for reading, in the new chair. Read books; books, books, books! They make the full man—just as newspapers make the smart empty man" (Frederic Misc. 1977, 314).[1] Frederic was already an established and well-respected journalist, but none of his three published novels *(Seth's Brother's Wife, In the Valley,* and *The Lawton Girl)* had achieved the success that he had envisaged for them.[2] He knew that he was a "smart" journalist, but did that make him a "smart empty man"? He desperately wanted success as a novelist in order to prove that he was more than a clever journalist. Behind his avuncular tone lurked the specter of failure. His ambitions for his novels remained unfulfilled. They neither attracted the interest that he hoped for nor brought him enough income to abandon journalism and live wholly by writing fiction.

Frederic had been hoping for literary success since his earliest days as a journalist. Although he could argue, according to a journalist friend, Arthur Warren, that "the journalism which influences public opinion along a high plane is the journalism that will endure," it is difficult not to be skeptical of Warren's claims of Frederic's allegiance to journalism (Warren 1898, 19). In this context Joseph Conrad's provocative comment is apposite though arguable: "Journalists, like labour leaders, only shout up their professions in order to get out of them" (Hart-Davis 1985, 186). One of Frederic's concerns was the ephemeral nature of the newspaper word. Writing to Howe on 9 April 1885, Frederic said that "a paper two weeks

---

1. Frederic had appropriated this from Francis Bacon's essay, "Of Studies," and Americanized it. Bacon had written, "Reading maketh a full man; conference a ready man; and writing an exact man. And therefore, if a man write little, he had need have a great memory; if he confer little, he had need have a present wit; and if he read little, he had need to have much cunning, to seem to know that he doth not" (Bacon 1911, 150–51).
2. *The Return of The O'Mahony* was not yet published in book form.

old is practically twenty years old," echoing Whitman, who calls the newspaper "so fleeting . . . is so like a thing gone as quick as come: has no life, so to speak: its birth and death are almost coterminous" (Frederic Misc. 1977, 56; Zweig 1985, 7). Frederic was attracted to the potential power newspapers could have, but hated the vapid daily routine and the anonymity of much journalism. The thought of being a successful novelist with a lasting reputation was more compelling than that of being a journalist. For several years prior to the letter of May 1892 Frederic had been writing to Howe predicting his imminent and permanent return to the United States. Although these predictions had become a regular theme in his letters to Howe, he was proving an increasingly unreliable reporter. His complicated personal life and concomitant financial difficulties made return a more remote and unlikely prospect. After 1890 he stopped visiting the United States altogether.

Frederic's diminishing expectations are captured in his letters. On 27 February 1886 he writes to Howe that he is confident about his forthcoming "permanent return" to the United States. England is "pleasant enough," but he writes that he wants to leave before he "lost touch" with what he calls "my own country" (the United States, but more important, New York State). He hopes that the success that he so confidently predicted for his first novel, *Seth's Brother's Wife*, would give him financial independence (Frederic Misc. 1977, 100).[3] This would prove to be another false prediction, but meanwhile he had enthusiastic plans for two more projects —a biography of Horatio Seymour, and a novel of the American Revolution. He writes, "if these beliefs of mine are not bubbles, I shall come back to America in 1887 with some money, with a reputation, and with the manuscript of a second story—the Mohawk Valley romance which I began five years ago [*In the Valley*]—in such shape that two months' pointing up on the ground will make it in American literature what Henry Esmond is in English. Then I need never, please God, ask what time a paper goes to press again."

In a letter of December 1886 Frederic's tone is calmer and more resigned. He tells Howe that his "exile" is only sometimes irritating and that much of the time he is happy in England: it is only the memories of American Christmas that makes an English Christmas seem "very hollow" (ca. 16 December, Frederic Misc. 1977, 150–51). Yet his moods fluctuated, and by 15 April 1887 he was again in despair. He writes to Edward Burlingame, an American publisher, that he has been made "nervous and despondent" by Burlingame's failure to give a prompt opinion of *Seth's Brother's Wife:* "No doubt it was silly, but I could not help construing your

3. Frederic writes, "I expect now to be in America in June; and at the farthest I do not expect to remain in Europe more than one year after my return from the coming vacation."

silence to mean that it was no good." His anxiety had been fueled by his increasing dissatisfaction with his job at the *New York Times:* he was "tired of newspaper work, and its ceaseless worrying and interruptions" and had written to the paper telling them that he wanted to return to the United States. His frustration explodes in a petulant and impassioned outburst: "I am giving the best years of my life to work I dislike, in a country I hate, and even if I have to make some sacrifices I feel that I ought to get out" (Frederic Misc. 1977, 169–70).[4]

He was losing control of his carefully planned future. The bravura with which he had resigned the editorship of the *Albany Evening Journal* and moved to London had been shaken, and his independence was beginning to feel like isolation. He was anxious that as a foreign correspondent, living and working away from an American readership, he would gradually be "de-Americanized," losing track of what his readers were interested in. He might lose his identity, and he might well jeopardize his career—"by absence, be crowded out of the rank in journalism to which I belong." On 9 April 1885 he had told Howe that "it is the only thing in all my future that I am nervous about—and my only reliance is in good friends like yourself, Sherlock, Atwell et al. who see that my grave is kept green" (Frederic Misc. 1977, 55). He knew that if he could not make a success out of his fiction, he would have to rely on journalism for an income. Seven years on, in 1892, his belief in his early return home had proved to be false and his confident predictions of easy success mistaken. He was struggling financially, and he had committed himself to what amounted to a second marriage with Kate Lyon without formally ending his first. He was more resigned and less nostalgic than he had been. On 11 May he wrote to Howe that "It seems many years since everything. I find myself no longer thinking much about returning for good. One settles into ruts" (Frederic Misc. 1977, 314).

His complex and changing responses toward both journalism and living in England are integrally linked. His job had taken him to England, and for this he was grateful, yet it kept him away from the United States—from his family and friends, and from membership in the American literary world to which he aspired. On 11 December 1896 he writes to the poet James Whitcomb Riley, "Expatriation has, on the whole, a tolerably level balance of losses and compensations—I suppose—but there are times when I feel very keenly my inability to get on a horse-car or a train, and go and say 'howdy' to men like you, and [Hamlin] Garland, and others whose work makes them close friends of mine, yet whom I never see" (Frederic Misc. 1977, 427). Frustration with the reception of his novels, and anxiety about his isolation, became bitterness at the job which kept him in En-

---

4. For more on Burlingame's publishing experiences, see Burlingame 1946.

gland. Frederic wanted to be a "full man."[5] Yet after Frederic's death a newspaper colleague described seeing him with his notebook crammed full of facts "with a grip of the whole political situation in England the like of which probably was possessed by not half-a-dozen other men, apart from the official wire-pullers" ("C.K.S." 1898, 4). He was, without doubt, a talented and well-informed journalist, and it was by having such a significant position as a foreign correspondent that he sustained his reputation.

Frederic's careful preparation for his journalism influenced the way in which he approached fiction. The Harold Frederic Papers in the Library of Congress contain intricate notes for his fiction as well as comprehensive plans, maps, and lists of names. In an interview he described his preparation for *The Damnation of Theron Ware:*

> "I am now writing a novel . . . the people of which I have been carrying about with me, night and day, for fully five years. After I had got them grouped together in my mind, I set myself the task of knowing everything they knew. As four of them happened to be specialists in different professions, the task has been tremendous. For instance, one of them is a biologist, who, among many other things is experimenting on Lubbock's and Darwin's lines. Altho [sic] these pursuits are merely mentioned, I have got up masses of stuff on bees and the cross-fertilization of plants. I have had to teach myself all the details of a Methodist minister's work, obligations and daily routine, and all the machinery of his church. Another character is a priest, who is a good deal more of a pagan than a simple-minded Christian. He loves luxury and learning. I have studied the arts he loves as well as his theology; I have waded in Assyriology and Schopenhauer; pored over palimpsests and pottery, and, in order to write understandingly about a musician, who figures in the story, I have bored a professional friend to death getting technical musical stuff from him. I don't say this is the right way to build novels; only it is my way."
> ("How the Popular Harold Frederic Works" 1896, 397)

Frederic is certainly indulging in blatant self-advertisement here, with a journalistic lack of self-abasement. He is also demonstrating his capability

---

5. His double response to his joint career has been ignored by several early critics who use his adherence to his journalistic career as evidence that he was not a serious or committed novelist. Clarence Gohdes misrepresents Frederic: "All of his books were rush work, prepared during hours when he was recuperating from newspaper tasks" (Gohdes 1951, 743). This judgment is inaccurate and suggests the prejudice he encountered in his own lifetime. Gohdes's assertion that Frederic's novels were "rush work" is entirely unsubstantiated, and his hostility is partly owing to moral outrage at Frederic's personal life. Gohdes continues his criticism quaintly, "soon the need for funds drove him with a lash, for he was a spendthrift and, moreover, was forced to provide not only for his own family but also for that of a mistress whom he kept in a separate bower." This combines coyness with sarcasm. Two pages later Gohdes writes that "His chief purpose as a writer was merely money-making, and, seemingly, he contributed as readily to *The Youth's Companion* as to *The Yellow Book.*"

as a journalist for, ironically, this comment on his working methods shows that he had taken the lessons that he had learned as a journalist and transformed them into his method for writing fiction.[6] As Charles Miller reminded him in a letter of 8 September 1893, "a newspaper man is supposed to know everything, or to be able to master any branch of human knowledge on the shortest notice" (Frederic Misc. 1977, 349). In practical terms, Frederic divided himself between journalism and fiction, and his working hours did not overlap. Certain days were for newspaper work, and others were for fiction. When writing fiction he would begin work punctually at half past nine in the morning, writing "slowly" in neat handwriting. With no set daily task, he would usually write between one and three thousand words a day, "though never more than that." He said that "I am conscientious about my books, and work on slowly and deliberately until about four in the afternoon. I never work at my novels after that hour" ("C.K.S." 1898, 4).

Frederic enjoyed the challenge of composition. He exclaimed in one letter of 13 August 1891, "Oh! the delight of sitting down at one's desk, with a ream of white cut sheets, and a book in the air about one!" (Frederic to Charles R. Sherlock, Frederic Misc. 1977, 288–89).[7] He developed scholarly habits of research for fiction and journalism, and he combined these with a strong practical approach toward his subject, learned from his newspaper experience Louise Guiney pointed out that though Frederic was not a "scholar, in the university sense . . . he was a 'fine old mouser': no Oxonian master of arts could find more quickly and surely the immaterial quarry which he sought" (Guiney 1899, 601).

A Newspaper Education

Frederic's formal education had ended shortly before he reached the age of fifteen. Like many young journalists, he was to find that his "university" was his newspaper experience. In the days before journalism became a formal academic discipline, the analogy between the newspaper and the university or school was commonplace, usually with a bias toward the "real life" experience of the newspaper. H. L. Mencken discussed his early days with the *Baltimore Herald* in terms of an alternative schooling, which recall Ishmael's claims in *Moby-Dick* (1851): "At a time when the respectable bourgeois youngsters of my generation were college fresh-

6. See also Sage 1975 and Kantor 1967.
7. This sentiment is echoed in *The Damnation of Theron Ware:* "He watched with his own eyes a whole ream of broad glazed white paper being sliced down by the cutter into single sheets, and thrilled with a novel ecstasy as he laid his hand upon the spotless bulk, so wooingly did it invite him to begin." (Frederic Novels 1986, 57).

men, oppressed by simian sophomores and affronted with balderdash daily and hourly by chalky pedagogues, I was at large in a wicked seaport of half a million people, with a front seat at every public show, as free of the night as of the day, and getting earfuls and eyefuls of instruction in a hundred giddy arcana, none of them taught in schools" (Weisberger 1961, 156–57).

In *Years of My Youth* (1916), W D. Howells calls the printing office his "school" and journalism his "university," and Mark Twain described his education as part school and part newspaper office. Bernard Weisberger makes a similar point about city journalists: "The city beat was for some . . . a literary academy. It was a curious one. The professors were tough city editors, the classrooms were docks, jails, morgues, and hospitals, and the dormitories were the cheap rooming houses which were all that salaries of five to fifteen dollars a week could command" (Howells 1975, 78 and 15–16; Twain 1960, 83; Weisberger 1961, 158). When Stephen Crane described his first sight of Frederic telling an anecdote to a keen circle of club members, "with all the skill of one trained in an American newspaper school," he inadvertently suggested how strong an influence Frederic's journalistic education had been and how much it had shaped his varied fictions. This education began in Utica and took him to Albany, to England, and from there all over Europe. It covered most aspects of journalistic work, from proofreading to international cable journalism. Journalism provided him with a steady income from his late teenage years until his death. It could exasperate and exhilarate him, but despite his contradictory remarks about it, he never left it.

Frederic's initial experience in journalism began in the summer of 1875 when he worked for several months at the fiercely Republican *Utica Herald* as a proofreader at twelve dollars a week. The *Utica Herald* (a morning paper) was one of the town's leading daily papers, and its rival was the Democratic paper, the *Utica Daily Observer* (an afternoon paper).[8] In September 1875, after a bout of ill health that he associated with night work, Frederic left the *Utica Herald*. In December 1875 he began work on the *Utica Daily Observer,* where he would be rapidly promoted, becoming editor of the paper in May 1880 at the age of only twenty-three. Frederic had come from what Haines calls a "fervently Democratic household," and his employment on the Democratic newspaper was more obviously to his taste

8. Their rivalry was not as bitter as that between Twain's Tennessee papers in his story "Journalism in Tennessee" (it was mainly theatrical—the proprietors were good friends); nevertheless, the *Utica Daily Observer* referred to the *Utica Herald* as "the morning cheese-press" (suggesting the Republicanism of the dairy farmers) and in its turn the *Utica Herald* refused to give its rival its proper name, dryly referring to "another paper of this city" (Haines 1945, 22). For an account of the traditional hostility between newspaper editors, see also Berger 1951, 7–8.

than his first short-lived newspaper experience (Haines 1945, 77). The *Utica Herald* would always resent his defection—in 1887 Frederic warned Charles Scribner that the paper would attack their review copy of *Seth's Brother's Wife*.[9]

It was first in his mother's home, and then in the offices of the *Utica Daily Observer*, that Frederic encountered serious and impassioned political debate. These were days of faction and strife within both political parties. In his early years as a journalist many important social, economic, and political changes were altering the tenor of American life—the increasing urbanization of the population, capital/labor unrest, the question of identity in a nation that was losing touch with its own origins, and the financial aspect of the age. The *Utica Daily Observer* saw itself as a self-appointed exponent of Democratic policies, and in the best tradition of the American political press, it indulged in controversy, attacked its opponents, and outlined the Democratic Party's political position. Its target area was not just Utica, but the whole of New York State. As Paul Haines writes, "The editors of the *Observer* engaged in ceaseless controversy with editors in Buffalo, Syracuse, Troy, Albany, Brooklyn, and New York City. Daniel Manning's Albany *Argus* and the *Observer* were among the chief batteries of the Democracy" (Haines 1945, 18–23). Utica had enjoyed a strong tradition of political writing since the days of the Civil War, and had boasted of papers with dramatic names such as *The Lever*, *The Emancipator*, the *Democratic Rasp*, the *Sledge-Hammer*, and the *Gridiron*.[10] At the time Frederic was working on the paper (1875–82), Utica had entered a quieter period and was

9. The *Utica Daily Observer* was founded in 1816. By 1875 it was a four-page daily paper (with eight pages on Saturday) and had a circulation of three thousand. The main feature of the paper was its editorials, forthright and political, and these were supplemented by domestic and foreign news, local stories, regular columns, and human interest incidents ("a poisoning in Bulgaria or an insane bride in Milwaukee"). It was owned and run by a trio of Democratic journalists who had a significant influence upon Frederic: Elijah Prentiss Bailey, Theodore Pease Cook, and De Witt C. Grove. The impact of the vigorous interests and experiences of these journalists would emerge throughout Frederic's life and work. (He would pay tribute to them by using their names in his fiction, in altered form—Frank Bailey, Theodore Madden, and De Witt C. Hemingway.)

10. Elijah Bailey, the *Utica Daily Observer's* part-owner, had served his apprenticeship on his father's abolitionist newspaper, *Friend of Man*. He had been on the *Utica Daily Observer* since 1853, was its "entire staff" during the Civil War, and had bought his interest in the paper in 1867. Bailey could be majestic in his authority, without being unduly aloof. Under his leadership the paper adopted a fiercely partisan position toward American political and economic life. Bailey had been a supporter of Horatio Seymour and was a tireless campaigner against the Tammany Democrats and their infamous associate, "Boss" Tweed. The Tweed ring's excesses had been exposed by one of the most famous early crusades of the *New York Times*. (See indexed references in Davis 1921 for details.) Theodore Cook, the other part-owner of the paper and older brother of the Utica poet Marc Cook, was a brilliant talker and fierce anti-Republican. He wrote the campaign biography of the Democratic governor and

experiencing less social and economic change than some of the neigh-boring towns and villages. The tenor of Utican life was altering slowly, but the effects of rapid industrialization (which Frederic describes vividly in *The Lawton Girl*) were felt more dramatically in nearby Rome than in Utica: the 1877 railroad strikes led to angry scenes in Rome, whereas the main emotion aroused in Utica was curiosity. The relative "steadiness" of Utica life was echoed in the *Utica Daily Observer:* despite the passion of its political polemic, the tone of its editorials was "judicious ... employers must have freedom in the labor market; agitators foment false notions of class distinc-tion where none exists; violence is un-American; our workmen strike not because they are Communists but because they are impoverished" (Haines 1945, 42–43). Whether or not these positions were shared by Frederic when he first joined the newspaper, they became his.[11]

As well as giving Frederic a thorough grounding in the political contro-versies of the day, his days on the *Utica Daily Observer* taught him every aspect of journalism. He read proofs, scanned through other papers for stories that he could copy, and covered local stories—art exhibitions, plays, and numerous incidents of rural brutality. Frederic used his early contact with a newspaper office as the basis of his first venture into sustained fiction. *Seth's Brother's Wife* has its basis both in his early experience with the *Utica Daily Observer* and in the political events that coincided with his editorship of the *Albany Evening Journal*.

When the paper's news editor, Edwin Westfall, died of tuberculosis in May 1879, Frederic was promoted to this position. He supplemented his newly augmented salary by working as a local reporter for the *New York Sun*. His ambitions went beyond the immediacies of writing for a provincial paper. He was already showing signs of literary ambition, beginning to write and publish fiction, and making earnest attempts at literary criticism that were not fully appreciated by his citified colleagues:

> One of his first attempts to shed the pinafore of routine was an elaborate piece of dramatic criticism which he sent down to us in a bulky envelope. Edwin Booth had been playing a one-night engagement at the opera-house and Harold Frederic had perceived how great a part Iago was and had written three or four columns about it for his New York newspaper. It was an ambi-tious and serious performance, worthy in some respects of the future author

---

presidential nominee, Samuel Tilden. Grove, the last of the trio, had been mayor of Utica from 1860 to 1862 and was a critic of Roscoe Conkling, the Republican brother-in-law of Horatio Seymour. A fourth journalist, the news editor Edwin Westfall, also came into regular contact with the young proofreader. Westfall had worked for the *New York Herald* during the Civil War and was a reader of classics, history, and German philosophy. The passionate interests of these men meant that the paper was characterized by its political position.

11. Compare chap. 34 of *The Lawton Girl*.

of "The Damnation of Theron Ware" and "Illumination,"[12] but of course lacking the aptness of proper occasion for such an essay. "How sorry the poor fellow will be," said Dana when I had reported, "to hear we city folks don't appreciate his discovery of Booth and of Shakespeare." (Mitchell 1924, 279)

Soon Frederic would obtain a promotion that would leave him little time for literary matters.[13] When the editor of the paper was forced to resign due to illness Frederic took on the job. His salary was raised to twenty-five dollars a week. He flourished in the editorship of the paper and enjoyed such prestige that in August 1882, aged just twenty-six, he was offered the editorship of the Republican *Albany Evening Journal*. Despite his own political preferences, he took the job. It was yet another advancement in a career characterized by remarkable early success.[14] The thrill and frustration of these early promotions is captured in "The Editor and the School-Ma'am."

The *Albany Evening Journal* had been established in 1830 by the great editor Thurlow Weed. It had a noteworthy history encompassing, among other dramas, a prolonged legal battle between Weed and James Fenimore Cooper.[15] In his first editorial, on 4 September 1882, Frederic paid tribute to his immediate predecessor, George Dawson, and fondly invoked Weed as "a giant who remains to us almost alone of a generation of giants, and toward whom the heart of every Albanian, of every newspaper man, and of every admirer of force, brains and will-power reverently warms." Frederic was still, at this early stage in his career, optimistic about the potential of journalism as an agent of civilization, and he admired masculinity and force. He was also keen to make an early statement of editorial policy—his first editorial is a carefully worded piece aimed to reassure the paper's Republican readership. He told his readers that the paper would not depart from its support for "so much of Republicanism as is Republicanism,"

12. The two are, of course, the same novel.

13. In May 1880 Theodore Cook was forced to leave his job as a result of what was called "tobacco craziness." In the middle of composing an editorial arguing that the president should only serve one term, Cook became "overwhelmed by the futility of polemic." Instead of writing newspaper copy he wanted to indulge more extravagant tastes, to see Barnum's tame stag Landseer, and to enjoy watching circus acts, to see Zazal being shot from a cannon (Haines 1945, 34–51). Frederic inherited both the unfinished editorial and the job.

14. Stanton Garner writes that "He told the owners that despite his former Democratic allegiance he had become an independent with Republican leanings" (Garner 1969, 9). I can find no other substantiation of this claim. Nevins describes Frederic as an independent Republican—but then he claims (inaccurately) that he came from an ardently Republican family (Nevins 1932, 118).

15. For detail on this, see "A Biography of Cooper," *Albany Evening Journal*, 23 December 1882, 2.

but it would "never fear to unmask and rebuke the remainder, no matter what its label." He was quick to act upon his threat.

He began his new editorship with the conviction that the *Albany Evening Journal* could play a significant role in state—and national—politics. He describes his duties at the paper in an article in the *Youth's Companion*, "A Day With the Managing Editor" (1889). He later claimed that the Albany paper had doubled in value in the term of his editorship because he had removed it "out of straight party lines . . . making it a sort of candid friend" (Sherard 1897, 537). This "friend" was not short of forthright advice as Frederic would quickly reveal.

The Republicans had split into two main factions in 1880, the Stalwarts (supporters of Ulysses S. Grant and Roscoe Conkling) and the Half-Breeds (who followed James Gillespie Blaine and James A. Garfield). The *Albany Evening Journal* was, both before and after Frederic's editorship, a Half-Breed paper. (As soon as Frederic resigned, the editorials began to praise Blaine.) Frederic had a natural antipathy to his fellow Utican, Conkling, but found Blaine equally distasteful. Within days of taking over as editor, Frederic was faced with an important political decision. Charles J. Folger had received the Republican nomination for the 1882 gubernatorial election. This was a direct snub to the incumbent Republican Governor, Alonzo B. Cornell.[16] Many saw the hand of Jay Gould in the Republican's rejection of an honest and able governor, and Republicans and Democrats alike were outraged. Henry Ward Beecher wrote, "When Cornell went out . . . Avarice and Revenge Kissed each other" (Nevins 1932, 105). Amidst these outcries, the *Albany Evening Journal* "bolted the ticket" on 21 September, refusing to support Folger—one of many traditionally Republican papers, including the *New York Times,* to do so. The paper had not openly expressed support for Folger's Democratic opponent—the "veto Mayor" of Buffalo, Grover Cleveland—but as Republican newspapers throughout New York State followed Frederic's lead, Folger's defeat was certain. (Frederic was later to style himself "pretty nearly the original Mugwump," [Sherard 1897, 537]. The *O.E.D.* definition of "Mugwump" is "One who holds more or less aloof from party-politics. . . . In 1884, *spec* applied to Republicans who refused to support the nominee of their party for president." Nevins writes that the name was taken from Eliot's *Indian Bible* in 1872 and popularized by the *New York Sun*.) (Nevins 1932, 156).

Frederic's tacit support of Grover Cleveland eventually led to a firm friendship between the men. Frederic soon began to visit Cleveland in the governor's office, which had become so accessible to the public that his lieutenant-governor suggested that he, Cleveland, should simply move his

16. Even Democratic newspapers were urging their readers to vote for Cornell. (Nevins 1932, 156–59)

desk outside—people would be able to see him easily, and he would get fresh air, too. Frederic had always admired strong-minded and able men, and in Cleveland he found one with whom he could be friends.[17] On 11 May 1883 the *Albany Evening Journal's* editorial page suggested that the Democrats nominate Cleveland as presidential candidate.

Some Republicans thought that Frederic had gone too far. When in March 1884 the *Albany Evening Journal* was sold to W. J. Arkell, a "more militantly Republican owner," Frederic was faced with a choice of resigning or of compromising his political opinions. He resigned from the paper, in the process becoming "something of a national journalistic hero because of his adherence to principle" (Frederic Misc. 1977, 9). Although he received a number of offers of editorships, he chose to turn his back on the editorial side of newspaper work: he wanted to have time to establish himself as a writer of fiction. With Apgar's help Frederic was offered the position of London correspondent for the *New York Times* at a salary of eighty dollars per week. He settled his family in rented accommodation in Bayswater on the advice of Gilbert Jones, the son of the newspaper's owner, and established an office in the Strand. He saw the move as a "temporary expedient."

The "Brotherhood of American Paper-Stainers in Exile"

When Frederic moved to England in 1884 he became the latest member of a group whom he dubbed the "Brotherhood of American Paper-Stainers in Exile" (Warren 1898, 19). Although it was clearly an honorific of sorts, the name also suggests that journalism is a reflexive rather than a reflective activity. There were few official American foreign correspondents in England at that time although there were numerous "hangers-on" who enjoyed the privileges of working on what Frederic called a "free-lunch basis."[18] Frederic despised these journalistic pretenders, for they gave the genuine American "Paper-Stainers" a bad name.

17. The two men had a good deal in common. Cleveland had spent much of his childhood close to Utica. He was fond of food and beer and fishing, and he enjoyed a relaxed personal moral code. Above all, he "presented a dual aspect to the world," as did Frederic. He could be "stiff, heavy, and stern" and also a "roystering [sic] blade," drinking heavily, singing drinking songs in saloons, and suffering severe hangovers as a consequence (Nevins 1932, 57). Frederic's most important friendships in Albany were almost entirely with leading Democrats, several of whom would later hold important office. They included Edgar Kelsey Apgar, then deputy treasurer of New York, Daniel S. Lamont, Cleveland's secretary and the editor of the *Albany Argus,* and William Gorham Rice, assistant secretary to Grover Cleveland. As Frederic got to know Cleveland better he became convinced that he had the honesty and strength to unite the American people.

18. See Frederic to editor, *Pall Mall Gazette,* 9 May 1885, Frederic Misc. 1977, 60.

Frederic soon found that American and English journalism were quite different, and that the English were wary of American smartness. Aaron Watson, an English journalist and friend, claims that though Frederic was usually proud of his "American smartness," he could also be unhappy with some of its consequences (Watson n.d., 159). Although "smartness" could be meretricious (which Frederic deplored), it was often shrewd. Watson tells an anecdote that shows Frederic's "smartness" at its best. One evening at the Savage Club Frederic overheard Watson being told that there had been an explosion at London Bridge. Watson quickly left, hoping for an exclusive story. He returned a while later, and was called over by Kay Robinson (later Kipling's editor in Lahore), who began to praise Frederic. Watson's laconic "What has he been doing now?" suggests that he was used to such confidences. Robinson told him, " 'he has been beating our English journalists into a cocked hat. He doesn't want it to be known, of course, but I don't mind telling you. There has been an attempt to blow up London Bridge. He heard of it somehow or other, I don't know how, and asked me to drive along with him to see what had taken place. He has just telegraphed two-thirds of a column to the *New York Times*. What English journalist could have done that in the time and under the circumstances?' My sole comment on this was to hand over my copy of the *Weekly Echo,* in which the account of the London Bridge affair occupied just two-thirds of a column" (Watson n.d., 160). Frederic had been alerted by Watson's suspicious behavior and had followed him in a cab. This was a notable piece of "smartness," made more effective by Frederic's secrecy about his sources.

Frederic's mock modesty, in this instance, contrasts with a genuine reluctance to have Watson read his weekly cable letters to the *New York Times.* He feared that Watson would attack "his method of dressing up English topics to suit readers 'on the other side,' " in other words, through translating them for an American audience used to innovative journalistic techniques and ideology about style. Frederic's method of "dressing up" was partly a counterpart to the stories that he told of his early life in upper New York State, and it was partly a response to the demands of New Journalism, which had begun to influence American journalists and newspapers earlier than it did their British counterparts.[19]

The difference between American and British journalists, pinpointed by Watson's anecdote, centered on the aggressive motivation of the American journalist. An anonymous article in the *New York Times* on 23 January 1898 outlines the significant distinction between the two. In it, the contrast in

19. For further accounts of New Journalism, see, for example, Brake 1994, chap. 5; Fyfe 1934, chap. 8; Schults 1972, chap. 2; Stokes 1989, chap. 1; and indexed references in Walkowitz 1994.

American and English journalists is used to represent the most marked difference between the two countries. The writer argues that in England, a "smart New York reporter" would quickly become embroiled in a libel suit, or would end up in prison if he worked "in the American way," in the same way that a British reporter would be fired from the "Yankee paper" for "not knowing news when it was handed to him." The American newspaper office feels more "modern": the journalist arrives at work and "receives the very latest information to hand by post, wire or 'ticker.' " British journalists expect to receive a wire or letter at their own homes in the morning. Failing that, they "are free for the day and draw their salary just the same." The "valuable" British journalist is the "literary chap" whereas the ideal New York journalist is the "wide-awake, enterprising, up-to-date fellow who gets out his own assignments and comes to the office every day primed with ideas for working up good news stories." The American journalist hates routine, pursues stories relentlessly, loves challenge, and thinks that shorthand is a mysterious hieroglyphic. Most British journalists are "first-class" at shorthand. The good piece of British journalism will report speeches exactly and allow the reader to draw her or his own conclusions. The good American piece "is a bright, entertaining article, with the salient points made the most of, the rest fading away in the perspective." The journalist is considered highly in America. In England "everybody takes you for a pennyliner." Frederic would find the transition between editorship in New York State and reporting for the *New York Times,* a difficult one. Through working "in the American way" he did indeed become embroiled in libel, and though he wanted to be "a literary chap," he found that his newspaper expected him to be an "enterprising, up-to-date fellow." [20]

The *New York Times*

The *New York Times* was founded in 1851. Two of its founders, George Jones and Henry Raymond, had earlier thought of buying the *Albany Evening Journal* from Thurlow Weed, but the deal fell through when a stockholder was unwilling to part with his shares (Mott 1962, 279). [21] The pair had worked on Horace Greeley's *New York Tribune,* Raymond on the news side and Jones in the business office. Jones had left to become a banker in Albany, and it was here, apparently crossing the frozen Hudson together, that the pair decided to found their own paper. By 1860 the *New York*

20. "Newspaper Work Abroad," 23 January 1898, 9. See also Healy 1928, 1:144. For a very useful and detailed account of British journalism in the nineteenth century see Brown 1985.

21. For further details of the history of the paper, see Berger 1951.

Times's circulation was just below the *New York Tribune*'s estimated daily circulation of forty-five thousand and some way behind the *New York Herald*'s circulation of sixty thousand. All three newspapers had similar formats. They usually consisted of eight pages and cost two cents. In the mid-1850s the *New York Times* joined the Associated Press, which was comprised of the *New York Tribune,* the *New York Herald,* and four other New York newspapers. The Associated Press had been formed in May 1848 for the purpose of sharing stories and communications overheads by dealing jointly with a telegraph agent in Boston to receive late news from steamships. The cost was $100 for three thousand words. By the middle of the 1850s the Associated Press had a commanding monopoly, although this gradually crumbled over the next decade. Frederic's new job kept him in close contact with the information that the Associated Press cables supplied, and this could be frustrating. By September 1885 Frederic called the Associated Press service in England "positively disreputable, in its willingness to send false things for sensation, and its childish inability to understand the simplest events. Its treatment of Irish 'news' is nothing less than scoundrelly. . . . Every editor in New York must long ago have seen what rot his paper pays for in the name of news, from that source" (Frederic to Charles R. Miller, 29 September 1885, Frederic Misc. 1977, 75–76). After the death of Raymond in 1869 the *New York Times* was headed by Jones until his own death in 1891. Frederic dedicated *The New Exodus* to the memory of Jones, calling him "The Founder of a Great Newspaper and The Lifelong Champion of Good Causes."

Jones took the position of a businessman rather than an owner-editor, and Frederic's contact with the paper was usually through Charles Miller, who was editor in chief from 1883 until 1921.[22] The letters between the two men suggest a relationship that was never wholly relaxed. Miller was a notoriously poor letter writer, and Frederic felt isolated and uncertain in London when he first arrived. He was frequently unhappy with Miller's style of management, and Miller thought him extravagant. On 23 September 1884 Frederic writes that he has lost hope of ever hearing from Miller except by the "sententious cable." Frederic resorted to Walter Mitty fantasies in which Miller and John Reid (the managing news editor) praised his work (Frederic to Charles R. Miller, 23 September 1884, Frederic Misc. 1977, 29–30). His dissatisfaction continued: on 12 November 1885 he writes, "Do you realize that I haven't heard a word from you since August last?" and on 6 March 1886 he explodes, "As you very properly said, I am unfamiliar with the kind of discipline which obtains in New York newspaper offices—but up in the remote quarters whence I came editors would at least not subject their subordinates to treatment of this sort" (Frederic to

22. For an account of Miller's career, see Bond 1931.

Charles R. Miller, Frederic Misc. 1977, 87 and 102). Frederic was especially irritated by the suggestion that he was a provincial—as his veiled reminder suggests. Their relationship improved after the two met on Frederic's 1886 vacation to the United States. Frederic later assured Miller that "of all the gratifying features with which my visit home was crowded, the best and pleasantest by far was the chance it afforded of getting to know you" (Frederic to Miller, 20 July 1886, Frederic Misc. 1977, 123).[23] Yet he remained uneasy about Miller's efficiency, lamenting to Daniel Lamont on 17 August 1888, "Mr. Miller is not always a prompt man—what editor ever was?" (Frederic Misc. 1977, 213).

Following the death of George Jones in 1891, the management of the *New York Times* changed. For a short time the paper was run by Jones's son, Gilbert Jones, and son-in-law, Henry Dyer. In 1893 Jones and Dyer sold the paper to the New York Times Publishing Company, run by Miller himself and a group of others, who, despite acute financial problems, kept the paper running until Adolph Ochs bought it in 1896. Ochs regarded Frederic's weekly cable as one of the paper's most valuable features, though it is not clear whether Frederic was made aware of this Frederic found the transition period following George Jones's death frustrating and felt that he was the subject of a vendetta. He found his position "intolerable" and claimed that he had "been as good as told that writing books is to be discouraged, or stopped, and every conceivable chance to write me quarrelsome and uncivil letters is leaped at nowadays" (Frederic to Daniel S. Lamont, 2 December 1892, Frederic Misc. 1977, 322). Faced with what he perceived as deliberate hostility, he searched for an escape from the newspaper and found it in a position that had special symbolic significance. He hoped to become the U.S. Consul to Liverpool under Cleveland's presidency, a position that Hawthorne had held at an earlier date. He invokes Hawthorne specifically in this context at another point in the same letter, "I would make a good consul, and the appointment would be a return to the old dignified Democratic days, as when Pierce sent Hawthorne there."[24] His dissatisfaction with the style of the management of

---

23. He begins the letter to "My dear friend."

24. He continues: "To be sure, I'm not a Hawthorne, but as the small Charleston darkey said to the old one, who insisted on God's superiority over the black Congressman from the Sixth district—'Yes, but don' you fohget—Bob Smalls he young man yet!' " This is a complicated discourse that should not simply be dismissed as racist: Frederic takes the side and the voice of the figure whom he sets up and imitates. Although it is certainly coolly patronizing and relies on blatant stereotyping, the discourse also enjoys the possibility of the improbable. It is a profoundly opportunistic moment in which elements of racism mingle with celebration. Frederic's avowal that he is not "a Hawthorne" leaves open the question of which Hawthorne —consul or novelist—he means. He hoped to take up the job of Hawthorne the consul, but it is surely the novelist whom he hopes to become In 1892 Frederic was a "young man yet."

the *New York Times,* combined with Miller's disapproval of his fiction writing, forced him to recognize the extent to which his two writing selves were being polarized. Arthur Warren's retrospective appreciation of Frederic puts this conflict into perspective: "When you knew him even passing well, you knew that there were two Frederics—the Frederic of the books and THE TIMES letters, and the high-voiced, careless, over generous, pugnacious, gentle-hearted, hardworked, dogmatic Frederic of Fleet Street and the smoking room. You had your choice. It depended upon yourself which of the two men you knew. But you liked the one you knew" (Warren 1898, 19).

Although Frederic could seem profoundly divided, he could also present a unified front. One example of the fusion of the "two Frederics" took place in 1887 when the "bookish" Frederic gave a precise and scholarly defense of the "journalistic" Frederic. On 8 March Frederic wrote an ironic letter to the editor of *Life* magazine. The magazine had criticized one of his regular Sunday cable "letters" in a patronizing manner: he responded to the attack with characteristic relish. He evidently enjoyed the challenge of undermining *Life's* assertion that "small boys and newspaper writers should not use big words that they do not understand." This conflation must surely have rankled, and Frederic rose to the challenge, using precise dictionary definitions (from the *Imperial Dictionary*) to justify his choice of words. The magazine had accused him of not understanding the meaning of the word "articulate." In his defense he writes, "its use as describing the one man of a class who can talk clearly is not novel; it runs all through Carlyle and Froude and Ruskin, and, what is more to the point, it conveys to the reader just the meaning which I wanted it to carry, and not to one out of ten thousand the meaning, or even a suggestion of the meaning, your small boy attaches to it." (Frederic Misc. 1977, 162–64).

His exuberant response to the magazine's assumptions reveals him at his best—playful, self-confident, precise—yet free from pedantry. He cheekily tells the editor that "I am glad you are reading my Sunday letters. You will get more actual information, from them—not to speak of delicate diction and effective imagery—than from all the other matter sent over to other papers combined. Perhaps you had not realized this before—and hence will thank me for pointing it out. . . . I don't want you to think I was vexed because my unapproachable—I might say ideal—letters were selected as the subject for a gag. I have been a mother myself."[25] Like Oscar Wilde, Frederic knew that there is only one thing worse than being talked about.

Although Frederic could, and often did, find satisfaction in his work for

25. This last sentence is repeated in *The Damnation of Theron Ware.*

the *New York Times,* he found many aspects of his job frustrating. In the same letter he told a fable that is both a witty defense of his position and a revelation of the irritations of international "cable" journalism: "There is a story of a brakeman on the Central [New York Central Line] who used to murder the old Dutch-Indian names along the Mohawk, shouting out 'Fundy!' and 'Palentine Bridge!' and 'o-RIS-kny!' until a passenger with an ear remonstrated. His sufficient retort was: 'Do you expect a first class tenor for $28 a month?' Lest you should leap to a false application of the parable, let me point out that preciseness is sometimes of necessity diffuseness, and that you can't be diffuse at fivepence a word."

The cost of transmission by cable significantly reduced the number of words that he could send to the *New York Times*.[26] This reduction was not the only irritant this type of journalism caused In order to reduce the cost of cabling his work, Frederic condensed it, relying on sympathetic "rewriting" in New York. Before he had even been in England for a year, however, he was complaining to Charles Miller of the "careless and badly informed rewriting" that undermined his articles, lamenting that "if I study all possible condensation compatible with strength and symmetry, at least as much pains and intelligence ought to be exerted on the other end of the wire in making the matter 'consist' " (Frederic to Charles R. Miller, 21 February 1885, Frederic Misc. 1977, 44). Miller responded to Frederic's complaint, for about a month later Frederic writes that there "is a notable improvement in the editing of my stuff" (Frederic to Charles R. Miller, 28 March 1885, Frederic Misc. 1977, 53).[27]

A large proportion of Frederic's correspondence with Miller, and with American and English publishers, relates to his continual financial struggles. He began to see the cable as a financial competitor: Frederic felt that the rest of his budget was limited on account of the cost of the cable and that this threatened his professionalism. Yet Charles Miller was willing to

26. Frederic usually used James Gordon Bennett's Commercial Cable Company. A price war, started by this company, significantly altered rates for transmission. In 1884, the year in which Frederic joined the *New York Times,* the rate dropped from one dollar per word to twenty-five cents. The *New York Times* of 3 December 1885, reported that the price per word had dropped to twenty cents. In slack times this was further lowered to ten cents. Nevertheless, the cost of cabling remained a significant factor. For more detail on the history of the cable and its relation to journalism, see Blondheim 1994.

27. The colloquialism is interesting: "stuff" is partly bluff and casual (he uses the word in many of his letters about his cabled material), but it is also pejorative. He usually described his cables either as "stuff" (which suggests insignificant "stuffing" padding out a newspaper) or as "matter" (significant writing that literally "mattered"). The way in which he wrote about his journalism depended upon the context of the letter, and his relation to the addressee. When he felt that Miller was not taking sufficient care with his work it was "matter," but when Miller treated it as though it was significant, it became "stuff."

pay a great deal for what he considered to be a worthwhile exclusive. In 1884 Miller had authorized payment of six thousand dollars to cover the cost of a cable from Madrid that revealed the full text of a secret treaty being negotiated between Spain and the United States. This text was revealed to the public in the *New York Times* on 8 December. Frederic certainly had this in mind when he complained, "If it is worth while to spend $6,000 on a treaty, it seems as if it ought to be worth while to let a poor fellow who is sent off to create a new service, make friends in a country where news and favors are strictly social things, and keep up a decent appearance,—it seems as if, I say, it ought to be worth while to let him be free in his mind about his weekly tradesman's bills, and, when he is trying all he can to get his balance down, to give him a fair chance" (Frederic to Charles R. Miller, 21 February 1885, Frederic Misc. 1977, 44–45).[28] He had said that he was not being given a "fair chance," that without being able to adapt himself to English life (that is, "return hospitalities in kind") he "should be as much outside the real life of London as . . . [he] would be in Yonkers." And it was at least partly the expense of cable journalism that was marginalizing him.

Frederic worked under other pressures too. When the *New York Times* wanted regular financial news Miller wrote to Frederic and told him that in the future he was to send the paper daily dispatches. Although quite aware that Frederic, on his own admission, knew nothing of the London market, Miller reassured him that "This is a new field for you, and you will most certainly read my letter with something like consternation. . . . I do not see the necessity of keeping two men in London when your own unusual and recognized abilities amply suffice for The Times' service there" (Miller to Frederic, 8 September 1893, Frederic Misc. 1977, 349). The pressure of demands of this sort was enormous. Frederic's work was time consuming, stressful, and relentless. He was expected to write financial news in addition to his regular weekly piece of between one and a half and three columns in length. He had to produce thoroughly researched and accurate information within a tight schedule. Furthermore, he was expected to conform to particular stylistic conventions—of length, context, and tone. And he was, as ever, restricted by his reliance on the ability of the people sending and rewriting the wretched cablegram.

When he first arrived in England he subscribed to a large number of European newspapers in order to broaden his knowledge of the huge area that he had been employed to cover but as yet knew little or nothing about. After a reprimand from Miller about the expense of the papers, and the inadvisability of reading so many, he canceled most of his subscriptions.

28. See also Davis 1921, 162–163 for details of the expensive cable.

He was excited by the prospect of being in a "rather novel position" but irritated that he was "forced to grub for news and indications of news through the medium of excessively bad and stupid papers" (Frederic to Charles R. Miller, 28 March 1885, Frederic Misc. 1977, 52). He rapidly realized the value of contacts and soon began to give and attend dinners and parties, and to join London Clubs. Miller constantly complained about Frederic's expenses, and Frederic was forced to explain his accounts, to his annoyance. Frederic's regular cables summarized English, European, and often especially Irish news, reported odd bits of gossip, announced the publication of noteworthy books, commented on theatrical productions, and gave a general impression of the events of London and Europe. As he became more assured he would mock British institutions, especially royalty, and he would use his column as a forum for discussing his particular interests. He might write a description of the Savage Club, or note the celebrations of George Meredith's seventieth birthday, or express sorrow at Aubrey Beardsley's death. He saw himself as both an interventionist and an explicator, both a sympathetic interpreter and "a chronicler, possibly of much that is foolish in the Britisher, but sometimes . . . of the greater side of the Anglo-Saxon character" (Frederic Misc. 1898, 19).

"Down Among The Dead Men"

Once in England Frederic quickly made a reputation for himself with a courageous piece of reporting on the cholera epidemic in southern France. Charles Miller wanted an account of the epidemic, and although Frederic had only been in England for about a month, he went himself. He was excited by the challenge and was glad of the opportunity to visit a land about which he had read so much through Erckmann-Chatrian. He spent five days (21–26 July) traveling through the cholera-infested regions of Marseilles, Toulon, and Arles, sending graphic and detailed cable reports back to New York.[29] When he returned to England he fainted in the cable office from hunger and exhaustion, and caused a panic among the clerks. Despite the shortness of his visit, he had been profoundly shocked by the conditions in which the poor lived—although he had already discovered that the poor of London lived in terrible slums. This was not an experience that would become the basis for anecdote: he writes to a friend that the thought of giving a second account of his trip made him "sick to

29. Frederic *NYT*, 1884b, 1. All quotations, unless otherwise stated, are from this piece of journalism. The title of the piece, "Down among the Dead Men," is taken from a toast, "Here's a Health to the King," by the British poet John Dyer (1699?-1757), "And he that will this health deny,/ Down among the dead men may he lie."

the stomach" (Frederic to Charles R. Sherlock, 26 July 1884, Frederic Misc. 1977, 26).

In the United States and England, public response to the disease had been extreme and irrational. Frederic was to investigate the spread of the disease and speculate upon causes and cures. Americans feared that immigrants would carry the disease with them from Europe and spark off an epidemic in the American cities. He realized that this American epidemic of what might be called "choleraphobia" (for it was a psychosomatic offshoot of cholera) was caused by ignorance and could be cured by a concentrated diet of fact. His journey in France might these days be called a "fact-finding tour." Yet a purely factual piece would not capture the intensity of his impressions. He decided to strike a distinctively personal tone combining what he calls "facts" and "scenes"—details of his research and episodes from his trip—in a method clearly using techniques that would become associated with the New Journalism. The narrative combines these fluently, achieving a dramatic effect on occasions, as when he follows a detached account of medical treatment with a moving description of a nun holding a dying baby in her arms:

> The treatment both here and at Toulon, in the first stages, is 20 drops of laudanum, with 3 grains of ether, and ice in the mouth to stop the vomiting. In the second stages the patients become very cold. From 10 to 15 grammes of acetate of ammonia, the same quantity of alcohol, and 2 injections of morphia are given daily. If the patient cannot breathe, artificial respiration of oxygen is produced and the limbs are rubbed with turpentine. The third stage is the coffin. . . . Of many pathetic sights, the most painful that I saw occurred in the female ward, where one room was mostly occupied by children. A nun held in her arms by an open window a dying babe 18 months old. Its three sisters, the oldest being only 10 years, lay on beds near by their parents, both of whom died the same day, and there was small hope for any of the remaining children save the oldest.

His report was not voyeuristic, although it was detailed and factual. Occasionally his control wavers and he slips into sentimentality.[30] Usually, though, he retains the impression of detachment.

Although the report was intensely dramatic, it had his characteristically humorous stamp. Frederic found that Dr. Koch, the discoverer of the cholera bacillus, had visited a Toulon hospital before his own visit, but had annoyed the hospital staff by his taciturnity. The light-hearted French

---

30. Calling a baby a "babe" is a cloying touch—yet the sight of dying children would have reminded Frederic of his own daughters Ruth and Ruby, and of his second daughter (also called Ruby), who had died in infancy.

doctors reported, and Frederic told his readership, that Koch kept his lips tightly closed "so that he might not swallow a single microbe." [31] Frederic might have taken his own writing method for this piece from the example of the French doctors, who were caring and professional without being glum. The first paragraph of the piece includes a brief outline of his exhaustive firsthand research and the conclusion that "the much-dreaded cholera, probably the most fatal and severe of all diseases to which human flesh is heir, is a thing of which no intelligent community of well-ordered lives and well-managed sewer pipes need have an alarming fear, even when brought into close contact with it, to say nothing of getting into a panic at a distance."

But by 1885 a more mature Frederic could see the narrowness of the *New York Times*'s briefing. Spain was experiencing an epidemic of far greater magnitude than that of France or Italy, yet the Spanish epidemic was being ignored. On 31 July 1885 he wrote a piece called "A Genuine Cholera Year" in the *Pall Mall Budget*. Discussing the extent and virulence of the Spanish cholera epidemic, he asks, "Is it not true, when all is said and done, that Spain is outside the Europe that civilisation knows and is interested in? Why we should be convulsed with sympathy and horror over a few thousand deaths in France and Italy and pay no particular attention to tens of thousands of deaths in Spain, I do not pretend to explain. But the fact is there" (Frederic Misc. 1885e, 9–10). He had recognized that Spain's ethnic and cultural inheritance and geographical location had alienated it from the relative unity of the Europe that England and the United States was interested in. He had become aware of the intellectual narcissism of his readership and of the market orientation of the newspaper. This was compounded in the same year when he received the cynical instruction from the *New York Times* to collate and accumulate material already collected from European agents from all over Europe, and then cable them to the *New York Times* to give the impression of a continent full of foreign correspondents all working for the paper (Frederic Misc. 1977, 23).

Once again he was forced to confront his own essential ambivalence toward his newspaper career. Journalism could confront the public with its

---

31. For one reaction to Koch's ideas, see Hillaire Belloc's "The Microbe": "The Microbe is so very small/ You cannot make him out at all,/ But many sanguine people hope/ To see him through a microscope./ His jointed tongue that lies beneath/ A hundred curious rows of teeth;/ His seven tufted tails with lots/ Of lovely pink and purple spots,/ On each of which a pattern stands,/ His eyebrows of a tender green;/ All these have never yet been seen—/ But Scientists, who ought to know,/ Assure us that they must be so . . . / Oh! let us never, never doubt/ What nobody is sure about!" (Belloc 1953, 120–21). Thanks, here, to Duncan Bennett for reciting nonsense verse to me throughout my childhood.

own hypocrisy (highlighting France and marginalizing Spain), but it could also deliberately deceive the public (inventing nonexistent European correspondents). Frederic had to face his culpability: he had focused public scrutiny on France (and away from Spain) by his heroic reporting, and he was colluding with the *New York Times* in a deliberate attempt to hoodwink its readers. He was caught in a conflict of loyalties, between responsibility toward his readership, the newspaper, and himself. This would become critical in 1887 with a dramatic piece of journalism that began in triumph and ended, in 1892, with a successful libel suit against him.

The *"Locrine* Incident"

Readers who paid the usual two cents for their daily copy of the *New York Times* on Thursday, 17 November 1887, were to have a surprise. Under the heavy gothic typeface of the paper's title, columns usually devoted to politics, national and international news, advertisements, and "human interest" stories had been transformed. Alert readers might have wondered if the paper's editorial team had been changed overnight. The less alert might, sleepily, have felt that they had picked up another paper by mistake. For the front page of the paper, the whole of the second page, and part of the third, were devoted almost entirely to Algernon Charles Swinburne's most recent piece, the verse tragedy *Locrine*. On Charles Miller's express request Harold Frederic had obtained a copy of Swinburne's tragedy and, using recent technology, had cabled eighteen thousand words to New York from London. *Locrine* was transmitted overnight via two cables—ten thousand words by the Commercial Cable Company and eight thousand by the Western Union company—at a cost of about three thousand dollars. Heading the front page of the paper was the title "Swinburne's 'Locrine': A Splendid Tragedy From The English Poet." An explanatory paragraph with a London dateline of 16 November said, "I send it [*Locrine*] to you by cable entire omitting only the dedication of some 600 words to Alice Swinburne, thus enabling THE TIMES to anticipate by several days its publication here." By publishing *Locrine* two days before its publication the England the *New York Times* knew that it would compromise the poem's copyright, a serious infringement of author's rights. It was an extraordinary day for the paper's readership and for international cable journalism. It may also have been something of a surpirse for Swinburne. The paper dubbed it "A Feat Without Parallel," and amidst the newspaper coups and crusades of the 1880s it is striking piece of journalism. The events leading up to the piracy, and the incident's personal consequences for Frederic are worth recounting in some detail. The narrative that unfolds is intriguing though incomplete.

Chatto and Windus had arranged the English publication of *Locrine* for 19 November.[32] Coincidentally, Andrew Chatto was arranging the publication of Frederic's first novel *Seth's Brother's Wife,* also published in mid-November. Chatto was highly considered by authors for his fairness, his businesslike methods, and his skill at protecting his author's work from piracy. Swinburne's American publisher, Richard C. Worthington, offered to sell the *New York Times* newspaper rights for simultaneous publication, requesting an answer within three hours of the offer. The price was to be one hundred dollars. Although Charles Miller was keen to accept, he failed to do so within the specified time, and the *New York Evening Sun* bought the poem. Miller was unbusinesslike, his writing was as illegible as that of Horace Greeley, and he was a notoriously poor letter writer who enjoyed working in chaotic conditions. The lapse was either a mistake caused by ineptitude, an attempt at beating the price of the poem down, or a calculated ploy aimed at obtaining an exclusive and outwitting competitors. He cabled Frederic and told him to obtain the poem and send it to New York.

Swinburne had at first pleased his public by *Atalanta in Calydon* (1865), and then outraged it by his infamous *Poems and Ballads* of the following year. He had not repudiated his "miry ways" (as the *New York Times* coyly called them). In a letter of 1 January 1887 to Jane Swinburne he naughtily describes his plans for *Locrine:* "I have begun a new dramatic attempt—in rhyme—founded on the legendary history of ancient Britain. The hero is the son of our first monarch, King Brute—a name that always delighted me, but I am afraid it must be "Brutus" in serious verse. His son (as all students of history will of course remember) was Locrine—who came to grief through imprudently marrying two wives" (Swinburne 1962, 5:179).

---

32. This dating of the first appearance of *Locrine* is consolidated by a footnote in Swinburne 1962, 5:179. This gives the date of the first publication of *Locrine* as 16 November. I would like to thank Cecil Y. Lang, the editor of the *Swinburne Letters,* for confirming this date and discussing its source with me. I must also thank Dr. Joanne Shattock, Mr. Peter Larkin, and Prof. Terry Meyers for their extremely generous help in my attempts to trace the exact date of publication at an earlier stage, as well as Mr. Mike Bott, the keeper of the Chatto and Windus archive at the University of Reading, who kindly searched the ledger and the letter books of the period in question. The first main reviews of *Locrine* appeared on 18 November, though further reviews did not appear until the following month. Dr. Elizabeth James of the British Library consulted the deposited edition of *Locrine* and found that it was dated 15 November, and then checked the catalogue for me. To her, and to Tim Burnet, also of the B.L., I also owe a debt of thanks for their enthusiasm and their scholarship. Frederic's note at the top of the cabled version of *Locrine* is dated 16 November and clearly states that the verse tragedy will not be published for several days. He and the *New York Times* certainly believed that they were publishing *Locrine* before it had been published elsewhere, and the paper fully intended to publish it first. In an article on 18 November ("Cabling a Whole Poem" 1887, 1) the paper reiterated the fact that *Locrine* had not yet been published elsewhere and two American publishers (Joseph Harper and E. D. Appleton) discussed the case in terms of the probable copyright implications.

The taint of the poet's risqué reputation may have been an additional inducement to secure the poem. *Locrine* might (in newspaper terms) be a scandalous story about a bigamist; his wife and son, who murder him; and his lover and daughter (or "lovechild"), who tragically kill themselves.

Sensationalism was the staple fare of the "yellow" journalism that was flooding the bottom end of the newspaper market. The *New York Times* appealed to a more serious readership, but it was losing out to a direct competitor—Joseph Pulitzer's New York *World* the pioneer of what would become the New Journalism—which was making the paper look increasingly conservative and old-fashioned by comparison.[33] The New York *World* combined "good news-coverage peppered with sensationalism, stunts and crusades, editorials of high character, size, illustration, and promotion" (Mott 1957, 4:439). The *"Locrine* incident" combines several of these features while retaining an air of dignity: the paper was unquestionably pulling a stunt—though by aiming it at the "judicious reader" it claimed it as an intellectual one. Yet it was also conducting a crusade for an international copyright agreement, albeit through questionable means. Pulitzer's paper plays an interesting role in the incident: both backstage and in a brief, ignominious, starring part.

Frederic (whose sexual entanglements are ominously presaged by those of Locrine) approached an Irish journalist, E. St. John Brenon, who had received a review copy of the poem. What followed may never be fully established, but it was never a simple newspaper assignment despite the way in which the *New York Times* represented it, and it rapidly became a feud. Aaron Watson, a contemporary member of the Savage Club, writes, "Frederic, who borrowed the book, telegraphed the whole of the contents to America, thus destroying Swinburne's copyright. He affirmed that he had paid ten pounds for the book, and that the purpose for which he required it was well understood; but this was denied by Brenon" (Watson n.d., 163). The incident led to a simmering hostility between Frederic and Brenon that continued over several years and culminated in a libel action that Brenon brought against Frederic in 1892, which centered around the issue of theft but had, at its heart, a question about the way in which the public and private can be or should be distinguished. Furthermore, a crucial aspect of the libel action concerned the way in which authorship can be said to be constituted, and this question clearly has implications for the issue of intellectual property and of copyright. The libel trial is, then, integrally allied, not just to the printing of Swinburne's tragedy, but to the whole question of authorship and to the relation of an author to the literary marketplace and of that author's place within that marketplace.

---

33. See Mott 1957, 4:428–29. The New York *Evening Sun* was conducting a vitriolic campaign against Pulitzer and his paper around the same period.

Whatever the precise nature of exchanges that took place between the two men in November 1887, it is clear that they both became acutely sensitive about the issue, and mutual distrust ensued. After Brenon wrote a slighting review of *In the Valley* in 1891, the two men argued together in the Savage Club, probably coming to blows. This public acrimony was no longer simply a private matter. Their argument was drawn to the attention of the Club Committee.[34] At this stage, the events of November 1887 were investigated with some thoroughness by the Savage Club itself. Brenon was accused of stealing *Locrine*—which he denied—and the subcommittee's report found that though he was not a thief, he "had not clearly established his use of the book, when obtained, to be in accordance with the conditions under which he received it, and to this extent he had been guilty of unbecoming conduct." He was not necessarily a thief, but he was guilty of indirection. He was suspended from the club for three months and would later say that he "never knew why" this had happened. Frederic resigned from the Savage, not (as Groucho Marx would say later) because a club that accepted him as a member was not worth belonging to, but because the scandal had made membership uncomfortable. Doubtless it had been suggested to him that club members should be more circumspect in their behavior. It is possible that Frederic recognized, for once, that discretion was the better part of valor: he may have been given a discreet warning that it would be more becoming to resign than to be expelled.

The committee's hearing was confidential, but an account of it was leaked to the New York *World*, appearing on 16 May 1891 on page 5 of the paper. The fifteen-line article headed "Harold Frederic Leaves the Savage" states that he had been "forced to resign" for calling Brenon "a thief within the precincts of the club and failing to prove his charge." Frederic was convinced that Brenon was responsible for the leak and was furious. Brenon later denied that he had instigated the story, but Frederic was already planning a counterattack. A number of Frederic's fellow "Savages" organized a private banquet in his honor at the Criterion as a gesture of solidarity Frederic, still smarting, suggested that the article of 16 May should be counterbalanced by an account of the dinner. He wrote a number of what he later called "suggestions" about the content of this new article, though it was not to be authored by him, and he later claimed that "The report . . . was not the account he wrote." The dinner culminated in a drunken visit to the office of the New York *World* in the company of Francis Scudamore, a *World* journalist. Scudamore sent a eulogistic dispatch about the banquet to the *World*. The article that resulted from this appeared in the paper on 30 May 1891 and included the damning com-

34. See "Queen's Bench Division: Brenon v. Frederic," *Times* (London), 6 May 1892, 13. Unless otherwise specified, references to the trial come from this source.

ment that "The Chairman, in the course of his speech, apologized for even mentioning the name of Brenon in an assemblage of gentlemen" and noted that it was impossible that Frederic could ever be "foreign to the interests of the Savage Club, of which he had been one of the chief ornaments for some years." These touches certainly suggest Frederic, and his "suggestions" may well have been a ghostwritten revenge upon his antagonist. Yet he claimed later that he "had no hand" in writing the article, and Scudamore argued in court that a "memorandum" was produced but that he himself wrote the article at the office of Dalziel's agency while Frederic "read the paper." It would be interesting to know just which paper Frederic was reading at the time.

Unsurprisingly, Brenon was incensed by the attack, accusing Frederic, Scudamore, and David Anderson (another journalist) of libel. He believed that Frederic cowrote or suggested the piece—a fair assumption. Frederic denied the charge, adding that the article was not libelous. The animosity between Frederic and Brenon was too deep to allow the matter to stand, although the actions against Anderson and Scudamore were eventually stopped. This again has significant implications for the question of authorship. The passage that so incensed Brenon was the indirect reporting of David Anderson's apology for mentioning Brenon's name. The action against Anderson was only stopped when he "solemnly assured him that the words he complained of in the libel were never spoken." Scudamore convinced Brenon less, and though he dropped the charges against him, he remained convinced that he was the "co-procurer" and "co-actor" with Harold Frederic. This language raises interesting questions of authorship and of the appropriation of another's voice: an actor is usually one who speaks another's words, one who may not be the author of those words but who is, however, the one who invests them with the activity needed for public utterance. Here, as elsewhere in this series of events, questions of voice, of stance, and of intent are crucial.

The case of Brenon versus Frederic loomed ominously. Faced with a potentially damaging lawsuit, Frederic wrote to Chatto and Windus in an attempt to clarify the conditions under which Brenon had received his copy of *Locrine*—for the dispute clearly originated in the events of November 1887. Andrew Chatto's reply of 18 March 1891 referred Frederic to a letter that Chatto had sent Brenon in December 1887. This letter—admirably restrained under the circumstances—informs Brenon that he (Chatto) has "just received" a copy of the *New York Times* that "seems to have published by cable the whole of Mr. Swinburne's 'Locrine.' " It continues, "You will remember that when you applied to me for an early copy of the book for a review which you were going to cable to this paper you asked permission to make 'a few quotations' to which I assented. The publication of the entire poem is so contrary to your undertaking to myself and is so obviously likely to give rise to vexatious complications, that I await with some anxiety your explanation" (Frederic Misc. 1977, 279). Brenon's "explanation" remains unrecorded, and it is tantalizing to speculate what it might have been. The findings of the Savage Club's subcommittee suggest that Brenon was, at best, indirect, but without additional testimony it is impossible to be certain of the exact circumstances under which Frederic obtained *Locrine*.[35]

The libel action of Brenon versus Frederic took place on 5 May 1892. It concentrated upon the newspaper report of 29 May 1891, the account of the private dinner. Brenon won his case and £50 damages, whereas Frederic was reprimanded for "printing trumpery gossip about private matters." Frederic was catapulted into a deep depression by the "swindle of a libel suit," writing to John Howe (an Irish-American Catholic) on 11 May 1892 that

> There never was a more heart-breaking misuse of court machinery since laws were invented—but least bearable of all was the humiliation of having my name bracketed in the public eye with that of the foulest blackguard that even Protestant Irishry has spawned. It is that that hurts—and I don't like to even think about it—much less write. I shall mention it no more—and I don't want ever to read of it again.
>
> However—I hear that the fellow is watching for the American papers, with a view to finding grounds for a new batch of libel suits in their comments on the case. He has also announced his intention of going to America, to bring these actions and pursue his task of further hurting me. And so—no more of him. (Frederic Misc. 1977, 313)

It is important to have more of him though, and more of the libel case that he brought against Frederic, too, for the very issues that constituted the cases for prosecution and defense—questions of authorship and of attribution; of the private and the public; of speech and writing; in other words, issues of the ownership of utterance either spoken or written, published or private; are all intimately related to debates surrounding intellectual property, authorship, and its associated rights, issues that are crucial to the debates on intellectual copyright that form the context for the newspaper events of 17 November 1887.[36] This plural is quite deliberate. Another event in a different New York paper on the same day forms part of this narrative. This event, though, will be described later.

As Mr. Justice Collins, who presided over the libel trial, summed up he

35. What is of course significant is that it is Brenon who was accused of theft and not Frederic.

36. For details of the realtion between the industry of publishing and copyright legislation in the 1880s, see Feltes 1993, chapter 2.

asked the jury to consider three questions: "(1) were the words complained of a libel; (2) if so, were they published by the defendant; (3) what were the damages sustained by the plaintiff." The jury had to make an evaluation of character, one of the question of the authorship of an anonymous newspaper article (despite the misleading or deliberately ambiguous way in which this is phrased), and an estimation of value based on the first decision. To reach a decision the jury had to decide upon which form of evidence (spoken or written) they should give credence to, and whose evidence was most plausible. Should they believe Brenon's claim that Frederic and Scudamore were coauthors and coconspirators; Anderson's written denial, in a private letter to Brenon of 4 November 1892, of words attributed to him; the oral testimonies of a number of men who had attended the event that the words attributed to Anderson, which appeared without quotation marks that might have acted as markers of property to, as it were "sanction" his voice, were indeed the words spoken by him?[37] In finding for Brenon the jury implicitly judged that an author (even the author of a speech) is better able to evaluate and to comment on and to recollect what she or he has said than an auditor. Anderson was better able to lay claim to his own precise utterance than anyone else even if others had witnessed it. He owned his speech and had privileged access to it. His spoken word was augmented by his written testimony (his letter to Brenon, which would certainly have been signed—stamped with the mark of authorship and authority), which carried more weight than the oral testimony of four other men present on the night in question. Although none of this argument is stated explicitly and it is impossible to have access to the jury's collective decision-making processes, it is clear that in the libel trial the conflicting discourses implicated in the labels "co-actor" and "co-procurer" are thrown together confusedly to produce a judgment that exonerated Brenon. Although feeling publicly humiliated in 1892, Frederic had been the stage manager five years earlier (in November 1887) of an event that brought plaudits from newspapers from all over the United States, as well as the self-congratulatory satisfaction of his own newspaper. It may have soothed him to look back upon the extraordinary coup he had pulled off, though it might equally have infuriated him that success should have such disastrous side effects.

The *New York Times* adroitly handled the *"Locrine* incident," ensuring maximum publicity both for the poem and for the means of transmission. An editorial of 17 November 1887, the day *Locrine* appeared, effectively operates as a public relations exercise. It is divided into two paragraphs, the entire first paragraph praising the paper for what it describes as "per-

37. For a fuller argument about the effects of quotation marks as forms of sanction, see de Grazia 1994, 289.

haps the most marvelous achievement of submarine telegraphy," the second praising the poem. This prioritizing is significant: the paper celebrated the possibility of sending such a cable more than the cabled material itself. It was important to the paper that the material should be worth the extraordinary lengths it took to obtain it. How was that worth quantified, and to what extent was it quantifiable? Charles Miller had been offered the poem, copyright intact, for one hundred dollars. He had eventually paid an estimated three thousand dollars for the cabled poem (minus copyright), plus ten pounds reportedly paid to Brenon—a steep mark-up. This huge amount was paid at a time when the paper's influence, readership, and profits were all in decline. Miller recognized the publicity value of such a coup and took pains to stress the technology that was responsible for it. The paper's editorial on 17 November 1887 announced that "To most readers, perhaps, the most remarkable fact about Mr. SWINBURNE'S new tragedy of 'Locrine' is the wonder of its transmission. The readers of THE NEW-YORK TIMES owe it to the Atlantic cables that they are able to enjoy, not the meaning only, but the music of a poem of which the music is not less important than the meaning, when it is still on the verge of publication in England. Various lyrics have been transmitted by cable, but seldom without mutilations that made the judicious reader await the printed copy to learn what the poet really wrote."

The paper followed this by a piece that appeared on 18 November It reprinted a significant extract from the editorial of the previous day's New York *Evening Sun* that with good humor accepted that the *New York Times* ("our neighbor" to the *New York Times's* "esteemed contemporary") has that day already printed Swinburne's poem. The paper notes that the dedication and last act are missing, which the *New York Times* quickly corrects as follows: "The fifth act was wanting in only a portion of the edition," though it avoids mention of the dedication, a significant omission that will be discussed shortly. The evening paper is gracious in defeat: "[W]e frankly and heartily congratulate our neighbor, upon a manifestation of enterprise so creditable. We feel at liberty to assume that the indiscretion which we are committed of advertising the tragedy and date of its publication so freely in our columns suggested to the editor of THE TIMES the really splendid stroke of journalistic spirit manifested this morning." This comment is a somewhat backhanded compliment suggesting first, that the New York *Evening Sun* provided the impetus for the *New York Times's* coup, and second, that the editor of the morning paper can be counted among the evening paper's readership. Miller, astute as ever, recognized the danger at once, and the *New York Times* gave the version of events already outlined, "But we may as well tell the story."

In this spirit then, the final part of this odd tale can be revealed, for it was in this climate of mutual and self-congratulation, forgiveness and neighborly good will, that the New York *Evening Sun,* acting no doubt in the spirit of one-upmanship even in defeat, published in its first pages on 17 November 1887 the whole of Swinburne's poem with the dedication and the last act intact. The price of this evening paper was one cent. In effect, the cost of *Locrine* had been slashed by 50 percent within a few hours. When one considers the price that the *New York Times* probably paid for *Locrine* that figure changes to one which is quite staggering.

A significant question, and one that neither paper was keen to address, was that of who actually wanted to read *Locrine,* and whether potential readers of Swinburne would wish to encounter him in their daily paper, or whether readers of the paper would wish to discover *Locrine* there. The New York *Evening Post* (the *Evening Sun*'s direct competitor) did raise the question, in acerbic tones. The *New York Times* repeated its comments in a brilliantly deflationary maneuver in which it simultaneously undermined both evening papers while representing the *Evening Post*'s position as being one of pure envy. In a column that appeared in the *New York Times* on 18 November the paper quotes the comments of the previous day's *Evening Post* as follows: "Nobody takes a newspaper, or would take one, in order to read in it long poems or essays. If THE TIMES had become possessed of an advance copy of SWINBURNE's tragedy in a book form it would have felt such a thing would be a shabby trick practiced on its subscribers. . . . We presume no busy man opened the paper at his breakfast table this morning without a sense of disgust and irritation at seeing one-fourth of it taken up with a long tragic poem—of all things in the world—in very poor type, and offered to him at an hour of the day when no human being thinks of reading either tragedies or comedies." The adroitness of the *New York Times*'s handling of this commentary lies in the positioning of the texts. It placed the *Evening New*'s critical comments within the same column, though just underneath, the New York *Evening Sun*'s account of its version of *Locrine,* which made the *Evening News*'s comments look like petty spite, and the *Evening Sun*'s exploits look like something of a "shabby trick." Since another article in the same issue assured the readership that the cabled verse led to a run on the paper that "exhausted the large edition," it is clear that the coup did indeed find readers.

By including the dedication to Alice Swinburne the New York *Evening Sun* had presented its readership with an unabridged verse tragedy, and had, indirectly, posed an interesting question about the status of this introduction and the way in which the *New York Times* and its London correspondent considered it. By leaving out the lengthy dedication the *New York Times* was implicitly splitting off Swinburne as author/individual from the poem as product or entity within the literary marketplace in a gesture that mimics the way in which the technology that made the coup possible itself helps to redefine spatial and temporal boundaries and hence to create a recognizably modern global market. For the paper was showing that a work can be cut loose from the boundaries of geography and time that were starting to totter in the latter part of the nineteenth century and also that the body of the work can be cut loose from itself, split up, taken apart, and can have its own boundaries and divisions questioned and rearranged for the sake of innovative technologies and possibilities. The *New York Times* explicitly and cannily recognized the value of its use of technology and celebrated the possibilities of the submarine cable in great detail for days.

On 18 November in an article titled, "Cabling a Whole Poem," on the front page of the paper, publishers gave their responses. On page 4 of the same issue " '*Locrine'* by Cable" described how the poem was obtained, gave the New York *Evening Sun*'s response, and argues that Swinburne's readership had been massively increased. The paper modestly refrained from mentioning its own readership and made little of whatever the copyright implications might be. On 20 November, once again on page 4, a series of further laudatory quotations appeared, culled from other American newspapers. This self-promotion continued on 21 November in an article titled, "A Feat Without Parallel." In an exultant passage the paper describes "HOW THE SWINBURNE CABLEGRAM WAS RECEIVED," elucidating in detail the difficulties of interpreting the thin blue line that the Thompson recorder produced. The line "was not beautiful" (it was compared with an outline of the Himalayas or a map of the walls of Troy after the invasion of the Trojan horse). Any electrical interference meant that the line became extremely difficult to read. Occasionally interference caused transmission to stop altogether. The manager of the Commercial Cable Company, G. G. Ward, told the paper that "the reading takes a first class man, and we have to keep a man two or three years before he can be trusted with such trying work." [38] The paper dwelt with relish on the technical aspects of its coup. The ten thousand words of the Swinburne cable that the Commercial Cable Company cabled covered 1,050 feet of paper. It was received at the rate of about seventeen words a minute, and took about five hours to cable using two cables, (making ten hours in all). The company's electrician explained that "cable telegraphing" and "land telegraphy" differ in respect to the energy of the current used. Despite what is "generally supposed," it took less energy to send a "sea" message than to send a land message. It took only thirty cells of energy to send the Swinburne cable twenty-five hundred miles. In contrast, he explained, a similar land message would have taken at least twelve hundred cells.

Beneath this article was a series of favorable quotations from other newspapers, suggesting the extent to which the piracy had operated as a public relations operation. These included this one from the *Altoona*

---

38. This might equally apply to Frederic himself.

(Pennsylvania) Tribune of 18 November, "It must have cost a pretty penny, but THE NEW-YORK TIMES never stops at expense when the information or pleasure of its readers is concerned," a welcome and explicit recognition of the paper's dedication to its readership. The *New York Times* quoted various favorable comments—"That's newspaper enterprise" *(Troy Press)* "the most remarkable achievement of its sort yet recorded for any newspaper in any country" *(New-Haven Palladium).* A quotation from the *Waterbury American* pinpoints one of the most controversial and contradictory aspects of the case: "[F]or 2 cents, New-Yorkers can buy a poem, whose publication is a literary event, days in advance of the date when Londoners can purchase the regularly issued copies. This is what journalism in the nineteenth century means." Mark Twain made the same point in a memorable and acerbic definition of journalism as "the one solitary respectable profession which honors theft (when committed in the [pecuniary] interest of a journal,) & admires the thief" (Twain and Howells 1960, 1:336.)

The paper carried on "puffing" for days more. On 23 November in a punning article titled, "It Beats the Record," on page 8, the Western Union Cable Company gave their side of the story and revealed, with no apparent irony, that the poem was sent by Morse from London to "that famous resort of melodious pirates, Penzance," and from there by cable to Cape Canso and then by Morse again to New York. It is hard to imagine how the paper might follow this, but it does, on the second page of the issue of 26 November, in an article from the *Weekly Utican,* and on the same day but two pages later in an article taken from the *Electrical World,* and culminates in another article on the same page from the *Shoe and Leather Reporter.* Underneath this is an article that seems to close the matter. It is not on Swinburne's poem, but rather is on submarine cables By this time that is enough. It does not have to say more. Yet did the *New York Times* have more creditable motives than the catalogue of articles implies, or was it simply living up to Twain's definition?

On 17 November, the day the *New York Times* printed Swinburne's poem, an editorial demanded an international copyright agreement. What is extraordinary about this appeal is its juxtaposition to an article that celebrates both the poem itself and the paper's cleverness at having obtained it. The editorial argues that author, publisher, and public are all impoverished by the lack of a copyright agreement that makes English books so cheap that American books and authors cannot compete. It moves toward a demand for a national literature that will be representative of the American people and way of life. This editorial was a version of an earlier phase of the argument that had emerged in the 1830s, and it was echoed throughout the end of the nineteenth century. Charles Dickens had, in 1842, announced at a public dinner in Hartford, Connecticut, "I would beg leave to whisper in your ear two words, International Copyright." But this state-

ment was taken less as a whisper than as a barbaric yawp.[39] A national
literature was to be the signifier that the United States was a truly civilized
and independent nation both culturally and politically, and it would attest
to the high political and cultural standards of the American people. The
New York Times argues that it would build up national fame and undermine
"Foreign, and especially English modes of thought" and would counteract
the effects of foreign political ideology that frequently oppose and threaten
the American political system.[40] This hope anticipates Frederic's ambition
for his historical romance *In the Valley*. Stanton Garner argues that the tone
and sentiments of the first editorial are "more typical of Frederic than of
an editorial office," suggesting that he might well have written the copyright article which, with its nationalistic and protectionistic tenor, allies the
New York Times with the Chace Bill (Garner 1973, 287). This is speculation,
though, and there is no other evidence for this claim.

The sensitivity of the debate on copyright is evinced by the passion it
inspired in authors and publishers alike. In this context it is important to
clarify Frederic's position. Paul Haines, perhaps confused by Aaron Watson's vague account of the Brenon-Frederic disagreement, could not locate
the pirated material in the *New York Times*. Thomas F. O'Donnell and Hoyt
C. Franchere go as far as suggesting that the incident did not occur at all.
The "story," they argued, was that "Frederic had either been given or had
purchased for £10 a copy of Swinburne's latest poems, yet to be published,
and had telegraphed the entire contents to the United States.... Since
the poems were not reprinted, at least not in the *Times,* the story is open
to some question" (O'Donnell and Franchere 1961, 169).

More questionable is the amount of effort all these men put into searching through back copies of the *New York Times*. Austin Briggs makes no
reference to the incident whatsoever (significantly, Briggs acknowledges
Haines's unpublished thesis and O'Donnell and Franchere's book to be
the fullest sources for his own critical study of Frederic). Although it is
clear that the incident did indeed take place, that it caused a major stir in
the world of journalism, and that it was responsible for permanent ill-
feeling between Frederic and Brenon, it is difficult to ascertain how the
printing of *Locrine* relates to the *New York Times*'s position on copyright.
Was it a copyright crusade or a cable coup? Was Frederic culpable for
betraying a fellow author for the sake of a piece of sensational journalism,
or were his actions prompted by the belief that he could help to achieve
an important piece of legislation? Insufficient evidence makes either argument unresolvable. The available facts suggest that the truth may be at
some point between the two extremes. Frederic and Miller were both

39. For an account of his reception see Welsh 1987, 33.
40. The fear of the foreign has, of course, already appeared in this case.

genuinely interested in the fight for international copyright legislation, which would protect American authors and encourage a national literature. Publishing *Locrine* in advance of its general release was both a clever stunt aimed at stimulating sales and a calculated maneuver to draw public attention to the inadequacy of copyright protection.

"An Empire's Young Chief" and "An Indictment of Russia"

In 1890 and 1892 Frederic wrote two long pieces of journalism for the *New York Times*. They represent the midpoint of his short writing career. The first, "An Empire's Young Chief," is a lengthy and ponderous character study of the Emperor William II of Germany. It was published in book form as *The Young Emperor*. It has not aged gracefully, although some of Frederic's more florid touches still resonate: of Charles of Württemberg and his brother Ludwig of Bavaria, he writes, "In these two brothers the fantastic Wittelsbach blood, filtering down from the Middle Ages through strata of princely scrofula and imperial luxury, clotted rankly in utter madness" (Frederic *NYT* 1890, 12).

For Frederic, William personified division. The article was the perfect foil for an extended piece of indirect analysis of his own familial and national history. The piece gestures backward toward Germany's imperial past, and forward to the reign of a young man who seemed to Frederic to combine a natural youthful innocence with an arrogance and harshness that was the inevitable inheritance of royal birth. (Frederic would tackle a similar subject in his penultimate novel *Gloria Mundi*.) In writing about William's ancestry he was writing of a history in which his own family had participated before they had left Europe for the New World. He began the series by a comparison between the coronation of the new emperor and preparations in the United States and France for celebrations of their freedom from imperial powers. By foregrounding the conflict between an optimistic belief in the future of the two young republics and ironic deprecation at William's appropriation of his magnificent titles—"a War Lord" and "a Mailed Hand of Providence" and "a sovereign specially conceived, created and invested with power by God, for the personal government of some fifty millions of people" he prepares the way for an examination of William's internal conflict: "one sees a constant struggle between two Williams—between the gentle, dreamy-eyed, soft-face boy of Cassel and the vain, arrogant youth who learned to clank a sword at his heels and twist a baby mustache in Bonn. Such conflicts and clashings between two hostile inner selves have a part in the personal history of each of us. Only we are not out under the searching glare of illumination which beats upon a Prince, and the records of those internal warrings are of interest to ourselves alone" (Frederic *NYT* 1890, 17). That "conflict" was a vivid part of Frederic's own personal history: his enthusiastic belief in the series of articles on William reflects his interest in his own "two hostile inner selves." He might have written the paragraph above about himself; certainly many of his friends wrote similarly about him. Sadly the article never lives up to its promise, but a second piece that appeared the following year is a more impressive achievement.

"An Indictment of Russia" appeared in regular long installments in the *New York Times* from 14 September to 21 December 1891. They were collected and published as *The New Exodus* the following year, following the pattern established by "An Empire's Young Chief." In July 1891 Frederic traveled, via Germany, to Russia, where he spent about three weeks collecting material on the persecution of Jews. It was a dangerous task because the authorities were sensitive about the activities of foreigners—the artist Joseph Pennell, visiting Russia on Frederic's advice, was arrested in Kiev for taking unauthorized photographs.[41] Frederic relied both on personal observation and on the help of informants. He protected the identity of his informants, knowing that they could "vanish" into Siberia if discovered: one diary entry notes that he was "With X.Z. (Perowna)" (Harold Frederic Papers). He received letters in cipher that were then translated into English via Russian and French—a complex procedure. His informants trusted him with damning evidence against the Russian authorities, and his lengthy report details systematic brutality and widespread blackmailing, extortion, pettiness, violence, and ignorance.

Frederic's piece was very different from the accounts of polite Russian society that predominated at this period. He had spotted a festering sore that Russian society had anxiously kept hidden from other observers, and the Russian authorities were furious to have their disfigurement so ruthlessly exposed. After Frederic's report was published they permanently banned him from the country Writing to Thomas Henry Huxley some seventeen months after his journey to Russia, Frederic says that the whole area had been "quite new" to him when he began his research and that it had been "dumped" upon him in addition to his regular newspaper tasks. Despite the justified disclaimer that it was "not the outcome of broad scholarship," the extent of his research and the depth and scope of his report are impressive under the circumstances (Frederic to Thomas H. Huxley, 21 December 1892, Frederic Misc. 1977, 324–24). His report is extremely powerful. His findings impassioned him to the extent that public exposure of Russian anti-Semitism became a personal moral imperative. Yet his response to Russia was ambivalent: he was disgusted by the Russian

41. Pennell's visit to Austria, Hungary, Poland, and Russia was published serially as an illustrated text in *The Illustrated London News* in December 1891. Hall Caine also traveled to Russia to investigate the persecutions. See Cowen and Cowen 1986.

state, but he was exasperated by what he interpreted as the passivity of the Jews who accepted persecution with a calm that came from seeing it as an inevitable repetition of the past. He threw himself into the journalistic task at hand and went to enormous pains to produce an important catalogue of evidence, yet the piece makes for uneasy reading as moments of moral outrage and calculatedly patronizing asides.

Like all his passions, his interest in Judaism spills over into his fiction—*The Damnation of Theron Ware, Gloria Mundi* and *The Market-Place* contain, respectively, references to Hebraism, Anglo-Jewish characters, and a protagonist whose most loathsome characteristic is his violent anti-Semitism.[42] The association between anti-Semitism and the competitive ethos of the financial buccaneer Joel Thorpe echoes "An Indictment of Russia." Frederic believed that "an unhealthy and unnatural competition" resulted on the one hand in the persecution of the Jews in Russia, and on the other, in the rise of a new class of powerful capitalists: "Whenever men engage in an unhealthy and unnatural competition those with the worst and most dangerous qualities rise to the top, trampling the weaker and softer ones under foot. We have seen something like that in Wall Street, where there are no laws abridging virtuous happiness or making dishonesty the condition of life" (Frederic *NYT* 1891, 1.) He might have called it the survival of the unfittest. Joel Thorpe's anti-Semitism is most striking in a violent outbreak in which he compares his own brutish physicality (which he associates with the amoral and inescapable movements of business) to the imagined nervous sensitivity of his Jewish antagonists: " 'That's the kind of hand . . . that breaks the Jew in the long-run, if there's only grit enough behind it. I used to watch those Jews' hands, a year ago, when I was dining and wining them. They're all thin and wiry and full of veins. Their fingers are never still; they twist round, and keep stirring like a lobster's feelers. But there ain't any real strength in 'em . . . when a hand like that takes them by the throat'—he held up his right hand as he spoke, with the thick, uncouth fingers and massive thumb arched menacingly in a powerful muscular tension—'when that tightens round their neck, and they feel that the grip *means business*—my God! what good are they?' " (Frederic *Novels* 1899, 184, [emphasis added]).[43] City men suspect that Thorpe's aim is a *"Judenhetze,"* and in an unwitting presentiment Thorpe is transformed by his success into a familiar Hitlerian figure: "It [his face] was palpably the

---

42. One of Frederic's earliest, sentimental stories was "The Jew's Christmas" (1882).

43. For a fascinating study of the representation of the body of the Jew see Gilman 1991. Thorpe's description of the hand of the Jew is close to George Du Maurier's illustrations of Svengali's hands. Both are part of an established anti-Semitic tradition. Nina Auerbach notes that Ellen Terry's son used to joke that his broad powerful thumbs (much like Thorpe's) were "murderous," relying on a Lombrosian reading of their significance (Auerbach 1989, 21). See also Naman 1980.

visage of a dictator. The moustache had been cut down to military brevity, and the line of mouth below it was eloquent of rough power. The steady gray eyes, seemingly smaller yet more conspicuous than before, revealed in their glance new elements of secretiveness, of strategy supported by abundant and confident personal force" (Frederic Novels 1899, 206). In Thorpe's relentless persecution of his Jewish antagonists; Hitler's Germany is presaged. Frederic had predicted a reemergence of German anti-Semitism in "An Empire's Young Chief" when he describes the German aristocrat dreaming "of a time when a beneficent fate shall once more hold Jerusalem up to conquest and rapine" (Frederic *NYT* 1890, 12). This, and other such comments, reveal an opportunistic streak in his journalism —a desire to shock through a certain brutality of style and polemic.

Frederic's travels in Russia aroused him to a ferocious anti-Russian prejudice. His personal animosity was aimed both at the Russian authorities and at an entire ethnic group. It is ironic that his passionate polemic against intolerance should partake of it so strongly. The implied racism of his reporting is restrained in comparison with the ugly tone of a letter that he wrote from Odessa. The suggestion of a "final solution" has an irony that he could not have appreciated at the time:

> One thing let me say briefly: never give a moment's credit to any tale you hear about Russian kindness, Russian honesty, Russian decency in public or political matters. I have been among them for a month with eyes tolerably wide open. I shall leave them with the abiding conviction that the human race would be rid of its most menacing and hopeless problem if they were all destroyed, root and branch. I think of myself as a merciful man,—but I have been brought to terrible lengths of pitiless inhumanity by viewing this great sprawling, monstrous camp of paganism called Russia. I feel that I could gladly see it not only whipped and humbled, but ravaged with fire and sword. Every evening before I go to bed I read over for personal delectation the historical accounts of how the Tartars formerly overran this country, putting everybody to the sword,—and I find myself quite restoring the Napoleonic idol in my mental shrine as I read of how he smashed and tore things all the way to Moscow. (Frederic to Charles R. Sherlock, 13 August 1891, Frederic Misc. 1977, 289)

He saw the situation in Russia as something that might in theory exist anywhere in the world. Specifically, he saw direct parallels between aspects of American life and the situation in Russia. He invokes these on several occasions, in part to provide a familiar context for de-familiarizing facts— to give a "pictorial idea" appropriate to a newspaper public—yet also because the comparison struck him so forcibly (Frederic to Thomas H. Huxley, 21 December 1892, Frederic Misc. 1977, 289). He saw Russia as an inversion of America: "Watching and pondering its various manifestations, I could never rid myself of the thought that it was a kind of America in which the early civilized settlers had been overwhelmed and absorbed by the aborigines. Everywhere one got the sense of departed glories, of vanished arts and forgotten knowledge. To the genuine aims and works of a real race had succeeded the squalid views and surface purposes of a mongrel and half-caste people, through whose feeble and fickle hands everything was slipping back into barbarism" (Frederic *NYT* 1891, 1). The piece is saturated in insulting references to Russian officials that slide over into more general attacks on the Russian people. Frederic's investigation is founded upon a broader argument on the competing influences that vie upon Russia: Europe versus Asia.

Traveling through Russia, receiving coded messages from brave individuals, wary of surveillance and arrest, Frederic developed a renewed realization of the political potential of newspapers. The Russian press suffered heavy censorship from the authorities; as a result the power of the independent press was crumbling, and anti-Semitic newspapers had a growing and pernicious influence. All but the most bland foreign commentary was prevented from entering the country. All of these factors conspired against the Jews by stifling news of persecution and inhibiting public comment— it is a familiar story. After the publication of "An Indictment of Russia" Frederic became a guest at a newly established Jewish club, the Maccabeans. In his 1891 appointments diary he notes the date of Yom Kippur. His initial encounters with Jewish culture were an echo of his earlier fascinated ventures into the lives of Utica Irish Catholics. The two experiences would combine in the complex intermingling of Hebraism and Hellenism in *The Damnation of Theron Ware*.[44] Yet his reaction to Judaism was, as ever, unstraightforward. Although he was a powerful advocate of Jewish causes and had Jewish friends (he dedicated *The Damnation of Theron Ware* to Marguerite Thomas, the Jewish wife of his friend, the dramatist Brandon Thomas), and was well thought of by many notable London Jews, he could also be profoundly anti-Semitic.[45]

Frederic's idiosyncratic likes and dislikes were also channeled into another extended piece of journalism. He displayed his impatience with the customs of a very individual British group, the matronly Mrs. Albert Grundy and her family.

Mrs. Albert Grundy: Observations in Philistia

The diversity of Frederic's journalistic output is well illustrated by a series of satirical sketches. "Observations in Philistia" was first published in

---

44. This works at many levels, some quite subtle. For instance, see Gilman 1991, 150–68, on the meanings of Heinrich Heine for Freud, and compare this with Celia Madden's invocation of Heine in her highly stylized "seduction" of Theron Ware.

45. See also Myers 1995, 107–9.

serial form in the *National Observer* between 20 February 1892 and 23 December 1893. All but two of the sketches were collected and reprinted in book form in 1896 as *Mrs. Albert Grundy: Observations in Philistia*. Frederic undoubtedly wrote the sketches for financial reasons. He later admitted that composition had been difficult: he had been "very busy and lazy," there had been "long intervals" between the appearance of the articles, and he frequently had trouble in "finding the mood for the sort of thing" (Frederic to editor *Brooklyn Times* ca. 25 February 1897, Frederic Misc. 1977, 444). The unevenness of the quality and tone of the sketches bears testimony to his acknowledged difficulties. Mrs. Grundy herself, exposed in the first sketch for her hypocritical moral double standards, is treated increasingly gently in the following sketches until she finally becomes the narrator's future mother-in-law in the last sketch. A pointed commentary on this final fall from grace ends the series—in the words of one character, "You ought to have married into the Grundys years ago. You were just born to be one of the family" (Frederic Misc. 1896a, 169).

Philistia is empire—both the domestic, interior, empire of Mrs. Grundy (centered upon her smoothly run semidetached villa, "Fernbank," with its dangerous borders and "outlying mantraps on the lawn"), and the British Empire itself, of which "Fernbank" is a small, though significant, satellite. In an echo of Rider Haggard, Philistia is described as "the land where She must be obeyed." This might aptly describe either Mrs. Grundy's Philistia or Victoria's England in the few years before her Diamond Jubillee: the husband of Mrs. Grundy is called Albert. Frederic was frequently hostile to the British Empire, condemning its "rapacious maw" and commenting wryly in a letter to Louis Becke on 3 August 1898 that "the angels have had very little to do ... with the development of the British Empire" (Frederic Misc. 1895, 137; Frederic Misc. 1977, 482). A romantic resolution to the series provided a neat ending for sketches that were rapidly losing momentum and direction. Equally though, the resolution reflects upon the pervasive quality of Philistia: it is unrivaled in its capacity for reproducing itself through conquest and colonization. In an after-dinner speech to the Omar Khayyam Club, of which he was a member, Frederic once warned of this quality when he, "in true Omarian spirit, bade hosts and guests alike 'gather rosebuds while they may,' and seize on some moments of the day for the self which the Minotaur of Convention and Custom devours" ("The Omar Khayyam Club Dinner" 1896, 60).

Despite his observations (the word neatly puns on the double aspect of being both an observer and commentator on Philistia), the American narrator, Tristram, never totally understands Philistia and is bewildered by the mysterious social rituals and strategies of Ermyntrude and her mother as they make wedding preparations. After the announcement of their engagement, Tristram notices a silent exchange between his future wife and mother-in-law. In describing it in militaristic terms ("manoeuvres and countermarchings"), he tacitly recognizes the supremacy of women in this area of the empire of Philistia. Later Tristram and Uncle Dudley, the worldly and well-traveled brother of Mrs. Grundy, together try to find a language to explain the "moment of preoccupied and surcharged silence" in which Ermyntrude and Mrs. Grundy challenge each other over Tristram. Tristram's version of the exchange is the stuff of popular romance: a "tender dialogue" between fond mother and timorous daughter. Dudley's interpretation is cynical comic realism, though later Tristram acknowledges that Dudley's interpretation is probably correct:

> MOTHER [*lowering brows*]. You may be sure that at the very best it will be Bayswater.
> DAUGHTER [*with quiver of nostrils*]. Better that than hanging on for a Belgravia which never comes.
> MOTHER [*disclosing the tips of two teeth*]. It is a chance of a title going for ever.
> DAUGHTER [*curling lip*]. What chance is ever likely here?
> MOTHER [*lifting brows*] He's as old as Methuselah!"
> DAUGHTER [*flashing eyes*]. That's my business! (Frederic Misc. 1896a, 163–64.)

Frederic's subjects are topical and his stance contemptuously patronizing. They include Mudie's circulating library and the censorship of books (Tess D'Urbeville, according to Mrs. Grundy, is "a farm-girl who for the most part skimmed milk or cut swedes in a field, and at other times behaved in a manner positively unmentionable"); English reaction to Americans (uninformed and prejudiced), the Royal Academy (institutionalized prudery), women journalists (generally worthless); the relation between the sexes (fraught); the vagaries of the Stock Exchange (unpredictable); the English and Germanic characters (lacking humor); and Rational Dress (leading to irrational responses in suburban women). He introduces characters of a Dickensian cast who include Lady Willoughby Wallaby; the Rev. Mr. Grayt-Scott; Sir Watkyn Hump and his son, Eustace; the Countess of Wimps; the Dowager Lady Thames-Ditton; and the Honorable Knobbleleigh Jones (son of the shipping magnate Lord Skillyduff). Sometimes Frederic's satire is accurate. Mrs. Grundy's attempts to be all things to all (middle-class and influential) people are treated with amused contempt. Her dilettantish movement between the Friendly Divided Skirt Association, via the Neo-Dress Improver League, to the Amalgamated Anti-Crinoline Confederacy is very funny. Her decision to defend the respectability of the Grundys by making Ermyntrude join the Crinoline Defense League to balance the family response to clothing is inspired. Yet of course both implicitly dismiss the ambitions behind the campaign for rational dress and with it demonstrate Frederic's real lack of interest in women's rights and his willingness to capitalize on the possibilities of a rather easy target group.

The sketches represent the point at which Frederic's journalism is at its closest to fiction. Here he wrote, as he did in the *New York Times,* of "much that is foolish in the Britisher," but this contemporary social commentary was allied to a narrative and a cast of fictional characters that differentiate it from both the main body of his journalism and his fiction.

4

The Novelist

The Promised Land of Fiction

In his introduction to the anthology *The New Journalism* (1990), Tom Wolfe writes that Americans have had, in the past, a particular fascination for the idea of writing novels. The "damnable novel" has had, he says, a key role in the fantasy life of America. From publishers to advertisers, English lecturers to convicts, there have been, in America's history, "a whole swarm of fantasizers out there steaming and proliferating in the ego mulches of America." He traces this idea, with characteristic gusto, from the 1930s to the 1960s, when, he argues, the "New Journalism" transformed the inner lives of Americans and created a new form that ironically (for it began as a homage to the dominance of the novel) would "wipe out the novel as literature's main event." Nearly twenty years on, the latter part of Wolfe's argument, fermented in his own peculiarly fertile "ego mulch," seems itself a fantasy. The novel has a peculiar staying power, a resilience greater than that of the 1960s "New Journalism," however significant, that Tom Wolfe and other writers, like Hunter S. Thompson, championed, though this undoubtedly continues to have enormous influence. Yet his evocation of the attraction of novel writing is revealing. The possibility of becoming a novelist was as thrilling, he says, as nineteenth-century dreams of finding gold or oil. It allowed for the sudden change of fortune in which the American could "over-night, in a flash, utterly transform his destiny" (Wolfe and Johnson 1990, 20 and 22).

Wolfe's idea of the extreme potency of such a desire, so strong that it gives such inclinations their power, is a convincing one. The possibility of rapidly acquiring riches, a compelling aspiration in a land of immigrants, has always had a central position in the American imagination and has been harnessed by many writers.[1] That the land itself, its farming land and

---

1. In *My Ántonia* (1918) Willa Cather uses the image of Coronado's restless and hopeless search for the Seven Golden Cities as a symbol of not only the soaring hopes that the American continent inspired but also its harsh reality. Coronado dies of a broken heart, a

mineral resources, were the inheritance of all and promised rich rewards to those who were lucky enough to uncover its secrets, as well as a dismal future to those who failed, was part of the meretricious fantasy. Land speculation, panning for gold, striking oil or other mineral deposits, or even discovering a lost inheritance: all these have been satirized, legitimated, or criticized in nineteenth-century fiction.[2]

Mark Twain wrote about American speculation with particular insight: it was a significant feature in his life. His father had purchased about a hundred thousand acres of East Tennessee land in 1830, believing that it would make his heirs wealthy for life. The land never lived up to his father's expectations, although fortunately he did not discover this. Yet, since it gave Twain material for *The Gilded Age*, it did bring the family something. In his autobiography Twain writes, "whenever things grew dark it rose and put out its hopeful Sellers hand and cheered us up and said, 'Do not be afraid—trust in me—wait.' It kept us hoping and hoping during forty years and forsook us at last. It put our energies to sleep and made visionaries of us—dreamers and indolent. We were always going to be rich next year— no occasion to work. It is good to begin life poor; it is good to begin life rich—these are wholesome; but to begin it poor and *prospectively* rich! The man who has not experienced it cannot imagine the curse of it" (Twain 1960, 24–25). In *The Gilded Age*, Washington Hawkin's heartfelt relief at his decision to sell his family's Tennessee land was shared by Twain: "The spell is broken, the lifelong curse is ended!" (Twain and Warner 1967, 417).

The idea of land ownership as curse had already been an important theme in Hawthorne's *The House of the Seven Gables* (1851). Colonel Pyncheon appropriates the land of Matthew Maule, and is cursed by Maule: "God will give him blood to drink!" (Hawthorne 1965, 8). Yet the Pyncheon family find that the real curse is the land itself, perpetually beyond their grasp because the deeds to it have been hidden by Matthew Maule's son, behind a portrait of Colonel Pyncheon (out of the Colonel's eyeshot). The portrait mysteriously communicates its secret to Clifford Pyncheon: " 'That picture!' said Clifford, seeming to shrink from its stern glance. 'Whenever I look at it, there is an old, dreamy recollection haunting me, but keeping just beyond the grasp of my mind. Wealth, it seems to say!—

---

shattered man, and Ántonia's father, destroyed by the bleak landscape of Nebraska and yearning for home, shoots himself. In *The Jungle* Upton Sinclair writes, "Jurgis, too, had heard of America. That was a country where, they said, a man might earn three roubles a day; and Jurgis . . . decided forthwith that he would go to America and marry, and be a rich man in the bargain. . . . America was a place of which lovers and young people dreamed" (Sinclair 1984, 29).

2. For example, in Mark Twain and Charles Dudley Warner's *The Gilded Age* (1873); in Frances Hodgson Burnett's *Little Lord Fauntleroy* (1886); in Twain's *The American Claimant* (1892); and in Howells's *The Rise of Silas Lapham*.

boundless wealth!—unimaginable wealth!' " (Hawthorne 1965, 315).[3]
The Maules' sole inheritance is the secret of where the deeds are kept,
whereas the Pyncheons inherit the fantasy of wealth, which, just as Twain
would discover, has a largely pernicious effect:

> This impalpable claim, therefore, resulted in nothing more solid than to
> cherish, from generation to generation, an absurd delusion of family impor-
> tance, which all along characterized the Pyncheons. It caused the poorest
> member of the race to feel as if he inherited a kind of nobility, and might yet
> come into the possession of princely wealth to support it. In the better
> specimens of the breed, this peculiarity threw an ideal grace over the hard
> material of human life, without stealing away any truly valuable quality. In
> the baser sort, its effect was to increase the liability to sluggishness and
> dependence, and induce the victim of a shadowy hope to remit all self-effort,
> while awaiting the realization of his dreams. (Hawthorne 1965, 19)

Matthew Maule's curse ends when the families are reconciled through the
idealized love between the artist Holgrave, a descendant of Maule, and
Phoebe Pyncheon.[4] Yet for Twain the curse on his family was only lifted,
not ended. Later Twain would speculate unsuccessfully in stocks, as well as
prospect for gold and silver, again without success. His interest in the Paige
typesetting machine would bankrupt him, forcing him to undertake a
world lecture tour to repay his creditors. He had inherited some of his
father's ruinous hopes after all.

Frederic's father, Henry De Motte Frederick, had also experienced the
lure of the new land, and he left his job in the early 1850s and, along with
his brother-in-law, went to California to prospect for gold. He was more
fortunate than Twain or his father and returned with enough money to
move into the house in which Frederic would be born. Yet Frederic shared
the fantasy of a lost inheritance. He told one interviewer in 1897 that he
came from "a whole list of people who abandoned fortunes for conscience
[sic] sake" (Sherard 1897, 533). Frederic wrote of the fantasy of discovering a lost inheritance in *Gloria Mundi;* although in *The Market-Place,*
he subverts the traditional form of such fantasies: Joel Thorpe makes his
fortune out of an imaginary rubber plantation, located on a piece of land
that does not even belong to him.

----

3. The novelist Gertrude Atherton writes that the financial interests of her wealthy grandfather were ruined by his partner's speculations, but that when the partner speculated successfully, "in a sudden access of conscience" he left her grandfather thirty thousand dollars
(Atherton 1932, 5–6).

4. For Hawthorne this is certainly a fable about the literary marketplace, at least in part.
The horror of exposure and publicity; fear of trade; the invasiveness of the market (which
even enters into Phoebe Pyncheon's house); its inescapabilty, and above all her enforced
dependence upon it and shrinking from it all suggest such a reading.

The same piece is used by Tom Wolfe to demonstrate that the nineteenth-century American dream of acquiring sudden wealth was transposed and translated into a parallel fantasy in the twentieth century, the desire for literary fame. He writes that

In the 1930s all the novelists had seemed to be people who came blazing up into stardom from out of total obscurity. That seemed to be the nature of the beast. The biographical notes on the dust jackets of the novels were terrific. The author, you would be assured, was previously employed as a hod carrier (Steinbeck), a truck dispatcher (Cain), a bellboy (Wright), a Western Union boy (Saroyan), a dishwasher in a Greek restaurant in New York (Faulkner), a truck driver, logger, berry picker, spindle cleaner, crop duster pilot. . . . There was no end to it. . . . Some novelists had whole strings of these credentials. . . . That way you knew you were getting the real goods. . . .

By the 1950s The Novel had become a nationwide tournament. There was a magical assumption that the end of World War II in 1945 was the dawn of a new golden age of the American Novel, like the Hemingway-Dos Passos-Fitzgerald era after World War I. There was even a kind of Olympian club where the new golden boys met face-to-face every Sunday afternoon in New York, namely, the White Horse Tavern on Hudson Street. . . . An! There's Jones! There's Mailer! There's Styron! There's Baldwin! There's Willingham! In the flesh—right here in this room! The scene was strictly for novelists, people who were writing novels, and people who were paying court to The Novel. There was no room for the journalist unless he was there in the role of would-be novelist or simply courtier of the great. There was no such thing as a *literary* journalist working for popular magazines or newspapers. If a journalist aspired to literary status—then he had better have the sense and the courage to quit the popular press and try to get into the big league. (Wolfe and Johnson 1990, 20–21).[5]

In the nineteenth century many young journalists tried to escape from the "little league" of hackwork or provincial journalism to the big league of the novel. Despite Wolfe's argument that journalism will kill fiction, in the nineteenth century the opposite seemed true. The movement from journalism to fiction was common enough to make journalism seem a necessary part of the training of the novelist, perhaps even an apprenticeship. Certainly the influence of fiction in the development of nineteenth century New Journalism is immeasurable. Frank Norris believed that all American artists needed a period of study or preparation, but for the writer, that meant an immersion into real life, since the writing of fiction "will not, will not flourish indoors." Writing in the *Boston Evening Transcript*

5. This type of publicity lent itself to parody. The cover of one of James Thurber's books reads, "He has not worked as a cow-puncher, ranch-hand, stevedore, short-order book, lumberjack, or preliminary prize-fighter" (Thurber, 1953).

on 27 November 1901, he argued that one way of writing within "the very heart's heart of life, on the street corner, in the market place" was through journalism (Norris 1964, 13). Many, perhaps most, of the well-known late-nineteenth-century American novelists were also journalists for at least some part (perhaps a substantial one) of their career. Wolfe's list of 1930s writers could be transposed into the 1880s or 1890s and read "journalist, critic, and reviewer (Howells); war correspondent (Crane); international correspondent (Frederic); critic, essayist, and commentator (James, Norris)." It could be extended almost indefinitely by adding figures from around the same period—Ambrose Bierce, Willa Cather, Theodore Dreiser, Hamlin Garland, Charlotte Perkins Gilman, Mark Twain. The interplay between American journalism and American fiction writing has always been productive and close.

The trailblazing character of the early lives of 1930s writers, as Wolfe sees them, can be contrasted with the pattern of late-nineteenth-century novelists. Journalism proved to be an important apprenticeship for many fiction writers: a way of working themselves out of one life and into another. Journalism was also a career in itself, or a means of supplementing the intermittent income of fiction writing. In many cases it proved to be a way out of a small-town life (and ideas), as it was for Harold Frederic escaping Utica, and W. D. Howells, Columbus, Ohio. In later life Howells wrote eulogistically of the town of his youth, but this again, is part of an established American writing tradition: escape and distance are often necessary preliminaries to celebration. All of Frederic's New York State fiction was written in England, and it is impossible to say how his writing would have evolved had he not left the United States.[6]

Frederic's career as a writer of fiction spanned just over twenty years and two continents. Fiction writing came first with Frederic: his earliest writing was undertaken while he was still at school, and his primary emotional investment was chiefly in literature rather than in journalism. He willingly and actively embraced the fantasy of being a successful novelist and saw his journalism as a way into the promised land of fiction. He wrote regularly throughout most of his adult life: novels, short stories, and plays, and also miscellaneous pieces of journalism, including book reviews and a regular philatelic column.[7] His first, tentative stories, written while he was a young proofreader, were slight works, and Frederic hid his identity be-

6. Frank Norris, writing about American expatriate novelists in the *Critic* in June 1902, argues that "Frederic of all of them seems to have been sturdiest in clinging to American traditions, but The Market Place [sic] is more English than native, and one is sure would—had not the author died—have marked a transition to a more Anglicized point of view" (Norris 1964, 202–3).

7. The columns have been collected in the files of the Harold Frederic Edition.

hind the assumed name of "Edgar" (probably after Poe), the first of many names that he would assume. In 1877 the assumption of a name expanded its dimensions: assumption became appropriation as he published a plagiarized essay, "The Mohawk Valley During the Revolution," under his own name.

Frederic also enthusiastically embraced anonymity in order to write radical social comment while protecting himself from personal attack. As "X" he wrote on contemporary Irish problems for the *Fortnightly Review;* as "An American in London" he commented on British life to several journals, and as "George Forth" he wrote the comic novel *March Hares.* Most notable in his list of noms de plume would be his journalistic sobriquet: from 1884 until his death in 1898 he was "Our London Correspondent" for The *New York Times,* though as his fame grew he was gradually identified by his initials and then by his full name.[8] He was a writer with many names and varied talents, and he found numerous outlets for publishing his work.

Finding the Way

Frederic was preoccupied with the power of words from an early age. At first his interest was largely passive. He read—newspapers, religious and historical books, novels—and he absorbed the conversations of those around him. Several surviving anecdotes tell of his early fluency, and one (from a reliable source, his mother) tells of him transforming a punishment (she had locked him in a closet) into an opportunity for indulging his passion for reading. Haines writes that "she found him sprawled on his belly to read by the light that came through the crack; the point of her story was that the book was far beyond his years" (Haines 1945, 12). Frederic was a precocious learner. His earliest encounters with fiction were with an oral tradition of storytelling. He had his grandmother's dramatic stories to inspire him, and as a child of a Methodist family he was familiar with the public ritual of Bible reading. This is memorably treated in Abner Beech's wrathful performance in the Civil War story "The Copperhead," after his son's rebellion and enlistment on the Union side, in the Civil War:

> He had the knack, not uncommon in those primitive class-meeting days, of making his strong low-pitched voice quaver and wail in the most tear-compelling fashion when he read from the Old Testament. You could hardly listen to him going through even the genealogical tables of Chronicles dry-eyed. His Jeremiah and Ezekiel were equal to the funeral of a well-beloved relation.

8. This was partly for copyright reasons.

This night he read as I had never heard him read before. The whole grim story of the son's treason and final misadventure, of the ferocious battle in the wood of Ephraim, of Joab's savagery, and of the rival runners, made the air vibrate about us, and took possession of our minds and kneaded them like dough, as we sat in the mute circle in the old living-room. . . . Then there came the terrible picture of the King's despair. I had trembled as we neared this part, foreseeing what heart-wringing anguish Abner, in his present mood, would give to that cry of the stricken father—"O my son Absalom, my son, my son Absalom! Would God I had died for thee, O Absalom, my son, my son!" To my great surprise, he made very little of it. The words came coldly, almost contemptuously, so that the listener could not but feel that David's lamentations were out of place, and might better have been left unuttered.

But now the farmer, leaping over into the next chapter, brought swart, stalwart, blood-stained Joab on the scene before us, and in an instant we saw why the King's outburst of mourning had fallen so flat upon our ears. Abner Beech's voice rose and filled the room with its passionate fervor as he read out Joab's speech—wherein the King is roundly told that his son was a worthless fellow, and was killed not a bit too soon, and that for the father to thus publicly lament him is to put to shame all his household and his loyal friends and servants.

While these sonorous words of protest against paternal weakness still rang in the air, Abner abruptly closed the book with a snap. (Frederic Short. 1971, 24–25)

Having first assimilated the sounds of words and the forms of stories, and then learned how to string his own narratives together, Frederic began to write—mainly fiction at first, dramatic stories of the American Revolution, then journalism, and a small quantity of drama.[9] He had little time for poetry, either as a producer or consumer: he did not have the temperament for it. Citing Meredith, he described it as resembling "the Polar bear, who walks up and down his cage, and is brought to a halt every time that he has taken a few paces ahead" (Sherard 1897, 540). He might, like Celia Madden of *The Damnation of Theron Ware* (who also echoes Meredith), have said that it was like talking on tiptoe. To Frederic, any form of tiptoe was anathema.[10] He claimed scarcely to be able to read poetry "with here and

9. See Haines 1945, 13. Frederic's friends liked him for "his quaint stories and droll, oblique comments."

10. See Frederic Novels 1986, 95–96. " 'It is a conventional way of putting it, but are you fond of poetry, Mr. Ware?' 'Well, yes, I suppose I am,' replied Theron, much mystified. 'I can't say that I am any great judge—but I like the things that I like—and—' 'Meredith,' interposed Celia, 'makes one of his women, Emilia in England, say that poetry is like talking on tiptoe; like animals in cages, always going to one end and back again. Does it impress you that way?' 'I don't know that it does. . . . As I get older, I find that I take less narrow views of literature—that is, of course, of light literature—and that—that—' Celia mercifully stopped him."

there a modern exception" (which remains unnamed).[11] What is certain is that he found *Paradise Lost* impossible.[12] His difficulty with Milton would be the subject of a wry literary joke: in his 1888 story "The Editor and the School-Ma'am" the protagonist misquotes *L'Allegro* and writes to a young school-ma'am that "Nobody cares a button about Mr. Milton's true place among English poets." Frederic, at least, did not, and he enjoyed putting down that great monument of English literature.[13]

Frederic made several (more modest) attempts of his own to establish his place among American poets. His first known piece was written ("but happily uncompleted") for the centennial celebrations of the Battle of Oriskany in 1877: "Wherewith, in grateful mood, we celebrate, / This anniversary. We stand / And listen to shouts of hoarse command, / No rifles' roar nor yells of long-nursed hate, / Nor moans of mangled men, marked out by Fate. / And with a spirit all divine, / Nature, ever kindest in these Autumn days / Peoples this vale with nymphs and fays. / Clio, Euterpe, Calliope combine. / We come to worship at their shrine" (Haines 1945, 30).

The poem is a painful debut, best passed over swiftly. It does not appear to have been published, but his next poem was among the earliest pieces of nonjournalistic writing to be published under his own name. "The Opium-Eater" is a self-consciously decadent piece aimed at impressing a small community with his awareness of worldly matters. Both early pieces

11. He also claimed never to have written a line of criticism on it in his life—yet he wrote a letter to the *Utica Daily Observer* on Marc Cook, the Utica poet, as well as contributing a preface to a collection of Cook's poetry (Frederic to editor, *Utica Daily Observer*, 5 October 1882, Frederic Misc. 1977, 12–13).

12. Visiting Ireland together, Frederic and T. M. Healy discovered two volumes of the poem at an inn and decided to combine intellectual and physical exercise: "I said to Healy, 'This is our chance; we must improve our minds,' and, he agreeing, we used to take one of these volumes down to our bathing-place, and either before or after our swim read out passages to each other. It was a most dismal performance. We then decided that Milton was not intended for reading aloud, and that we must read it to ourselves, and here again we failed." (Sherard 1897, 540). The American and the Irishman found the Englishman's lengthy sentences and Latinate words unpalatable, even unpronounceable. Frederic's frankness is engaging. He was self-confident enough to be unafraid of seeming a philistine.

13. Hamlin Garland is also reputed to have had an unfortunate encounter with Milton: one anecdote tells how American prairie life was incompatible with *Paradise Lost:* "[o]n his fifteenth birthday his mother presented him with a copy of *Paradise Lost,* which he read thoroughly but with more bewilderment than enthusiasm. 'The extraordinary harangues of Satan,' which greatly impressed him, became a part of his declamatory material, until one day when his audience, the team of mules before his plow, bolted in protest at the vigor of his delivery" (Frederic Short. 1888, 14; Holloway 1960, 9). Compare Twain's attack on Scott in chapter 46 of *Life on the Mississippi* (1883) and Twain on Michelangelo in chapter 27 of *The Innocents Abroad* (1869).

are imitative and are directed outward, to a prospective audience, from a young man keen on having his worth recognized. Later Frederic would turn away from his early imitations. In 1897 he misleadingly claimed that he had never written a line of poetry in his life, unwilling to claim this early offspring of his fancy,

> My fairy comes at the death of day—
>   Comes with the stars and pall of night,
>   Comes with a face aglow with light,
> And whispers—what, I may not say.
>
> Paints for me fantasies so strange—
>   Glimpses of beauty beyond all thought,
>   Glimpses of loveliness peril-fraught,
> Unreal and weird. With ceaseless change
>
> They whirl and chase before my eyes—
>   These visions of my waking dreams,
>   These spectres of the things that seem,
> Yet would I not from the world arise,
>
> Nor break the spell which binds me close
>   With songs of sirens witching fair,
>   With madd'ning music in the air,
> While the flesh lies cold and comatose.
>
> Why should I grieve if the world is lost?
>   My fairy knocks at the death of day
>   My soul is hers. Insensate clay!
> I drink my dreams; you pay the cost.[14]

"The Opium-Eater" recalls elements of *Kubla Khan,* especially in its repetitive alliteration (compare Frederic's "ceaseless change" with Coleridge's "mazy motion" or "ceaseless turmoil seething"). It is another false start, as Frederic later realized: like the opium addict's "waking dream" the poem revealed itself (in the cold light of day) to be something of a nightmare. A third poem, written in the birthday book of Ruth Frederic, is an affectionate tribute to her. It is quite different in tone from his other poetry and in its simplicity is quite touching: "If 'Werner' had but lived my life, / And could have learned to tell the truth—/ Had had the sense to take a wife—/ He then had learned that better, forsooth, / Than

---

14. Reprinted in the *Frederic Herald,* 1, no. 3 (1968): 2.

health, wealth, fame, successful strife, / It was to have a daughter Ruth" (Harold Frederic Papers). The impetus behind the poem's simple style is Emerson's "Concord Hymn," which also uses a succession of monosyllables for their "rhetorical force," notably in the line "And fired the shot heard round the world" (Emerson 1950, 783). In Utica days, one of Frederic's drunken arguments with John Howe was on the dramatic possibilities of the monosyllable. Frederic liked to recite Emerson's poem as a dramatic finale (Other lectures were less elevated: one on the evil of drink followed the loss of his own and Howe's wages at pinochle.) (Haines 1945, 42).

One brief piece of nonsense poetry, written at an unknown date, has survived him. Frederic's self-proclaimed interest in the monosyllable is evident in the second line, and the couplet is nicely sharp and abrupt: "The feathered race with pinions cleave the air, Not so the mackerel—still less, the bear" (Frederic Misc. 1977, 479.) He also wrote two poems for *The Return of The O'Mahony* that were accredited to O'Daly, the hereditary bard of the O'Mahony family. The O'Mahony calls one of them "downright po'try," but it is obviously a spoof:

I

"What do the gulls scream as they wheel
    Along Dunmanus' broken shore?
What do the west winds, keening shrill,
    Call to each other for evermore?
        From Muirisc's reeds, from Goleen's weeds,
            From Gabriel's summit, Skull's low lawn,
        The echoes answer, through their tears,
            'O'Mahony's gone! O'Mahony's gone!'

II

"But now the sunburst brightens all,
    The clouds are lifted, waters gleam,
Long pain forgotten, glad tears fall,
    At waking from this evil dream.
        The cawing rooks, the singing brooks,
            The zephyr's sighs, the bees [sic] soft hum,
        All tell the tale of our delight—
            'O'Mahony's come! O'Mahony's come!'

III

"O'Mahony of the white-foamed coast,
    Of Kinalmeaky's nut-brown plains,
Lord of Rosbrin, proud Raithlean's boast,

Who over the waves and the sea-mist reigns.
Let Clancy quake! O'Driscoll shake!
The O'Casey hide his head in fear!
While Saxon's [sic] flee across the sea—
O'Mahony's here! O'Mahony's here!"
(Frederic Novels 1892, 62–63) [15]

Although Frederic's enthusiasm for poetry seems to have been minimal (except when he could use it to score points in an argument), he was a keen theatergoer, an enthusiasm that was developed more fully when he moved to London. Utica had what Paul Haines calls "a respectable and emininent culture" though it was necessarily limited. Traveling troupes brought *Camille, The Rivals,* and *The Lady of Lyons* (with Mary Anderson) to the Mechanics' Hall from September to May. Such productions regularly visited small towns and cities, and Frederic reviewed such productions for the *Utica Daily Observer.*[16] He learned to recognize the particular tastes of Uticans. In a letter to the theatrical impresario Augustin Daly, he wrote that "I know a Utica audience thoroughly, and have felt its pulse for years" (Frederic to Augustin Daly, 1878, Frederic Misc. 1977, 10).[17] Traveling lecturers often stopped off in Utica: Oscar Wilde lectured on "The English Renaissance" at the City Opera House in 1882 (Ellmann 1987, 178 and 183).[18] Middle-class Uticans listened to lectures on "The Dignity of Labor" and "What Poetry Owes to a Belief in a Future Life." The apothecary's shingle boasted a quotation from *Romeo and Juliet.*

15. The poem is to be sung to the tune of "The West's Awake." Later in the novel, before he is roundly told to keep quiet, the irrepressible O'Daly reads three lines of his latest piece, "Hark to thim joyous sounds that rise—/Making the face of Muirisc to be glad! / 'Tis the devil's job to believe one's eye—" (Frederic Novels 1892, 327.)

16. In *My Ántonia,* Willa Cather (a theater reviewer for some years) writes a brilliantly comic and perceptive account of Jim Burden and Lena Lingard's reactions to *Camille* (Cather 1984, 271–78). The actress, Clara Morris, had been one of the leading ladies of the theater impresario Augustin Daly. See also Cather's review on *Camille* and Clara Morris in the *Journal,* of 25 March 1894 (Cather 1970, 1: 42–49). Frederic would later negotiate with Augustin Daly regarding a production of *Seth's Brother's Wife.*

17. See also Frederic's letter to Genevieve Ward, 19 February 1879, 10–11 of the same work. He predicts failure for *The School for Scandal* because the public is unfamiliar with it. To the performer Genevieve Ward he criticizes a Utica audience that is "not accustomed to make distinctions between plays and players, or to distinguish with any degree of nicety artifice from art." See also *The Damnation of Theron Ware,* in which Sister Soulsby lectures Theron on the difference between appearance and reality: "Did you ever see a play?—in a theatre, I mean. I supposed not. But you'll understand when I say that the performance looks one way from where the audience sit, and quite a different way when you are behind the scenes. *There* you see that the trees and houses are cloth, and the moon is tissue paper, and the flying fairy is a middle-aged woman strung up on a rope" (Frederic Novels 1986, 171).

18. It is very likely that Frederic saw him there.

Although Frederic had access to live drama in his early years, it was less available than novels and short fiction. It was inevitable that his first sustained attempts at creative writing should take the form of fiction writing. His first published pieces of fiction were short stories, yet in the course of his wide-ranging writing career he also aspired to be a dramatist. He tried to arrange productions of *Seth's Brother's Wife,* for which he completed a script, and also *The Damnation of Theron Ware,* planned several new plays, and completed one. This is a play about mesmerism, the theme of George Du Maurier's best-selling novel, *Trilby* (1894), which also had a fantastic stage success. It is based, Frederic claimed, upon a true story, but it was never produced. Frederic had a brief career as an actor. While a schoolboy in Utica he participated in a play entitled *Fing Wing Coming Man.* Later, in London, he acted in a copyright production of J. M. Barrie's *Little Minister* (1891) Richard Harding Davis, who was also in the play, wrote a letter home describing the production, exclaiming, "At one time there were five men on stage all talking Scotch dialects and imitating Irving at the same time. It was a truly remarkable performance" (Birkin 1979, 44).[19] Frederic, like so many American writers at this time (including Bret Harte, Howells, James, Joaquin Miller, and Twain), was keen to be a dramatist as well as a novelist. The desire was partly financially motivated (Twain claimed to have made seventy thousand dollars out of the dramatization of *The Gilded Age*) and partly motivated by the hope to participate in the creation of a national drama—Twain hoped to make the character of Sellers into "permanently . . . *the* American character, to be used by generations of authors and actors" (Felheim 1956, 300).[20]

Frederic always enjoyed telling stories himself and knew that he was good at it, so it was unsurprising that his earliest short stories were predominantly first person narratives. "The Blakeleys of Poplar Place" is narrated by an old Dutch woman in the style of his grandmother and also in the style of a theatrical monologue. He worked out dramas and conflicts in these early writings that are scattered through newspapers and magazines of the 1870s and 1880s, from which they have never been reprinted. When he began the elaborate formal preparation for his novels, his mind went back to the early stories, and he took up the themes of several of them and explored them more fully. "The Two Rochards" and "The Blakeleys of Poplar Place" are models for *In The Valley.* "Cordelia and the Moon" is

19. See "Frederic as a Bit Player in *The Little Minister*" 1969. The performance was at the Haymarket Theatre on 13 July 1897 at 10:30, admission five guineas. Frederic was one of the men on stage—"imitating Irving"—whom he knew from the Savage Club. A character in *March Hares* has an absurd and stagy Scottish accent, and in notes for a planned play about a boisterous adventurer, *Strathbogie,* he writes that Strathbogie himself "affects Scotch dialect when drunk . . . very badly" (Harold Frederic Papers).

20. For an account of James' ambitions for *The American* see James 1987, 52–3.

close to *The Damnation of Theron Ware*. He would continue to write and plan short stories throughout his life, even setting himself up as an expert among experts in a magazine seminar called "How to Write a Short Story" (Frederic et al. Misc. 1897a, 42–46).

Staking a Claim

In his "Preface to a Uniform Edition" Frederic writes that no map exists, even in his own mind, of the fictionalized landscape of New York State that was the subject of so much of his writing. This absence is a curious one. Frederic's intensive research included drawing maps and plans of battle-fields that feature in his stories, in one sense, only indirectly. If he mapped out peripherals with such care, it seems strange that he should leave his own chosen terrain uncharted. The reader who expects the cartography of, say, Thomas Hardy, with its carefully planned juxtaposition of the real and the imagined, will be disappointed. Frederic's fictionalized version of New York State remained uncharted—much like his work, which is still largely unexplored and unmapped. His fiction celebrates the landscape of his childhood, writing a landscape of the memory in the space he made for himself by leaving New York State. Although his writing is partially a celebration, it is also ironic, often fiercely critical, and can be pastiche. The geographical area of Frederic's fictional world is huge, stretching from New York State eastward to Europe. The themes and historical range of that world are equally broad, ranging from a play he once planned set in early Christian England to a novel dealing with a corrupt capitalist at the end of the nineteenth century.[21] His fictional writing is often set in a period of social, political, or economic upheaval—the American Revolution or Civil War, the postwar years of the Gilded Age, late-Victorian England with its collapsing empire. These historical moments are the landmarks on the map of Frederic's fiction. The troubles of these changing times are re-flected in the psyches of his protagonists, forced to stand at the crossroads of desire and possibility, fantasy and reality.

The main body of Frederic's fiction falls into three broad groups, which can be classified according to locale and chronology. Such a classification is useful, though reductive. Its utility is in its placing of emphasis on the unity of what otherwise might seem an erratic and diverse oeuvre. Yet its reductiveness is in its apparent denial that what is interesting about Frederic's writing is that it ranges so broadly and responds so closely, even oppor-tunistically, to the demands of the market. Such a classification is

21. There are several references to this planned play in his *Correspondence*. See, for exam-ple, his letter to Henry Irving, 6 July 1895 (Frederic Misc. 1977, 399–400). Details of it can also be found in the Harold Frederic Papers.

convenient, then but little more. The "American" writings consist of four novels and a group of Civil War stories, all published between 1887 and 1896: *Seth's Brother's Wife* (1887), *In the Valley* (1890), *The Lawton Girl* (1890), and *The Damnation of Theron Ware* (1896). They are all set in the fictionalized landscape of his native New York State, his birthplace and the home to which he intended to return. An interim, outwardly comic phase, forms the second group, which consists of the "Irish" novel *The Return of The O'Mahony* (1892), and the "English" novel *March Hares* (1896). These form a transition from the earlier writing to the more somber tone of the final, late novels, the two other "English" novels *Gloria Mundi* (1898) and *The Market-Place* (1899).

The pattern of Frederic's writing, with its movement from the United States to England, mirrors that of Frederic's own life. His later writing shows a distinct shift from the landscape of New York State to that of Europe. He gradually became distanced from the life and people of his birthplace, and whereas his early writing draws upon the resources offered to him by New York State, his later writing is less obviously "American." Frederic moved away from the local color realism at which he excelled, instead using European settings—Ireland and England—and placing, at the center of his novels, a protagonist who is either an outsider, like Christian Tower, or an outsider and a fake—an impostor like The O'Mahony, or a crooked capitalist like Joel Thorpe.[22] An increasingly pessimistic outlook accompanied this shift, and the neat resolutions of his early novels are a striking contrast to the ambivalent endings of *The Damnation of Theron Ware, Gloria Mundi,* and *The Market-Place.*

In January 1887, two and a half years after Frederic moved to London, two literary premieres coincided: Frederic's first novel, a realist piece called *Seth's Brother's Wife,* began its serial run in the first issue of *Scribner's Magazine.* In an age in which magazines proliferated, this publication was destined to have great success. It would enjoy a long and distinguished career as a quality monthly, combining fiction, poetry, miscellaneous articles, and illustrations. Contributing to the first issue was a distinguished start to any novelist's career: future contributors would include Stephen Crane, Richard Harding Davis, Joel Chandler Harris, W. D. Howells, Sarah Orne Jewett, Rudyard Kipling, Octave Thanet, and Edith Wharton. The magazine was an offshoot of the publishing house of Charles Scribner's Sons. Its editor, Edward Burlingame, maintained close links between the magazine and the main publishers. Burlingame and Frederic began a long business association that was polite but never intimate. Charles Scribner's Sons became Frederic's main American publishers, but only "The Copper-

---

22. Even Theron aspires to be a "good fraud," and David Mosscrop describes himself as a confidence man.

head" and *In the Valley* were published in the magazine, in addition to *Seth's Brother's Wife.*

Burlingame had been educated at Harvard and Heidelberg and was respected as an able and astute publisher with exacting literary standards. He was anxious to create a strong base from which the magazine could compete with the three established "qualities"—the *Atlantic Monthly*, the *Century*, and *Harper's New Monthly Magazine.* The new venture would combine the topical with the literary, with literature as its main emphasis. Burlingame called his "formula" a combination of "intrinsic interest" and "pure literary work," and this combination was reflected in the magazine's content. William James published in it, and Jacob Riis's exposé "How the Other Half Lives" was an early success and was followed by a number of articles on the theme of urban poverty and unemployment. The "outstanding contributor" in the early part of the twentieth century was Theodore Roosevelt. (Mott 1957: 717–32).

When Joseph Kirkland and Henry Cuyler Bunner (both born in New York State) praised *Seth's Brother's Wife* as it appeared serially, Frederic became impatient for book publication.[23] The magazine provided him with a significant audience. It had a much publicized initial distribution of a hundred thousand (though it took two years before its circulation regularly reached this number). Yet Frederic was anxious to find a reading public of his own—to test himself against other writers and to compete within a wider market. The novel was published in book form in New York and London in autumn 1887, but it was not a success, falling "dead on the market in both places" (Frederic 1977, 156). Frustrated by the evaporation of his hopes, he wrote a short story, "The Editor and the School Ma'am," a dramatized defense of Howellsian realism that draws directly upon Howells's notorious and misconstrued "smiling aspects" article of September 1886.[24] Between 1886 and 1892 Howells's "The Editor's Study" appeared regularly in *Harper's Monthly*, introducing the serious American reading public to a range of European writers who included Tolstoy (a literary discovery that came to Howells with the impact of a religious revelation), Dostoyevsky, Gogol, Valdés, Valera, and Zola. Howells's championing of American writers was personally generous as well as critically astute. He wrote enthusiastic early criticism of many American writers and in September 1886 wrote a pioneering piece of criticism on *Crime and Punishment* (1866). Dostoyevsky's achievement is, he argues, impressive—but the novel is a specifically Russian piece of writing. A tragedy of that order would be inappropriate to the United States: "whoever struck a note so

23. For Frederic's reaction to their comments, see Frederic to Edward Burlingame, 15 April 1887, Frederic Misc. 1977, 169.

24. For a defense of Howells's often misunderstood position see Howells 1973, 89–90.

profoundly tragic in American fiction would do a false and mistaken thing." American writers should not attempt to reproduce works that are essentially a "natural expression of such a life [Dostoyevsky's] and such conditions." Instead, they should capture the idiosyncratically American rhythms of American life, concentrating upon "the more smiling aspects of life which are the more American" (Howells 1973, 89–96).

Howells's own novels provide a critical blueprint for his argument—he delighted in being a mentor. The moral dilemmas of his novels are less about whether characters should commit (or confess to) murder, but rather whether they have committed unwise or morally unjust acts of a lesser variety. In *The Minister's Charge* (1886), the minister David Sewell struggles with the consequences of his uncritical advice to a young writer, Lemuel Barker, and in *The Rise of Silas Lapham,* Lapham is caught in an ethical dilemma between the conflicting demands of business and conscience.

Stung by the failure of his first novel, Frederic used "The Editor and the School-Ma'am" to give vent to his frustrated hopes and vindicate his writing. He incorporates Howells's argument into the story, which becomes an indirect, off-hand manifesto. The story's genesis is in Frederic's early days as editor of the *Albany Evening Journal.* As a young editor and aspiring novelist he had rejected an essay submitted by a woman reader, writing to recommend Russian realism to the hapless aspirant. Frederic fictionalizes this in an encounter between a youthful newspaper editor and a school-teacher. Alexander Waring writes to Agnes Corbett brusquely dismissing her worthily titled essay, "The True Place of Milton Among English Poets," and advising her to give up Milton in favour of Dostoyevsky, Tolstoy, and Gogol. (Waring's antipathy toward Milton is reminiscent of Frederic's own struggles with the poet.) Waring's most particular piece of advice is to study *Crime and Punishment:* "Then, with your eyes newly opened, observe the people close about you. Study the butcher, the baker, the candlestickmaker. . . . [W]rite me articles about these people—what they think, say, do, and leave undone" (Frederic Short. 1888, 14).[25]

The story is both a comic portrayal of his youthful pretensions and an avowed enlistment onto Howells's side in the "realism war." In 1897 Frederic called himself "a Howells man to the end of the war" (Frederic to Hamlin Garland, 12 May 1897, Frederic Misc. 1977, 455). Part of the comedy of the story is in Waring's unrelenting sentimentality. He pictures the young school-ma'am struggling through great snowdrifts from an isolated schoolhouse to collect her mail. Later she will explain that the

25. His imitation of Howells takes into account an article written some years after he had left the *Albany Evening Journal.* See also Frederic to Edward L. Burlingame, 7 March 1888, Frederic Misc. 1977, 205.

butcher delivers the post in harsh weather. With splendidly bathetic effect she describes the difference between Dostoyevsky's characters and her own butcher: "[N]ow, you must know, our butcher isn't the least bit like that. He is the mildest little old man your [sic] ever saw, and he goes about three days in the week in a wagon and rings a bell, and the farmers' wives come out and look inside the green and yellow box at the back and buy whatever they want—or rather, whatever he has got. You see, I couldn't imagine him getting hungry—like the poor stick of a young man in the novel—because he has all that meat in his wagon. And even if he were hungry—very, very hungry—he would never dream of killing even the oldest and most harmless of all the farmers' wives. He would go and kill what he calls a 'beef critter' or something—instead." Waring eventually accepts her witty send-up of his pretensions, but Frederic could never reconcile himself to Milton.

The American Fiction: "My Little Part of the North"

Frederic's first three novels are best read as a triptych: separate, though strategically connected. Frederic describes *The Lawton Girl* as being "a kind of sequel" to *Seth's Brother's Wife*.[26] Taken collectively, the three constitute an inquiry into the social, economic, and political life of upstate New York (hence America itself) from Revolutionary times until the last decade of the nineteenth century. *In the Valley* centers on the birth of the young republic, and *Seth's Brother's Wife* and *The Lawton Girl* look at what has happened to the nation, examining the political health of the democracy and the prospects of a country that has lost its direction through its intoxication with industrial capitalism. *The Damnation of Theron Ware* complements the three earlier novels, though it goes well beyond them, too.

Frederic constructs a thinly veiled set of names and references to reinvent the fictionalized landscape of his childhood and early adult life. These are used throughout the "American" fiction, creating what he calls an "indefinite milieu" of the real and the imagined (Frederic to W.B. Wemple [?], 21 April 1895, Frederic Misc. 1977, 394). Frederic's birthplace, Utica, was formally named only in 1798, so the act of naming was still part of the relatively recent history of the region—Frederic was simply continuing "the quaint operation of the accident which sprinkled our section, as it were, with the contents of a classical pepper-box."

The Lawton Girl is set in Thessaly, a small American manufacturing town close to the Fairchild farm in *Seth's Brother's Wife*. Tecumseh, Tyre, and Octavius are all real names though applied to invented places, although

---

26. All quotations, unless otherwise stated, are from Frederic Misc. 1977, 1–6, "Preface to a Uniform Edition."

they have their origins in places that Frederic knew well. Their significance extends beyond their resemblance to a topology that Frederic wanted to recreate: they suggest a landscape that he thought of as characteristically American. The device is familiar: Richard Russo uses it in his recent novel *Mohawk* (1986), in which the upstate New York town of Mohawk both denotes a generic small town and acts as a specific reference. Octavius, the setting for *The Damnation of Theron Ware* is more or less an anagram of Utica. The other names could easily be real places close to Utica. These are still today an eclectic collection of Native American, European, and classical names—Sauquoit; Florence; Pompey. Slightly further from Utica, Liberty is ominously close to Lookout—the early settlers recognized the fragility of freedom. Frederic's invented names allowed him to create a recognizable but appropriated landscape that became a fictional trademark. He indulged in an affectionate joke with upstaters who could recognize "real" landscapes and people, linking himself with his readers in an esoteric and intimate relationship that drew them together. In England he re-created his New York State birthplace, writing novels using its familiar landscape and naming his Surbiton home "Oneida Lodge." Confused London tradesmen called it "One-Eyed" Lodge (Rideing 1909, 398).[27] In the *Harold Frederic Papers* in the Library of Congress there is a long list, which Frederic compiled from memory, of names familiar to him from his childhood. He put a cross by those he used in his fiction. This was a premeditated action, strategic—not accidental.[28]

The novels are not simply linked by naming but also by the device of characters who appear in more than one work, giving the effect of reality and continuity. Jessica Lawton of *The Lawton Girl* is mentioned obliquely in *Seth's Brother's Wife*, as is Reuben Tracy, the ambiguous protagonist of *The Lawton Girl*. Frederic often used a single character in more than one novel. The hard-drinking Sylvanus Boyce figures as a younger man, General Boyce, in the Civil War stories. Some years after his appearance in *Seth's Brother's Wife* the political "boss" Abe Beekman would lend money to the impecunious Alice and Theron Ware. Celia Madden, the femme fatale

27. One of Frederic's publishers anticipated similar pronunciation problems with "Douw Mauverensen"—Frederic's preferred title for *In the Valley*—which he thought would cause "difficulties in pronunciation . . . to the average man in other parts of the country" (Edward L. Burlingame to Frederic, 5 January 1888, Frederic Misc. 1977, 202–3). See Burlingame 1946, 98–99: "Dear to the heart of Harold Frederic was the title *Douw Mauverensen* for his second novel. When the Scribners saw it on his fine manuscript they shuddered in unison. The very stenographers and office boys shuddered. Possibly in sections of upstate New York, which were the setting of Frederic's story, the name would be pronounceable. But in the Deep South, the Middle West, Philadelphia or even Boston tongues would twist over it until they gave up. 'Give me that book beginning with a D by the man who writes for *Scribner's Magazine.*' It was not easy, however, to divert the author."

28. A glance at the Forest Hill Cemetery records in Utica or at the City Directories for the 1850s to 1860s reveals that many of these names had Utica counterparts.

of *The Damnation of Theron Ware*, reappears in Frederic's last novel, *The Market-Place*, in a chastened form.[29] These details suggest Frederic's identification with the fictional landscapes that he creates and peoples. *In the Valley* is set in the landscape of his ancestors, the Civil War stories in the landscape of his childhood, and the three contemporary American novels in that of his young adulthood. He conjured up his own terrain, carefully staking out and claiming his territory with fictional names—like one of the early pioneers.[30] He peopled this fictional terrain with characters whose dialects, interests, and beliefs were entirely familiar to him and, to some extent at least, were shared. He evokes a convincing and detailed picture of upstate New York with the degree of intimacy and knowledge that a number of writers bring to the regions they chronicled with care: Sherwood Anderson to *Winesburg Ohio* (1919); William Faulkner to his evocation of Yoknapatawpha County; Hamlin Garland to *Main-Traveled Roads;* and Sarah Orne Jewett to *The Country of the Pointed Firs* (1896). Frederic's tone is not elegiac, nor is it usually nostalgic. His writing is closer to that of pessimistic realism than it is to the epic quality of some American writing, yet it shares something of both.

Seth's Brother's Wife *(1887)*

In his "Preface to a Uniform Edition" Frederic gives an interesting account of how he came to write his first novel. He had spent about eight years and made as many attempts to write a historical novel set in the American Revolution. Frustrated by failure, he decided temporarily to abandon the attempt and write an "apprentice piece." This would teach him how to write a novel and prepare him for the great historical work that was evading him. He was inspired by the enviable ease with which his friend T. P. O'Connor had written his autobiographical novel, *Dead Man's Island,* which had appeared serially in the *Weekly Echo.*

"T. P." was often considered the model of a successful journalist by

29. "I had my own way in my teens—my own money, my own power—of course only of a certain sort, and in a very small place. But I know what I did with that power. I spread trouble and misery about me—always, of course, on a small scale. Then a group of things happened in a kind of climax—a very painful climax—and it shook the nonsense out of me. My brother and my father died—some other sobering things happened . . . and luckily I was still young enough to stop short, and take stock of myself, and say that there were certain paths I would never set foot on again, and stick to it" (*Frederic Novels* 1899, 241).

30. Twain would do something similar, though in an idiosyncratically satirical way, when Colonel Sellers, of *The Gilded Age,* maps out and names the towns on his imaginary railroad on the table—St. Louis; Slouchberg; Doodleville; Brimstone; Belshazzar; Catfish; Babylon; Bloody Run; Hail Columbia; Hark-from-the-Tomb; Hawkeye; Stone's Landing; Napoleon; Hallelujah; and Corruptionville (Twain and Warner 1967, 178–79). In *The American Claimant* Sellers plans to create a vast city in Siberia called "Libertyorloffskoizalinski" and a capital city called "Freedomolovnaivanovich" (Twain 1892, 11).

his peers.[31] He treated his deadlines as challenges, only beginning each installment on the day it was due at the printers. Unimpressed by the perilous closeness of the deadline, he would march up and down dictating the story in a loud voice to drown the sound of his secretary's typewriter. Frederic's reaction to this straightforward and businesslike approach to writing is candid. He was jointly inspired by T. P.'s enviable fluency and his capacity for exacting payment from publishers. He wanted to learn both the art of fiction and the business of writing, and T. P.'s example was more likely to teach him the latter. Financial inducement fired Frederic's imagination. He loved to tell autobiographical stories—here was an opportunity to be paid for it. T. P. received just over three times Frederic's monthly salary for *Dead Man's Island*.[32] Frederic writes that he rushed off to begin his own attempt at once. He soon found out that it was not so simple after all. He took the first chapter of this "story" to Aaron Watson, the editor of the *Weekly Echo*, who said that it was "too American" for the English papers.[33] Frederic's initial depression gave way to what he called a "helpful reaction," as he writes "I realized that I had consumed nearly ten years in fruitless mooning over my Revolutionary novel, and was no nearer achievment [sic] than at the outset, simply because I did not know how to make a book of any kind, let alone a historical book of the kind which should be the most difficult and exacting of all. This determined me to proceed with the contemporary story I had begun—if only to learn what it was really like to cover a whole canvas." This combines an image of the book as artifact with that of it as art, yet it is not self-conscious in this respect. He worked steadily at his "canvas" for two years, producing a lengthy novel that revolves around the main experiences of his life until that time. Its protagonist is an aspiring young journalist who gets involved in a gubernatorial election. Writing to Daniel Lamont, then Grover Cleveland's presidential secretary, on 24 April 1886, Frederic tells him, "The story is laid in rural Central New York, and deals with farm-life, politics and newspaper work in a provincial city. The action lies in the campaign of 1882 [Cleveland's gubernatorial election]. . . . Its political side will particularly interest you—and, I hope, thousands of others. The words Republican and Democrat are never mentioned; the whole thing is between the good and bad in politics. There are some suggestions of portraiture in it, too, which you will enjoy" (Frederic Misc. 1977, 115–16.)

31. For a biography of T. P. O'Connor, see Fyfe 1934

32. Although he writes that "Certainly its completion, and perhaps still more the praise which was given to it by those who first saw it, gave me a degree of confidence that I had mastered the art of fiction which I now look back on with surprise—and not a little envy."

33. All quotations, unless otherwise stated, are from the "Preface to a Uniform Edition." Also see Frederic to Aaron Watson, 12 December 1887, Frederic Misc. 1977, 197–98.

The novel participates in a tradition of political writing. In the years before the publication of *Seth's Brother's Wife*, three political novels had received a good deal of attention. Henry Adams's sophisticated political satire, *Democracy* (1879), had delighted and scandalized Washington society when it appeared anonymously. Its polished and accomplished display of wit and inside knowledge thrilled and anguished politicians in equal measure. John Hay's antilabor novel *The Bread-Winners* (published anonymously in 1883), and John Keenan's antithetical "reply," *The Money-Makers* (1884) (in which he casts Hay himself as the corrupt Archibald Hilliard), had also prepared the way for both *Seth's Brother's Wife* and *The Lawton Girl*, although they are more overtly polemical than Frederic's novels.[34] Like Frederic, Keenan never mentions the names Democrat and Republican, though his Ultrocats and Optimates are recognizable. All three political novels indulge in portraiture, though Frederic claimed (despite what he had told Lamont) that with regard to the journalistic portion of the novel he "did not aim at portraiture, or keep any particular office in mind" (Frederic to editor, *Boston Herald*, 23 August 1893, Frederic Misc. 1977, 346).[35] He seems to have had at least one other political novel in mind when he wrote *Seth's Brother's Wife*. This was F. Marion Crawford's popular novel *An American Politician* (1885), which Albert Fairchild attacks for its portrayal of a tea-drinking reformer. (Frederic Novels 1968, 223). Frederic's pen-portraits of well-known politicians are not satirical to any great degree. They operate more like his fictionalized "real" landscapes, defamiliarized yet recognizable. For instance, Richard Ansdell, the highly principled politician and bachelor playboy, was probably based upon a combination of Grover Cleveland and the Democratic politician Edgar Apgar.[36]

Politics are at the center of the novel—as they were in Frederic's life—but they are never fully integrated within the novel. *Seth's Brother's Wife* reflects the jubilation Frederic felt as he was writing the novel, the relief and pleasure he was given by Grover Cleveland's election to the presidency.

34. In 1887 Frederic compared the reception of *Seth's Brother's Wife* with that of *The Bread-Winners*. (Frederic to Charles Scribner, 13 December 1887, Frederic Misc. 1977, 200). Later he would meet Hay when he came to London.

35. In *Democracy* Senator James G. Blaine was ruthlessly satirized as Senator Silas P. Ratcliffe. The mercilessness of the satire had infuriated him so much that he publicly cut Clarence King, who he believed had written the novel. Keenan was also clever, though crude, in this respect: two rich speculators, Risk and Fould, are clearly Fisk and Gould; Amasa Stone, John Hay's father-in-law, becomes Aaron Grimstone, the ruthless, self-made businessman.

36. Richard Ansdell combines a zealousness towards public duty with a relaxed and generous personal moral code. "There was much more both in his theories and his practice which would not commend itself to the moral statutes of the age; he attempted no defense, being incredulous as to the right of criticism upon personal predilections But he had a flaming wrath, a consuming, intolerant contempt, for men who were unable to distinguish between private tastes and public duty" (*Frederic Novels* 1968, 35).

A sense of this emotion is given by an extraordinarily idealistic congratulatory letter that he wrote to Cleveland on 8 November 1884:

> So long had I seen and hated these modern tendencies in our people; so trivial and selfish and unworthy had seemed to me the aims and ends for which Americans worked, the gods before which they did fetish worship, and the political harangues by which they justified themselves, that I may be said to have grown up with more indignation at, than pride in, my country and my countrymen. In my little way, I tried to do what I could to set things right —and you know how I was broken on the wheel for it. But, as in a burst of sunlight, the pride of country, of race, yes, of State, comes to me now, and I am almost intoxicated by its radiance and power. It is true, after all, that nobody who through the years behind us has worked for the right has wrought in vain. It is true that in the end corruption wins not more than honesty, that there is a public conscience—that all the greed and scoundrelism and prejudice and folly of our political, race and business sides, massed into one grand desperate effort for control, were not able to stand before the simple weight of an honest man and an upright cause. (Frederic Misc. 1977, 36–37.)

He concludes his letter "there is not a fibre in heart or brain which does not have its place in the congratulations I send you." It was in this mood of jubilation and relief that Frederic began his first novel, a piece that would culminate in the election of an independent reformer to Congress —a retrospective campaign biography.

In this novel Frederic's writing has a documentary quality. His texts are punctuated by public events—political conventions, Methodist fundraisings, funerals. He excels at mordant details of country life. Peripheral characters are better observed than the protagonists, for his caricaturing works best in brief moments, and he is good at describing kitchen gossip or the mundanities of newspaper or political life. He is also excellent at vignettes of rural life. The funeral at the start of the novel has a grim, comic realism that is as brilliant and well observed in its way as Hamlin Garland's or Flannery O'Connor's depictions of farm life.

At the start of the chapter Frederic remarks that the "grim, fatalist habit of seizing upon the grotesque side, which a century of farm life has crystallized into what the world knows as American humor, is not wanting even in this hour" (Frederic Novels 1968, 35). He portrays characters both as grotesque and as "grotesques," as Sherwood Anderson does, and uses dialect to capture the idiosyncratic voices of country people.[37] Certainly the humor of this chapter has its grotesque moments. Nosy neighboring

---

37. See Howells 1973, 231–42, on dialect in literature. Frederic's reliance on phonetic rendering of regional accents is, unfortunately, often clumsy.

women test the quality of the carpet at the Fairchild farm with their feet, and check to see if furniture has been revarnished or when the ceiling was last whitewashed, and guess at the value of the curtains and melodeon. Sitting close to the coffin in which Cicely Fairchild lies—"the embodiment of the eternal silence" and raison d'être of the gathering—they gossip about mortgages and marriages, financial and physical declines (42). The undertaker slips in and out of roles, one moment a dictator, the next affably drinking cider and gossiping, his black clothes rusty-hued with age. The Baptist minister goads his Episcopalian counterpart over the midday meal (while the Episcopalian grapples miserably with the unaccustomed fork or "split spoon") and monopolizes the funeral service leaving the Episcopal clergyman at the mercy (or mercilessness) of the locals. They ask him, "What air you here fer, mister, if you ain't goin' to say or dew nothin'?" His miserable reply ("I officiate at the grave") no doubt convinces no one (44).[38] The writing is ironic, often wry, and observant. He is often excellent at the immediacies of description, at dialogue, or at details of behavior or character.

Frederic hoped to dramatize the novel and worked on a collaboration, first with Maurice Barrymore, and then with Brandon Thomas. The American theatrical manager Augustin Daly (whose policy was to produce new American plays in order to encourage a national drama) bought and cast the play, but it was never produced. Among the suggestions that Frederic made to Daly was that the following hymn should be sung, for it especially reflects "the tone of farm-life" in the play: "O where shall rest be found, / Rest for the weary soul? / 'T were vain the ocean-depths to sound, / Or pierce to either pole; The world can never give / The bliss for which we sigh; / 'T is not the whole of life to live; / Nor all of death to die" (Frederic to Augustin Daly, 27 January 1891, Frederic Misc. 1977, 273–76). The mournful lines best reflect what is most vivid about the novel, not its political polemic, but its rural realism, the unrelenting picture of farm life that was praised by Hamlin Garland and W. D. Howells.

In the Valley (*1890*)

In 1897 Frederic wrote that in one sense he was always preparing for what would eventually become *In the Valley:* it seemed "in retrospect to have been always in my mind."[39] At its most explicit this preparation took the

---

38. This is clearly a joke—compare *The Damnation of Theron Ware,* 242: "But I don't see," observed Theron, "granting that all this is true, how you think the Catholic Church will come out on top. I could understand it of Unitarianism, or Universalism, or the Episcopal Church, where nobody seems to have to believe in anything except the beauty of its burial service."

39. All quotations, unless otherwise stated, are from Frederic Misc. 1977, 1–6, "Preface to a Uniform Edition."

form of planning, note taking, and interviewing informants about their family histories.[40] Yet this was only the final stage of a less formal rehearsal involving both a self-conscious journalistic saturation in the daily detail of life in the Mohawk Valley and his grandmother's evocation of the past. Lucretia Ramsdell's stories, gripping yet factually based versions of her own and the valley's history, mediated between the past and the present. To her grandson she embodied a historical moment. Distinctions between a distant, learned history and personal family narratives vanished. Frederic wrote that "by a single remove I came myself into contact with the men who held Tryon County against the King, and my boyish head was full of them."

Her stories were of "local heroes"—the unsung performers of deeds whom few knew of or cared about. But Frederic cared passionately, and before the age of twelve he had written "several short but lurid introductions" to a "narrative" centering on the Battle of Oriskany. His boyish imagination dwelled upon the gory aspects of the Revolutionary War, though *In the Valley*, like his other war writing, would concentrate rather upon the effects that violent upheaval has on local communities. As a boy (whose early reading included a history of George III) he was inspired by the prospect of the Valley people holding out against the British army. *In the Valley* is essentially a story of a successful rebellion, and Frederic could not resist paralleling one clash with authority with another. He claimed to have been expelled from school after being caught writing one of these early "narratives" and refusing to give the manuscript to his teacher. Actually he completed his studies and left school at the age of fifteen like most young Uticans of his generation. But the drama of revolt shines through this characteristic fiction even when the truth of it is undermined. Frederic knew what it was to want to be a "local hero," whatever sort of "fiction" he was writing. He continued to work through the details of the novel and seems to have had it in his head years before he began to write it. His friend Charles Sherlock recalls being told the story of the book on a fishing trip in terms that seem clichéd: "I remember, almost as if it were yesterday, the rainy afternoon when, in the shelter of an old oak tree on the banks of the Mohawk, I sat with my back against its trunk and heard Harold Frederic tell the absorbing story of *In the Valley*. . . . This was in the early summer of 1883. . . . The sport in the shallows of the river had been none too good, so that the wretched weather came as a sort of blessing in disguise as Frederic became more and more absorbed in the romance which he was unfolding" (Haines 1945, 98).

40. Frederic referred to "the immense amount of material in the shape of notes, cross-references, dates, maps, biographical facts and the like which I had perforce to drag along with me."

When Frederic began planning his novel he was indignant that New England historians had, as he felt, written out New Yorkers from histories of the Revolution and so denied them their proper place in the history of the formation of the United States. This was a long-standing New York complaint, to which Frederic, through the mouthpiece of his narrator Douw Mauverenson, added an acerbic reflection: "[W]e of New York have chosen to make money, and to allow our neighbors to make histories" (Frederic Novels 1890a, 419). By choosing a financial destination, New York, he believed, had turned its back upon its past. He would debate throughout his writing the terms in which worth can be quantified, most strikingly in Theron Ware's conflict between being a "good fraud" and a godly minister, but most explicitly in the social debate of his penultimate novel, whose title draws from a phrase offering a précis of the conflict—*sic transit Gloria Mundi.*

Frederic's interest in the valley's past was cemented by a speech given by his earliest and best-loved hero, Horatio Seymour. In 1877 Frederic had become a charter member of the newly formed Oneida Historical Society and was soon involved in planning the Oriskany Centennial celebrations that were held on 6 August 1877. He even dramatized this "membership" by pretending later that although he helped form the society, he did not have the money to join it. Seymour addressed the huge crowd that had assembled, calling upon New Yorkers to investigate their own history and make New York State's significance in the history of the United States public: "Historians have done much, and well . . . in making up the records of the past. But their recitals have not yet become, as they should be, a part of the general intelligence of our people. . . . There is a dimness in the popular version . . . about this great centre, source and theatre of events which have shaped the civilization, usages, and government of this continent. This is not only a wrong to our State but to our Union" (O'Donnell and Franchere 1961, 40).

Frederic listened to the speech and reported on the celebration for the *Utica Daily Observer.* He would dedicate the novel to Seymour, acknowledging that he had given him the real inspiration for it. He began working on the novel in earnest at this stage, collecting anecdotes and information from old New York families whose ancestors had played significant parts in the war. This documentary, not to say journalistic, method of collecting material was characteristic of the way in which he prepared for his novels, and it was particularly appropriate for this one. Seymour's call for a public and personal education in the history of New York appealed to Frederic's sense of the way in which serious journalism should aim to educate and enlighten. The novel is explicitly polemical and was always Frederic's favorite of his works, partly for that reason. His lofty ambitions for it, and high opinion of it, are suggested by a letter to Grover Cleveland in which he says that he is so fond of its political message that he felt like working hard enough to give every young American male a free copy to read! (Frederic to Grover Cleveland, 13 November 1889, Frederic Misc. 1977, 243). The central event of the novel is the Battle of Oriskany. The novel enacts Frederic's thesis, not one widely shared by historians, that the battle marked the turning point in the war. (The battle was undoubtedly crucial, though not as much as Frederic believed.) Several stories and articles would find echoes in the completed work.[41] Although he worked intensively at the notes and maps he compiled, he remained naïve about the project. In 1886 he wrote to the American historian Moses Coit Tyler asking for advice on which books to read and enclosing a list headed "BOOKS THAT I KNOW OF." (Frederic to Moses Coit Taylor, 18 August 1886, Frederic Misc. 1977, 131). This unsophisticated candor is entirely characteristic. Despite two years of living in a great metropolis, and all his attempts to hide the fact, Frederic had a guilty secret—he was always something of an ingenue.

Like James Fenimore Cooper's *The Spy* (1821), which it resembles, Frederic's novel combines the political plot with a romance. Daisy Mauverensen's complex role is like that of Cooper's Frances Wharton. Cooper and Frederic both saw society's treatment of woman as an indicator of the civilization of that society. Cooper writes, "The good treatment of their women is the surest evidence that a people can give of their civilization; and there is no nation which has more to boast of, in this respect, than the Americans" (Cooper 1960, 399).[42]

Daisy Mauverensen embodies the tensions between the old order and the emerging one just like Marian Forrester in *A Lost Lady* (1923), or Lily Bart in *The House of Mirth* (1905), or Jessica Lawton in *The Lawton Girl*. Each of these women enact their difficult roles through sexual dramas. By failing to negotiate the slippery slope between propriety and pleasure, Marian, as the title of the novel insists, is "lost" (though perhaps only in the eyes of the novel's priggish narrator), and Jessica dies, though her last words (and the last words of the novel) are "I tell you I *have* lived it down!" (Frederic Novels 1890b, 346). She has—but to little avail, as inevitable death follows immediately, and implicitly. In contrast, Daisy is always a mediator. Her guardian, Thomas Stewart, names her Desideria (a compound of Greek and Latin) after the great Dutch humanist scholar Desiderius Erasmus, both to signify her Dutch ancestry and to indicate that she is loved above all others. She is both an object of desire and a proto-American. Stewart's other ward, Douw Mauverensen, swiftly shortens and

---

41. Two of these were "The Two Rochards," and "The Blakeleys of Poplar Place," and Frederic also produced an early, plagiarized piece called "The Mohawk Valley During the Revolution."

42. Another significant influence on the novel is quite clearly Walter Scott.

Americanizes her name to Daisy, the name of a common flower, which suggests her origins. She is a "flower plucked from the rapine and massacre of the Old War" (Frederic Novels 1890a, 75). The full name has an epic or classical quality that the shortened name deflates, suggesting that the epic might be familiar—vernacular.

Frederic thought of the Revolution as an idiosyncratically American epic, one not of classical heroic grandeur, but of the common people. The desire to produce an American epic was shared by both Frank Norris and Willa Cather writing of, respectively, California and Nebraska. In *The Octopus* (1901) the poet Presley wants to write an epic poem:

> It was his insatiable ambition to write verse. But up to this time, his work had been fugitive, ephemeral, a note here and there, heard, appreciated, and forgotten. He was in search of a subject; something magnificent, he did not know exactly what; some vast, tremendous theme, heroic, terrible, to be unrolled in all the thundering progression of hexameters.
>
> But whatever he wrote, and in whatever fashion, Presley was determined that his poem should be of the West, that world's frontier of Romance, where a new race, a new people—hardy, brave, and passionate—were building an empire; where the tumultuous life ran like fire from dawn to dark, and from dark to dawn again, primitive, brutal, honest and without fear. (Norris 1986, 9)

The desire of Norris/Presley to write an "Epic of Wheat" or a "Song of the West" is echoed by Willa Cather, whose hopes for her female epics of her native Nebraska are suggested by the conversation of the mysterious Gaston Cleric in My Ántonia: " '*Primus ego in patriam mecum . . . deducam Musas*'; 'for I shall be the first, if I live, to bring the Muse into my country.' " Cleric had explained to us that "patria" here meant, not a nation or even a province, but the little rural neighborhood on the Mincio where the poet was born. This was not a boast, but a hope, at once bold and devoutly humble, that he might bring the Muse (but lately come to Italy from her cloudy Grecian mountains), not to the capital, the *palatia Romana,* but to his own little "country"; to his father's fields, "sloping down to the river and to the old beech trees with broken tops" (Cather 1984, 264).

The subject of Frederic's epic is the moment at which a new nation was born (Desideria is found in the second chapter of the novel). Desideria functions both as mother and daughter: motherless, she becomes a mother for generations of other Americans. Her great-granddaughter is Kate Minster of *The Lawton Girl.* Her name echoes that of another American, Henry James's Daisy Miller. Daisy Miller is also from New York State: she is from Schenectady, a short distance from Daisy Mauverensen's home. Randolph Miller's comment on his sister could apply equally to Daisy Mauverensen —"She's an American girl" (James 1984, 157). On his lecture tour to the United States, Oscar Wilde found that she really was a recognizable type.

"He remarked in Louisville on 21 February [1882] that he had met a Daisy Miller, and 'the sight of her has increased my admiration for Henry James a thousand fold' " (Ellmann 1987, 171).

The steady corruption of America from an Eden state of nature to the rapacity of late-nineteenth-century America can be traced through the trope of flowering. From the innocence of Daisy Mauverensen, an American Eve, via the innocent poisonousness of Rappacini's daughter, to the dubious morality of Daisy Miller, there are a line of women figuratively deflowered by men. In 1887 Oscar Wilde called America the "Paradise of Women," though adding wryly that "This, however, is perhaps the reason why, like Eve, the women are always so anxious to get out of it" (Wilde 1982, 64). Several of Frederic's women try to return to a lost Eden. Edith Cressage of *Gloria Mundi* and *The Market-Place* retreats to the flowers in her conservatory after a disastrous marriage, and Alice Ware (in Frederic's novel of temptation and damnation), frustrated by her failing marriage, creates a wonderful garden only to have it destroyed by a sharp frost (to the pleasure of her husband, who has already had his reptilian credentials established by having a lizard named after him). Daisy is little more than an item of exchange (a highly desirable one, as her full name suggests), a token of the changing society that produces her. She plays a complex part in the affections of four men who represent the dominant forces contending against each other for the future of America. The men, an Anglo-Irish soldier, Anthony Cross; his old comrade-in-arms Thomas Lynch (alias Thomas Stewart); Cross's son Philip; and Stewart's ward, Douw Mauverensen, respond to Daisy in ways that indicate their attitude to America itself. Stewart and Anthony Cross suggest an idealized version of the relationship between England and America before the war: courtly and comradely. Cross's son, Philip, and Stewart's other ward, Douw Mauverensen, represent the new relationship between the two countries: hostile, jealous, and competitive.

In the Valley aspires to be more than a historical documentation of New York State's role in the Revolution or an account of the changing relationship between England and America. Frederic's research took account of minute details of every aspect of life in the Mohawk Valley—language, religion, ritual, clothing, fauna, wildlife, fur trading, furniture. In its exactitude it offers itself as a cultural index to the changing desires of American society. He considered the work required reading for those wishing to understand the origins of the United States. The minutiae that he collects combine to create a realistic picture of valley life and to illustrate the distinctions among the inhabitants of the Mohawk Valley. In 1883 he wrote to the writer Benjamin P. Blood, "For half a dozen years I have dreamed of a great historical and human romance of the lower Mohawk settlements in the Colonial-Revolutionary period, which should study the race types,

Palatine, Dutch, Scotch-Irish and aboriginal, which group themselves about the baronial life of Johnson and Van Rensselaer" (Frederic to Benjamin P. Blood, 9 May 1883, Frederic 1977, 16).

It is significant that (in this description at least) he chose to suggest an ethnographic basis for the novel. With its exacting attention to historical fact and social documentation, and its crude attempts to provide a rationale for action based on inherited cultural or racial predilection, the novel attempts to account for the distinctive character of the people of the Mohawk Valley. As well as providing an account of a historical moment, the novel relates that moment to the historical present. It describes the transformation of the valley people from immigrants without a common vernacular and with distinct social and cultural idiosyncrasies, to a heterogeneous group of English-speakers. Douw Mauverensen says, "The United States of the Netherlands was the real parent of the United States of America, and the constitution which the Dutch made for the infant State of New York served as the model in breadth and freedom for our present noble Federal Constitution. In that much my faith was justified. But it is true that my State is no longer Dutch, but English, and that the language of my mother has died out from among us" (Frederic Novels 1890a, 125). If Douw's mother-tongue, Dutch, has died out, it is because it has been replaced by the language of another mother, that of Daisy, who has been brought up speaking English. Daisy might figure as America itself her origins ("roots") are uncertain, though European. Once "discovered," the name that she uses for herself is considered barbarous—"not a good name to the ear"— and she is renamed (45). Her new name, drawn from two great European civilizations, is unique, one that "no other woman [or nation] bears," one that suggests "home love" (patriotism). Her classical name had an imperial origin, and when Douw shortens and democratizes her name to Daisy, her new name explicitly links her to nature, to the earth. Although *In the Valley* does function as history, it is also (and the pun is irresistible) her story. The "American" group of novels and the Civil War stories trace the history of America from colonial times to a modern, capitalist, democracy. With its special stress on the emergence of a heterogeneous and multiracial nation, *In the Valley* is a specifically American treatment of American life in its self-conscious attempts to evaluate the qualities that have gone into the making of America and the American people.

The Lawton Girl *(1890)*

On 7 February 1890 Frederic wrote to John Howe giving the *Utica Daily Observer* advance warning of the publication of *The Lawton Girl:* "The story is some 15,000 words longer than 'Seth's Brother's Wife'—and 15,000 000 000 000 times better and stronger, to my thinking" (Frederic to John B.

Howe. Frederic Misc. 1977, 252). Six months before this he had written describing the ill-fated *In the Valley* in similar terms (it was 10,000 words longer than *Seth's Brother's Wife* and about 10 to the power of 24 volts better)(Frederic Misc. 1977, 229, Frederic to John B. Howe, 3 August 1889). As usual, Frederic's enthusiasm was genuine, but he was also keen to entice Howe's readership. His previous two novels had not had the sales he had desired, and he hoped that local publicity might stimulate interest in his novel. None of his three early novels achieved much popularity or success, despite Frederic's huge claims for them. Frederic began *The Lawton Girl* in the summer of 1887, using work as an escape from sorrow at the death of his eldest son and namesake, just as Howells buried himself in *A Hazard of New Fortunes* (1890) after the death of his daughter Winifred. By August 1889 Frederic was complaining that the book was behind schedule, "like the grasshopper in the old school reader, I have wasted my summer in gaily jumping about, and now I must grind at my book, to finish it by a given date" (Frederic to ?, 8 August 1889, Frederic Misc. 1977, 231). He looked forward to a time when, as he said, he would be able to "divert myself among my fellow beings." By February 1890 he had finished the novel and was in a position to enjoy diversions—including that represented by Kate Lyon. He returned the concluding proofs of the novel to Charles Scribner's Sons, having already pocketed a cheque from Chatto and Windus for the English copyright, and looked forward to the publication of a book whose hoped-for success would enable him to give up journalism and live as a man of letters.

If *In the Valley* catalogues the birth of a nation, then *The Lawton Girl* examines its troubled teenage years—the eruptions of industrialization and urbanization, the rebellion against the values of its fathers, and its widespread rejection of the mere "pocket-money" of an agricultural economy in favor of more substantial wealth—what Frederic calls "the hateful and ruinous spirit of dollar-getting which has seized upon our people" (Frederic to Grover Cleveland, 8 December 1888, Frederic Misc. 1977, 215). Thessaly epitomizes the changes of the Gilded Age years: it has quadrupled in population since the war, and is building factories, warehouses, and cheap housing for workers, at an astonishing rate. Thessaly is intellectually bankrupt, yet is getting richer every year. It is "drifting citywards on a flowing tide" (Frederic Novels 1890b, 107). The people of Thessaly and the surrounding countryside, though "not precisely intolerant" of its earlier history, prefer the present. Frederic's cynicism about the moral values of postbellum America is thinly veiled.

Like *Seth's Brother's Wife* and *In the Valley* the novel has several complicated plots that work together, not always successfully. The first, as the title suggests, is the story of the doomed Jessica Lawton. Like Daisy Mauverensen, she is the agent of human connection, uniting the oppositional.

She is the product of the divided society in which she lives. Jessica resembles Edith Wharton's Charity Royall of *Summer* (1917): both come from poor families—Charity from what are called the "white trash" mountain people, and Jessica from the shiftless Lawton family. Both are seduced and abandoned by wealthy lovers. The history of Jessica's lover, Horace Boyce, (like Theron Ware's) a story of moral disintegration. As the protagonist in an ironic and often comic tale of vanity and delusion, Horace resembles Howells's Bartley Hubbard, or Dreiser's Clyde Griffiths, or Lewis's Elmer Gantry, in his capacity for fantasy. The lives of Horace and Jessica are ironically juxtaposed. His story ends with his ignominious fall, though he (like Theron) is treated gently by Frederic, mocked rather than attacked for his vanity. Frederic had taken Howells's dictums to heart.

All of the plots have some connection with the "grimy bulk and tall, smoke-belching chimneys" of the Minster Ironworks that dominate Thessaly, a symbol of the industrial capitalism that cast its shadow over late-nineteenth-century America (Frederic Novels 1890b, 107). The Ironworks were started by the ghostly (and now dead) figure of Stephen Minster, who had single-handedly established a huge fortune, speculating in ore, financing the erection of the works and an infrastructure to support it, and employing workers. Such a figure would have been treated more fully by, say, Frank Norris, who cleverly portrayed the paradoxical character of the American businessman in *The Octopus*. Later, in *The Market-Place*, Frederic would evoke a frightening image of a capitalist, but in his earliest novels characters are not so clearly delineated.[43] The dominant protagonist of his first three novels is, rather, the United States itself. Stephen Minster exists either as an absence or as a series of negatives: he is dead, no one can remember him committing a dishonest or unkind deed, no one knows the extent of his personal (financial) worth. This last negative (or absence) suggests ambivalence: the equation of personal and financial worth is inevitable though uneasy. Since he is dead, he is difficult to judge. But in his will there is another curious absence, which troubles Thessalians, "the absence of public-spirited bequests" (18). When details of his will are made public after his death, the local community, after momentary disappoint-

43. See "Preface to a Uniform Edition": Frederic Misc. 1977, 4: "In 'Seth's Brother's Wife' I had made the characters do just what I wanted them to do, and the notion that my will was not altogether supreme had occurred neither to them nor to me. The same had been true of 'In the Valley,' where indeed the people were so necessarily subordinated to the evolution of the story which they illustrated rather than shaped, that their personalities always remained shadowy in my own mind. But in 'The Lawton Girl,' to my surprise at first, and then to my interested delight, the people took matters into their own hands quite from the start." It is interesting to trace Frederic's fascination for the figure of the capitalist back to this point, to a novel that centers in part on capital/labor unrest and in the relation of a single powerful figure to a group of employees.

ment, put this last omission down to his sudden death. Yet such a detail, though mentioned in passing, has a disquieting effect. As if to compound this effect, his original heir, his only son and namesake, has died of alcoholism shortly before his father's death. The younger Stephen's lack of moral fiber (as it is described) augments the sense that something is missing in the male line of the Minsters, just as Lemuel Fairchild's undistinguished intellectual prowess in *Seth's Brother's Wife* suggests the same for the Fairchild family.

The Lawton Girl is closer to *Seth's Brother's Wife* than to any of Frederic's other works. The drama of the first novel was enacted through the question of who would win the gubernatorial election—whether political integrity could hold out against self-interest, greed, and corruption. In *The Lawton Girl* the central issue is who will control the Minster Ironworks, and by extension the United States itself. This is addressed by a romantic plot (who will marry Kate Minster?) and an economic plot that anticipates *The Market-Place*. Horace Boyce and two shady businessmen, Schuyler Tenney and Pete Wendover, scheme to divide capital and labor—to discredit the Minsters with the workers at the Ironworks and to manipulate their stocks. The portrayal of the relationship among these three is the most convincing part of the novel, despite Frederic's occasional tendency toward the banal —once, Wendover announces that "Business is business; time is money." Tenney and Wendover, respectively a local hardware businessman and a New York financier, more or less blackmail Horace into joining their plan to combine against the Minster fortune. When the plot is foiled Frederic explodes with righteous fury: "Great and lasting good must follow such an exposure as he would make of the social and economic evils underlying the system of trusts. A staggering blow would be dealt to the system, and to the sentiment back of it that rich men might do what they like in America. . . . The effect would be felt all over the country. It could not but affect public opinion, too, on the subject of the Tariff—that bomb-proof cover under which these men had conducted their knavish operations" (Frederic Novels 1890b, 278).

Frederic's first three novels, all set in the same region of New York State, deal with the challenges that political, social, or economic corruption force the people of the state to confront. The optimistic conclusions of the first three novels would be challenged in his fourth novel of New York State, *The Damnation of Theron Ware*.

Civil War Stories: "Home Life In the North"

The seven pieces that comprise Frederic's Civil War stories differ from other, better known, accounts of the war by Ambrose Bierce, Stephen Crane, or Walt Whitman, in the perspective which they offer on the war.

Whereas other writers focus predominantly on soldiers and the effect war had on those directly involved in it through fighting or hospital work, Frederic concentrates on what he calls "home life in the North," on the broad repercussions of warfare. Unlike the writings of Louisa May Alcott, Bierce, Crane, or Walt Whitman, which mainly center on battlefields, hospitals, or transit between such locations, only two of the stories shift focus to accounts of the battlefields or hospitals of war themselves. Of the people who figure most prominently in the novels, most are young boys, women, or farmers—civilians caught up, in one sense indirectly, by the events of war. The stories concentrate on the devastating effects war had on the lives of the people left behind, the relatives and friends of those who went off to earn their badges of war. Frederic drew upon his own experience of living through the war: many of the stories are narrated by a series of young boy narrators, or adult men describing their youth. The narrators are usually fatherless in some sense, as Frederic was, and live with strong female figures (mothers or aunts) who suggest Frederic's own capable mother and grandmother. Frederic writes that the stories "are by far closer to my heart than any other work of mine, partly because they seem to me to contain the best things I have ever done or ever shall do, partly because they are so closely interwoven with the personal memories and experiences of my own childhood—and a little also, no doubt, for the reason that they have not had quite the treatment outside that paternal affection had desired for them" ("Preface to a Uniform Edition," Frederic Misc. 1977, 5).

Stephen Crane wrote an appreciative piece on these stories, one of his rare ventures into the realm of literary criticism. He praises *In the Sixties* (a collection of five of the seven stories) for its vivid evocation of the "Titanic conflict" as it was felt in the homes of ordinary people. He laments the fact that certain unnamed critics were so vehement in their attacks on romantic fiction and their demands for writing of "the impressive common life" of the States that their "din" has drowned out Frederic. He adds a characteristically colloquial and ironic afterthought: "All this goes to show that there are some painful elements in the art of creating an American literature by what may be called the rattley-bang method" (Crane 1898, 359). Edmund Wilson makes a similar point when he calls the stories "too sober and unobtrusive, too instinct with fundamental irony, too dependent on social criticism for their point, to have interested the public at the period when America was supposed to be booming" (Wilson 1972, 94–95).[44] Yet they also bear an interesting relationship to developments in journalism, for while Frederic was writing his Civil War stories, Crane and Richard Harding Davis were turning war reportage into something of an art form.

Frederic's vision is not that of Whitman, whose vivid accounts of ampu-

---

44. For further comments by Wilson on Frederic, see also Wilson 1970.

tated limbs, bleeding torsos, and dying boy-soldiers, have a grim, poignant, and obtrusive reality. They do share something of Whitman's insistence on showing the corruption of war: profiteering, exploitation, looting. Whitman writes that "the real war will never get in the books," but in some ways Frederic's war, alternately poignant and thrilling as it must have been to a small boy, is the real war, with its family conflicts and the local divisions caused by the wider disagreements of civil war. Although Frederic had written of the Revolutionary War as a new American epic, he never treats battle in grandiose or epic terms: it is never a "Titanic conflict" despite Crane's claim, it is brutal, sometimes an "awful sustained carnage," sometimes "an awful fight" or "this terrible battle." Adjectives are repeated, language fails. Although occasionally Union victories are treated as exciting, the devastating result of any battle always eclipses the momentary thrill of victory. War eventually becomes part of everyday life, and waves of enlistment, or returning dead bodies, leave civilians "seasoned veterans in sightseeing" (Frederic Short. 1971, "Marsena," 208; "The Eve of the Fourth," 309; "Marsena," 191).

There are many splendid vignettes of the women and men of New York State: the bloomer-wearing and peevish Mrs. Watkins, a Women's Rights' woman ("which some held was much the same as believing in Free Love"); "Jee" Jehoiada Hagadorn (the Biblical names of the upstaters are often quaint), a "Shouting Methodist" whose loud scriptural war against Abner Beech, a Copperhead, is unfairly assisted by possession of a Cruden's Concordance from which he picks useful quotes. The stories provide a rich and vivid evocation of village and town life in upstate New York, a complement to the earlier New York State novels. Many contain realistic domestic detail and intricate accounts of minor details of village life: in "Marsena," family histories; gossip; social hierarchies; entertainment (traveling shows such as a "Whaler's Life on the Rolling Deep," complete with boat, harpoons, panorama sheets, whale's jaw and music-box, or a magic-lantern show with pictures of Kossuth, Garibaldi, Lincoln, and an upside-down picture of Jefferson Davis, comics, landscape, and statuary). Into the contained narrative of "My Aunt Susan," the facts of war's influence away from the front are interspersed within the text partly as the virtual commonplaces that they became, and partly as registers of the extent to which life at home was changed by the war. Women cut up and sew carpet rags (of depressing blues and blacks—the colors of uniform and mourning) in the evening while men read "news from the front" from the *Weekly Tribune*. The young narrator lives in the constant fear that the new kerosene lamp will explode and burn the house down. He fails to recognize his soldier-father when he returns from the war but instantly, "cruel familiarity of my war-time infancy," recognizes his uniform and knows him to be an officer.

The story takes place around an act of memory—the recollected act of cutting up a dead pig. The narrator alternately feels guilt and glee as he recalls the pig's early life as a companion whom he played with and fed, and anticipates his reincarnation as sausages, gravy, headcheese, jelly and spareribs. The scene of dismemberment, though dispassionately told, is both macabre and cannibalistic (for human flesh is also known as "long pig"). In the bloody inversion of the pig there is an unmistakable implied reference to the slaughter on the battlefields of the war in which former friends, the Confederates, as well as present ones, were becoming cannon fodder. Whitman captures the horror of this unforgettably in "A Night Battle, Over a Week Since," "Then the camps of the wounded—O heavens, what scene is this?—is this indeed *humanity*—these butcher's shambles? ... the groans and screams—the odor of blood mixed with the fresh scent of the night, the grass, the trees—that slaughter-house! O well is it their mothers, their sisters cannot see them—cannot conceive, and never conceiv'd, these things" (Whitman 1938, 639). Here the double play on "conceive" and "conceiv'd" suggests the unnaturalness of the monstrous sights that wars give birth to. Whitman's war is not the war that generally figures in Frederic's writing. As Edmund Wilson describes "A Day in the Wilderness," "The call of the bugle is heard but from afar and not always irresistibly" (Wilson 1966, xiv).

Yet the horrific fact of being at war is never forgotten. When reports of the "desperate battle" of Malvern Hill reach the villagers of "Marsena," "The village streets were filled with silent, horror-stricken crowds. The whole community seemed to have but a single face, repeated upon the mental vision at every step—a terrible face with distended, empty eyes, riven brows, and an open drawn mouth like the old Greek mask of tragedy" (Frederic Short. 1971, "Marsena," 208). Still more desperate is the scene at Malvern Hill after the battle is over. Frederic describes this in a rare encounter with the actuality of the battleground, the air foul with smells of blood and sulphur, the ground covered by butchered men: "The vine-wrapped fences, stretching down from the plateau toward the meadow lands below, were buttressed by piles of dead men, some in butternut some in blue. Clumps of stiffened bodies curled supine at the base of every stump on the fringe of the woodland to the right and among the tumbled sheaves of grain to the left. Out in the open, the broad, sloping hillside and the valley bottom lay literally hidden under ridge upon ridge of smashed and riddled human forms, and the heaped debris of human battle" (216–17). This image of violence and bloodshed is unusual. The stories present images of human reconciliation as being transcendent and uniting: one man buries his rival in love after they have both been rejected by their flirtatious lover; two women cry in each other's arms after their husbands are killed in battle; two families are united after years of bitter enmity when the daughter of one family marries the son of another. Four of the seven stories end melodramatically, with bonds of family or community being revitalized, and by acts of emotion (crying, embracing, or hugging) serving a cathartic function for communities divided and bereaved by war. The images of reconciliation within small communities and families suggest an optimistic belief in a broader reconciliation between North and South, an optimism seemingly expressed by Abner Beech, the Copperhead farmer of the story of the same name.

"The Copperhead" deals with the way in which the war spilled over from the battlefields, dividing not only the North from the South, but whole communities, families, and individuals. Abner Beech is an out-and-out Copperhead in his total rejection of the war, but not a Southern sympathizer, as some Copperheads were. His refusal to support the war outrages his neighbors, who verbally (and in one case physically) attack him, try to tar and feather him, and eventually are the cause of his house being burnt around him. His political position, though provocative, is rational and held with deep conviction. His opponents, who include the religious fanatic "Jee" Hagadorn, the "tiresome fanatic of the fifties" whom the community has taken as "the inspired prophet of the sixties," eventually are reconciled with him and agree to help him rebuild his home, a tradition in those parts (Frederic Short. 1971, 38). Beech comes to a new understanding of his neighbors at the end of the story, saying, "I've despaired o'the republic. I admit it, though it's to my shame. I've said to myself that when American citizens, born an' raised on the same hill-side, got to behavin' to each other in such an all-fired mean an cantankerous way, why, the hull blamed thing wasn't worth tryin' to save. But you see I was wrong—I admit I was wrong. It was jest a passin' flurry—a kind o' snow-squall in hayin' time" (106).

Frederic's belief in democracy is less ingenuous than this quotation suggests. Despite the images of renewed communality that the stories present, a latent pessimism threatens. Beech's belief in the Republic is undermined by a curiously ambivalent passage in which he looks across the remains of his farmhouse to the surrounding farmland. As his eyes travel across the "further prospect," words that invite a double interpretation suggesting both geographical and temporal distance, Beech (who has the appearance of an Old Testament prophet) has "the far-away look of one who saw still other things" (Frederic Short. 1971, 106).[45] Despite the apparent optimism of the conclusion of the story, one is left questioning what it is that Beech sees.

45. Frederic would use a similar image at the start and the end of *The Damnation of Theron Ware* with just such an uneasy effect.

The Irish Fiction: *The Return of The O'Mahony* (1892) and the Irish Stories

On 2 February 1891 Frederic's appointments diary notes, "Began Irish novel." By 17 February he records that he has finished three chapters, and throughout March progress is noted in the form of regular word counts. By 29 March he had written 29,700 words, and he put the novel to one side when, on 11 April, he left for a two-week visit to Ireland. Although his diary notes are spartan, they do give an impression of his holiday: he photographed the coastline; fished for trout; drove about with a driver called Jerry (probably the original of Jerry Higgins, a Queenstown driver in the novel); climbed Mount Gabriel (which also features in the novel as well as playing an important role in O'Mahony myth); visited druidical sights and the castles of the O'Mahonys; and relaxed, "Cork at noon/ Books and gaiters and black thorns./ Skibbereen and sunset drive to Baltimore" (Harold Frederic Papers). The trip to Ireland was rounded off by a visit to the Royal Irish Academy with T. M. Healy, who was already being acknowledged as Home Rule leader after Parnell's marriage with Kitty O'Shea. Frederic returned to England with plenty of material for the novel and renewed wonder and despair at the rugged beauty of the coastline of the Southwest of Ireland and the apparent hopelessness of the Irish cause.[46]

The Return of The O'Mahony is, like *March Hares,* a skittish romp. Yet it combines the playfully comic with a more serious recognition of Ireland's political and economic situation. The two novels provide an interim phase between the optimistic realism of the early fiction and the more serious tone of the last three novels. *The Return of The O'Mahony* blends farce, fantasy, gothic, broad humor, and lingering melancholy that is partially pastiche. Despite its broad slapstick, its tone is often solemn. Frederic's Ireland, like the Ireland of his friend T. P. O'Connor, was a "Dead Man's Island": looking down from Mount Gabriel, Kate O'Mahony says, "'Twas like dreaming . . . and a strange thought came to me: 'Twas that this lovely Ireland I looked down upon was beautiful with the beauty of death; that 'twas the corpse of me country I was taking a last view of. . . . Ah, poor, poor Ireland!" (Frederic Novels 1892, 228–29).

The opening of the novel might have been suggested by a section of O'Connor's *The Parnell Movement* (1886). The American Civil War had

46. Some of his photographs of Ireland are reproduced in "The Coast of White Foam" (1896). For more detail on the friendship between Healy and Frederic and an account of partisan journalism, see Lyons 1977, 437–40. See also Garner 1967, 1968.

given new impetus to the ailing Fenian movement. Systematic repression had broken down the movement, but with the outset of the Civil War many Irish exiles began to have practical experience of weaponry and warfare. O'Connor writes that this "gave a stimulus to the idea of liberating Ireland through insurrection." The idea gained currency and "With the close of the American war hundreds of Irish-American officers were released from their duties. They poured into Ireland, and the air became thick with rumours of the impending rising" (O'Connor 1886, 206 and 208). The Irish Republican Brotherhood (Fenianism) was founded in 1858 by J. O'Mahony. O'Mahony is a common name, but Frederic saw the possibility of humor: on the boat journey from New York to Ireland The O'Mahony's taciturnity convinces the Fenians that he is their leader, one of them remarking, "Faith, I'm bettin' its the general himself!" [47]

Frederic's *Fortnightly Review* articles of 1893 and 1894 had argued that the Irish were less interested in abstract political theorizing than they were in an inspired leader—"The Celt does not want a constitution. He wants a man." In 1891, the year in which Parnell died, "that strange shadowy figure, prophet, desperado, ruler, charlatan, madman, martyr all in one— the last commanding personality of hapless Ireland's history"—Frederic created just such a leader in the figure of the impostor Zeke Tisdale, The O'Mahony of Muirisc (Frederic Misc. 1893a). The O'Mahony is a kindred spirit to Twain's Connecticut Yankee. If The O'Mahony's gumption, and his speech—"I'm your huckleberry"—suggest Twain's Yankee, then O'Daly suggests Twain's Merlin in his capacity for boring anecdotes. Frederic caricatures the Irish in the same way that he does the American rustics of his earlier novels. [48]

The novel was indifferently printed and circulated by Robert Bonner's Sons of New York, and it sold badly. On 19 March 1897 Frederic wrote to Charles Scribner's Sons, who were trying to purchase the novel from Bonner's: "I should shriek like a mandrake at the notion of your reprinting from their plates. . . . [N]obody outside the mysterious Bonner public so much as knows it. Even inside that public, the knowledge cannot be very exciting—for since Jan 1893 I have not had a penny in royalties on it. . . .

47. In a passage describing a number of the men who traveled to Ireland from the United States with The O'Mahony, Frederic writes, "They were all Fenians—among the advance guard of that host of Irishmen who returned from exile at the close of the American War— and they took it for granted that the solitary and silent O'Mahony was of the Brotherhood." He adds that "The O'Mahony had never so much as heard of the Fenian Brotherhood" (Frederic Novels 1892, 42–43).

48. His attempts to render the rhythms and wit of Irish speech are similar both to his own representations of New York State dialect, and to J. M. Barrie's reproduction of Scots speech and dialect. They are highly theatrical.

[F]rom a shuffling sort of note I get [sic] this week I suspect that I am to hear shortly that a mistake has been made, and that some small sum is due me for accrued royalties" (Frederic Misc. 1977, 449). Despite its poor sales Frederic remained excited by the history of the O'Mahonys, just as he had been by historical accounts of the American wars. In the three years or so after finishing *The Return of The O'Mahony* Frederic wrote a series of Irish stories, each relating to one of the O'Mahony castles dotted around the Southwest of Ireland. The stories were set in the years between 1170 and 1602 and were the product of prodigious research. In 1895 he writes, "I have been toiling for years on the archeology & history of their district and family, and when these stories are all written and made into a book, I fancy the work will be unique in more ways than one" (Frederic to James N. Dunn, 1 March 1895, Frederic Misc. 1977, 392). Most of the Irish stories are based around the O'Mahony family and its legends, though one, "The Martyrdom of Maev" (1890), is a contemporary story. Although at least one of these stories has been lost, several can be traced to journals of the 1890s, from which they have never been reprinted. They include "The Path of Murtogh" (1895); "In the Shadow of Gabriel" (1895); "The Truce of the Bishop" (1895); and "The Wooing of Teige" (1896). They are part of the fin de siècle interest in Irish matters, yet it is not clear that Frederic simply cashed in upon the Celtic Revival. It seems rather to have conveniently developed at a time when it might prove useful to him, and he just as conveniently saw what it might offer to him. The central concern of the Irish stories is mythic Irish history: a historical past that has both the dimensions and potency of a myth, and is yet actually unreal.

In the Valley had filled a gap in the history of the Revolution and shown that a different sort of history was a possibility. Frederic created a patriotic history that he hoped would inspire the people of New York State beyond what he saw as being their immediate, commercial, interests and involve them in their own past. Yet paradoxically *The Return of The O'Mahony* shows the paralyzing effect of a falsely romanticized history (a theme shared with Twain) while also suggesting the possibility of the transformative power of a single figure. The two constitute a confused message.

The English Fiction

March Hares *(1896)*

March Hares and *The Return of The O'Mahony* are steeped in the pessimism that also runs through Twain's writing. By 1896, the year in which *March Hares* appeared, Frederic's marriage had broken down, and he was supporting two independent households on a woefully inadequate income.

Kate Lyon wrote short stories in an attempt to support their young family.[49] By the end of 1896 he had finally achieved popular success and short-lived financial security with *The Damnation of Theron Ware.* Yet the long wait for success had left him bitter. "The Connoisseur," published at the end of 1896, depicts a man who, like David Mosscrop in *March Hares,* has wasted his talent.

The novel was published pseudonymously (Frederic called himself "George Forth") in order not to compete with *The Damnation of Theron Ware.* The pseudonym was carefully chosen, suggesting the colorful and flamboyant rake, George IV of England. In *The Damnation of Theron Ware* Frederic had played with anagrams and palindromes (Celia Madden can be read as "Alice Damned," and the name "Ledsmar" is an inversion of the name of Frederic's maternal grandmother, Lucretia "Ramsdell"). In *March Hares,* Vestalia Peaussier is the mock-French alias for Vestalia Skinner (the word "alias" is contained in the letters of "Vestalia"). Frederic combines mockery of English royalism with a joyful celebration of naming in 1894. He wrote a tongue-in-cheek letter to the *Daily Chronicle* suggesting that the yet unchristened prince (the future Edward VIII) should be named Henry, his own middle name. Spouting ironically in a vein of Wildean excess, he exclaims, "Merely to think of a coming Henry IX, is to be conscious of a new incentive to live on." The letter lists the eight Henrys who have already ruled England, before arriving at more recent kings: "The island was first inundated by an exotic nomenclature—with George on the crest of the wave, and minor Ernests, Fredericks, Christians, Augustuses, and Adolphs billowing along underneath, to complete the Teutonic flood. Just as this was spending its force, along came the equally un-English Albert, sweeping all before it like a tidal wave, and breaking with a spray of Leopolds and Helenas, of Alfreds and Louises and Arthurs and Beatrices, which were beautiful enough of themselves, no doubt, but conveyed no sense at all of English grip and grit." (Frederic to editor, *Daily Chronicle,* 13 July 1894, Frederic Misc. 1977, 367).

The name "George Forth" also suggests two other pseudonymous Georges—George Eliot and George Sand. Frederic was probably familiar with the work of both writers, invoking George Sand explicitly in *The Damnation of Theron Ware* (the prudish Theron Ware gloats over his titillat-

---

49. Tracing her writing is difficult. It is probable that she wrote under several assumed names. I have read one story by her, "Lorraine's Last Voyage," which appeared in the *New York Ledger* in 1895. She is known to have assisted Stephen Crane in researching a number of articles toward the end of his life and after Frederic's death. Her contributions even extended to writing. Furthermore, she was still supporting herself much later in her life, at least in part, by writing.

ing discovery of Sand's relationship with Chopin).⁵⁰ The name "George Forth" has a veiled reference to these two other writers as well as a suggestion of the frolicsome, playful excesses of the Regency. Henry Harland noted this aspect of the novel in an extensive review in *The Yellow Book*. Harland (calling himself "The Yellow Dwarf") divides writing into "Cat-Literature" and "Dog-Literature," lamenting that the "Average Man" loves the obvious (Hall Caine, Marie Corelli, Jerome K. Jerome, A. Conan Doyle, to cite a few of his examples) while suspecting the "complex shaded language" of the subtle and enigmatic "Cat-Literature." The *prix d'honneur* belongs to Henry James, whereas for one seeking "the artificially educated Cat, in green apron and periwig," Harland recommends Max Beerbohm. (Safely incognito, "The Yellow Dwarf" asserts that Henry Harland has produced some "very pretty Grey Kittens".) The main part of the review is devoted to *March Hares,* which Harland praises for its capriciousness and surprises and hopes that it is written to give the Average Man a headache ([Harland] 1896, 11–23).⁵¹ Frederic was not averse to upsetting the Average Man. Unconventional in dress as in domestic arrangements, he scorned the expectations of the average and openly attacked British pomposity and hypocrisy. His "royal" letter (cited above) had already pained J. Page Hopps, a Baptist minister and author who had begun a personal epistolary campaign against him in the 1890s, showing exactly the "Dog-loving" characteristics that Harland complained of. Irritated and misled by the mannered style of Frederic's letter, Hopps lacked the wit to appreciate its irony. Bristling with indignation, he had growled to the editor of the *Daily Chronicle,* "Surely it is time to put in a word for sobriety and commonplace sense." The editor published his outraged letter, appending a weary note saying, "We thought Mr. Hopps had some sense of humour" (J. Page Hopps to editor *Daily Chronicle,* Frederic Misc. 1977, 368).

March Hares, despite Frederic's somberness at the time at which he wrote it, is a fantasy of meetings and separations, discoveries and denouements. It is an 1890s novel of London that moves between high aestheticism (a gourmet's appreciation of food, for instance) and a highly materialistic pleasure in consumer items and display. This movement culminates in the way in which it poses: it is a detective novel manqué. It skips and frolics its

50. Henry James was completely fascinated both by the Sand/Chopin menage, and by Sand's relationships with her other lovers. See his essay on Sand in James 1981, 155–71. Also see James and Wharton 1990, indexed entries, but especially the extraordinary passages on 66 and 215–16. See also Showalter 1991, 59–75. Chopin emerges frequently in British and American fiction of the turn of the century. Celia Madden, Dorian Gray, and Edna Pontellier of *The Awakening* (1899) all either play Chopin or have him played to them.

51. One of Harland's other pseudonyms was "Sydney Luska," and as Luska he had written realist fiction about Jewish immigrants. For a biography of Harland, see Beckson 1978.

way from the initial encounter between David Mosscrop and Vestalia Peaussier on Westminster Bridge to the romantic resolution of the story with their marriage. Early in the novel Vestalia tells Mosscrop that, having met him, she feels as though she is in fairyland. The two agree to act as though they are. This none-too-subtle device allows Frederic a degree of lightness that he exploits fully. As the novel progresses it begins to take on the attributes of a fairy tale: false identities are uncovered, family histories exposed, a rich and generous uncle appears, a secondary love-plot entwines itself with the first. The good all end happily, and the bad (in the form of the grasping wife of Archie Linkhaw, a Scottish nobleman) unhappily. She dies, leaving him free to marry the beautiful and rich American, Adele Skinner, who turns out to be the cousin of Vestalia. It is partly the stuff of popular romance, but Frederic plays with the genre, undermining the narrative by irony and bathos, and by introducing embellishments and whimsy that subvert conventions and threaten to destabilize the plot. The novel is parodic, or at least masquerading, in a way similar to Arnold Bennett's *The Grand Babylon Hotel* (1902). *March Hares* subverts itself openly and joyously, enjoying its contradictions and uncertainties, celebrating its own willfulness. Reality is seldom allowed to obtrude, or to interfere with the plot. When it does, it is swiftly undermined. The novel has many moments of darkness—Mosscrop is torn by regret and disgust at the way in which he has wasted his life—but these are often deflated or trivialized, though never finally dismissed.

At the start of the novel Mosscrop stands on Westminster Bridge early on an August morning. He decides to kill himself, and in a section that anticipates musings on a different London Bridge in *The Waste Land* (1922), he contemplates the possible histories and futures of what Eliot would call the "undone," "the book-keeper who was probably short in his accounts, the waiter who had been backing the wrong horses, the barmaid with the seraph's face who at luncheon time would be listening unmoved to conversation from City men fit to revolt a dock labourer" (Frederic Novels 1896, 4). The procession is initially presented as a simple spectacle —a series of people with hidden, interior realities that Mosscrop attempts to imagine—but the section that follows this one suggests its fictional and theatrical possibilities. It undermines both its reality and verisimilitude, and by dissolving the boundaries between what is real and what can be imagined, it transforms the London scene into that of an "Unreal City."[52] To Mosscrop, momentarily a *flâneur,* its unreality is exposed in the swift transformation from life into representation: "It was indeed as good as a play, this marvelous aggregation of human dramatic possibilities surging

52. Dreiser would write of the "hypnotic city" in 1900.

tirelessly before him. He wondered that he had never thought of seeing it before."[53]

This final sentence of the passage is a key to the novel, a novel in which people choose their own realities—their ways of seeing and of being seen by others. Vestalia and Mosscrop decide to be in fairyland; Mosscrop poses as Drumpipes, a Scottish nobleman; Laban Skinner acts out the part of an archetypal American, though he is English-born; Vestalia pretends to have mysterious and romantic parentage; Skinner's daughter Adele claims not to know who the real Drumpipes is (though she knows all along). This is fiction posing as reality posing as fiction, teetering on modernism but finally resisting it and resorting instead to sending up established forms. Frederic's overt and tantalizing shift between reality and imagination (a shift that anticipates the plot manipulations necessary to a fairy tale) develops into a marvelous mock-naturalistic piece of daydreaming. The following might have been written by Dreiser or Norris on Chicago in its evocation of a mechanical, law-governed universe in which individuals are of little value: "He [Mosscrop] thought of the mystery of London's vast economy; of all its millions playing dumbly, uninstructedly, almost like automata, their appointed parts in the strange machinery by which so many droves of butchers' cattle, so many thousands of tons of food and trunks of clothing and coals and oil were bought in daily, and Babylon's produce was sent out again in rebalancing payment. The miracle of these giant scales always being kept even, of London's ever-craving belly and the country's never-failing response, loomed upon his imagination" (Frederic Novels 1896, 4–5). Unlike Dreiser or Norris, Frederic cannot resist undermining his own narrative: Mosscrop yawns suddenly and decides that a brain capable of such fantasies deserves better than being drowned. He determines to change his life, an impossibility in a strictly naturalist or realist novel, and to start again. It is at this point that he meets Vestalia.

In a piece of invention that anticipates Flann O'Brien's creation of the metaphysical philosopher de Selby in *The Third Policeman* (1967), Frederic makes Mosscrop a Professor of Culdees. The Culdees, according to the founder of Mosscrop's chair, were the Biblical Chaldeans. For his annual salary Mosscrop has only to lecture for three weeks a year. He believes himself to be a fraud: "I am not quite a confidence-man, because nobody ever reposes an atom of confidence in me. Mine is a peculiar form of case" (Frederic Novels 1896, 50).

It is an absurd situation: but only as unlikely as the rest of the novel.

---

53. For an account of the *flâneur* in American fiction of the last century, see Brand 1991.

Gloria Mundi *(1898)*

In the final chapter of *Gloria Mundi,* Christian Tower, the new Duke of Glastonbury, finds himself lost on his own estate. The episode is the culmination of a series of quests. Christian has been traced to France, where he is an obscure language tutor, and called to England, where he is revealed to be the lost heir to enormous wealth and title. He is a reluctant figure, confused by English customs, despising most of the aristocrats that he meets, and rejecting Edith Cressage (who will later marry Joel Thorpe in Frederic's final novel) for Frances Bailey, a serious and high-minded career woman. Christian looks across a moor, part of the ancestral domain that he had visited only once before, in the previous autumn. His first glimpse of the landscape was in the closing phases of the old Duke's life, and the last months of years of inept and vicious management of the estate. Christian finds his way from the house to the moor, but is not sure how to get to where he wants to go from there: he cannot move forward. The narrative describing his moment of negative recognition is curiously flat: "Christian realized blankly, all at once, as he stood and gazed out over the moor, that he did not know his way" (Frederic Novels 1898, 337).

The halting clauses suggest his sudden realization. He is not surprised by it—it registers as a blank. Nor is it surprising in the context of the rest of the novel. Christian has never known his way. His progress to England and to Caermere, the vast ancestral home of which he has never heard—an antithetical Celestial City—has not been accompanied by any intellectual advance. As he stands on a fraction of his seventy-five or eighty thousand acres (no one is sure of the actual size, as if five thousand acres matters little as a proportion of such a large amount) he finds himself lost, unable to decide which path to take, and often unable to see a path at all. With the growth of reawakened nature, autumn's landmarks have vanished:

> The path which had led along the wall, for example, was now nowhere discernible. Or had there really been a path at any time? It was clear enough, at all events, that his course for some distance lay beside this massive line of ancient masonry, even if no track was marked for him. At some farther point it would be necessary to turn off at a right angle towards the Mere Copse— and here he could recall distinctly that there had been a path. But then he came upon several paths, or vaguely defined grassy depressions which might be paths, and the divergent ways of these were a trouble to him. At last, he decided to strike out more boldly into the heath, independently of paths, and to try and get a general view of the landscape. He made his way through creepers and prickly little bushes toward an elevation in the distance, realis- ing more and more in his encumbered progress that his quest was like that of one who should search the limitless sea for a small boat. There seemed no boundaries at all to this vast tract of waste land. (Frederic Novels 1898, 337–38)

The probing, stumbling, syntax suggests the uncertain nature of Christian's quest, raising questions that the novel never adequately resolves: how far will Christian stay on the paths of tradition or convention and how far will he strike out across the waste land "boldly" and "independently"? As a lost (and therefore unexpected) claimant his role is uncertain, potentially radical—"no track was marked for him." Free of a restrictive and traditional aristocratic upbringing, his choice of paths is equally unfettered. Frederic was interested in how far such a figure might try to get "a general view of the landscape" and to what extent he might allow himself to be restricted by the ancient institutions and traditions of which his title is a product. The passage is the first real indication that he will not aimlessly follow the "massive line of ancient masonry," that is, follow convention, but will take up the challenge of searching for mobile and elusive challenges.

Christian is the tentative and unlikely protagonist of a novel that reveals the underlying seriousness of Frederic's late writing. It is a novel of ideas, laboriously worked out and ponderous in tone, and conforms, to some degree, with Ian Fletcher's category of a decadent "aesthetic of failure" that is without doubt characteristic of *March Hares*.[54] Notes for the novel in the Library of Congress show that Frederic was concerned with a wide range of large issues. Scattered through columns of writing are quotations from books and varied observations. Some of them are trite, some—especially his comments on women—are dismissive, many are interesting for the perspective they offer on Frederic's mental state. He describes artistic temperament as "the impulse to belong to the losing side" and gives an uncomfortable reason for not returning to the United States: "In America women always hunt up the wives of men. (Trades Union spirit) apologize for not inviting them, when fact of their existence comes out" (Harold Frederic Papers). The notes are sardonic, often somber, suggesting a sort of hopelessness that characterizes Christian himself. It is tempting to read into Christian's dilemma the confusion of Frederic himself, arriving in a strange land in 1884, trapped in his dual career, bewildered by alien customs, and meeting and setting up home with Kate Lyon. The solemn and earnest Christian Tower, the feeble Theron Ware, and the formidable Joel Thorpe, together form a composite alter ego for Frederic. Frederic worked out the contradictions and inconsistencies of his lives throughout his fiction, but especially through these three distinctively different protagonists.

Gloria Mundi is the most intellectual of Frederic's works: it is as self-consciously earnest as Christian himself and often quite as dull. An outsider, Christian questions traditions and conditions much as Howells's Altrurian in *A Traveller from Altruria* (1894). Just as Theron encounters figures who represent a range of ideas and possibilities, Christian contemplates a bewildering array of ideologies suggested by friends and relatives.

54. See "Decadence and the Little Magazines" 195, in Fletcher, assoc. ed., 1979.

Frances Bailey, a bicycle-riding New Woman has enlightened ideas about employment and is a reader of Edward Carpenter. Emanuel Torr, Christian's cousin, has conceived of an elaborate and benevolent system of feudalism (called, unimaginatively, the "System") that he is testing out on his own estate. Emanuel's father, Julius, has married a Jewish woman whom the pair idolize, and this relationship allows Frederic to debate at some length the beneficial influence of a woman upon a man within the institution of marriage, as well as the issue of mixed marriages. Two of his other cousins represent the worst aspects of the aristocracy, and his half brother who lives in the United States is a Christian Socialist. All this might have produced interesting debate, but the novel is overburdened with (often irrelevant) detail and progresses slowly, with little direction. Christian's frail build cannot withstand the weight of the expectations he encounters —and the flimsy plot is strained by bulky ideas.

Yet Frederic was clearly attempting to go beyond his earlier novels, and though he enjoyed working out some clever and somewhat caricaturing character sketches, notably of the English aristocracy, he shows a determination to engage with a range of social problems that he had been interested in for some time. The chief problem with the novel is that there are simply too many subplots, and they are too complex and detailed for a single novel, even a long one. Among the influences at work in the novel are the theories and practices of the Arts and Crafts movement that are elaborated upon in descriptions of Emanuel Torr's "System" in which architecture, art, and social welfare are woven together.[55] Frederic was certainly familiar with the ideas of William Morris—for instance, on 2 April 1898 he wrote to the *Philistine* and admitted ownership of several books printed by the Kelmscott Press (Frederic Misc. 1977, 471).[56] The "System" is not a socialist one however—Emanuel is violently antisocialist—and breaks down as the novel progresses, to the relief of several women in the novel who argue that it is premised upon the subordination of women. This is only one of the many points in the novel at which the situation of women in late Victorian England is addressed, for the Woman Question is another large issue that Frederic tackles here, dealing with the possibility of careers and marriage for women that will be both fulfilling and emancipatory. Like many of the New Woman novelists, Frederic "sought to improve or redefine rather than abolish the institution of marriage" in this novel (Miller 1994, 15). Yet eventually he becomes evasive rather than explicatory or even evangelical, and the conclusion of the novel, with Frances Bailey taking a sexually active position in relation to the rather

55. See Richardson 1983 for architectural examples that consolidate this point.
56. For an illuminating account of visual aesthetics, Kelmscott, and the 1890s, see McGann 1993, 3–41.

feminine Christian Tower is disappointing. It is hard not to feel that the anticipated marriage will be of great benefit to Christian and simply satisfactory to Frances Bailey, who is obviously intellectually superior to her future husband; furthermore, it seems that Frederic himself would be quite content with that outcome.

Gloria Mundi is an ambitious piece of work, yet it reads as if it would much better have been broken down into several novels, or even several extended journalistic essays, rather than a single, elaborate, and worthy piece of fiction.

❧ 5 ❧

The Damnation of Theron Ware
or Illumination (1896)

The Reverend of Real Estate

Reading *The Damnation of Theron Ware* is a disquieting process. The title of the novel promises revelation. Initially, the process of this revelation—the illumination of the reader—appears to be linear. It is only late in the novel that its full permutations make themselves known. It is not only Theron who is misled about his "illumination," but the reader, too. The novel is powerfully absorbing because it promises so much yet reveals so little. As a morality tale, it is inadequate, for it lacks a clear moral. It is an embodiment of its own message—the difference between appearance and reality. Almost every significant character provides, within the text, a rereading of the novel, but none of the rival readings have much authority. For instance Michael Madden tells Theron that he is a "barkeeper," his sister, in the most systematic and ruthless rereading, calls Theron a "bore." The chronology of the novel embodies forward movement—its progression is seasonal—but each advance in knowledge proves to be an illusion. The movement toward illumination is not smooth. Like Theron, the reader experiences a loss of faith.

In June 1896 Harold Frederic wrote to his friend Sir Charles Russell, currently Lord Chief Justice of England, describing the Reverend Theron Ware in affectionate terms. Russell had recently finished reading Frederic's latest novel, *The Damnation of Theron Ware*. In response to Russell's comments, which are unrecorded, Frederic writes, "All that you say is charming. I think I like best of all the judgement of those who, like you, feel that our friend Theron was badly treated. I couldn't save him from it, but it was a grief to me none the less" (Frederic to Sir Charles Russell, 15 June 1896, Frederic Misc. 1977, 417). The two men had weighed up the case of Theron Ware and decided it in his favor. Yet neither man could "save" him, as Frederic put it, punning both on Theron's religious calling and on his encounter with the saintly Michael Madden, a consumptive archangel.

Both Frederic and Russell had good reason to empathize with the "badly treated" Theron. Frederic had felt victimized for years by his newspaper, by Grace Frederic's refusal to give him a divorce, by the public that was not buying his books, and by his main American publishers, Charles Scribner's Sons, who were not, Frederic believed, marketing his work with sufficient care. Frederic's "grief" that he could not "save" Theron was partly self-pity emerging from his sense of futility when confronted with an oppressive predicament. Russell would also shortly experience a difficult public ordeal. When he first encountered Theron, he may already have had intimations of the scandal that was brewing around him.[1]

It is curious that Frederic should speak of Theron in a way that does not acknowledge his responsibility for his protagonist's fate. Something of his impotence—"I couldn't save him from it"—applies equally to the dilemma that he found himself in, in 1896. His description of writing *The Lawton Girl* compounds this sense of powerlessness. In 1897, Frederic described the act of writing the earlier novel as being like a "spectator" who followed the movements of characters at a distance and was able to participate in their activities only through their courtesy. He had been in control, he writes, of his first two novels, *Seth's Brother's Wife* and *In the Valley*, but in his third the characters took on a life of their own, independent of his authority. It is to this that Frederic alludes when he tells Russell that he "couldn't save" Theron from his downfall. In his letter to Russell, his tone is that of a parent helplessly watching as his offspring "goes to the dogs," becoming, in the penultimate chapter, and after a series of canine images, "just one more mongrel cur that's gone mad, and must be put out of the way" (Frederic Novels 1986, 336). Despite Frederic's affection for "our friend Theron," he maintains that he could not interfere with the inevitability of Theron's downfall, suggesting that, like *The Lawton Girl*, the novel had developed a momentum of its own. Stylistically, Frederic had learned restraint. At the end of *The Lawton Girl* Frederic did, as he says, "assert my authority" in order to kill Jessica. He had planned to do the same to Theron—early jottings for *The Damnation of Theron Ware* suggest that Theron commits suicide at the end of the novel. The penultimate chapter of the finished work leaves Theron's fate tantalizingly open until the last

---

1. In the autumn of 1896 his mother-in-law, Tina Scott, circulated leaflets accusing him of immorality, specifically, sexual acts with two young men who worked upon his yacht. Russell sued for libel, and the case against him collapsed when one of the men died and the defendants were forced to plead guilty. Frederic reported on the case in the *New York Times*, summing up "with heavy bias in favor of Russell" and probably particularly enjoying the humiliation of Lady Scott. Frustrated by having to sit through a half-hour lecture from the judge before being sentenced (she was given ten months of "comfortable imprisonment"), she expostulated, "For goodness sake let me have my sentence, I am only a woman" (Frederic Misc. 1977, 430–31).

chapter reveals it.[2] To have Theron kill himself would be as "false and cowardly" as Jessica's stage-managed death, but Frederic had seriously considered the possibility. Theron was to have jumped off Brooklyn Bridge, opened a few years earlier in 1883.[3] Two years later, some of Frederic's acquaintances believed that his own death was effectively suicide, and certainly his heavy drinking was self-destructive.

The idea of suicide may have been suggested to Frederic by a famous suicide that took place while Frederic was writing the novel, in 1893, which had an enormous impact. Ernest Clark, a young carpet designer, shot himself in the waiting room of Liverpool Street Station. He left a poem by his body that the *Daily Chronicle* translated from the French, and printed on 18 August: "Life is short:/ A little love,/ A little dream,/ And then— Good day!/ Life is vain:/ A little hope,/ A little pain, / And then—Good night!" (Frederic Misc. 1977, 344). George Du Maurier used a version of this in the final lines of *Trilby* after the deaths of Svengali, Trilby, and Little Billee. The novel was published just one year after Clark's suicide.[4] Clark's death prompted, or seemed to prompt, the reporting of numerous suicides, and the affair became one of public concern, not least because of the care with which he made sure that his private death was likely to become public. In what John Stokes calls an "ingeniously modern variation" on the suicide note, Clark advertised his forthcoming death by writing to the *Daily Chronicle* shortly before his suicide and informing them ghoulishly that by the time the letter had reached them he would already be dead (Stokes 1989, 116–18). As he no doubt expected it was published in the paper, on 16 August.

Frederic was one of many contributors to the ensuing debate, writing to the *Daily Chronicle* on 20 August 1893. He called suicide a subject so old that no one "can hope to say any more about it," though of course this did not silence him. He writes that the Ancients made their image of death "a beautiful youth, twin brother of Sleep, holding his torch downward," which suggests that it is time to go home (Frederic Misc. 1977, 341–44). Although the debate that took place in the *Daily Chronicle* largely concerned questions of sanity and insanity (was suicide a result of lunacy or was it rather a sane and rational response to an unbearable world?), what was also at issue, as Stokes argues, was that "the suicidal individual was exceptionally

2. Evidence from the Harold Frederic Papers gives details of Frederic's original ending, with the words of the Soulsbys ending the book. Also see Van Der Beets 1969, 358–59.

3. For a study of the symbolism of the Brooklyn Bridge, see Trachtenberg 1965.

4. "A little work, a little play/ To keep us going—and so, good-day! / A little warmth, a little light/ of love's bestowing—and so, good-night! / A little fun, to match the sorrow/ Of each day's growing—and so, good-morrow! / A little trust that when we die/ We reap our sowing! And so—good-bye!" Du Maurier 1994, 278.

sensitive to the world around him, as the Decadent hero might be"; or indeed as Theron believes himself to be (Stokes 1989, 118).[5]

So what, then, is the significance of Frederic's decision to keep Theron alive and yet deliberately to give the impression, as he does at the start of the final chapter of the novel, that Theron is dead (though not from the suicidal leap he had originally planned)? Part of what is at stake for Frederic is Theron's delusion: keeping him alive and sending him off West (lighting out for the Territory, as it were) is a far more ignominious ending both for him and for the future prospects of the United States than killing him off might be. Allowing him the drama of a leap from Brooklyn Bridge is more than he deserved, or, by contrast, might suggest that Theron does indeed have heroic potential—might even be a sort of Decadent hero after all. Finishing the novel with a soggy death through drink would be merely melodramatic and somewhat conventional. Yet the ending that Frederic eventually opted for is far more grimly ironic than suicide and is so brilliantly unexpected that it makes uneasy reading. The eternal hellfire that Michael Madden warned Theron of is the steady suicide of real estate that Theron adopts at the end of the novel.

Frederic's letter to the *Daily Chronicle* is echoed in Celia's outburst to Theron and Forbes at the Catholic picnic, but is at the forefront of the novel in another way, too.[6] When Frederic designed the frontispiece of the English edition of the novel he chose the image of a hand holding an upheld torch. This literally inverts the iconography of suicide, and the image becomes one of light, or *"Illumination,"* the title of the English edition of the novel. It also suggests the most famous of American icons, the Statue of Liberty. The frontispiece of the English edition of the novel adds another dimension to the novel. The Statue of Liberty is the guardian of the entrance to the New World. In the 1890s, its illuminated flame, partly a great overt symbol of welcome and arrival, partly functioning in a double role as a lighthouse beacon, guided the traveler from the Old World into the safe harbor of Manhattan, close to the dominant span of the Brooklyn Bridge. Had Frederic ended the novel with Theron's suicidal leap it would have completed the neat architectural structure of the novel. Although Frederic chose to underplay the possibilities of the New York cityscape, for Theron's stay in the metropolis is short and disastrous, he does explore the idea of new worlds. Early in the novel Theron reflects

5. As Stokes notes, Hubert Crackenthorpe drowned himself in the Seine in 1897. See also Crackenthorpe 1977, 126–58.

6. Frederic Novels 1986, 240. Celia says, "The Greeks had a religion full of beauty and happiness and light-heartedness, and they weren't frightened of death at all. They made their image of death a beautiful boy, with the torch turned down. Their greatest philosophers openly preached and practised the doctrine of suicide when one was tired of life."

upon his meeting with Dr. Ledsmar and Father Forbes at the Catholic Pastorate. He decides that Ledsmar and Forbes belong to "an intellectual world, a world of culture and grace, of lofty thoughts and the inspiring communion of real knowledge, where creeds were not of importance, and where men asked one another, not 'Is your soul saved?' but 'Is your mind well furnished?' " (Frederic Novels 1986, 132). Once Theron begins to distance himself from the world that he knows—a process that Frederic questions throughout the novel, in regular registers of mistrust ("was it, after all, an advance?")—and to propel himself into one in which he is as "curiously alien" as the Irish once were to him, he is as ill-equipped to save his own soul as he is to "furnish" his mind (15 and 48). Theron's conspicuous failure is suggested by his inability even to furnish his house without the regular assistance of generous friends and well-wishers—the marriage "donation" of his first congregation, Abram Beekman's offer to clear his debts, and Celia Madden's gift of a piano.

His romantic fantasy of transition fails to take into account the significance of what he has to lose—the tools he needs to acquire in order to help him survive, and the customs and expressions of a new world. Theron must develop different strategies in order to read and understand its language, whether it is the importance of correctly interpreting a kiss, or of convenient attacks of rheumatism. In the continuation of this passage, one of the most significant in this complex and coded novel, the inevitability of Theron's doom is apparent: "Theron had the sensation of having been invited to become a citizen of this world. The thought so dazzled him that his impulses were dragging him forward to take the new oath of allegiance before he had had time to reflect upon what it was he was abandoning" (Frederic Novels 1986, 132). Although Theron has "the sensation of having been invited," the invitation is never forthcoming, and it is difficult to see what form it might ever take. Each invitation that he is offered is quickly regretted: the scientist, Doctor Ledsmar, and the Catholic priest, Father Forbes, vow not to ask him to their homes again, and Celia admits that she has made a mistake in inviting him to kiss her. Theron is less illumined, as he believes, than literally blinded by the people and ideas that he encounters. It is in this debilitated state of hysterical blindness that he seems most like a moth helplessly circling a source of light that he believes to be the catalyst of his illumination, singeing himself every time he gets too close to it, and inevitably floundering into it. *The Damnation of Theron Ware* is a catalogue of that self-destructive trajectory.

Frederic became increasingly pessimistic in his later years. His youthful belief in the likelihood of progress was gradually shaken. Unlike Hawthorne and James, who retained some "Edenic" sense of American character, Frederic, like Twain, doubted. When Frederic lay dying, John Scott Stokes read to him from Twain rather than from his "literary parent,"

Hawthorne. Frederic had long hoped to be "a Hawthorne," but on his deathbed he must have realized that in his ambivalent relationship to the world he resembled Twain. Evidence from the *Harold Frederic Papers* in the Library of Congress suggests that Frederic shared Father Forbes's pessimistic view that civilization was constantly in danger of collapsing, taking all moral values with it. Forbes tells Theron that "of all our fictions there is none so utterly baseless and empty as this idea that humanity progresses" (Frederic Novels 1986, 241). Frederic's notes for the novel show his own skepticism: "People do not improve as the world grows older. . . . They still fluctuate, as they always did, between imitating good models and then forgetting why they did so. . . . [There is] no earthly reason why [we] shouldn't all wallow back into the blackest barbarism. Think electric light [will] save you, do you?" (Harold Frederic Papers).

Frederic's journalistic experiences, which brought him into contact with war, disease, violence, social inequality, and political corruption, had long suggested to him that civilization was simply a veneer. One of his *New York Times* pieces, "A Return To Barbarism," shows a preoccupation shared by many writers of the period, especially the naturalists: "When I was a boy we used to be taught that civilization had at last become the permanent state of man There remained, therefore, nothing for civilized man to do but go on peacefully and develop his improved civilization indefinitely til the crack of doom with none to make him afraid. But Nobel's discovery of what happened when twenty-five parts of silicous earth were saturated with seventy-five parts of nitro-glycerene has absolutely swept that theory from the human mind" (Frederic *NYT* 1892, 1). That an advance in knowledge can mark a retrograde step is the sort of paradox that is depicted in *The Damnation of Theron Ware*. Nobel's discovery literally blasted away illusions, showing the fragility of civilization. Frederic's youthful belief in the perfectibility of mankind was replaced by a well-founded fear of the consequences of Nobel's discovery.

By the time of the publication of *The Damnation of Theron Ware* some months before his fortieth birthday in August 1896, Frederic was indeed tired of life. In notes in the Library of Congress under the heading of "Man at 40" he writes, "He becomes in essence Grave, if he has any brains." He adds, in an abbreviated sentence, "He still full of humor or wit, seems to himself as young and gay as ever, but he doesn't fool young girl" (Harold Frederic Papers). The passage toward the despondency of his fortieth year had been inexorable. He had learned of the depths of corruption of American political life, as well as of its moments of honor, through watching the careers of two Uticans, Roscoe Conkling, and Horatio Seymour.[7] This early lesson was reinforced by his days on the *Utica Daily Observer* and *Albany*

7. Dr. Ledsmar's house resembles the Deerfield home of Seymour.

Evening Journal, where he watched and reported on "machine" politics, and rural murders and suicides, as well as more elevated matter. He was not overly pessimistic in those days, but he could be a cynic in the best tradition of the newsman. His gloomy cogitations upon the moral impoverishment of American life had been challenged for a short time in 1884 with the election of Grover Cleveland as president.[8] Yet the burden Frederic was placing upon a figure that he was obviously idealizing hopelessly was always doomed. The regeneration for which Frederic had hoped did not last. It may have seemed to him that no single man was enough to counter the deterioration of the Gilded Age.

The year of Cleveland's retirement from the political stage, 1896, was also the year in which Theron Ware was to make his appearance and have his "confiding ignorance . . . tampered with." In a scene that resembles a political convention, Theron is first introduced at the "annual Nedahma Conference of the Methodist Episcopal Church," in terms that suggest a familiarity with Lombroso, as "the tall, slender young man with the broad white brow, thoughtful eyes, and features moulded into that regularity of strength which used to characterize the American Senatorial type in those faraway days of clean-shaven faces and moderate incomes before the War." [9] By invoking the Civil War and associating him with a halcyon prewar period, Frederic initially appears to be emphasizing Theron's exemption from the general decline that characterizes the younger Methodist ministers at the conference. Theron certainly looks like an aspiring idealist, a figure with the potential to counter the moral decline that was blighting postbellum America. Yet Frederic had always distrusted idealism, even his own, when it existed without a balance of practicality and good sense, conservative qualities that his mother had tried to instill into him. This early description of Theron, read in the light of the rest of the novel, is undercut by an ironic tone that pervades the novel and warns the reader against making superficial judgments.[10]

8. In a letter of congratulation to Cleveland, Frederic had compared him with Luther, Washington, and Lincoln. He had called him "the Regenerator of your country," telling him, "I do not know whether you feel as fully as I do that the public tendency since the war, in business, in politics, in social life, has rotted and infected almost every condition of our existence. Moral sensibility has been blunted, the keen edge of honor turned, the standards of justice clogged, the ardor of patriotism chilled, the confiding ignorance of the half-educated tampered with, the ambitions of good men perverted" (8 November 1884, Frederic Misc. 1977, 37)

9. See "Criminal Degeneracy: Adventures with Lombroso," Chapter five of Greenslade 1994.

10. Austin Briggs writes that, "in the Fairchild family in Seth [*Seth's Brother's Wife*], it is the corrupt Albert who looks like his grandfather, the pre-Civil War Senator. Judge Wendover, one of the villains of *The Lawton Girl*, is described as having the appearance of the pre-war gentleman" (Briggs 1969, 115).

Later in the novel Sister Soulsby tells Theron that the performance of a play "looks one way from where the audience sit, and quite a different way when you are behind the scenes" (Frederic Novels 1986, 171). So it is with the novel, in which Theron's character "looks one way" at the Nedahma conference, "and quite a different way" as the novel progresses. Theron eventually leaves the ministry to "go West," to move to Seattle, Washington, and go into real estate: the bleakest ending Frederic could conceive of, worse, even, than suicide. Theron also develops senatorial ambitions: "What Soulsby said about politics out there interested me enormously. . . . I shouldn't be surprised if I found myself doing something in that line. I *can* speak, you know, if I can't do anything else. Talk is what tells, these days. Who knows? I may turn up in Washington a full-blown Senator before I'm forty" (344). In this parody of the frontier spirit, Theron's political aspirations reveal his damnation more succinctly than much of the sometimes labored symbolism of the novel. To be "full-blown" is to be past one's best, even rotten. All of Frederic's distrust of the corruption of Gilded Age business and political life goes into Theron's transformation. The circularity of this—from Senatorial look-alike preaching pulpit oratory to potential Senator hoping for a political platform—is complete. Theron moves to Washington State, but his real ambitions are centered upon Washington, D.C., even, as Sister Soulsby jokes, the White House: a political nightmare, but the ultimate American real estate dream.

In the fourth and last of his full-length examinations of life in upper New York State, Frederic questions what has happened to the promise of the Revolution. *In the Valley* had ended on an optimistic note that little suggested that within five years Frederic's attitude toward his native country would be considerably less hopeful. From the description of the ministers in the opening pages of *The Damnation of Theron Ware* it is clear that the moral integrity and genuine worth of the early American settlers and of the generation of people idealistically represented in *In the Valley* with such aching precision and optimistic zeal has not been passed down to their children and grandchildren.

The Damnation of Theron Ware is a novel of loss and of longing, the last novel of American life written by a man who had been out of his country for twelve years. Frederic had carefully charted and created a fictionalized version of rural New York State in his novels, but he had lost contact with the real landscape that it resembled. Although he had written about the harshness of American life, he had idealized the landscape of his native region and, personally, he had perfected the development of an "American" character. Now, owing to the circumstances of his divided personal life, he had been shut out of this idealized vision, just as Theron figuratively loses access to the his wife's Eden-like garden. Theron's deteriorating relationship with Alice Hastings is an echo of Frederic's failed marriage with

Grace Williams. The first names of the two women are close, and the name "Williams" is obliquely indicated by Alice's surname, "Hastings." The reference is more significant than this, though. It was Harold who lost the Battle of Hastings to William the Conqueror. In the despair that Frederic experienced in the early 1890s he may have felt that he had lost his long conflict with his wife.

In *The Damnation of Theron Ware* the theme of loss works most obviously through Theron's religious doubt, but this is only one of its most superficial manifestations, since there is never much depth to Theron's belief. Although the novel draws upon the vogue for the novel of religious doubt, in Britain contributed to most famously by Mark Rutherford and Mrs Humphry Ward, this is not its sole, or even chief preoccupation.[11] The most poignant "loss of faith" is the shrinking promise of American life, encapsulated by the shift in attitude and beliefs from those of the early mendicant Methodist preachers to those of the young Theron Ware. The drama of the first chapter of the novel centers upon the issue of which minister will move to Tecumseh. The Tecumseh Methodists are presented "with particularly cutting irony," and Theron's credibility is called into question by their eagerness to associate themselves with him. Austin Briggs argues that Frederic treats the oldest ministers—"venerable Fathers in Israel"—with ambivalence. When Abram C. Tisdale is chosen as Tecumseh's preacher, Briggs points out that, "Brother Abram not only bears the name of the Father in Israel but is one of the church veterans, 'a spindly, rickety, gaunt old man' " (Briggs 1969, 114–15). He is the leftover representative of what Frederic calls the "heroic times" of early American Methodism. Briggs's examination of the evasive nature of Frederic's irony is also made by Luther Luedtke, who says that "the reader's perceptions are filtered by constantly sliding screens of irony." (Luedtke 1975, 85.) The depth and complexity of the irony is suggested by Forbes's revelation to Theron that "The word 'Abram' is merely an eponym—it means 'exalted father' " (Briggs 1969, 69).

Abram Tisdale, the feeble old man whom even the Licensed Exhorters laugh at, is one of Methodism's "exalted father[s]." Briggs is right to argue that Frederic is ironic at the expense of both Theron and Tisdale. This does not mean that Frederic is dismissive of the older ministers. The de-

---

11. Morey (1992) writes about the novel in terms of its relation to this tradition, and deals interestingly with Frederic's representation of sexuality. Some critics have argued that the novel's roots are in a proliferation of novels of religious doubt—*The Autobiography of Mark Rutherford Dissenting Minister* (1881) and *The Revolution in Tanner's Lane* (1887), by Mark Rutherford; *Robert Elsmere* (1888), by Mrs. Humphry Ward; and *John Ward Preacher* (1888), by Margaret Deland. This is true in a broad sense, but Theron's loss of faith is only a symptom of a deeper deterioration:one aspect of the novel rather than its central preoccupation. See also Davies 1959.

scription of the ministers is imbued with a nostalgic sense of loss, of stunted potential. The ministers suggest the history of America itself. The oldest ministers have a dignity despite their physical infirmity and evoke memories of the earliest days of both American Methodism and the United States. In their youth they were fervent idealists who traveled between "the rude frontier settlements" of pioneers. As survivors of "heroic times" these men embody a masculine virility, attractive to Frederic at least, that is far from evident in their current physical state. In old age they are as simple and humble as ever. Their lack of finesse and their present physical inferiority to the younger ministers is balanced by their clear moral superiority. Frederic is explicit about the younger generation's loss of moral credibility: "The impress of zeal and moral worth seemed to diminish by regular gradations as one passed to younger faces, and among the very beginners, who had been ordained only within the past day or two, this decline was peculiarly marked. It was almost a relief to note the relative smallness of their number, so plainly was it to be seen that they were not the men their forbears had been" (Frederic Novels 1986, 2–3).

The absence of significant beliefs is the deepest loss that Frederic registers within the novel. Each character seeks to compensate for this loss in different ways. Michael Madden retreats into the mysteries of Catholicism when its dogma perplexes him, Father Forbes develops an interest in etymology and origins when he can no longer believe in "this Christ-myth of ours." Celia Madden is determined to behave according to new rules of conduct for women while calling herself a "Greek," yet her philosophy is unsystematic and willful at best, and Doctor Ledsmar pursues science through experimentation and empirical observation when he can no longer accept the discipline and ideas of the medical profession. The theme of loss works further through the deaths of Jerry Madden's friends and family, through famine and tuberculosis, through Levi Gorringe's search for a woman to replace the one he "lost" years before, and through Alice's attempt, Eve-like "most worshipful of womankind," to entice her American Adam back into the garden of innocence and prolusion that she has created, only to find that his keenest pleasure comes from watching as it is destroyed by frost. Despite its comedy, which comes, predominantly, from its clever character sketches (particularly in its outrageous presentation of Celia Madden), the novel is pervaded with a deep sense of gloom that reflects Frederic's belief in the impossibility of "returning to the garden."

The Novelists' Novel

Writing in 1910, the American novelist Gertrude Atherton claimed that "No American writer was ever more appreciated in England than Harold

Frederic, and whatever he wrote was received by the press with the same consideration and distinction accorded to the leading British novelists. . . . The best men all read him, his books were seriously discussed, his next eagerly awaited" (Atherton 1910, 637). Although she exaggerates, it is certainly true that none of his novels were better received than *The Damnation of Theron Ware*. William Heinemann, its English publisher, wrote to Frederic that "it is from beginning to end almost perfect. . . . I want to have it on record that I am its first enthusiastic admirer." Yet he was not quite first. Three months before this Frederic had already announced that "No doubt I take a prejudiced view, but I am sure it is a great book." A year later he would write gleefully, "my book is the success of the season" (Heinemann to Harold Frederic, 17 June 1895, 391; Frederic to William Heinemann, 20 February 1895, 390; Frederic to Charles R. Sherlock, ? March 1896, 412. Frederic Misc. 1977, 397). By December 1896 there had been nine reprints of the book. (O'Donnell and Franchere 1961, 172). Three were in that month alone. The novel was favorably reviewed in the United States and Britain. Ernest Earnest suggests that "By comparison the British response to Henry James was tepid" (Earnest 1968, 221). This is an exaggeration, but the novel was rapidly hailed as an important piece of American writing, and its good sales gave Frederic fresh hope that he would at last be able to escape from the frustrations of the world of journalism. Writing to Hamlin Garland in 1897, Frederic regretted that he never discovered what "the big man, Mr. Howells" thought of the novel. (Frederic to Hamlin Garland, 12 May 1897, Frederic Misc. 1977, 454). Evidently he did not come across Howells's favorable review in *Munsey's Magazine* of April 1897, praise repeated after Frederic's death, when Howells described *The Damnation of Theron Ware* as one of his favorite novels. The novel has had, and has continued to have, a remarkable following among writers. The poet Edward Arlington Robinson was made uneasy by its reputation, writing to a friend in October 1896 that "You make me uncomfortable with your talk about *Illumination*. I have not read the book, but, if I am ever to believe half that I read about it, it must be a bigger book than I am ever likely to put my name to" (O'Donnell and Franchere 1969, 108).

Robinson's professional envy over the tributes which the novel received is understandable. Gladstone thought it a "masterpiece of character drawing." (Mary Gladstone Drew to William Heinemann, 14 April 1896, Frederic Misc. 1977, 413).[12] Frank Harris thought the first hundred pages unequaled by any "English novelist in our time save Meredith" (Harris 1898b, 527). Harris's anxiety to "claim" the novel for Europe is added

---

12. Drew, Gladstone's daughter, writes that "it was interesting to see how unable he was to put it down."

testimony to his belief in the force of the novel. Willa Cather, writing on 10 June 1899, called the first two hundred pages "as good as anything in American fiction, much better than most of it" (Cather 1970, 2: 711).[13] It is not surprising that amidst such acclaim from writers, the novel was to be an important inspiration for others. Arnold Bennett, struggling with *Anna of the Five Towns* (1902), wrote to the novelist George Sturt on 31 January 1897, "All day, & a beastly day too, I have been wanting to begin again with my novel, but couldn't centre my wits on it at all. . . . I wait only for one little incident to shape itself and then I can march on up to, & right through, my great revival scene in the Wesleyan Methodist Chapel, which is to beat Harold Frederic in his own chosen field" (Bennett 1968, 2: 75).

For many years Frederic's literary reputation, such as it was, depended upon this one novel, and although he was neglected by literary historians, he maintained an underground reputation among writers. Oscar Wilde read the novel while in prison and found it "very interesting in matter." Theodore Dreiser, in his diary for 1903, notes that he has read the novel (Dreiser 1983, 85–86).[14] Fitzgerald's *This Side of Paradise* (1920) mentions *The Damnation of Theron Ware* specifically and is "filled with echoes of the work." Writing to Sinclair Lewis in 1920, Fitzgerald was emphatic. He told Lewis that *"Main Street* has displaced *Theron Ware* in my favour as the best American novel" (Briggs 1969, 195). In *Main Street* (1920) Lewis has Carol Kennicott tell Miss Sherwin that she is rereading *The Damnation of Theron Ware:* "I've been re-reading "The Damnation of Theron Ware." Do you know it?' 'Yes. It was clever. But hard. Man wanted to tear down, not build up. Cynical. Oh, I do hope I'm not a sentimentalist. But I can't see any use in this high-art stuff that doesn't encourage us day-laborers to plod on" (Lewis 1950, 66). Seven years after *Main Street* Lewis was to write *Elmer Gantry* (1927). Although this has many obvious thematic similarities with *The Damnation of Theron Ware,* Theron is treated with more psychological subtlety than Elmer, and Elmer more cleverly caricatured than Theron. Both Frank Shallard and Elmer Gantry are partially modeled on Theron. Elmer's first appearance is as a bar-room drunk, and later the Dean of Mizpah seminary tells him, "Now I don't suppose you're bright enough to become a saloon-keeper, but you ought to make a pretty good bartender," which suggests Theron's meeting with Michael Madden, as well as his

---

13. Cather continues, "They [the first two hundred pages] are not so much the work of a literary artist as of a vigorous thinker, a man of strong opinions and an intimate and comprehensive knowledge of men. The whole work, despite its irregularities and indifference to form, is full of brain-stuff, the kind of active, healthful, masterful intellect that some men put into politics, some into science and a few, a very few, into literature" Charlotte Perkins Gilman records being given the the novel in her diary of 13 December 1896. See Gilman 1994, 2:650.

14. Dreiser also records reading *March Hares.*

alcoholic binge at the end of the novel. Elmer, like Theron, is described as a sort of senator—"He was born to be a senator. He never said anything important, and he always said it sonorously" (Lewis 1927, 174 and 9). The irony is much closer to outright sarcasm than the subtler tone of *The Damnation of Theron Ware* though Lewis is good on the well-meaning, disappointed, naïve, provincial American—notably George Babbitt—a secularization of Theron Ware.

What writers enjoyed about *The Damnation of Theron Ware* was Frederic's portrayal of a characteristic aspect of American life, that is, idiosyncratically American in the sense that Frederic suggested when he praised Howells's *The Rise of Silas Lapham* for capturing a "distinctive phase" of American life (Frederic to W. D. Howells, 5 May 1885, Frederic 1977, 58). Frederic's earlier novels had brought him some recognition, but here, finally, was a new and specifically American voice. Frederic had captured accent and idiom without being overburdened with phonetic writing, as he had been in *Seth's Brother's Wife* and *The Lawton Girl;* he had a central character who was not only psychologically convincing, but was dramatic and compelling. Theron's anxiety about how others perceived him, his eagerness to please and naïve belief in his own intellectual and social advances captured a painfully familiar aspect of American national character. The novel was more skillful than the two earlier contemporary American novels, making it less stuffy, didactic, and melodramatic than either. Furthermore, it is brilliantly unsettling, particularly in the representation of Theron himself.

The novel has had a devoted following and in consequence had a material influence among later writers. Its literary debts are to Hawthorne, and Frederic's overt use of symbolism and careful naming of characters reveals the extent of his reliance. The novel has been compared with *The Scarlet Letter* (1850), "Rappaccini's Daughter" (1846), "Young Goodman Brown" (1846), and *The Blithedale Romance* (1852), and its closest affinities are certainly with *The Scarlet Letter.*[15] At its most obvious, the resemblance between Frederic's novel and *The Scarlet Letter* is specific and contextual. The crowd scenes at the beginning of each novel, the retreat into the forest with its entwining paths and possibilities, the patterns of allegory and symbolism, the relation of science and revealed religion in the Dimmesdale/Chillingworth and Ware/Ledsmar relationships, all reinforce the close connections between the two novels. Like Theron, Dimmesdale is excited by the potential that friendship with Chillingworth offers him, and as Hawthorne writes, "There was a fascination for the minister in the company of the man of science, in whom he recognized an intellectual cultivation of no moderate depth or scope; together with a range of ideas, that he would have vainly looked for among members of his own profession" (Hawthorne

---

15. See Coale 1976, 29–45, and Johnson 1962, 361–74. See also Luedtke 1975, 82–104.

1962, 123). Dimmesdale finally stands up in the market-place with Hester Prynne and Pearl and confronts his own hypocrisy, whereas for Frederic, and for Theron, redemption is more remote. This is the crucial difference between Frederic and Hawthorne. The tone and temperament of American life had shifted radically since Hawthorne was writing. Although Frederic provided neat resolutions to his first three novels, by 1896 he had found that he could no longer do the same with any credibility. Had Frederic followed Hawthorne and ended the novel with Theron's death, the result would have been evasive and unsatisfactory. Theron's death could only be inglorious since the certainties of Heaven and Hell no longer existed for him, or for Frederic either.

A further parallel between the two novelists is the titles of two of their novels. While Hawthorne prevaricated about the title for his forthcoming novel, his English publishers chose a title based, they said, on one of his early suggestions for the novel. Their title, *Transformation: or the Romance of Monte Beni* (1860) was finally accepted by Hawthorne as the title of the English edition of *The Marble Faun* (Hawthorne 1968, xxv-xxvii).

Hawthorne is not the only source of the novel. In an article on *The Damnation of Theron Ware,* John Henry Raleigh has noted the "remarkable" similarities between Frederic's novel and James's first novel, *Roderick Hudson* (1875). He compares the characters within the novels, concluding that "James's great theme is duplicated almost point by point in *The Damnation* without any of the characters ever setting foot aboard ship" (Raleigh 1958, 220). The similarities are certainly close, yet Frederic's major achievement is that he is able to set the novel in small-town America and still bring "Jamesian" themes to bear on the characters.

It is difficult to know whether Frederic ever read James's novel. Frederic liked to affect to despise James. The difference between the two upstate New Yorkers is encapsulated by one episode. While James advised a visiting American to take a tour around the Cathedral cities of England, elaborating on their beauties in some detail, Frederic broke in to suggest that a tour of the London slums might be more instructive as to the real condition of England. Frederic clearly enjoyed trying to shock James, and James probably obliged by being shocked by his boisterous compatriot. Yet despite the unlikelihood of friendship between the two men, it seems as though there was a bond between them. Although it is likely that Frederic would have read James's novels even if it was simply in order to find grounds to be critical of them, in the absence of any evidence it cannot be certain when he read James. What is certain is that *The Damnation of Theron Ware* is thematically similar to *Roderick Hudson,* and that James's novel owes a great debt to Hawthorne's *Marble Faun.*

Hudson goes to Europe in order to escape from a stultifying New England village and experience an atmosphere that will stimulate his artistic creativity. In contrast, Theron experiences Europe in Octavius, through the Catholic Church, and his acquaintances the Irish Forbes, and Celia Madden, and Germanic Ledsmar. Both Theron and Roderick go through a process of what they think is intellectual expansion that marks the beginning of moral degeneration. Both are deluded about themselves, and both are victims of overexposure to culture. Soon after Hudson arrives in Rome he tells Mallet that Europe has transformed him: " 'It came over me just now that it is *exactly three months to a day* since I left Northampton. I can't believe it!. . . It seems like ten years. What an exquisite ass I was!' 'Do you feel so wise now?' . . . 'Haven't I a *different* eye, a *different* expression, a *different* voice?' " [Emphasis added] (James 1983, 223). Mallet suggests that Hudson has become "in the literal sense of the word, more civilized." Hudson's jesting reply is that his fiancée, Mary Garland, would think that he was already "corrupted." This ironic relation between civilization and decay is a major theme of *The Damnation of Theron Ware* Hudson's discussion of his "transformation," one of the many within the novel, is strikingly like a conversation that Theron has with Forbes. Theron tells him, "It is really only *a few months ago* since I was here—in this room —before. . . . Yet it might have been *years many long years,* so *tremendous* is the *difference* that the lapse of time has wrought in me date such a *tremendous* revolution in my thoughts, my beliefs, my whole mind and character, from my first meeting with you . . ." [Emphasis added] (Frederic Novels 1986, 277–78).

Both Theron and Roderick believe that they are "transformed" or "illumined," and both believe that they have been damned, Roderick by stupidity (James 1983, 502). Both eventually come to blame their degeneration on their contact with forces for which they were not intellectually prepared. Theron, never willing to accept responsibility for his own situation, tells Celia, "This is what you have done to me, then!" (Frederic Novels 1986, 323). Hudson, like Theron, reacts too quickly to every new impression. Both reject the stability of their past in order to embrace a future that seems more stimulating. Neither is emotionally or intellectually prepared for the consequences of his choice. It is appropriate, though somewhat obvious, that the first work in Europe of Hudson, an American Adam, is a life-sized sculpture of Adam.

The Degenerating Deacon

In "The Idea of Degeneration in American Fiction, 1880–1940," George Spangler argues that the "idea of degeneration" is a central theme within post-Civil War American fiction. It exists as "a counter-myth of the degenerate American," and as such, it is in opposition both to the "earlier myth of regeneration in America—the American Adam in a New Eden," and to "the popular nineteenth century belief in progress." He calls it a "primary element" in the works of "such dissimilar minds and sensibilities" as "Henry Adams *and* Jack London, Edith Wharton *and* Frank Norris, Gertrude Stein *and* Upton Sinclair" as well as Stephen Crane, John Dos Passos, William Faulkner, Scott Fitzgerald. He mentions, though briefly, that the idea of degeneration is the basis for *The Damnation of Theron Ware* (Spangler 1989, 407 and 424).[16] Since he refers to the novel only in passing, one might be inclined to simply add his voice to that of other critics who have read it as a straightforward account of "damnation." Yet his discussion of Howells's work, specifically *A Modern Instance* (1882), provides a useful way of confronting the complexities of *The Damnation of Theron Ware,* "this designedly ambitious and problematic novel" (Luedtke 1975, 82).

Spangler calls *A Modern Instance* "a seminal work because it establishes a pattern that other novelists will repeat over and over again in their portrayals of American life." He characterizes Howells's model as "an ironic version of the American success story." The rise of the protagonist, Bartley Hubbard, accompanied by a moral or spiritual fall, acts as a warning to society. He points out that in *A Modern Instance* Howells's analysis of degeneration concentrates primarily on moral degeneration: "As obvious as the insistence on Bartley's degeneration is Howells' intention that it embody a cautionary analysis of the moral tone of American life." Howells accounts for this tendency toward degeneration in two ways. The first is the rootlessness of Hubbard himself, and of both Boston and Equity. Neither have " 'principles' and 'traditions' " behind them. The second is "the decline of religious conviction, which the churches in fact encourage with the gross compromises they make to hold their congregations." What Hubbard lacks is an identifiable moral code that might act as a guide for his actions. As Spangler shows, Hubbard can only be morally "bad" if first, such a code exists, and second, he is aware of it. Yet since Howells himself is uneasy about what this entails he "mitigates Bartley's offenses and undercuts his critics." Ultimately the novel lacks moral stability, and this is due to "the bewildering manner in which Howells oscillates between endorsing and undercutting the authority of their [the moralists'] voices" (Spangler 1989, 407–10). The novel becomes an example of what it attempts to illustrate. The problem that it never faces is partially a question both of whether a moral law exists and also of where moral authority resides.

Atherton, one of the moral voices of *A Modern Instance,* explains the inevitability of the failure of unrestrained individualism within the United States. Atherton is by no means an ideal source of moral authority. His opinions are confused and sometimes contradictory as a result of Howells's

16. See also Stein 1972.

own poorly defined moral stance: "We're all bound together. No one sins or suffers to himself in a civilized state, or religious state—it's the same thing. Every link in the chain feels the effect of the violence more or less intimately. We rise or fall together in Christian society" (Howells 1977, 418). Atherton's conflation of civilization and religion is not shared by Frederic. The cynicism of Atherton's idea of human nature, however, is essentially similar to that of Frederic: "The natural man is a wild beast, and his natural goodness is the amiability of a beast basking in the sun when his stomach is full. . . . No, it's the implanted goodness that saves,—the seed of righteousness treasured from generation to generation, and carefully watched and tended by disciplined fathers and mothers in the hearts where they had dropped it. The flower of this implanted goodness is what we call civilization" (Howells 1977, 416). If, as Atherton implies, the state of religious institutions are a measure of the state of society, then the decline of Methodism in *The Damnation Theron Ware* bodes ill for America. There is no "seed of righteousness" possible.[17]

A different issue is addressed in Fritz Oehlschlaeger's "Passion, Authority and Faith in *The Damnation of Theron Ware.*" He argues that Frederic questions the nature of authority in the novel and both "systematically discredits every authority figure in the novel" and shows Theron's constant search for an authority that would counteract his own decentered self (Oehlschlaeger 1986, 239). His reading of Frederic's novel raises issues that compare interestingly with *A Modern Instance*. Like Bartley Hubbard, Theron lacks stability. Oehlschlaeger is revealing about Theron's lack of fixity. He has no family, and Alice's family has rejected the couple after their marriage. His job means that his life is an itinerant one, and "Frederic even emphasizes the brevity of Methodism's own life, contrasting it with the long history and continuity of Catholicism." Both Hubbard and Theron find that their background is inadequate: they have no well-established traditions from which to draw for moral guidance. In *The Damnation of Theron Ware* Frederic shows that authority itself may be a corrupting influence. Although lack of true authority may lead to degeneration and damnation, power has its own capacity to corrupt. Theron's quest for self-improvement and his endless self-rejection are treated ironically by Frederic, and "despite the novel's consistent criticism of authority, Frederic shows in Theron that the self which lacks anything to shape or confirm it is very likely to become a void." Oehlschlaeger concludes that Frederic attempts two things in *The Damnation of Theron Ware*. The first is that he "depicts in Theron the problems caused by nineteenth-century Protestant America's lack of well-established authorities." The second is that he "reveals the proscription of female sexuality by male authority and systemati-

---

17. For a discussion of degeneration and the a British novel, see "Max Nordau and the 'Degeneration' Effect." Chapter one of Greenslade 1994.

cally undercuts all the authority figures in the novel" (Oehlschlaeger 1986, 250–53).

The idea of authority, in a number of guises, had already been threatened by a tradition of individualism that had gained new impetus in the Jacksonian era. The consequences of unrestrained individualism form part of the context for *The Damnation of Theron Ware.* As Jacksonian individualism gave way to the rapacious and corrupt self-interest of the Gilded Age businessmen and politicians, Social Darwinism provided a justification for social inequality and injustice. With the idea of a responsible individualism capable of transcending institutions undermined, hope for the perfectibility of mankind waned. Evidence for this in *The Damnation of Theron Ware* is Frederic's careful documentation of the simultaneity of Theron's degeneration with his search for an external authority to which he can turn. The question of authority is also addressed by Howells's *The Minister's Charge.* David Sewell's advice to the would-be poet Lemuel Barker is given in bad faith. When Barker is let down by Sewell his social and moral decline begins, and is only halted by his self-sacrificing faithfulness to his lover. The inadequacy of existing authorities and desire for well-established authorities, explains why Theron falls victim to the Soulsbys. Plausible, articulate, and charming, they epitomize a late nineteenth-century "authority," which is as corrupt as it is fraudulent.

Several critics have seen the debt-raising Soulsbys, especially Candace Soulsby, in diabolic roles. Scott Donaldson calls Candace "the true villain of the piece" and says that she "plays Mephistopheles to his [Theron's] Faust" (Donaldson 1975, 442). Luther Luedtke calls her "the agent of a *damnation* that has moral as well as social reality." He too sees her as a "Mephistophelian tempter of Theron's soul and a minion of spiritual darkness" (Luedtke 1975, 82 and 84). Samuel Coale suggests more reservedly that she "may in fact be the Devil of the piece" (Coale 1976, 41). Other critics have responded to Candace in a more positive way. Neither Paul Haines, John Henry Raleigh, Ralph Robert Rogers, or O'Donnell and Franchere have diabolized her. Although Frederic was undoubtedly aware of the possibilities of a Faustian dimension to the novel, he invokes it tangentially and then minimalizes it. It is significant in this respect that he associates Candace Soulsby with the stage. In 1885 Henry Irving had scored a significant hit with W. G. Will's *Faust,* playing Mephistopheles. The performance was very successful and famous for its special effects. It had several revivals and two tours of the United States, and was even sent up in a cross-dressing performance at the London Lyceum in 1889, with Fred Leslie imitating Irving to perfection, dressed in a ballet skirt, much to Irving's fury.[18] Candace, however, is neither Satan nor the pragmatic

18. See Rowell 1981, 2, and Auerbach 1989, 216–17. Ellen Terry played opposite Irving and was delighted by the transvestite performance.

savior of an overidealistic young minister. Frederic presents her as a self-appointed authority, a "good fraud," but not as a worthwhile alternative to the other authority figures whom Theron encounters.

The Soulsbys are recognizable figures within nineteenth-century folklore. They are related to the Western "backwoodsman, with his gift for masquerade and his mastery of the tall tale," the Southwestern "cardsharp and the horse-race 'fixer' . . . the bogus lawyer and doctor and banker and long-lost relative," and the New England "master trickster"—the Yankee. They are confidence tricksters who prey on the gullibility of their victims (Halttunen 1982, 30). The confidence trickster has a long and dishonorable pedigree in American literature, indeed, in world literature too. Arguably the most famous and intriguing early manifestation of the confidence trickster in American literature is in Herman Melville's *The Confidence-Man and his Masquerade* (1857). This novel is unusual because it explicitly places the confidence trickster at the center of the work, but conmen and women figure, often in peripheral roles, in American folklore, in tall tales, and in mainstream literature. Confidence tricksters are celebrated in much of Twain's work, including *The American Claimant* and *The Adventures of Huckleberry Finn* (1885); criticized in Horatio Alger's novels, which often show these cons at work; and described as a menace to society in W. D. Howells's *The Minister's Charge*—in which the minister David Sewell cons Lemuel Barker as much as the real conmen that he meets. Sewell pretends that Barker's poems are better than they really are because he wants to save his feelings. Fresh from this piece of trickery, Barker travels to Boston to make his name as a writer and is immediately set upon and robbed by conmen. The proximity of these two events compounds the sense that Barker has been robbed twice in quick succession, both times by people whom he thought he could trust, people in whom he had "confidence." This was the essence of the confidence trick, as Melville had realized.

The Soulsbys resemble the "duke" and "king" of Twain's *Huckleberry Finn,* notable swindlers even within this celebration of trickery and game playing.[19] One conman claims to be "the rightful Duke of Bridgewater," and the other says that he is "the pore disappeared Dauphin, Looy the Seventeenth, son of Looy the Sixteenth and Marry Antonette" (Twain 1950, 396 and 398). In other respects their lives are less distinguished. Their account of their careers reads much like that of the Soulsbys. Candace has been a dancer, an actress, a fortuneteller, a medium, and a clairvoyant. Her husband or lover, Brother Soulsby, has also been an actor, a medium, and a "travelling phrenologist, and for a time he was advance agent for a British Blondes show," and a lecturer on "female diseases." Both have faced a grand jury, and Candace was acquitted when a jury

19. Several critics have noticed this similarity.

member was bought off by "the smartest and most famous train gambler between Omaha and 'Frisco, a gentleman who died in his boots and took three sheriffs deputies along with him to Kingdom-Come" (Frederic *Novels* 1896, 177).

The curricula vitae of Twain's confidence men are similar. Twain's "duke" describes himself tersely; "Jour printer by trade; do a little in patent medicines; theatre-actor—tragedy, you know; take a turn to mesmerism and phrenology where there's a chance; teach singing—geography school for a change; sling a lecture sometimes—oh, I do lots of things—most anything that comes handy, so it ain't work." The career of the "king" is much the same: "I've done considerble in the doctoring way in my time. Layin' on o' hands is my best holt—for cancer and paralysis, and sich things; and I k'n tell a fortune pretty good when I've got somebody along to find out the facts for me. Preachin's my line, too, and workin' camp meetin's, and missionaryin' around" (Twain 1950, 395). His "workin' " of a camp meeting is a fraud worthy of Candace herself. Posing as a reformed pirate, he acts his part so well that the earnest congregation propose collecting money for him. They give him over eighty-seven dollars so that he can return to the Indian Ocean and convert other "pirates." [20] Huck's comment on the pair is revealing, "It didn't take me long to make up my mind that these liars warn't no kings nor dukes at all, but just low-down humbugs and frauds" (Twain 1950, 399). Huck is something of a con-man himself, though not an entirely unprincipled one.

When Frederic wrote *The Damnation of Theron Ware* and created Brother and Sister Soulsby, he had this tradition of writing to draw upon. Yet he was also contributing to a sociological debate about the dangers that confidence tricksters posed to society. In *Seth's Brother's Wife*, Seth moves to Tecumseh overburdened by advice about what and whom to avoid in the treacherous city. Theron, visiting New York for the first time, is virtually assaulted by a group of "savage hackmen" and clutches his bag fearfully. Both had little experience of crowds or urban life, but both were aware of what to expect. They were afraid of their innocence being spotted and exploited by professional tricksters.

In *Confidence Men and Painted Women: A Study of Middle-Class Culture in America 1830–1870* (1982), Karen Halttunen outlines the threat that urban confidence men were thought to pose to nineteenth-century American society. They were dangerous through their numbers, the threat they posed to American democracy, and their corrupting influence on American youth. The confidence game was dependent on the vulnerability of American youth, which usually fell victim to the tricksters. These victims were thought to be dangerously susceptible to the pernicious "influence"

20. Frederic would tell a similar story about his friend, the one-time pirate Louis Becke.

of their companions. Although influence was never clearly defined, the belief in its contaminating powers owed much to the popular pseudoscience of mesmerism.[21] Their own success at conning the public with regard to the properties of mesmerism confirmed the public estimation of the dangers confidence tricksters posed. The corruptibility of American youth was the corruptibility of the youthful republic itself; confidence tricksters threatened individuals and the national character alike. If, as Karen Halttunen argues, the youth signifies the "American-on-the-make," then, by extension, he is also "America-on-the-make." The liminality of the youth was that of his youthful country. His susceptibility to the conman was American society's vulnerability to the unscrupulous self-made man, who included the capitalist. Halttunen lists the dominant institutions in seventeenth-and eighteenth-century America as "the family, the local community, and the church" and argues that "the prevailing pattern of social relationships was authority and deference." By the early nineteenth century the pattern had changed because of changing economic and demographic conditions, so that "the pattern of authority was not one of mastery and deference, but one of equality." With the changing nature of American society, an individual of personal magnetism, a Jackson or a Napoleon, could "in the absence of a clearly defined, hierarchical authority structure . . . [use] the power of charisma to bend others to their will"[22] (Halttunen 1982, 5, 3, 20 and 21, 24). Frederic was intrigued by the possibilities of Napoleonic charisma, as his final novel would reveal.

Although these leaders fascinated the American people, some considered that their charisma was not an acceptable criterion for the appropriation of power from legitimate rulers. Proponents of this view included "the writers of antebellum advice manuals."[23] They warned America's youth of the dangers of the charismatic confidence trickster, who was guilty of illegitimate usurpation of power. In order to protect himself against contamination by the confidence man, the youth was advised to develop fixity of principles, for this "was the youth's only defense against the powers of marginality." The trickster was a marginal figure in society, moving on the edges of society with no real position or stability. Yet, as Halttunen con-

21. Interestingly, Howells's criticism of *Trilby* centers on his objection that Du Maurier's "whole story was a confidence. . . . A trick? Yes; but none of your vulgar ones; a species of legerdemain . . ." (Howells 1973, 264–65).

22. See chapter 6. For a further account of confidence tricksters in the American novel, see Lindberg 1982. For new challenges to the category of tricksterism in some noncanonical writing of the turn of the century, see Ammons and White-Parks 1994.

23. "The conduct manuals were aimed at an audience of aspiring men and women who hoped to fulfill the promise of the allegedly open society of Jacksonian America, either by entering the ranks of the middle class from below or by rising within those ranks to higher levels of gentility" (Halttunen 1982, xv).

cludes, "If a fixed character alone could protect the youth against the contaminating powers of the trickster, then the young man addressed by the advice manuals was in fact no match for the confidence man. For he, like his enemy, was a liminal man" (Halttunen 1982, 26–27).

The real fear of the writers of advice manuals was that the young American could not combat the confidence man because of the similarities between them. Both were liminal characters, and although the confidence man was selfish in his desire to make money, the youth also hoped for worldly rise. Youths might then be influenced adversely by confidence tricksters, yet another possibility was even worse: the writers' "deepest fear" was "that the youth himself might become a confidence man, that his worst enemy lurked not in the city streets but within his own breast. And here lay also the attractive powers of the confidence man. For the youth to become successful, he himself might have to learn the tricks of the confidence man" (Halttunen 1982, 32).

Frederic draws upon both literary tradition and social debate for *The Damnation of Theron Ware,* making the Soulsbys less straightforwardly comic than Twain's "Duke" and "King" and less downright criminal than the conmen in Howells's *The Minister's Charge.* Candace Soulsby has been a criminal, and she is certainly comic, but she is more complex than either of those words suggest. Frederic uses a series of theatrical associations to undermine her moral credibility. He stresses the special part that her eyes play in conversation. Her eyes seem to devour the speaker, in a look "probably employed by eminent actresses like Ristori and Fanny Davenport." At one point she "rolled them at him [Theron] in a curve of downward motion which suggested to his fancy the image of two eagles in a concerted pounce upon a lamb" (Frederic Novels 1986, 137 and 142).[24] Yet Theron is not lamblike for long. His attempt to be a successful fraud is a fulfillment of the advice writers' fears. He systematically tries to learn the tricks of a confidence man, studying the "tricks" of pulpit oratory, and determining to "master them" (Frederic Novels 1986, 21). Although Candace is right to say that Theron will never make a truly good fraud, she nevertheless compliments him on his intentions, and these become part of Theron's boast to Celia that "I've learned to be a showman. I can preach now far better than I used to, and I can get through my work in half the time and keep on the right side of my people, and get along with perfect smoothness.... I've taken a new measure of life. I see now what life is really worth, and I'm going to have my share of it" (179, 251).

Candace's explanation of how her "good fraud" works explains why the Methodist Church is vulnerable to debt-raisers like herself. The Catholic

24. For interesting discussions of the techniques of Sarah Bernhardt, Ellen Terry, and Eleanora Duse, see Stokes, Booth, and Bassnett 1988.

Church has a formal hierarchical system of authority, it is "chuck-full of authority—all the way from the Pope down to the priest," whereas the Methodists reject this system: "No, we won't have any authority, we won't obey any boss." Then she describes how the fund-raising works: "We who are responsible for running the thing, and raising the money and so on—we have to put on a spurt every once in a while, and work up a general state of excitement, and while it's going, don't you see that that is the authority, the motive power, whatever you like to call it, by which things are done? Other denominations don't need it. We do, and that's why we've got it" (Frederic Novels 1986, 174).

The Catholic Church has a system of authority that safeguards its people. Father Forbes can discuss "this Christ-myth of ours," and Celia can tell Theron that she is a Catholic "only in the sense that its symbolism is pleasant to me" without endangering their Catholicism. Ledsmar explains Forbes's role as priest to a confused Theron: " '[H]e should be the paternal, ceremonial, authoritative head and centre of his flock, adviser, monitor, overseer, elder brother, friend, patron, seigneur—whatever you like—everything except a bore. They draw the line at that. You see how diametrically opposed this Catholic point of view is to the Protestant.' 'The difference does seem extremely curious to me,' said Theron" (Frederic Novels 1896, 71, 258, 74). It is appropriate that when Celia dismisses Theron at the end of the novel she tells him "we find that you are a bore" (321). Before Celia's final and devastating dismissal of Theron, Michael Madden warns him of the difference between having an identifiable external authority and being an autonomous individual: " 'Keep among your own people, Mr. Ware! When you go among others . . . You do not realize that they are held up by the power of the true Church, as a little child learning to walk is held up with a belt by its nurse. They can say and do things, and no harm at all come to them, which would mean destruction to you, because they have help, and you are walking alone" (298).

As Theron rejects the values of his youth he has less and less to hold him up and he becomes increasingly vulnerable. Lacking the primitive faith of the early preachers, he has even his flimsy beliefs shaken by Forbes. The Catholic Church is a source of both moral authority and of virtue for its people. When Forbes describes it as a "police force" he means that it provides moral and social guardianship for Catholics. It creates a community in which Catholics can meet with like-minded people. It regulates their activities and provides a social focus. It ensures that no member of the church is alone. The Catholic picnic, described in chapters 22 and 23, is an occasion for drinking beer, paddling in streams, swinging on swings, dancing and pleasure, all supervised by priests. In contrast, the Methodist camp meeting, which takes place in another part of the woods, is a combination of the extreme decorum of the daytime and the frenzied religiosity of the evening prayers and the sexual dramas outside. Only Theron makes his way through the woods that separate these two quite different gatherings, thrilled and terrified by the risks that he is taking, excited by the thought of a double life, keen to impress his own people with his pulpit oratory and his would-be friends with his worldliness. Theron participates uneasily in both events, and Frederic empathizes.

Like Joel Thorpe, Frederic's final and powerful protagonist, and like Frederic himself, Theron tries to find a path for himself out of the possibilities that he encounters. He fears exposure and being thought negligible, yet admires manipulators and aspires to be a conman. At the end of *The Damnation of Theron Ware* Theron indulges in megalomaniacal fantasy which is then taken up by Frederic at the beginning of *The Market-Place*. Theron looks forward to a time when he will be an adored orator, and Joel to the prospect of being a rich man.

ᏼ 6 ᏼᏼᏼ

The Market-Place (1899)

The Master of Capital

Among Frederic's notes in the *Harold Frederic Papers* in the Library of Congress, this observation appears: "Business! Business! . . . You can read in histories, memoirs, state papers, every conceivable detail of how such a war was waged, such a revolution created; everything in political and social history can be investigated. But in financial history, the great capitalists who [are the] true rulers of [the] world work in impenetrable mystery" (Harold Frederic Papers). This quotation suggests two things. The first is a profound dissatisfaction with the paucity of documentation surrounding the "great capitalists." The second is a desire to remedy this, to write the unwritten, penetrate the "impenetrable."

Frederic fulfills this wish in *The Market-Place* in what could be described as a piece of investigative journalism. He traces the fictional career of Joel Thorpe up to the moment when Thorpe decides that he will "Rule England" (Frederic Novels 1899, 346). By conceiving of Thorpe as a self-appointed social and political leader, Frederic completes and actualizes the metaphor of capitalist-as-ruler. By stressing the self-made aspect of Thorpe's achievements, and by comparing him at one point with Napoleon, Frederic echoes an established tradition. He invokes the figure of Napoleon as a representative of the nineteenth-century man-on-the-rise. Yet to suggest that Thorpe is simply one of the "great capitalists" would be to underestimate the complexity of Frederic's last novel. Thorpe is a buccaneer, a pirate, a swindler on an enormous scale, a man who gets more pleasure from spending money than from making it. As a "great capitalist," Thorpe falls far short of the mark—one of his most endearingly human qualities is his bewilderment at the tireless industry of the Rothschilds:

He had heard it said that the very head of the house listened to quotations from the tape while he ate his luncheon, and interrupted his conversations with the most important of non-commercial callers, to make or refuse bargains in shares offered by brokers who came in. What impulse lay behind this extraordinary devotion to labour? Toward what conceivable goal could it be striving? To work hard and risk great things for the possession of a fortune in order to enjoy it afterwards—he could understand how that attracted men. But to possess already the biggest of human fortunes, and still work— that baffled him. He wished he knew some of the men in there, especially if they belonged to the place. It would be wonderfully interesting to get at the inner point of view of New Court. (Frederic Novels 1899, 309)

Contemporary critics were as perplexed by the character of Joel Thorpe as Thorpe himself was by the Rothschilds. Frederic had undoubtedly got to the "inner point of view" with Joel Thorpe—Frederic's realistic description of Thorpe's wheeler-dealing is impressive—but what sort of a man was Thorpe, and where had he come from?

Frederic's interest in a finance novel with a central, dominating character, goes back some way, although his formal preparation for the novel was less prolonged. Some years earlier, having completed *In the Valley*, he had thought of writing a second novel set in Revolutionary America, which would look at the war from the perspective of a nonaligned adventurer. One of his ancestors had fought on both sides of the war, and Frederic was interested in his motivation. Fiercely partisan himself, he found his ancestor's cool premeditation attractive. Frederic's plans for this novel came to nothing, but he retained his interest in figures who combined audacity with self-control. One such protagonist is Zeke Tisdale, who deserts from the American Civil War to pose as The O'Mahony of Muirisc and then fights for the Fenians and travels all over Europe as a mercenary. Another, only briefly developed in the sketchy outlines of a play, is the genial liar Colonel Strathbogie. Joel Thorpe combines the energy of Tisdale with the mendacity of Strathbogie. These two were partial models for Thorpe—early prototypes—but their influence, though significant, was not complete.

Thorpe emerges, in a general sense, from the American magnates and capitalists who were the evil geniuses of the last decades of the nineteenth century, but contemporary reviewers wanted to find a specific counterpart. Was he "Whittaker Wright, the blower of bubbles, the prodigious swindler" who poisoned himself in the manner of Trollope's Augustus Melmotte, or was he Ernest Terah Hooley, whose fraudulent behavior was exposed shortly before Frederic's premature death allowed details of his own double life to leak out into the press (Rideing 1909, 398)? Both Hooley and Wright may have been partial models for Thorpe, and at least three other men, George Lewis ("Louis") Becke, John Richard Somers Vine, and James Lorimer Graham, may also have suggested Thorpe to Frederic. Becke, an Australian novelist, had once been the supercargo to the pirate W. H.

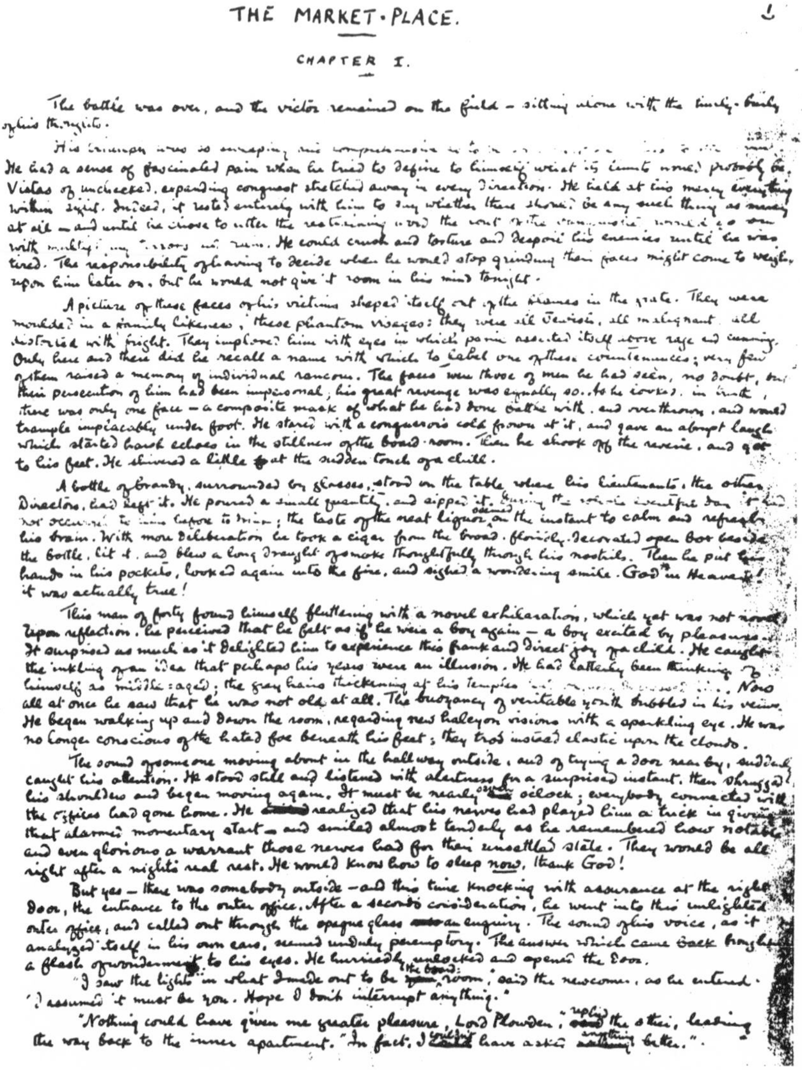

THE MARKET-PLACE. 1

CHAPTER I.

The battle was over, and the victor remained on the field — sitting alone with the lively-bright of his thoughts.

His triumph was so sweeping and comprehensive [illegible]. He had a sense of fascinated pain when he tried to define to himself what its limits would probably be. Vistas of unchecked, expanding conquest stretched away in every direction. He held at his mercy everything within sight. Indeed, it rested entirely with him to say whether there should be any such thing as mercy at all — and until he chose to utter the restraining word the rout of the [illegible] would go on with multiplying terrors and ruin. He could crush and torture and despoil his enemies until he was tired. The responsibility of having to decide when he would stop grinding their faces might come to weigh upon him later on. But he would not give it room in his mind tonight.

A picture of these faces of his victims shaped itself out of the flames in the grate. They were moulded in a family likeness, these phantom visages: they were all Jewish, all malignant, all distorted with fright. They implored him with eyes in which pain asserted itself above rage and cunning. Only here and there did he recall a name with which to label one of these countenances; very few of them raised a memory of individual rancour. The faces were those of men he had seen, no doubt, but their persecution of him had been impersonal; his great revenge was equally so. to be [illegible]. in truth, there was only one face — a composite mask of what he had done battle with, and overthrown, and would trample implacably under foot. He stared with a conqueror's cold frown at it, and gave an abrupt laugh which started harsh echoes in the stillness of the board-room. Then he shook off the reverie, and got to his feet. He shivered a little at the sudden touch of a chill.

A bottle of brandy, surrounded by glasses, stood on the table where his lieutenants, the other Directors, had left it. He poured a small quantity, and sipped it. During the whole eventful day it had not occurred to him before to drink; the taste of the neat liquor seemed on the instant to calm and refresh his brain. With more deliberation he took a cigar from the broad, floridly-decorated open box beside the bottle, lit it, and blew a long draught of smoke thoughtfully through his nostrils. Then he put his hands in his pockets, looked again into the fire, and sighed a wondering smile. God in Heaven! it was actually true!

This man of forty found himself fluttering with a novel exhilaration, which yet was not novel upon reflection. he perceived that he felt as if he were a boy again — a boy excited by pleasures. It surprised as much as it delighted him to experience this frank and direct joy of a child. He caught the inkling of an idea that perhaps his years were an illusion. He had latterly been thinking of himself as middle-aged; the gray hairs thickening at his temples [illegible]. Now all at once he saw that he was not old at all. The buoyancy of veritable youth bubbled in his veins. He began walking up and down the room, regarding new halcyon visions with a sparkling eye. He was no longer conscious of the hated foe beneath his feet; they trod instead elastic upon the clouds.

The sound of someone moving about in the hallway outside, and of trying a door near by, suddenly caught his attention. He stood still and listened with alertness for a surprised instant, then shrugged his shoulders and began moving again. It must be nearly seven o'clock; everybody connected with the offices had gone home. He ~~[illegible]~~ realized that his nerves had played him a trick in giving that alarmed momentary start — and smiled almost tenderly as he remembered how notable and even glorious a warrant those nerves had for their unsettled state. They would be all right after a night's real rest. He would know how to sleep <u>now</u>, thank God!

But yes — there was somebody outside — and this time knocking with assurance at the right door, the entrance to the outer office. After a second's consideration, he went into this unlighted outer office, and called out through the opaque glass ~~[illegible]~~ an enquiry. The sound of his voice, as it analyzed itself in his own ears, seemed unduly peremptory. The answer which came back brought a flash of wonderment to his eyes. He hurriedly unlocked and opened the door.

"I saw the lights in what I made out to be ~~your~~ the board-room," said the newcomer, as he entered. "I assumed it must be you. Hope I don't interrupt anything."

"Nothing could have given me greater pleasure, Lord Plowden," ~~said~~ replied the other, leading the way back to the inner apartment. "In fact, I ~~could~~ couldn't have asked ~~nothing~~ anything better."

First page from the manuscript of *The Market-Place.*
Note Frederic's tiny copperplate writing, and the minimal corrections.

"Bully" Hayes on his ship, *Leonora.* When the ship was sunk Becke was tried and acquitted in Brisbane. Frederic liked to tell strangers that Becke had received a death sentence for piracy but was let off owing both to his youth and to "a promise to return to the Islands to preach the Gospel" (Frederic

Misc. 1977, 476).[1] Vine was a journalist and was well known to Frederic as the secretary of the Savage Club. Graham was an "audacious swindler" and "soldier of fortune" whom Frederic supported financially when, as an old man, he found himself destitute in London. Frederic wrote of him that "He impersonated a nobleman, which was easy. He imposed upon noblemen, which is not so simple a matter" (Frederic Misc. 1977, 83–84). Thorpe (indeed, Hooley too) imposed upon noblemen with ease; Thorpe finds transformation into a nobleman a less easy matter.

The qualities that Frederic found compelling in all of these figures were their force and audacity, their disregard for conventionality, and their irrepressible belief in themselves, characteristics he shared. When he began writing the novel in late 1898 his enjoyment of their unconventionality and disapproval of certain of their actions (including, curiously, Graham's sexual improprieties) formed the basis of his attitude to Thorpe. Frederic wrote to Becke on 6 July 1898 suggesting that he and Vine should meet. His letter is tantalizingly vague: he mentions a company (of which Vine is the "chief figure") which "has its grip on British New Guinea" and reminds him of the "plans about the Carolines which once occupied your mind—perhaps do still" (Frederic Misc. 1977, 475–76). Frederic also remarks upon the self-interest of the promoters, who are "thinking more of the London Stock Exchange than they are of New Guinea." The letter ends with a whimsical comparison between Vine and Becke: "Vine is also a pirate. He is a fatter and more cheerful buccaneer than you are, and he is incapable of your smaller vices, such as promising to visit people over and over again, and putting up paltry bluffs afterward which would not deceive a wart-hog. In larger crimes, however, I think you two would understand each other readily. Together, you might plunder a hemisphere—and really, when I come to think it over, I'm quite unable to guess which of you would then be most likely to return . . . with the loot as the survivor. You would have to take your own chances on that." The word "pirate" had a double aspect for Frederic: it was partly pejorative, but could be affectionate.[2]

A second letter to Becke, written on 3 August 1898, suggests that Becke did not relish Frederic's jocular tone. Frederic reassures him that he did

1. Frederic appropriated this idea from Twain.
2. When he addressed Becke as "You old pirate" he celebrated his roguishness and past career, but when he described Thorpe as a pirate he suggests the darker elements of piracy: "All his voyages and adventures and painful enterprises had been informed by the desire of the buccaneer—the passion to reap where others had sown, or at the worst to get something for nothing" (Frederic Novels 1899, 19). In Kate Chopin's The Awakening (1899) Edna Pontellier and Robert Lebrun entertain each other by telling pirate stories to each other. Here piracy operates as a metaphor for potential sexual experimentation but it may also reflect tangentially upon Edna's husband, who is a speculator. In other words it may represent both financial and sexual speculations.

not deliberately propose "anything illicit" in his earlier letter, and that he respects Becke's "feelings" (presumably reservations about both the project and Frederic's manner of representing it) and "like you a lot better for having them." He also writes, archly, "I did not assume that the Company we are speaking of is composed of cherubim; the angels have had very little to do, I am told, with the development of the British Empire" (Frederic letter to Louis Becke, 3 August 1898, Frederic Misc. 1977, 482). Becke, as an Australian, was probably in sympathy with this sentiment.

Long before this, Frederic had already encountered, and suffered from, shady speculations that had little to do with "cherubim." He had written a summary of a project concerning the Panama Canal after being approached by a character who sounds much like Thorpe, as he ruefully admits to Charles Miller:

> The first eight pages were prepared last summer, at the instance of a man who had a plan for making several millions of pounds—a million more or less didn't matter much to him—out of bearing the stock. I was to master the subject and prepare a statement summarizing the situation, and he was to do all the rest. I think I was to have a hundred thousand pounds for my share of the proceeds,—I forget exactly. Then the man borrowed four pounds of me, and I have never heard any more of either the speculation or the loan. . . . (In parenthesis I may say that I have reason to believe that most of the bear operations here which have knocked the stock down were based on my presentation of the case, although I have netted a loss of $20 by it.) I have put on a postscript, explaining one or two later developments—and I hope the thing may prove of more service to the [New York] *Times* than it has been to me. (Frederic to Charles R. Miller, 12 November 1885, Frederic Misc. 1977, 86–87)

This early bitter experience may have prepared him for the machinations of City men that he encountered in the later part of his career. From 1893 onward Frederic had been, in addition to his other duties, covering London financial news for the *New York Times*. The paper hoped to broaden its appeal in a highly competitive market, and Charles Miller decided to save money by getting Frederic to gather material for its financial columns. The City was a world of which Frederic had little experience, but Miller was imperturbable. Writing to Frederic in September 1893, Miller says:

> You wrote me the other day that you were absolutely ignorant of City affairs, and this opinion of your own capacities was frankly and good-naturedly confirmed by your friend, Mr. Ivins, who says that you know nothing of finance and have no financial acquaintances. Of course, I knew this very well before, but inasmuch as you are within a short time to send The New York Times its daily financial dispatches, and inasmuch as they must be thoroughly accurate and well informed, must convey frequently inside news, and give intelligent

interpretations of matters and movements that affect the stock market and the financial situation, you will, I trust, see the necessity of getting up your equipment and laying your lines of acquaintances without delay (Miller to Frederic, 8 September 1893, Frederic Misc. 1977, 348–49)

Frederic was so persistent and effective at making "financial acquaintances" and at mastering the complexities of the world of finance that he was able to conceive of Thorpe's stock market coup and construct an entire novel around it. Yet, though the novel reads to some extent like a muckraking exposé it does not take a moral stance. As he read financial papers, listened to City gossip, and set out to "master" the world of finance he began to realize that this was an area that had been neglected by writers of fiction. Another paragraph of Miller's letter may have provided Frederic with extra motivation: "I ought to warn you that in fixing your mind upon the precise and sometimes sordid details of the money market and the Exchange, you will run a serious risk of impairing your imaginative faculties to a degree which would probably incapacitate you for the writing of further acceptable fiction. But what you lose as a novelist you will probably gain as a financial writer—provided you show a capacity for growth and attain to a high proficiency."

Miller's tone is deliberately pointed. His teasing words gently undermine Frederic's obvious aspirations toward fiction writing, and he may have intended a deliberate double entendre with his reference to being a "financial writer." Frederic's complaints about money had been part of the earliest correspondence between the two men—to this extent he had long been a "financial writer"—and Miller was aware of his London correspondent's hopes that his novels would bring him financial independence from the paper.

As Frederic began to understand more of the business life of London, he found that working in the City was frequently a dirty business, and that this dirt rubbed off on those who dealt in it. Although not easily shocked, he found the language of City men disturbing, commenting in *March Hares* that it was "fit to revolt a dock laborer," although his own language was often choice. His friends included successful businessmen: he dedicated the English edition of *Gloria Mundi* to the industrialist Sir Joseph Lawrence, and named one of his children Barry, after John Barry, an Irish member of Parliament and businessman. His earliest introduction to business had been, of course, through his mother. He spoke highly of "practical self-reliant businessmen," whom he praised for their solid qualities, but he might have added the word "businesswomen," too (Frederic to John B. Howe, 11 May 1892, Frederic Misc. 1977, 314).[3]

These were the models for *The Market-Place*. On the one hand there

---

3. For an account of the representation of the businesswoman, see Albertine 1990.

were piratical buccaneers who broke the rules and formed their own boundaries, and on the other there was the forceful example of Frances De Motte. The freedom and unconventionality of the former were highly attractive to Frederic, but he saw the dangers of their corrupting influence and in his final novel offered two potential models for business and for finance at the turn of the century. Louisa Thorpe, stable, bourgeois, and conservative, stays in the family bookselling business, whereas her brother Joel fights his way through an international marketplace, displacing convention and challenging and redefining boundaries as he goes. Louisa Thorpe and the Thorpe bookshop are the representatives of a tradition of business against which Frederic defines the emerging figure of the capitalist, Joel Thorpe.

Many writers before and after Frederic had written or would write about traditional American businessmen and businesswomen whose old-fashioned values were becoming increasingly out of place. Writing of the novelist Robert Herrick, Van Wyck Brooks says:

> He admired the older business types, the pioneers of trade who had floated their merchandise down the Western rivers, who had had more elbow-room in the years before the World's Fair and had kept their faith in the goodness of American life. They had had the adventure of the frontiers, their fights had been free, in the open, they had had their exciting round-ups in finance and construction, and their wide contacts with other men had often made them generous and kind. . . . There had been something poetic in them, spacious, courageous, self-reliant, fatherly towards their employees, sincerely democratic, unlike the new "damned money-getters," as his Jarvis Thornton called them, who abused their giants' strength in a world of graft. (Brooks 1955, 188)

These "older business types" were celebrated by Willa Cather in her story "Two Friends," and in the figure of Captain Forrester in *A Lost Lady*.[4] These businessmen and businesswomen (much like Frederic's mother) were local, respected, well liked, and trusted. Their political opinions were sought, their advice was taken, they occupied a significant position within the local community. The money they made could be seen to be at some level commensurate with the amount of work they put into their businesses, unlike that of the new capitalists, who were compared with gamblers.[5] Whatever their actual position within local communities, there was no doubt that in comparison with the "damned money-getters" they were

4. Interestingly, Forrester is compared with Grover Cleveland.
5. F. Marion Crawford writes of the fictional Mrs. Sam Wyndham, an aristocratic Bostonian, that "she understood business to some extent, and called it finance, but she despised the New York Stock Market and denounced its doings as gambling" (Crawford 1885, 9).

attractive figures. They were part of an old mythology of the United States. Yet these "older business types" were passing into American folklore as a new figure, the Napoleonic capitalist, was emerging as the dominant figure in an American mercantile democracy.

The Market-Place is a transference of the American myth of the self-made man into England and London society. In one sense this transference is straightforward. Thorpe is the capitalist of the Gilded Age, opportunistic, rapacious, vulgar, and upwardly mobile. His philosophy is Darwinistic— the survival of the fittest—though Frederic's writing is not self-consciously naturalistic, and he seldom uses the discourses of Social Darwinism in his writing.[6] Frederic uses the currency of naturalism on occasion without a systematic investigation of what it involves. He dips into it, appropriating aspects that suit him—notably animal imagery—and abandoning the rest.[7] Thorpe's business ethics are at best, questionable. His father, from whom he breaks away, is like a Puritan "founding father," and the Thorpe book-shop is the family firm that he should have joined. Frederic's irony turns the legend into a satirical vision of the usual rags-to-riches success story. One could see Thorpe as a representation of the United States. The divi-sions within his personality are those of the United States, partly new, partly old; partly breaking with the past, partly being molded by it. The space and enclosure suggested by both Thorpe's many overseas adventures and the confines of the family bookshop is that of the vast American continent gradually being tamed by its settlers. It is at once infinite and intensely finite.

Part of Thorpe's recital of adventures includes a description of his over-seas travel. He has traveled in countries with ancient historical pasts as well as in those with more recent, known histories. He has lived in the United States and traveled to Colorado, as well as to China, the Dutch Indies, Australia, Argentina, Brazil, British Columbia, and Mexico. He represents a previously inconceivable freedom of movement, yet his dynastic back-ground is also stressed. Frederic makes him suggest both movement and fixity, the new and the old, for he is at some point between all of these It is significant that the rubber plantation that secures his fortune is in Mexico, geographically between the "new" United States and the "older" South American countries, independence and empire.

Frederic makes Thorpe the direct source of almost all the information that is given about him. His early life is exposed through self-revealing

6. Dreiser, in his representation of Frank Cowperwood, uses Social Darwinism mediated through naturalism to give an account of Cowperwood's predisposition to capitalism. Frederic certainly carried out some research on Darwinian theory in preparation for *The Damnation of Theron Ware*.

7. See Walcutt 1939.

dialogue, and he controls, edits, and glorifies his past without contradiction. Like Fitzgerald's Jay Gatsby or Trollope's Augustus Melmotte, he seems to have come from nowhere. His lack of accountability to others, and at times even to himself is the most consistent aspect of his characterization. The only two characters who threaten his absolute freedom to create his own history, Gafferson and Tavender, are ineffectual most of the time. Gafferson has a conveniently poor memory so any threat he poses is more accidental than malicious. Thorpe buys his silence by promising to finance his horticultural experiments—Gafferson has moved from British Honduras, where Thorpe knew him, to become a gardener in England—and to pay for him to exhibit any successful hybrids. Thorpe, a "new species" himself, and something of a hybrid, has little interest in Gafferson's creations, but is always astute at recognizing the purchase power of his money. Tavender, Gafferson's brother-in-law, is the real owner of the land Thorpe claims to possess. He is usually drunk and unreliable, so is no real threat to Thorpe. When Tavender becomes dangerous to him, Thorpe pays General Kervick (his future father-in-law) to keep Tavender quiet by plying him with drink, and Tavender is permanently silenced when he dies in an alcoholic stupor. Thorpe is quite literally a self-made man. He creates himself financially through his market success, mythically through dramatic retellings of his past adventures, and symbolically through the icons of prosperity with which he surrounds himself—his beautiful house and his beautiful wife.

In order to create this "new" figure, Frederic uses repeated images to define and refine Thorpe. Three main image patterns are used to describe him. The first set of images is that which portrays him as a larger-than-life heroic figure: he is a vengeful and omnipotent ruler, a military hero, an invincible soldier, a "conqueror," a dictator, a "hero and chieftain among City men," Napoleonic, and an aspiring Cromwell. The second set of images portrays him as an adventurer, a conman, a barbarian, a pirate, and a criminal. The last portrays him as bestial: a "surprising and bloody-minded lamb," a bird of prey, a spider, a snake, and is "as strong as an ox" (Frederic Novels 1899, 1; 22; 197; 2; 206; 276; 205; 313; 345; 18 and 52; 29; 164–65; 360; 203; 212; 259; 271; 343). At one point in the novel his imagination proves itself to be unbounded and he conceives of himself as having mountainous dimensions: "His lip curled once at the conceit that he was one of the Alps himself" (Frederic Novels 1899, 144). Frederic's intention is certainly ironic: the word "conceit" is barbed, suggesting both Thorpe's pride and a formal notion of wit (a Metaphysical "conceit"). Yet the implication is unclear. To be one of a range of mountains has no particular distinction, and Thorpe, above all, is an individualist. It was Napoleon who said, "There shall be no Alps," but it is the Napoleonic Thorpe who deludes himself that he is a part of that range (Emerson 1950, 507).

The first two groups of images portray an image of Thorpe as a man wielding a very particular type of power. His power is characterized by brutality, rawness, and machismo. It is used against other men in male-ordered structures, and the masculine bias of the first two sets of images conveys men's dominance of the money market. Taken together, they suggest a moral ambivalence. The first images are of a powerful military conqueror and leader; the second temper the way in which we read the first. If the first portray Thorpe as a soldier, the second define him as a mercenary, and indeed he is profoundly anti-Semitic, too. The word most frequently used to describe Thorpe is "big." Its extended meaning—beyond sheer stature—is of potential, of ego, of imaginative capacity. On one occasion, however, he is described as a "brute," again qualifying the adjective and suggesting a different set of connotations (Frederic Novels 1899, 270).

Thorpe is actually rejuvenated as the novel progresses. By the second day of the action of the novel his appearance and actions have begun a process of transformation, as if he is evolving into a new being throughout the novel. He arrives "fully ten minutes too soon" for his train, a "deviation from his deeply-rooted habit of catching trains at the last possible moment." He has bought entirely new clothes and bags, and he feels that "the thousand familiar things that made up the Thorpe he had been—were becoming strange to him." He is "a new kind of being, embarked upon a voyage of discovery in the unknown," an appropriate description for an adventurer (Frederic Novels 1899, 39). This feeling of newness also characterizes Henry James's protagonist of *The American* (1877), Christopher Newman who says, "I seemed to feel a new man inside my old skin, and I longed for a new world" (James 1983, 536). (Newman is teased about being a Columbus.) Thorpe reflects that "even his face was new," for he has shaved his beard, and by this he believes that he has "revived his youth." He has in fact lost years so rapidly that the previous day he felt "distinctively boyish" in the excitement of buying an entirely new outfit. His satisfaction in his new life was more gratifying than it would be if he were younger, for "He had this wonderful advantage, that he supplemented the fresh-hearted joy of the youth in nice things with the adult man's knowledge of how bald existence could be without them" (Frederic Novels 1899, 40).

This new boy-man suffers from adolescent traumas. He finds himself on the verge of "tearful profanity" when he thinks that he will miss the train which is to take him to Plowden's ancestral home (Frederic Novels 1899, 41). Such fluctuations between austere self-control and childlike terror and frustration characterize Thorpe and suggest the paradoxical character of the capitalist. This temperamental behavior suggests a self-interested immaturity: like the moneyed classes of America, Thorpe begins to believe that money will overcome every difficulty of his life. He is like Tom and Daisy Buchanan of *The Great Gatsby* (1925), of whom the narrator, Nick Carraway, says, "They were careless people, Tom and Daisy—they smashed up things and creatures and then retreated back into their money or their vast carelessness, or whatever it was that kept them together, and let other people clean up the mess they had made. I shook hands with him; it seemed silly not to, for I felt suddenly as though I was talking to a child" (Fitzgerald 1974, 186).

Joel Thorpe shares the childishness of the Buchanans. He combines the tearfulness of a boy with the language of a man of the world, resulting in the contradictory "tearful profanity." His behavior is often that of a willful and demanding child, a child who has often had his whims thwarted and is now determined to indulge them. His dreams of power, of being respected, thanked, and worshipped are partly the result of a somber and truncated childhood spent outside the Thorpe bookshop guarding the books. A photograph of his father, a "scowling old man" dominates the gloomy atmosphere of the shop, and when Thorpe visits his sister he frequently glances up at the portrait "automatically." Thorpe thinks that it is responsible for the "cheerlessness of the room" (Frederic Novels 1899, 13). As a symbol of the past, imposing its values upon the present, it recalls the portrait of Colonel Pyncheon in *The House of the Seven Gables* (1851), which depicts "the stern features of a Puritanic-looking personage ... holding a Bible with one hand, and in the other uplifting an iron sword-hilt" (Hawthorne 1965, 33).[8] Hawthorne darkly hints that the sword is much more visible than the Bible, and like Thorpe, Hepzibah and Clifford Pyncheon look fearfully up at their ancestor. The two gloomy ancestors look down, disapproving and stern, and pass their judgment upon the present generation. Thorpe tells Lord Plowden, a member of his dummy board of directors, that his father "had precisely the same kind of dynastic ideas ... that you fellows have. His father and grandfather had been booksellers, and he was going to hand on the tradition to me and my son after me" (Frederic Novels 1899, 51).

He tells himself that "It was of no real significance that the law-student

---

8. In *The American Claimant*, Twain parodies this obsessive interest in portraits of ancestors. The protagonist, Mulberry Sellers, has portraits all around his room: "All the portraits were recognizable as dead Americans of distinction, and yet, through labeling added by a daring hand, they were all doing duty here as 'Earls of Rossmore.' The newest one had left the works as Andrew Jackson, but was doing its best now, as 'Simon Lathers Lord Rossmore, Present Earl.' On one wall was a cheap old railroad map of Warwickshire. This had been newly labeled 'The Rossmore Estates.' " (Twain 1892, 10–11). "Labeled" might more accurately be renamed "libeled" throughout. Melville had already subverted this splendidly in *Moby-Dick* (1851), with his descripion of Queequeg as "George Washington cannibalistically developed" (Melville 1992, 56).

grew to be Lord Chancellor, and the bookseller remained a bookseller; in the realm of actual values the Thorpes were as good as the Plowdens" (101). This same point is made later on when Thorpe tells himself that his nephew looks "infinitely more like the son of a nobleman . . . than that big dullard the Honourable Balder" (147). A similar transformation is described in *The American* when Valentin Bellegarde tells Newman, "you have got something that I should have liked to have It is not money, it is not even brains. . . . It's sort of an air you have of being thoroughly at home in the world. When I was a boy, my father assured me it was by just such an air that people recognized a Bellegarde" (James 1983, 608).

The capitalist and his relatives are acquiring more than wealth. Thorpe fantasizes about the country mansion he intends to buy "with gardens and horses and hounds and artificial lakes and deer-parks and everything" (Frederic Novels 1899, 128–29). "Everything" is a key word: in its expansiveness it becomes meaningless, though it is both vast and menacing, too. Later, Christian Tower (who appears briefly at the end of the novel) tells him that "Everything which used to be exclusively the nobleman's is now within everybody's reach, including the sins. And it is not only that others have leveled up to him: they have leveled him down." Plowden's old title is no match for Thorpe's new money, as Christian explains: "As an institution, he [the nobleman] descends from a period when the only imaginable use for wealth was to be magnificent with it; but now, in this business age, where the recognized use of wealth is to make more wealth, he is so much out of place that he has even forgotten to be magnificent" (354–55). British institutions are unable to withstand the purchase power of the *nouveaux riche*. Frederic predicts the future of the United States by creating a figure who negotiates his way around social barriers with ease. If Thorpe represents the American capitalist, or the United States itself, or simply the American dollar, English society's inability to resist him suggests the continuing breakdown of traditional class structures. Frederic represents the English aristocracy as so willing—even eager—to embrace this new figure that they are little better than Thorpe.

By the conclusion of the novel Thorpe has evolved into a country gentleman, fulfilling Celia Madden's prophesy of an inevitable transition: "Having made his fortune it is the rule that he must set up as a gentleman." She says that Thorpe is being ruined by his more civilized nephew and niece: "I'm afraid they are spoiling him, just as the missionaries spoil the noble savage. They ought to go away and leave him alone. As a barbarian he was rather effective, but they will whitewash him and gild him and make a tame monstrosity of him" (Frederic Novels 1899, 164). Although Thorpe does become a metaphorical "alderman" for a time, the description is ambivalent: Ambrose Bierce defines an "alderman" as "An ingenious criminal who covers his secret thieving with a pretence of open marauding"

(Frederic Novels 1899, 336; Bierce 1972, 195). Thorpe soon realizes that the role of "tame monstrosity" is not for him. He is bored by his country estate, by his leisure time, and of leading the centuries-old life of a country aristocrat. His Scottish broker, Semple, explains his dissatisfaction to him: "You've set out to live the life of a rich country squire, and it hasn't come off. It couldn't come off I never believed it would. You haven't the taste for it inbred in your bones. . . . It doesn't come to you by tradition, and you haven't the vacancy of mind which might be a substitute for tradition" (Frederic Novels 1899, 312). Still, it is the American woman who, in the last few lines of the novel, recognizes Thorpe's potential: " 'I still maintain,' said Miss Madden, interpolating her words through the task of lighting a cigarette, and contriving for them an effect of drollery which appealed to Thorpe most of all—'I shall always insist, just the same, that crime was his true vocation' " (360).

The Napoleonic Capitalist

The figure of Napoleon was weighted with potent significance for many nineteenth-century writers, European and American. George Bernard Shaw's 1895 play *The Man of Destiny*, which he wrote for Ellen Terry, Victorien Sardou's play *Madame-Sans-Géne* (1897), in which Terry starred, both demonstrate Napoleon's significance for the theater as well as the novel.[9] Wilde considered Napoleon one of the "three great personalities" of the nineteenth century (Ellmann 1987, 509).[10] For some he epitomized the possibility of a single man triumphing over the great structures of European society. He was a figure about whom many felt ambivalent, but he was, at best, the representative of American aspirations. His (undoubted) symbolic force is attested to by Emerson's essay *Napoleon or The Man of the World* (1850), and by Carlyle's less laudatory portrait of him in *Heroes and Hero-Worship* (1841). Emerson portrays him as self-reliant, independent, energetic, direct, bold, brave—"the incarnate Democrat" (Emerson 1950, 501). Yet to these celebratory adjectives he adds a parallel list of pejorative ones. Napoleon is opportunistic, egotistical, false, selfish, vulgar, unscrupulous—and addicted to gossip; "in short, when you have penetrated through all the circles of power and splendor, you were not dealing with a

9. In 1900 Sarah Bernhardt would appear in a triumphant production of Edmond Rostand's *L'Aiglon*.

10. Allusions to Napoleon are too numerous to cite individually, though admiration of him is usually gendered. It is very often male figures (famously, for example, Julien Sorel) who seek to imitate him. In *A Portrait of the Artist as a Young Man* (1916) Stephen Dedalus chooses a plain style of dress in order to be more like Napoleon, and in *The Scarlet Letter* Napoleon is one of the favored topics of conversation of the Naval Officer in the Custom-House.

gentleman, at last; but with an impostor and a rogue, and he fully deserves the epithet of *Jupiter Scapin*, or a sort of Scamp Jupiter" (Emerson 1950, 518).

Despite Emerson's reservations about Napoleon, his keenest celebration of him is as "representative" of "the class of business men in America, in England, in France and throughout Europe; the class of industry and skill." For Emerson, Napoleon suggested the struggle between "the interests of dead labor," (old money tied up in property and stocks) and "the interests of living labor, which seeks to possess itself of land and buildings and money stocks." The aim of "living labor" is materialistic, selfish, and anti-intellectual, subordinating everything to its single aim—yet Emerson found that it had a compelling degree of energy (Emerson 1950, 501). For Emerson, Napoleon was essentially modern, a man of the people who through ability and destiny combined achieved enormous power for France. He embodied the desires of his people, personifying their secret aspirations and unspoken fantasies. To the extent that he achieved power, the self-made emperor was an exciting iconoclast. Yet he set himself up as an icon, intent on retaining his own power at all costs, thus confounding expectations. His megalomaniac ambition, his selfishness and egotism, flawed the image his people had of him. It is owing to the conflicting emotions he inspired, desire and fear, that Emerson likens Napoleon to the figure of the American businessman. Napoleon was the representative of the vigorous new businessmen, the capitalists who were the forces of "living labor," and they, like Napoleon, were concerned with challenging entrenched traditions and setting themselves up in their place.

Emerson's fascination with Napoleon, and ambivalence toward him, strike a similar tone to Frederic's presentation of Joel Thorpe, who is emphatically both an "impostor" and a "rogue." Henry Nash Smith points out that Emerson perceives the extent to which the quest for power becomes "a kind of tropism, an irrational compulsion" that determines the actions of the Napoleon/businessmen. (Smith 1967, 91). This "compulsion" is a characteristic that Thorpe shares with Napoleon, climaxing in Thorpe's outrageous claim that he wants to rule England. Another shared characteristics is the overwhelming egotism of both men—Thorpe's "pride in his own brains and power was his weakest point" (Frederic Novels 1899, 270). Yet Emerson's anticlimactic dismissal of Napoleon, at the end of his essay, and with this gesture the trivialization of what Henry Nash Smith calls the "subversive threat of commercialism," is diametrically opposed to Frederic's response to the threat. Frederic, writing at the end of America's huge transformation from an agrarian to an industrial society, shows Thorpe to be the most "subversive threat" of the time. Bullying, buccaneering, amoral, and selfish, he is proof that Emerson's "metaphysical optimism" was misguided (Smith 1967, 92). At the end of *The Market-Place*

Frederic's bullying buccaneer shows every intention of "ruling England." Carlyle's description of Napoleon reveals more ambivalence than Emerson's. Carlyle criticizes the "fatal charlatan-element" that undermined Napoleon once he became emperor. Frederic may well have had Carlyle in mind when he wrote *The Market-Place*. Thorpe is compared with both Cromwell and Napoleon, two of Carlyle's kingly heroes, and like Carlyle's Napoleon, he is a charlatan. Edith Cressage, who eventually marries Thorpe, makes an inaccurate but direct reference to Carlyle when she tells Thorpe, "I fancied a rut was the one thing there could be no question about with you. I had the notion that you were incapable of ruts and conventional grooves. I thought you—as Carlyle puts it—I thought you were a man who swallows all the formulas" (Frederic Novels 1899, 300).

The force of the idea of Napoleon would undoubtedly have come to Frederic through the novels of Erckmann-Chatrian. A number of their novels center on the Republic and Empire. Two of them, *The History of a Conscript of 1813* (1864), and its sequel, *Waterloo* (1865), together sum up the phenomenon of Napoleon *The History of a Conscript of 1813* begins with a statement of extraordinary certainty, confrontation, and assurance, setting up an idea that will pervade the novel, remaining with the reader throughout all the catalogue of death, poverty, and fear: "People who did not see the glory of the Emperor Napoleon during the years 1810 to 1812 cannot realize the height to which the power of man can rise" (Erckmann-Chatrian 1909, 3).

The centrality of Napoleon as idea is established at the very outset of the novel. Napoleon is not simply a man, not merely emperor, but a possibility, a reminder of "the power of man." Within a few pages his status is confirmed. The first chapter presents the horror of being a nation continually at war. Oxen used to draw the wagons of the grenadiers serve as food when the provisions that they transport are exhausted. The animals are thin, diseased, and dying; their meat becomes unfit for consumption; the local priest warns that hundreds of thousands of men will also die to satisfy Napoleon's passion for war. The fate of the oxen is somberly symbolic. Yet the chapter ends with a reaffirmation of Napoleon's power: " '[T]hat man has the life of every one of us in his hands. He has to breathe upon us, and we are destroyed. Let us bless Heaven that he is not a bad man' " (Erckmann-Chatrian 1909, 8).

Waterloo continues the story of *The History of a Conscript of 1813*, and in the last chapter of the novel the anti-Royalist watchmaker Goulen muses bitterly on what Napoleon has brought France to: "When Napoleon took France into his hands she was the greatest, the freest, the most powerful of nations; all the others admired and envied us! But now we are vanquished, ruined, and bled to exhaustion; the enemy fills our fortresses, and has got his foot on our throat. We see what has never been seen since France existed—the stranger master of our capital. . . . That is what one pays for putting one's liberty, fortune, and honour in the hands of an ambitious man!" (Erckmann-Chatrian 1909, 358). This "ambitious man" has first been presented as a god of war, destroying his enemies but taking care of his people. By the end of *Waterloo* he has become a vampiric figure, bleeding France of its youth and capital to finance his lust for conquest and war, its liberty to further his absolutism.[11] He is both hero and monster, saint and villain. Napoleon represented both the best hopes and worst fears of a nation. As such he was an ideal "representative man" to compare with the paradoxical figure of the capitalist. If Napoleon wanted to be the "master of our capital," the capitalist wanted to be "master of capital."

Napoleon enjoyed emphasizing the role that chance had in his career, and liked to speak of himself as the "Child of Destiny" (Emerson 1950, 505). In a discussion of Julien Sorel in *Ideas and the Novel* (1980), Mary McCarthy recognizes the attraction this held for would-be Napoleons; and an apposite comment of hers extends the Napoleon/capitalist conflation: "To many minds, Napoleon was not just the man of destiny but destiny itself in a tricorne. It was natural, therefore, that youths seeking to be his avatars would feel they bore the stamp of destiny on them. . . . [T]o put it coarsely, they thought they had a 'future' and they gambled in their futures like speculators buying next year's wheat shares on the grain exchange" (McCarthy 1980, 74). It is in the context of a "gamble" that Napoleon is invoked in Twain and Warner's *The Gilded Age*.

The most compelling character of the novel, Colonel Sellers, is an unsuccessful and charming speculator continually failing in his elaborate and frequently ridiculous business ventures. His best commodity is certainly his charm—his only "selling" point. *The Gilded Age* is partly a satire on the American obsession with speculation, a preoccupation shared by Hawthorne's *The House of the Seven Gables*. Twain and Warner show that speculation has a particular attraction for American youth because of its sense of the space of the country, and the opportunities which it offers: "To the young American, here or elsewhere, the paths to fortune are innumerable and all open; there is invitation in the air and success in all his wide horizon. He is embarrassed which to choose, and is not unlikely to waste years in dallying with his chances, before giving himself to the serious tug and strain of a single object. He has no traditions to bind him or guide

---

11. Compare Emerson: "And what was the result of this vast talent and power, of those immense armies, burned cities, squandered treasures, immolated millions of men, of this demoralized Europe? . . . He left France smaller, poorer, feebler, than he found it, and the whole contest for freedom was to be begun again. . . . So this exorbitant egotist narrowed, impoverished and absorbed the power and existence of those who served him; and the universal cry of France and of Europe in 1814 was, 'Enough of Napoleon;' 'Assez de Bonaparte'" (Emerson 1950, 519).

him, and his impulse is to break away from the occupation his father has
followed, and make a new way for himself" (Twain and Warner 1967, 76).[12]
The novel's irony is often biting, and Twain and Warner use satire to great
effect.

The Gilded Age, rambling and weak though it often is, explodes American
mythologizing and explores the emptiness of the philosophy of the Gilded
Age. Sellers, constantly speculating, acting a part, spinning yarns, is the
mouthpiece for the myth of the limitless bounty of the American nation.
The United States, he says, is "The place for a young man of spirit to pick
up a fortune, simply pick it up, it's lying round loose here" (Twain and
Warner 1967, 89). The myth had already been punctured by the expatriate
Welshman Henry Morton Stanley, who in 1867 accompanied General Han-
cock (and later, General Sherman) on their respective Indian campaigns.
In *My Early Travels and Adventures in America* (1895) he recalls an event that
proved to him that the fantasy of America's bounty was largely illusory:
"This country strikes a person at first glance as being immensely rich in
the precious metals. But 'All that glitters is not gold' I found a very true
proverb. In my prospecting tour over the mountains, I saw quantities of
yellow metal which I believed to be gold. I filled my pockets with the
precious stuff, as there was so much of it. I filled a satchel with it, and had
a very good mind to fill my hat also. I carried my treasure to the hotel, and
up to my room, and, choosing a small piece, I took it down, and carelessly
asked a rough-looking fellow what he thought of it. Imagine my surprise
and disappointment when he pronounced it a 'pretty nice species of pyrites
of iron' " (Stanley 1982, 186–87). Stanley avoids the mineral's popular
name—"fool's gold"—but his anecdote nicely reverses stereotypes. It is
the smart journalist who must retreat to the *American Cyclopaedia* for a
definition of the gilded mineral, and the "rough-looking fellow" who has
a glib instant recognition of it. Stanley has a last stab at salvaging his
self-respect, adding in conclusion, "I retain a belief that Colorado is as rich
in gold as any territory in the United States, though capitalists are just now
shy of Colorado mining stock, and prefer to invest their money in other
speculations." The America Stanley describes in this passage is Sellers's
America, part myth and part reality. This is the breeding place for the
American self-made man. The name that Sellers wants to call one of the
towns he is planning is "Napoleon." It is the ideal name for a town that
remains the potent fantasy of a man whose destiny has failed him.

---

12. Also compare with Edward Bok's comments in his autobiography which unironically
reiterates the myth, "he found every avenue leading to success wide open and certainly not
overpeopled. He was surprised how few there were who really stood in a young man's way"
(Bok 1921, 125). Emerson is also useful on this point, arguing that the class represented by
Napoleon "desires to keep open every avenue to the competition of all, and to multiply
avenues" (Emerson 1950, 501).

Chance and destiny play no part in Henry R. Elliot's "After Business Hours." The story appears in the same limited edition volume as Frederic's "Cordelia and the Moon."[13] It opens with a millionaire arriving home to find a reporter waiting to interview him "on 'How Rich Men Get Rich' . . . this ever interesting topic" that echoes the start of Howells's *The Rise of Silas Lapham* and that demonstrates New Journalism at work, for the interview was an innovative technique[14] (Elliot 1893, 219). Trumbull, the millionaire, gives a practical demonstration of his talents by selling the reporter a house on which he owns the mortgage. His philosophy, he explains, is to get rich by helping others to get rich. In this way one can avoid making enemies. In an age when Carnegie was preaching the laws of business competition, Trumbull's explanation of his success sounds a little unconvincing. His methods are outlined in more detail later when he describes his investment strategies to a persistent dinner guest: "Let it be granted, as the school-books say, that the United States is gaining on the world, and that in the United States the cities are gaining on the country, and he who backs the averaged growth of the averaged American city is sure to win" (Elliott 1893, 221). Believing that American cities must expand, he buys up plots of land around the circumferences of selected cities at regular intervals. Which ever way the city grows, he makes money. In this way he eliminates chance as a determining factor in his success, replacing it with a combination of patriotism and good sense. Trumbull is explicitly linked to the transformation of America into a market-based urban economy and is exposed for his mock philanthropy and his petty miserliness.[15] Like Joel Thorpe, Trumbull is compared with Napoleon, though only in passing: the newspaper reporter notices "the masterful bearing of this king of trade, and the large brilliant eyes lustrous with what Napoleon called the glance of conquest" (Elliot 1893, 221).

The "Representative Man"

The capitalist was too important a figure to be ignored, but writing about him or her (though the capitalist was usually represented as male) presented novelists with dilemmas. Writers were forced to question the nature of the society from which these figures had emerged. In an unpublished doctoral thesis, "Representative Men: Businessmen in American Fiction 1875–1914," (which uses Emerson's phrase) Clare Eby argues that

13. Since Frederic was not a member of the Author's Club, which published the collection of stories, he did not automatically receive a copy of the book, and may not have been familiar with the story.

14. It might be interesting to read Frederic's description of the early career of Jeremiah Madden in this way too: it is presented as if it were just such a description of the self-made American man.

15. Compare Howells 1971, 29.

the contradictions involved in writing about the businessman stem from the fact that American response to business is "inextricably bound up with our [i.e., an American] sense of national identity" (Eby 1988, 8).[16] As late-nineteenth-century society was transformed from an agrarian to industrial society, a new social order was created with power and money concentrated in the hands of fewer people. The enormous expansion in business in the late nineteenth and early twentieth centuries was accompanied by a huge population expansion—from 31 million in 1860 to 92 million in 1910. This created a vast market that further compounded the transformation in American society. She concludes that "Standing astride the rubble of a society faced with such upheavals seemed to be the businessman. . . . Demons who attempted to corner gold markets, princes who endowed universities, Machiavellian instigators of panics, philanthropic patrons of art museums and libraries, the businessman seemed to embody much of the good and evil of the new age. He was, in short, the new Representative Man of America" (Eby 1988, 3–4). Despite Eby's use of the word "businessman" it is more appropriate to use the word "capitalist" to epitomize the phenomenon she describes. The old style of businesswoman or man (though he tended to be a man), as has been argued earlier, was figured differently within American fiction.

As "Representative Man" this new figure was ideally suited to be the protagonist of a distinctively American literature. He was the uniquely American hero of an idiosyncratic plot He demanded new treatment. At last Americans had found an area, business, in which they could, and would, dominate the rest of the world. (To some extent the American novel of finance anticipates, and partakes in, this victory.) America could compete financially with other nations where it could not in terms of history. The newest part of American society, its capitalists, became its version of the aristocracy. In various fictional treatments of the business theme the new American aristocracy challenges established American society or European aristocracy (for example, in both *The American* and *The Market-Place*). Their aristocratic status is established by a process of naming; names in themselves indicate society's ambivalence toward this new class. Newspapers popularly referred to some capitalists as "Robber Barons," suggesting both criminality and aristocracy. Eby points out that Joel Thorpe is jocosely referred to as the "Rubber King" at one point, and Newman chaffed about being "Duke of California." (Eby 1988, 6). A 1905 article from the *Wall Street Journal* shows how overused such titles had become:

16. "My argument is that our attitudes as a nation towards business are inextricably bound up with our sense of national identity, and that these attitudes were being reconstructed during the formative years of modern business in the late nineteenth and early twentieth centuries."

"the king of petroleum John D. Rockefeller, who is also prince of financial concentration, duke of trusts, earl of banks, marshal of railroads, knight of the golden fleece of billions, and decorated with the brass medal of the order of Ida M. Tarbell" (Eby 1988, 5).[17] She might have added that mock-aristocratic sobriquets are associated, in American folklore, with nomadic conmen such as the "Duke" and "King" in *Huckleberry Finn*—and that Joel Thorpe is just such a conman Frederic's misgivings about Thorpe are most succinctly suggested by the title "Rubber King." (One of Robert Maxwell's nicknames was the "Bouncing Czech.")

In a discussion of James, Frederic, Wharton, and Dreiser, Eby argues that their representation of the businessman is characterized by "contradictions and ambivalences" (Eby 1988, 15). Indeed, Frederic's difficulties in writing about Thorpe were considerable. As a person commanding a certain sort of power Thorpe is an exciting and challenging figure, yet as a ruthless philistine he is often personally distasteful. Frederic's tone is always ironic, and he views Thorpe with detachment. Other writers had different strategies for writing about a figure who was portrayed as half-angel, half-demon. Hawthorne, himself deeply reticent about his own relationship with the literary marketplace, spends an entire chapter of *The House of the Seven Gables* verbally attacking the dead body of Judge Pyncheon. Like Hepzibah Pyncheon, fearfully and shame-facedly opening her "cent" shop in certain knowledge of the stern disapproval of dead ancestors, Hawthorne wrote and sold his romances. Yet he registers his deep distrust of the market by his lengthy attack on Judge Pyncheon, which is both vengeful and cathartic.

Frederic concentrates more on an analysis of Thorpe's motives and less on the painstaking details of transactions than does another journalist/novelist, Theodore Dreiser, in his treatment of Frank Cowperwood, the protagonist of Dreiser's *Trilogy of Desire — The Financier* (1912), *The Titan* (1914), and *The "Genius"* (1915). Dreiser bombards the reader with a bewildering quantity of facts and figures, whereas Frederic is content to economize. Nevertheless, Dreiser's realism provides a commentary on

---

17. Twain and Warner send this process up in *The Gilded Age*. Sellers says, of Washington D.C., "when we first came here I was Mr. Sellers, and *Major* Sellers, and *Captain* Sellers, but nobody could ever get it right, somehow, but the minute our bill went through the House I was *Colonel* Sellers every time. And nobody could do enough for me; and whatever I said was wonderful, sir; it was always wonderful; I never seemed to say any flat things at all. . . . Well, the Senate adjourned, and left our bill high and dry, and I'll be hanged if I warn't Old *Sellers* from that day till our bill passed the House again last week. Now I'm the *Colonel* again; and if I were to eat all the dinners I am invited to, I reckon I'd wear my teeth down to a level with my gums in a couple of weeks." "Well, I do wonder what you will be tomorrow, Colonel, after the President signs the bill?" "*General*, sir! General without a doubt" (Twain and Warner 1967, 383).

Frederic's less detailed prose when it comes to the terminology of the Stock Exchange. Thorpe's explanation of his financial situation to his sister is not especially revealing: "We've got what's called a corner on the bears. They're caught short, and we can squeeze them to our heart's content. What, you don't understand now?" (Frederic Novels 1899, 34). Louisa claims that she does understand, and indeed she seems to, but this may have to do more with sisterly telepathy than the definitive nature of the explanation. Dreiser provides the necessary elucidation, writing that a " 'bear' was one who sold stocks which most frequently he did not have, in anticipation of a lower price, at which he could buy and satisfy his previous sales. He was 'short' when he had sold what he did not own. . . . He was in a 'corner' when he found that he could not buy in order to make good the stock he had borrowed for delivery and the return of which had been demanded" (Dreiser 1946, 41).

Dreiser's descriptions are often more journalistic than Frederic's. Whereas Frederic alludes to complexities, Dreiser pursues them relentlessly. The detail of Dreiser's naturalism often inhibits the movement of the plot. He clarifies the minuscule to such an extent that he obscures the larger outlines. His interest is primarily in the mechanistic aspect of the enormous forces he believes shape human destiny. Frederic is not so much concerned with impersonal forces as with individual, Napoleonic ambition —Thorpe's desire for power and for revenge. Frank Norris, deeming the individual of little significance compared with the forces that shape things, treats the capitalist of *The Octopus* with more subtlety. Presley goes to meet Shelgrim, the capitalist, and discovers that the seventy-year-old man usually leaves his office late in the evening and often comes back to work there at night. Presley's immediate response is highly conventional: "It is an ogre's vitality. . . . Just so is the man-eating tiger strong. The man should have energy who has sucked the life-blood from an entire People" (Norris 1986, 571).[18] His assumptions are challenged and overcome when he listens in on a conversation between Shelgrim and an assistant manager about a worker who has occasional days of bitterly regretted drunkenness. The manager wants to sack him, but Shelgrim insists on doubling his pay as an incentive. Presley, astonished at this, is even more surprised when Shelgrim expresses a sound knowledge of art criticism. He concludes that Shelgrim is a more complex figure than he had given him credit for being "who understood with equal intelligence, the human nature in an habitual

18. The vampiric overtones of this passage recall the tone of Erckmann-Chatrian's *Waterloo,* yet they also suggest another significant aspect of the representation of the figure of the capitalist, which is the "racial chain of signification that links vampirism to anti-Semitic representations of Jewishness." See Halberstam 1993, 348 The relation of anti-Semitic discourses within *The Market-Place* is highly complex and contradictory.

drunkard, the ethics of a masterpiece of painting, and the financiering and operation of ten thousand miles of railroad" (Norris 1986, 575).[19]

The Romance of Money

In Howells's *The Rise of Silas Lapham,* Bromfield Corey, explaining the attractiveness of finance, resignedly admits that it is "the poetry of our age" (Howells, 1971, 64). Corey, a wealthy dilettante artist (whose family money has come from trade) sees the romantic allure of money and money making, tangentially suggested by his son's courtship of Lapham's daughter. Basil March, in Howells's *A Hazard of New Fortunes,* accepts that business-men like Jacob Dryfoos are "the ideal and ambition of most Americans," but inveighs against the warping effect that money making has had on his character and the threat that it poses to an American public that idolizes Dryfoos: "He must have undergone a moral deterioration, an atrophy of the generous instincts, and I don't see why it shouldn't have reached his mental make-up. He has sharpened, but he has narrowed; his sagacity has turned into suspicion, his caution to meanness, his courage to ferocity" (Howells 1976, 224–25).

The romance of money reaches its apotheosis in *The Great Gatsby,* in the character of Jay Gatsby, who has, the narrator feels, "an extraordinary gift for hope, a romantic readiness such as I have never found in any other person and which it is not likely I shall ever find again." Yet despite Fitzger-ald's lush and haunting evocation of Gatsby, the novel is punctuated by regular registers of the narrator's disapproval of him and what he repre-sents—"everything for which I have an unaffected scorn" (Fitzgerald 1974, 8). A radically different writer, Sinclair Lewis, had already savagely and unequivocally attacked American consumerism and the businessman in *Babbitt* (1922), in which—like Arthur Miller in *Death of a Salesman* (1949) —he focused upon the "ordinary" man of more commonplace experience. When George Babbitt meets a group of like-minded men on a train, Lewis's contempt reaches a pitch: "To them, the Romantic Hero was no longer

19. Presley's response to Shelgrim resembles the perplexed double response that the public had to William Randolph Hearst. "An ominous message came from Henderson, the [San Francisco] *Examiner's* stiff-necked editorial manager:/ 'Chamberlain drunk again. May I dismiss him?' Hearst, who was fond of Chamberlain, replied: 'If he is sober one day in thirty that is all that I require' (Swanberg, 1962, 65). Swanberg also writes that "General Weyler and the Brooklyn Bridge engineers could logically say that he was an unmitigated liar. Hum-ble citizens of New York for whom he had fought and won a lower gas rate regarded him as the soul of virtue. Upper-crust New Yorkers who recoiled at his newspapers felt that he must be the most vulgar of men; yet people who met him were personally struck by his shy charm and genuine courtesy. Rival newspapermen regarded him as a monster of misrepresentation, but they had to admit that his own dispatches from Cuba were able and accurate" (173).

the knight, the wandering poet, the cowpuncher, the aviator, nor the brave young district attorney, but the great sales-manager, who had an Analysis of Merchandising Problems on his glass-topped desk, whose title of nobility was 'Go-getter,' and who devoted himself and all his young samurai to the cosmic purpose of Selling—not of selling anything in particular, for or to anybody in particular, but pure Selling" (Lewis 1945, 143). Jay Gatsby and Willy Loman both live and die for their single-minded dreams. Loman sells himself short and kills himself when he recognizes his own redundancy and the bankruptcy of his dream. Gatsby lives and dies amidst his, paying "a high price for living too long with a single dream," a dream that romanticizes his "dirty" money hiding the reality of his business deals behind his Platonically created self. (Fitzgerald 1974, 168).[20] Gatsby is a consummate artist, possessed of a "creative temperament" and an all-consuming romantic fantasy. This conflation of art, romance, and finance was a consistent aspect of early novels of finance.

Dreiser's fascination with the relation between the capitalist and the artist is apparent throughout *The Financier.* His interest centers on the question of vocation and genius—whether financiers were actually organically different from other men, whether the titans of finance really were a new breed. This preoccupation was shared by Frank Norris: their comments on it are similar. The narrator of *The Financier* calls finance "an art." The young Cowperwood's transformation into a financier, comes from a combination of this natural instinct and a certain amount of training, including visits to his father's bank. Cowperwood's natural instinct is to be a financier, and his training enhances this—both Norris and Dreiser would agree that the effects of environment are incalculable. In an article of 1901 entitled "Novelists to Order—While You Wait" (which nicely combines art and commerce), Norris argues that "genius" is simply a combination of ability and training. The artist and the capitalist both possess this "genius," but in different areas, indeed, every capitalist of "genius" could, under different circumstances, have been an artist of "genius," (and presumably vice versa). Although both Carnegie and Rostand might be called "geniuses," it is unlikely, or at least debatable, that we would say that their "genius" differed "in kind." He goes on to say that "As for my part, I suspect that, given a difference in environment and training, Rostand would have consolidated the American steel companies and Carnegie have written *L'Aiglon*" (Norris 1964, 14–15). Norris's argument was also being taken up, with different emphasis, by apologists for the capitalists. Clare Eby points out that "One recalcitrant literature professor at the University of Chicago, delighted by John D. Rockefeller's generosity to the University,

---

20. See also Godden 1990, 78–103, especially his discussion of connoisseurship on 52–53.

published a study asserting that the Standard Oil tycoon was more of a creative genius than Homer, Dante or Shakespeare" (Eby 1988, 21). Amidst the enormous implications of such claims, these figures become far more intriguing figure to writers.

Emerson's essay *Napoleon; or The Man of the World,* which comes to mind again in relation to Norris, argues that if Napoleon has a special appeal it is to what is similar to us in him: "[I]f Napoleon is France, if Napoleon is Europe, it is because the people whom he sways are little Napoleons" (Emerson 1950, 501). The analogy with Norris is not exact, yet it is sufficient to explain the implications of Norris's conjecturing. If the artist can see the possibilities of the capitalist in him, not because he himself is a potential capitalist but because he recognizes the "genius" that is common to them, the capitalist becomes a less remote, less fabulous figure—the two have a shared humanity. Emerson quotes Napoleon as saying, "The market-place . . . is the Louvre of the common people" (Emerson 1950, 501). With a deft transference of terms, the capitalist—whose gallery is the marketplace—is the artist of the common people. Yet tycoons in American fiction usually have an extremely limited sense of beauty or art, except in terms of its commodity value. Adam Verver, of *The Golden Bowl* (1904), conceives of himself as almost the equal of the artist because he is a collector of art. Elmer Moffat, self-made business tycoon of *The Custom of the Country* (1913), compares his sense of business with that of Raymond de Chenes, a French aristocrat. He tells Undine, who is currently married to de Chenes, that he can understand why de Chenes is reluctant to part with a number of tapestries his family owns, for "His ancestors are his business: Wall Street's mine" (Wharton 1965, 389). Eventually Moffat marries Undine and gets the tapestries.

Dreiser's Cowperwood is far from being an artist. Although he appreciates beauty in the two women that he marries, he has no feeling for literature. The desirability of these women simply confirms his own sense of purchase power. When he praises their looks he is celebrating his own business acumen. His second wife is younger and more beautiful than his first. As a commodity, his first wife is slightly shop-soiled (she is a widow) and has a short shelf life (she is older than he). His second wife is top-quality goods. Christopher Newman, of *The American,* has a similar notion of marriage. He says, "I want to possess, in a word, the best article in the market" (James 1983, 549). The contractual nature of marriage is a commonplace. It often involves exchanges that benefit both parties. The marriage between Maggie Verver and Prince Amerigo of *The Golden Bowl* (1904) is a fine example. Maggie has "wealth," Amerigo, "wealth of kinship" (James 1987, 53). Ralph Marvell of *The Custom of the Country,* is explicit about the nature of the exchange: "The daughters of his own race sold themselves to the Invaders; the daughters of the Invaders bought their husbands as they bought an opera-box. It ought all to have been transacted on the Stock Exchange" (Wharton 1965, 74). Thorpe's appreciation, like that of Cowperwood, is allied to a desire to appropriate. Thorpe thinks of Edith Cressage as an elaborate and decorous possession. Marrying her will enhance his reputation as a man of taste: "Why, all the world is going to have living proof very soon . . . living proof that I'm the greatest judge of perfection in beauty of my time" (Frederic Novels 1899, 240).

The Dual Man

In a letter to his main American publisher in November 1896 Frederic writes that he has "two or three tentative American-serial suggestions in hand," and before he died he was negotiating with another publisher over a proposed novel, *Kenley*. His description of the plot suggests James and Wharton, for his theme was to be the American in Europe: "The book is to be a study of two Americans in Europe—a boy and a girl in Boston in the late seventies, (which will be largely autobiographical)—then in England. . . . It will be a book of character studies of painters, opera singers, actors, and the like, in the London of our day" (Frederic to Frederick A. Stokes, ca. July 1898, Frederic Misc. 1977, 481).

It is indisputable that Frederic's last three novels show a movement away from his early preoccupation with New York State, but the transition from American to European settings was not smooth. The protagonists of his last novels are uneasy with their positions within European society. *Gloria Mundi* and *The Market-Place* both center upon characters who are never fully integrated into English life. In *Gloria Mundi* Christian Tower finds that his background is sometimes painfully at odds with his newly discovered heritage. Throughout the novel his French upbringing is revealed by spontaneous gestures or by outbreaks that jar with the more restrained behavior of his English family. At one point he kisses the butler and cries on his shoulders only to be gently told by his uncle that "Under ordinary circumstances, men in England do not kiss their butlers, or even sob on their bosoms" (Frederic Novels 1898, 99 and 103). In *The Market-Place* Frederic represented Thorpe as being characterized by movement. He says, "I always intended to come back here; or, no, I won't say that, because most of the time I was dog poor, and this isn't the place for a poor man. But I always said to myself that if ever I pulled it off—if I ever found myself a rich man—*then* I'd come piking across the Atlantic as fast as the triple-expansion engines would carry me" (Frederic Novels 1899, 9). Thorpe first meets Lord Plowden (who joins his dummy board of directors) crossing the Atlantic, a midway point between the New World and the Old, at which the rigid value-systems of the Old World give way to the more egalitarian mores of the Republic. Plowden has spoken to him only because he has mistaken him for an American. Being a rich "American" guarantees him a certain flexibility within English society and is one of the easiest ways of cutting through a normally rigid class hierarchy. The point is also made by Howells's Bromfield Corey: "[T]he suddenly rich are on a level with any of us nowadays. . . . [T]here's no doubt but money is to the fore now. It is the romance, the poetry of our age. It's the thing that chiefly strikes the imagination. The Englishmen who come here are more curious about the great new millionaires than about anyone else, and they respect them more" (Howells 1971, 64). In *March Hares* Frederic had exploited this curiosity in his representation of the oil millionaire Laban Skinner, yet Skinner is a one-dimensional figure and is not intended to be more than that. Joel Thorpe is a very different creature.

Thorpe, the most complex character in Frederic's fiction, dominates *The Market-Place,* personifying contradiction and duality. Frederic's attitude toward him is curiously ambivalent: one is never sure whether Thorpe is the hero or villain of the piece. He quite literally has the last laugh on every occasion, and when the novel ends he is laughing last, and loudest. His laugh is sometimes that of a pantomime antihero, yet it can also be chilling. To many of the figures within the novel Thorpe is an enigma who acts on whim and has tremendous capacities both for revenge and for generosity. He can be unpredictable and freakish in his mood swings. Although he thinks and talks about himself and his projects incessantly, his self-knowledge is limited. He sees himself as a compound of two separate but complementary types—a good Thorpe and a bad Thorpe—perhaps a sort of socially acceptable Jekyll and Hyde.

The comparison with Stevenson's divided protagonist is significant. *The Strange Case of Dr. Jekyll and Mr. Hyde* (1886) centers around a figure whose dual and dueling personalities depend upon each other. "Jekyll" and "Hyde" are not two separate halves of a person, one good, one bad, but are a single personality within which the two parts exist symbiotically. The personality that represents Jekyll/Hyde becomes unstable only when the natural relationship of Jekyll to Hyde, which keeps the two in balance, is broken. At this point both Jekyll and Hyde begin to deteriorate. The chemical "purification" of the elements that make up the compound of Jekyll/Hyde is an illusion. The experiment turns out to be one, not of purification or distillation, but of destruction. So it is appropriate that the conditions of the original chemical experiment on Jekyll/Hyde can be recreated only for a finite amount of time, for the initial chemicals contained an unknown impurity. Jekyll cannot rid himself of Hyde—he is inescapable.

Frederic greatly admired Stevenson and would certainly have been familiar with the novel. At the beginning of *The Market-Place* Thorpe is described in terms that suggest Hyde, and also suggest familiarity with Lombroso's phrenological theories of criminality. Thorpe is Neanderthal in appearance—"burly and slouching," his face "thick-featured, immobile, undistinguished," his clothes, hair and beard, unkempt and neglected.

Most significantly, his hands "resting on his big knees were coarse in shape, and roughened and ill-kept" (Frederic Novels 1899, 360). If Hyde, troglodytic, with hands that are "lean, corded, knuckly, of a dusky pallor, and thickly shaded with a swart growth of hair" is the "beast within" (an ancestral ape), then the early Thorpe is a close cousin (Stevenson 1987, 88). Thorpe's transformation into "Stormont" Thorpe, the well-groomed capitalist, is almost as rapid as Hyde's materialization back into Jekyll, but is more stable.[21] Frederic's equivalent of Stevenson's chemical concoction is money: Thorpe is an alchemist who turns rubber into gold and uses that gold to turn himself into a member of the landed gentry. It is not free from impurity—far from it—but unlike Jekyll, Thorpe is under no illusions about its purity. So long as it is in regular supply, Thorpe is safe. He can contain Joel Thorpe within the vast personality of "Stormont" Thorpe, though on occasions Joel does threaten to burst out—most notably, toward the end of the novel.

Throughout the novel Thorpe reinvents himself, changing from a ruthless capitalist to a respectable country gentleman, as he has already changed from a lower-middle-class shopkeeper to an adventurer. Already implicated in the death of one of the two men who could have revealed his duplicity, he stops himself when he is on the verge of murdering the only other man who knows about his history. In a moment of remarkable self-delusion Thorpe convinces himself that his personality has been transformed:

> With a singular clearness of mental vision he perceived that the part of him which brought bad dreams had been sloughed off—like a serpent's skin. There had always been two Thorpes, and one of them—the Thorpe who had always been willing to profit by knavery, and at last, in a splendid coup as a master thief, had stolen nearly a million, and would have shrunk not at all from adding murder to the rest, to protect that plunder—this vicious Thorpe had gone away altogether. There was no longer a place for him in life; he would never be seen again by mortal eye. . . . There remained only the good Thorpe—the pleasant, well intentioned, opulent gentleman; the excellent citizen; the beneficent master, to whom even Gafferson, like the others, touched a respectful forelock. (Frederic Novels 1899, 343)

Thorpe may be a snake with a new skin, but he is indubitably a snake, a reptilian capitalist all the more dangerous for his facade of gentility, for his multiplicity of skins and his ability to consume, to regurgitate, and to reconstitute: a version of the novelist.

---

21. William Veeder's discussion of the importance of preserving one's name in *The Strange Case of Dr. Jekyll and Mr Hyde* is instructive here. See Veeder and Hirsch 1988.

Afterword

In February 1897 Harold Frederic wrote to Charles Scribner, of his main American publishers, Charles Scribner's Sons, enclosing the completed preface to a Uniform Edition of his work. The letter contains several suggestions for the forthcoming edition and possible future writing, but it was prompted by the simple necessity of sending the preface. The first paragraph is a brief, blunt reflection upon the commissioned piece: "Here is a preface. I am quite frank in saying that I have no notion whatever whether it is too long, (it can hardly be too short) too introspective, too autobiographical, too everything" (Frederic to Charles Scribner, 16 February 1897, Frederic Misc. 1977, 441).

In contrast with the flat, businesslike, and reluctant tone of this paragraph, Frederic's "Preface to a Uniform Edition" is playfully self-assured in tone. He had expressed a concern, in the preface itself as well as in his letter to Scribner, that it was "over-long," and his main anxieties were stylistic. He had never before written a preface to his own work. It was unexplored territory. As he writes in the preface, it was "strange ground." The preface is a self-referential peregrination, and Frederic plays with the imaginative possibilities of the metaphor that he had used. He argues that writing prefaces is an American fashion. Since he was "doomed to be doing in England at least something of what the English do" he adds, self-consciously parodying his genuine disquietude, he had "never before chanced to write one." What happens next is interesting. He "abruptly" finishes what he calls "the apology of the exile" and begins an apotheosis. He extends the "strange ground" metaphor. The mock-solemnity of "exile" and doom are part of this. He backtracks rapidly: despite his "exile," he argues, he is nonetheless an American. Once again he returns, through his fiction, to his childhood in upstate New York. He calls the history of his family one of the most important inspirations behind *In the Valley*. He writes about his early attempts at the novel, produced while he was still at school. He argues his position using his fiction as evidence. The American subject matter of his writing becomes necessary proof of his adherence to American life.

This argument is not altogether compelling, given his writing shift toward Europe, but he is selective in his choice. He projects the "Americanness" of his personality solely through the medium of the fiction reproduced in the Uniform Edition. His subject, he writes, is the United States, and though the contents of the Uniform Edition (*Seth's Brother's Wife, In the Valley, The Lawton Girl,* and several of the Civil War stories) were written in England, "they do not belong to the Old World in any other sense." The implication is that it is England itself that is "strange ground," and Frederic who does not belong. Although he was estranged from the United States that he knew and loved, the estrangement was physical. Emotionally, intellectually, he was as captivated by American life as ever. Thirteen years after Frederic had left New York State for England, this position is not persuasive. He had regularly chronicled English life throughout his entire residence in England. He had visited the United States infrequently. It was he who was becoming the stranger, and his denials of strangeness and estrangement act as poignant testimonials to his alienation. Even at this late stage in his writing career Frederic was still anxiously defending himself against the imagined criticism of others, in this instance his American readership. Twenty months later he would become one of what he called the "defenseless dead," but while he was alive he would fight out his own position. The question of nationality and patriotism still troubled him. He was still explaining, arguing, exhorting. Early in Frederic's life he had set out on an intellectual and geographical journey away from Utica. He would find that he had traveled too far and too fast. He could not return, he was unwilling to remain where he was, and the possibility of moving out of his predicament was complicated. Uncertain of what to do next, he had the choice taken from him. His journey was cut short by his premature death. It was a solution, of sorts, but it could not be called a resolution.

On Tuesday, 25 October 1898, a short article appeared in the *Daily Chronicle.* Headed "The Late Mr. Harold Frederic," it gives details of Frederic's cremation. More precisely, it gives details of the journey to the event. Initially it appears to be strictly to the point, but the narrative rapidly becomes dislocated:

> The body was conveyed from . . . Waterloo by the quarter-past ten train yesterday morning, and a few friends of the deceased went down to Woking to attend the funeral service by the five minutes to one train. Two saloon carriages were placed at their disposal, one of the saloons being nearly filled with beautiful wreaths. . . . Unfortunately several friends of the deceased were directed to the wrong platform at Waterloo, and so lost the train which conveyed the rest of the mourners. Mrs. Harold Frederic desires us to express her grateful thanks to the large numbers of her friends who have sent her

letters and messages of sympathy in her bereavement. ("The Late Mr. Harold Frederic," 3)

The wonderfully bathetic penultimate sentence transforms the unemotive prose, lending an unfortunate air of farce to the narrative. As readers we enjoy the imagined spectacle and grimace at the sheer awfulness of it: the wrong platform; the missed or "lost" train; the presumed horror of the mourners; the depleted funeral service; all of which mock the stateliness of the saloon "nearly filled with beautiful wreaths" and radically destabilize the rhetoric of precision associated with the detail of the narrative (the carefully outlined train times) but which is also associated with the mode of cultural production, to the mechanics of newspaper journalism, and to that elusive concept, "newsworthiness." Other possibilities or variants of the story are thrilling, too. What if the body had also gone astray? Our glee and our anxiety pivot upon such possibilities and focus on the unlikeliness of the route on which the narrative has led us. Like the hapless mourners, it seems that we, too, have been sent off in the wrong direction or at least one that was not anticipated. The story turns out to be, at one level, grotesque comedy or low humor, though it had seemed to be about something else. Ultimately that is exactly what it is: a story that is not what it seems, one that turns out to be about something else or at least available for multiple readings or meanings. It might be necessary to begin again, to retrace our steps and start upon a new narrative journey.

The problematic rhetoric of discovery, revelation, analysis, and construction is one this anecdote neatly illustrates: here the newspaper account is presented as if it is a single privileged discourse, one that fills in gaps and produces an authoritative narrative of prescence rather than absence, but that is clearly only contingent, provisional, another voice or testimony, and indeed, one that is highly partial. In presenting the case of Harold Frederic I have had to demonstrate the processes by which I came to interrogate his death and also the way in which I decided to go about researching and writing it. Even when I finally found the location of his body I found that the questions I had about his death were not solved. I had, it seemed, found the final resting place of his ashes—I had certainly found a tomb marked with his name; it read:

Harold Frederic
Author & Journalist
1856–1898

Yet other testimony, that of his daughter Ruth, suggested that his ashes had been interred a few thousand miles away, in England, and she was undoubtedly confused by the question of where Frederic's ashes were lo-

Stone marker at Forest Hill cemetery, Utica, New York.

cated. Cemetery records revealed that though Frederic was indeed interred in the Forest Hill cemetery in Utica, and though only his name was marked on the tombstone, the ashes of Grace Frederic, and of their daughter Ruby, had been interred with his. Having found what I thought was the end of his story and my journey, I found new texts to investigate: the misleading (or was it?) inscription on his tombstone, and then, as I investigated that, the texts proliferated; I found myself immersed in cemetery records and city records, notices of births and deaths, and cemetery plot purchases.[1]

1. Frederic's eldest daughter confessed herself "frankly confused" by the details of the family plot. She wrote (of her parents) that "the ashes of both were disposed of in England." Yet it seems that she was simply mistaken, and that time had played tricks with her memory. In the same letter she admits that dates mean little to her, and though she seems to be

Might Frederic be located there, too? I found myself attempting to construct a body of evidence that would help me ascertain the circumstances of his death and its aftermath, and trying to find the real location of Harold Frederic. I found myself asking innumerable questions—why had Frederic and his wife been forcefully reunited after death? Who had paid for the looming marker in which his ashes had been placed? Who had chosen the inscription, and why? Finally, why, if the presence of Frederic in this "strange ground" was to be marked, were the names of Grace and Ruby Frederic left out altogether?[2] Indeed, I was doing exactly what I had always cautioned against, for I found myself wanting to construct the last word, the definitive text. Yet I knew that this was impossible and that I must go about my work without making special claims for myself or for him. In doing this I found that I had to return to the newspaper accounts of his death that had appeared on two continents; to correspondence, memoirs, and diaries; and to the evidence I had collected about his coded double life.

His body had formed and had provided evidence for his travels, and his body, the subject of an autopsy after his death, was also to some degree the key evidence in the manslaughter trial. The mute body, mutilated after the doctors had finished their final examinations, was made to speak, and it told of a life of excess. Yet it did not respond to questions of a pressing nature, did not tell whether it was that of a suicide or that of a man who had been killed by another or other parties. The body did not provide evidence for either argument and indeed, could not. It was clear that other documentation or forms of evidence would have to be uncovered if the case of Harold Frederic was to be solved. The body, a site of competing articulations and accounts, did not speak for itself and indeed, could not. The beginning, like the end, could only be the word.

---

mistaken about facts on occasion, she is remarkably sharp and quirky, as ever (Ruth Frederic to Hoyt Franchere, ? Jan. 1960, Harold Frederic Edition). Robert Woodward describes an interview of 1963 with Harold Frederic Baxter, Frederic's second cousin and godson (the spelling of his name is interesting). Baxter claimed that the ashes of Harold and Grace Frederic were kept on a mantelpiece by Frederic's mother, and on the death of their daughter Ruby in 1901, the ashes were all interred together. He also suggested that the cemetery records contained inaccuracies (Woodward 1967, 5).

2. Baxter indicated that the inscription had been made a few years prior to 1963, and though in Woodward's brief article there is no account of why the family might have chosen to have the inscription made, it is no doubt related to the emerging interest in Frederic, as well as to the fact of the passing of time. The inscription is interesting for the way in which it splits off the words "author" and "journalist" as if a journalist is not also an author.

WORKS CITED

INDEX

Works Cited

Primary Sources: Unpublished Works

Harold Frederic Edition. Department of English, University of Nebraska, Lincoln. The papers here include unpublished letters, bank statements, and so forth, and also all of Frederic's known writing for the *New York Times*.

Harold Frederic Papers. Washington, D.C., Library of Congress.

Harold Frederic Papers, Personal Miscellaneous. Ernest L. Oppenheim Papers, Rare Books and Manuscripts Division, The New York Public Library, Astor, Lenox, and Tilden Foundations.

Stephen and Cora Crane Papers. Rare Books and Manuscripts Library, Butler Library, Columbia University.

Frederic's collection of press clippings. Utica College of Syracuse University, Utica, N.Y.

Primary Sources: Published Works

Novels

1890a. *In the Valley.* New York: Charles Scribner's Sons.

1890b. *The Lawton Girl.* London: Chatto & Windus.

1892. *The Return of The O'Mahony.* New York: Robert Bonner's Sons,

1896. *March Hares.* New York: D. Appleton.

1898. *Gloria Mundi.* London: William Heinemann.

1899. *The Market-Place.* London: William Heinemann.

1968. *Seth's Brother's Wife: A Study of Life in the Greater New York.* 1887. Reprint, Grosse Point: Michigan Scholarly Press.

1981. *The Market-Place.* Vol. 2 of *The Harold Frederic Edition.* Edited by Charlyne Dodge. Fort Worth: Texas Christian University Press.

1986. *The Damnation of Theron Ware or Illumination.* New York: Penguin Books.

Shorter Fiction

1876a. "Barbette's Christmas." *Utica Daily Observer,* 23 Dec., 2.

1876b. "A Fortunate Coincidence." [by "Edgar"] *Utica Daily Observer,* 18 Nov., 2.

1877. "The Blakelys of Poplar Place: A Legend of the Mohawk." *Utica Daily Observer,* 30 June, 2.

1882. "The Jew's Christmas." *Albany Evening Journal*, 23 Dec., 4.

1886. "Brother Angelan." *Harper's New Monthly Magazine* 73 (Sept.), 517–28.

1888. "The Editor and the School Ma'am." *New York Times*, 9 Sept., 14.

1890. "The Martyrdom of Maev." *New York Ledger* 46 (22 Mar.), 1–3, and (29 Mar.), 3.

1891. "The Song of the Swamp-Robin." *Independent* 43 (12 Mar.), 394–432, and (19 Mar.), 430–31.

1893. "Cordelia and the Moon." In *Liber Scriptorum, The First Book of the Authors Club*, 241–52. New York: The Authors Club.

1894. *Marsena and Other Stories of the War-time.* New York: Charles Scribner's Sons. ["Marsena," "The War Widow", "The Eve of the Fourth," "My Aunt Susan"]

1895a. "In the Shadow of Gabriel." *Black and White* (Christmas), 21–26.

1895b. "The Truce of the Bishop." *Yellow Book* 7 (Oct.), 84–111.

1896a. "Brother Sebastian's Friendship." 1879. Reprint, in *Stories by American Authors*. New York: Charles Scribner's Sons, 6: 145–64.

1896b. "The Connoisseur." *Saturday Review* 82 (Christmas), 18–21.

1896c. "The Wooing of Teige." *Pall Mall Magazine* 10 (Nov.), 418–26.

1901. "The Path of Murtogh." 1895. In *Tales of Our Coast*. New York: International Association of Newspapers and Authors, 81–130.

1966. *Harold Frederic's Stories of New York State.* Edited by Thomas F. O'Donnell. Syracuse, N. Y.: Syracuse Univ. Press.

1969. *The Deserter and Other Stories: A Book of Two Wars.* 1898. Reprint, New York: AMS Press. ["The Deserter," "A Day in the Wilderness," "How Dickon Came by His Name," "The War Avon into Severn Flows"]

1971. *In The Sixties.* 1897. Reprint, New York: AMS Press. ["The Copperhead," "Marsena," "The War Widow," "The Eve of the Fourth," "My Aunt Susan"]

New York Times *Writing*

1884a. "Cholera's Grasp Relaxed." *New York Times*, 6 Aug., 1.

1884b. "Down Among the Dead Men." *New York Times*, 27 July, 1.

1884c. "Figures of the Cholera." *New York Times*, 2 Nov., 4.

1884d. "Stricken French Towns," *New York Times*, 30 July, 1.

1884e. "The Trip to Marseilles." *New York Times*, 10 Aug., 2.

1890. "An Empire's Young Chief." *New York Times*, 22 June-24 Aug. Collected and published as *The Young Emperor William II of Germany: A Study in Character and Development on a Throne.* New York: G. P. Putnam's Sons; London: T. Fisher Unwin, 1892.

1891. "An Indictment of Russia." *New York Times*, 14 Sep.-21 Dec. Collected and published as *The New Exodus: A Story of Israel in Russia.* New York: G. P. Putnam's Sons; London: William Heinemann, 1892.

1892. "A Return to Barbarism," *New York Times*, 1 May, 1.

1893. "Joy in Methodist Churches." *New York Times*, 30 Oct., 9.

1896a. "The Coast of White Foam." *New York Times*, 1 Nov., 4–5.

1896b. "Stephen Crane's Triumph." *New York Times*, 26 Jan., 22.

1898. "London Expects War." *New York Times*, 3 Apr., 19.

Miscellaneous Writings

1877. "The Mohawk Valley During the Revolution." *Harper's New Monthly Magazine* 55 (July), 171–83.

1882a. "A Biography of Cooper." *Albany Evening Press,* 23 Dec., 2.

1882b. Untitled editorial. *Albany Evening Journal,* 4 Sept., 2.

1883a. "How It Is Worked." *Albany Evening Journal,* 13 Jan., 2.

1883b. "Prefatory Words." In Marc Cook, *Vandyke-Brown Poems.* Utica: Bristol and Smith, v-xiii.

1884a. "An American View of the Nicaraguan Canal." *Pall Mall Budget* 32 (26 Dec.), 13.

1884b. "The Latest American Novel." *Albany Evening Journal,* 19 Jan., 2.

1884c. " 'The New President' by 'One of his Countrymen in London.' " *Pall Mall Budget* 32 (14 Nov.), 12–14.

1885a. " 'American Free Traders' by 'An American in London.' " *Pall Mall Budget* 33 (19 Nov.), 11–12.

1885b. " 'England, America and the Dynamiters." *Pall Mall Budget* 33 (13 Mar.), 13–14.

1885c. "English and American Electioneering' by 'An American in London.' " *Pall Mall Budget* 33 (12 Nov.), 9.

1885d. "From a Saunterer in the Labyrinth." *Pall Mall Gazette* 33 (24 July), 22.

1885e. "A Genuine Cholera Year." *Pall Mall Budget* (31 July), 9–10.

1885f. " 'Musings on the Question of the Hour' by 'A Saunterer in the Labyrinth.' " *Pall Mall Gazette* 33 (13 Aug.), 11–12.

1885g. " 'The New American Administration' by 'An American in London.' " *Pall Mall Budget* 33 (13 Mar.), 13–14.

1885h. " 'The War Upon Dr. Walsh' by 'An American in London.' " *Pall Mall Budget* 33 (19 June), 22.

1885i. " 'What do Irishmen Want?' by 'An American in London.' " *Pall Mall Budget* 33 (17 Dec.), 9.

1889. "A Day with a Managing Editor." *Youth's Companion,* 13 June, 330.

1891. "A Painter of Beautiful Dreams." *Scribner's Magazine* 10 (Dec.), 712–22.

1892. *The New Exodus: A Study of Israel in Russia.* London: William Heinemann.

1893a. " 'The Ireland of Today' by 'X.' " *Fortnightly Review* 60 (Nov.), 686–706.

1893b. " 'The Rhetoricians of Ireland' by 'X.' " *Fortnightly Review* 60 (1 Dec.), 713–27.

1894a. " 'The Ireland of To-morrow' by 'X.' " *Fortnightly Review* 61 (Jan.), 1–18.

1894b. " 'Irish Railways: To The Editor of the Fortnightly Review' by 'The Writer of the First "X" Article.' " *Fortnightly Review* (Jan.), 138–140.

1895. "An Opera Bouffe Kinglet." *Saturday Review* (London), 3 Aug., 137.

1896a. *Mrs. Albert Grundy: Observations in Philistia.* London: John Lane; New York: Merriam Co.

1896b. "The War of 1812." *English Illustrated Magazine* 14 (Mar.), 573–82.

1897a. "How to Write a Short Story." *Bookman* (New York) 5 (Mar.), 42–46. By Frederic; Robert Barr, Arthur Morrison, and Jane Barlow.

1897b. "In the Sixties." ["Preface to a Uniform Edition"]. *Literary News* 18 (May), 130.

1898. "On Historical Novels Past and Present." *Bookman* (New York) 8 (Dec.), 330–33.

1968. "The Opium-Eater." *Frederic Herald* 1, no. 3, (Jan.): 2.

1977. *The Correspondence of Harold Frederic.* Vol. 1 of *The Harold Frederic Edition.* Edited by George E. Fortenberry, Stanton Garner, and Robert H. Woodward. Fort Worth: Texas Christian Univ. Press.

Secondary Sources

Adams, Henry. 1959. *A Henry Adams Reader.* Edited by Elizabeth Stevenson. Garden City, N.Y.: Doubleday.

———. 1973. *The Education of Henry Adams.* Edited by Ernest Samuels. Boston: Houghton Mifflin Co.; Cambridge, Mass.: Riverside Press.

"Aid for Jewish Refugees." 1891. *New York Times,* 21 Dec., 9.

Albertine, Susan. 1990. "Breaking the Silent Partnership: Businesswomen in Popular Fiction." *American Literature* 62 (June): 238–61.

Ammons, Elizabeth, and Annette White-Parks, eds. 1994. *Tricksterism in Turn-of-the-Century American Literature: A Multicultural Perspective.* Hanover, N. H.: Univ. Press of New England.

Andrews, Ernest. 1982. "Mind Over Matter: Manslaughter in Kenley." *Local History Records* 21: 32–36.

Anesko, Michael. 1986. *"Friction with the Market": Henry James and the Profession of Authorship.* Oxford: Oxford Univ. Press.

Atherton, Gertrude. 1910. "The American Novel in England." *Bookman* (New York) 30 (Feb.), 633–40.

———. 1932. *Adventures of a Novelist.* New York: Liveright.

Auerbach, Nina. 1989. *Ellen Terry: Player in Her Time.* New York: W. W. Norton.

"Authors Have a Matinee: James Russell Lowell Acts as Chairman." 1887. *New York Times,* 29 Nov., 5.

Avery, Gillian. 1994. *Behold the Child: American Children and Their Books, 1621–1922.* London: The Bodley Head.

Bacon, Francis. 1911. *The Essayes or Counsels and Morals of Francis Bacon Lord Verulam.* 1906, Reprint, New York: E. P. Dutton.

Beckson, Karl. 1978. *Henry Harland: His Life and Work.* London: The Eighteen Nineties Society.

———. 1992. *London in the 1890s: A Cultural History.* New York and London. W. W. Norton.

Beer, Thomas. 1924. *Stephen Crane: A Study in American Letters.* New York: Alfred A. Knopf.

Belloc, H. 1953. *Cautionary Verses.* Melbourne: Penguin Books.

Benfey, Christopher. 1993. *The Double Life of Stephen Crane.* London: André Deutsch.

Bennett, Arnold. 1968. *Letters of Arnold Bennett.* 3 vols. Edited by James Hepburn. Oxford: Oxford Univ. Press.

Berger, Meyer. 1951. *The Story of the New York Times 1851–1951.* New York: Simon and Schuster.

Bergmann, Frank, ed. 1985. *Upstate Literature: Essays in Memory of Thomas F. O'Donnell.* A New York State Study. Syracuse, N.Y.: Syracuse Univ. Press.

Berryman, John. 1950. *Stephen Crane*. The American Men of Letters Series. New York: William Sloane Associates.

Bierce, Ambrose. 1972. *The Collected Writings of Ambrose Bierce*. 1946. Reprint, Secaucus, N. J.: Citadel Press.

Bigsby, C. W. E. 1968. "The 'Christian Science Case': an Account of the Death of Harold Frederic and the Subsequent Inquest and Court Proceedings." *American Literary Realism 1870–1910* 1 (Spring): 77–83.

Birkin, Andrew. 1979. *J. M. Barrie and the Lost Boys*. London: Constable.

Blackall, Jean Frantz. 1971. "Perspectives on Harold Frederic's *Market-Place*." *PMLA* 86 (May), 388–405.

Blondheim, Menahem. 1994. *News Over the Wires: The Telegraph and the Flow of Public Information in America, 1844–1897*. Camridge, Mass.: Harvard Univ. Press.

Bok, Edward. 1921. *An Autobiography*. London: Thornton Butterworth.

Bond, F. Fraser. 1931. *Mr. Miller of the "Times": The Story of an Editor*. New York: Scribner's.

Brake, Laurel. 1994. *Subjugated Knowledges: Journalism, Gender and Literature in the Nineteenth Century*. Basingstoke, Eng.: Macmillan.

Brand, Dana. 1991. *The Spectator and the City in Nineteenth-Century American Literature*. Cambridge: Cambridge Univ. Press.

Briggs, Austin Jr. 1969. *The Novels of Harold Frederic*. Ithaca: Cornell Univ. Press.

Brooks, Van Wyck. 1955. *The Confident Years: 1885–1915*. New York: E. P. Dutton; London: J. M. Dent and Sons.

Brown, Lucy. 1985. *Victorian News and Newspapers*. Oxford: Clarendon Press.

Burgess, Anthony. 1979. *Ernest Hemingway and His World*. London: Thames and Hudson.

Burgess, Gelett. 1898. "Some Mad Americans in London." *Illustrated London News*, 17 Sept., 399.

Burlingame, Roger. 1946. *Of Making Many Books: A Hundred Years of Reading Writing and Publishing*. New York: Charles Scribner's Sons.

"By an Old Friend: Some Recollections of Harold Frederic." 1898. *Saturday Review* (London), 29 Oct., 571–72.

Cabanne, Pierre. 1975. *Van Gogh*. London: Book Club Associates.

"Cabling a Whole Poem." 1887. *New York Evening Sun*, 18 Nov., 1.

Cady, Edwin H. 1958. *The Realist at War: The Mature Years 1885–1920 of William Dean Howells*. Syracuse, N. Y.: Syracuse Univ. Press.

Cather, Willa. 1970. *The World and the Parish: Willa Cather's Articles and Reviews 1893–1902*. 2 vols. Edited by William M. Curtin. Lincoln: Univ. of Nebraska Press.

———. 1984. *My Ántonia*. 1983. Reprint, London: Virago Press.

"C.K.S." [Clement Shorter]. 1898. " 'The Sketch' Regrets the Loss to London of Mr. Harold Frederic, the Well-Known Author and Novelist." *Sketch*, 26 Oct., 4.

"Charge Against Christian Scientists, The." 1898. *Times* (London), 22 Nov., 9; 29 Nov., 11; 6 Dec., 77.

"Cholera News Bad Again." 1884. *New York Times*, 3 Aug., 1.

"Christian Science Inquiry." 1898. *New York Times*, 16 Nov., 1.

"Christian Scientists." 1898. *Croydon Advertiser and Surrey County Reporter*, 17 Dec., 3.

"Christian Scientists, The." 1898. *New York Times*, 13 Nov., 12.

"Christian Scientists Free." 1898. *New York Times*, 6 Dec., 4.

"Chronicle and Comment." 1896. *Bookman* (New York) 3 (July): 383–84.

"Chronicle and Comment." 1898. *Bookman* (New York) 8 (Dec.): 303.

Coale, Samuel. 1976. "Frederic and Hawthorne: The Romantic Roots of Naturalism." *American Literature* 48: 29–45.

"Concerning Pulitzer." 1887. *New York Evening Sun*, 17 Nov., 4.

Conrad, Joseph. 1986. *The Collected Letters of Joseph Conrad: 1898–1902*. Vol. 2. Edited by Frederick R. Karl and Laurence Davies. Cambridge: Cambridge Univ. Press.

Conrad, Peter. 1980. *Imagining America*. London: Routledge and Kegan Paul.

"Copyright and the People." 1884. *New York Times*, 17 Nov., 4.

Cooper, James Fenimore. 1960. *The Spy: A Tale of Neutral Ground*. New York: Harper.

Cowen, Anne, and Roger Cowen. 1986. *Victorian Jews Through British Eyes*. Oxford: Oxford Univ. Press.

Crackenthorpe, David. 1977. *Hubert Crackenthorpe and English Realism in the 1890s*. Columbia: Univ. of Missouri Press.

Crane, Stephen. 1898. "Harold Frederic." *Chap-Book* 8 (15 Mar.), 358–59.

———. 1968. *The Letters of Stephen Crane*. Edited by R. W. Stallman and Lillian Gilkes, with an introduction by R. W. Stallman. 1960. Reprint, New York: George Braziller.

———. 1988. *The Correspondence of Stephen Crane*. 2 vols. Edited by Stanley Wertheim and Paul Sorrentino. New York: Columbia Univ. Press.

Crawford, H. Marion. 1885. *An American Politician*. Boston: Houghton Mifflin; New York: 11 East Seventeenth Street; Cambridge: Riverside Press.

Davies, Horton. 1959. *A Mirror of the Ministry in Modern Novels*. Oxford: Oxford Univ. Press.

Davis, Elmer. 1921. *History of the New York Times: 1851–1921*. New York: New York Times.

Davis, Tracy C. 1992. "Indecency and Vigilance in the Music Halls." In *British Theatre in the 1890s: Essays on Drama and the Stage*, edited by Richard Foulkes, 111–31. Cambridge: Cambridge Univ. Press.

"Death of Frederic." 1898. *New York Times*, 23 Oct..

"Death of Harold Frederic, The." 1898a. *Daily Graphic* (London), 6 Dec., 9.

"Death of Harold Frederic." 1898b. *New York Times*, 22 Oct., 6.

"Death of Harold Frederic." 1898c. *Utica Daily Press*, 20 Oct., 3.

"Death of Mr. H. Frederic, The." 1898. *Times* (London), 10 Nov., 10.

"Death of Mr. Harold Frederic, The." 1898a. *Croydon Chronicle Caterham Oxted and Godstone News and East Surrey Advertiser*, 29 Oct., 6.

"Death of Mr. Harold Frederic, The." 1898b. *Croydon Guardian and Surrey County Gazette*, 5 Nov., 7; 12 Nov., 3.

"Death of Mr. Harold Frederic, The." 1898c. *Daily Graphic* (London), 27 Oct., 9.

"Death of Mr. Harold Frederic, The." 1898d. *Times* (London), 22 Oct., 13; 27 Oct., 4; 3 Nov., 10.

de Grazia, Margreta. 1994. "Sanctioning Voice: Quotation Marks, the Abolition of Torture, and the Fifth Amendment." In *The Construction of Authorship: Textual Appropriation in Law and Literature*, edited by Martha Woodmansee and Peter Jaszi, 281–302. Durham, N.C.: Duke Univ. Press.

Dickens, Charles. 1985. *American Notes.* London: Granville Publishing.

Donaldson, Scott. 1975. "The Seduction of Theron Ware." *Nineteenth Century Fiction* 29 (Mar.): 441–52.

Dreiser, Theodore. 1946. *The Financier.* Cleveland: World Publishing.

———. 1959. *The Letters of Theodore Dreiser.* 3 vols. Edited by Robert H. Elias. Philadelphia: Univ. of Pennsylvania Press.

———. 1983. *American Diaries: 1902–1926.* Edited by Thomas Riggio et al. Reprint with corrections, Philadelphia: Univ. of Pennsylvania Press.

Du Maurier, George. 1994. *Trilby.* London: Penguin Books, 1994.

Eby, Clare Virginia. 1988. "Representative Men: Businessmen in American Fiction 1875–1914." Ph.D., diss., Univ. of Michigan,

Eichelberger, Clayton L. 1968. "Philanthropy In Frederic's *The Market-Place.*" *American Quarterly* 20: 111–16.

Eisenstadt, Norma L. 1968. "Harold Frederic Stages a Comeback: Ex-Utica Author 'Reclaimed.' " *Utica Observer-Dispatch,* 7 Jan., 6B.

Elliot, Henry R. 1893. "After Business Hours." *Liber Scriptorum, The First Book of the Authors Club,* 219–25. New York: The Authors Club.

Ellmann, Richard. 1987. *Oscar Wilde.* London: Hamish Hamilton.

———, ed. 1969. *The Artist as Critic: Critical Writings of Oscar Wilde.* Chicago: Univ. of Chicago Press.

Emerson, Ralph Waldo. 1950. *The Selected Writings of R. W. Emerson.* 1940. Edited by Brooks Atkinson. The Modern Library. Reprint, New York: Random House.

Erckmann-Chatrian [Erckmann, Émile, and Louis-Alexandre Chatrian]. 1909. *The History of a Conscript of 1813 and Waterloo.* [First published as *L'Histoire d'un Conscrit de 1813* and *Waterloo.*] Translated by Russell Gilman. London: J. M. Dent; New York: E. P. Dutton.

"F." 1898. "Some Recollections of Harold Frederic." *Saturday Review* (London) 86 (29 Oct.), 571–72.

"Faith Cure Murders." 1898. *New York Times,* 11 Nov., 6.

"The Faith Healers at Kenley." 1898. *Croydon Chronicle Caterham Oxted and Godstone News and East Surrey Advertiser,* 12 Nov., 6.

"Faith Healing and Fee Grabbing." 1898. *New York Times,* 20 Nov., 21.

"Feat Without Parallel, A" 1887. *New York Times,* 21 Nov., 4.

Felheim, Marvin. 1956. *The Theater of Augustin Daly: An Account of the Late Nineteenth Century American Stage.* Cambridge, Mass.: Harvard Univ. Press.

"Filthy Imported Rags." *New York Times,* 2 Aug., 4.

Feltes, N. N. 1993. *Literary Capital and the Late Victorian Novel.* London: Univ. of Wisconsin Press.

Fitzgerald, F. Scott. 1960. *This Side of Paradise.* Vol. 3 of *The Bodley Head Scott Fitzgerald.* London: The Bodley Head.

———. 1974. *The Great Gatsby.* Middlesex, Eng.: Penguin Books.

Fitzpatrick, Ellen P., ed. 1994. *Muckraking: Three Landmark Articles.* The Bedford Series in History and Culture. Boston: Bedford Books.

"Five Hours with Christian Scientists at Kenley." 1896. *Croydon Chronicle Caterham Oxted and Godstone News and East Surrey Advertiser,* 5 Nov., 6.

Fletcher, Ian, assoc. ed. 1979. *Decadence and the 1890s.* Stratford-upon-Avon Studies 17. London: Edward Arnold.

Foulkes, Richard, ed. 1992. *British Theatre in the 1890s: Essays on Drama and the Stage.* Cambridge: Cambridge Univ. Press.

"France and England." 1898. *New York Times,* 6 Nov., 19.

"Frederic as a Bit Player in *The Little Minister.*" 1969. *Frederic Herald* 3, no. 2 (Sept.): 3.

Fryer, Judith. 1976. *The Faces of Eve: Women in the Nineteenth Century American Novel.* Oxford: Oxford Univ. Press.

Fryer, Peter. 1963. *Mrs. Grundy: Studies in English Prudery.* London: Dobson Books.

Fyfe, Hamilton. 1934. *T. P. O'Connor.* London: George Allen and Unwin.

Garland, Hamlin. 1960. *Crumbling Idols: Twelve Essays on Art Dealing Chiefly with Literature Painting and the Drama.* Edited by Jane Johnson. Cambridge, Mass.: Belknap Press of Harvard Univ. Press.

——. 1962. *Main-Travelled Roads.* New York: Signet.

Garner, Stanton. 1967. "Some Notes on Harold Frederic in Ireland." *American Literature* 39 (Mar.): 60–74.

——. 1968. "More Notes on Harold Frederic in Ireland." *American Literature* 39 (Jan.): 560–62.

——. 1969. *Harold Frederic.* Pamphlets on American Writers, No. 83. Minneapolis: Univ. of Minnesota Press.

——. 1972. "Harold Frederic." In *American Writers.* Vol. 2 of *A Collection of Literary Biographies,* edited by Leonard Unger, 126–49. 1959. Reprint, New York: Charles Scribner's Sons.

——. 1973. "Harold Frederic and Swinburne's 'Locrine': A Matter of Clubs, Copyrights, and Character." *American Literature* 45 (May): 285–92.

Garner, Stanton, and Thomas F. O'Donnell, eds. 1969. *The Merrill Checklist of Harold Frederic.* Charles E. Merrill Checklists, edited by Matthew J. Bruccoli and Joseph Katz. Columbus, Ohio: Charles E. Merrill.

Genthe, Charles V. 1964. *"The Damnation of Theron Ware* and *Elmer Gantry." Research Studies* (Washington State) 33: 334–43.

Gilkes, Lillian. 1962. *Cora Crane: A Biography of Mrs. Stephen Crane.* London: Neville Spearman.

Gilman, Charlotte Perkins. 1994. *The Diaries of Charlotte Perkins Gilman.* 2 vols. Edited by Denise D. Knight. Charlottesville: Univ. Press of Virginia.

Gilman, Sander. 1991. *The Jew's Body.* New York: Routledge.

Gilmore, Michael T. 1985. *American Romanticism and the Marketplace.* Chicago: Univ. of Chicago Press.

Gissing, George, and H. G. Wells. 1961. *George Gissing and H. G. Wells: Their Friendship and Correspondence.* Edited by Royal A. Gettman. London: Rupert Hart-Davis.

——. 1978. *London and the Life of Literature in Late Victorian England: The Diary of George Gissing Novelist.* Edited by Pierre Coustillas. Hassocks: Harvester Press.

Godden, Richard. 1990. *Fictions of Capital: The American Novel From James to Mailer.* Cambridge: Cambridge Univ. Press.

Gohdes, Clarence. 1951. "The Later Nineteenth Century." In *The Literature of the American People: A Historical and Critical Survey,* edited by A. H. Quinn, 569–809. New York: Appleton-Century-Crofts.

Greenslade, William. 1994. *Degeneration, Culture and the Novel 1880–1940.* Cambridge: Cambridge Univ. Press.

Guiney, Louise Imogen. 1899. "Harold Frederic: A Half-Length Sketch From the Life." *Book-Buyer* (New York) 17 (Jan.): 600–604.

Haines, Paul. 1945. "Harold Frederic." Ph.D. diss., New York Univ.

Halberstam, Judith. 1993. "Technologies of Monstrosity: Bram Stoker's *Dracula.*" *Victorian Studies* 36, no. 3 (Spring): 333–52.

Halttunen, Karen. 1982. *Confidence Men and Painted Women: A Study of Middle-Class Culture in America 1830–1870.* New Haven: Yale Univ. Press.

[Harland, Henry] "The Yellow Dwarf." 1896. "Dogs, Cats, Books, and the Average Man." *Yellow Book* 10 (July), 11–23.

"Harold Frederic." 1898. *Illustrated London News*, Oct., 625.

"Harold Frederic Dead." 1898. *New York Times*, 20 Oct., 7.

"Harold Frederic to be Cremated." 1898. *Times* (London), 21 Oct., 7.

Harris, Frank. 1898a. "A Contemptible Verdict." *Saturday Review*, 12 Nov., 629–30.

———. 1898b. "Harold Frederic: Ad Memoriam." *Saturday Review*, 22 Oct., 526–28.

———. 1931. *Frank Harris on Bernard Shaw: An Unauthorised Biography Based on Firsthand Information.* London: Victor Gollancz.

———. 1958. *My Life and Adventures.* [First published as *My Life and Loves*, 1923–27]. London: Elek Books.

Hart-Davis, Rupert. 1985. *Hugh Walpole: A Biography.* London: Hamish Hamilton.

Hawthorne, Nathaniel. 1962. *The Scarlet Letter.* Vol. 3 of *The Centenary Edition of the Works of Nathaniel Hawthorne,* edited by William Charvat et al. Columbus: Ohio State Univ. Press.

———. 1965. *The House of the Seven Gables.* Vol. 2 of *The Centenary Edition of the Works of Nathaniel Hawthorne,* edited by William Charvat et al. Columbus: Ohio State Univ. Press.

———. 1968. *The Marble Faun: or The Romance of Monte Beni.* Vol. 4 of *The Centenary Edition of the Works of Nathaniel Hawthorne,* edited by William Charvat et al. Columbus: Ohio State Univ. Press.

Healy, T. 1928. *Letters and Leaders of My Day.* 2 vols. London: Thornton Butterworth.

"Heroism in Journalism." 1884. *New York Times*, 30 July, 4.

Herron, Ima Honaker. 1971. *The Small Town in American Literature.* New York: Haskell House.

Herzberg, Max J., ed. 1963. *A Reader's Encyclopedia of American Literature.* London: Methuen.

Hind, C. Lewis. 1922. *More Authors and I.* London: John Lane.

Hirsch, J. C. 1984. "The Frederic Papers, the McGlynn Affair, and The *Damnation of Theron Ware.*" *American Literary Realism 1870–1910* 17 (Spring): 19.

Holloway, Jean. 1960. *Hamlin Garland: A Biography.* Austin: Univ. of Texas Press.

Howells, W. D. 1968. *Literary Friends and Acquaintance: A Personal Retrospect of American Authorship.* Edited by David F. Hiatt and Edwin H. Cady. Vol. 32 of *A Selected Edition of the Works of W. D. Howells.* Bloomington: Indiana Univ. Press.

———. 1971. *The Rise of Silas Lapham.* Introduction and notes by Walter J. Meserve, with text established by David J. Nordloh. Vol. 22 of *A Selected Edition of the Works of W. D. Howells.* Bloomington: Indiana Univ. Press.

———. 1973. *W. D. Howells as Critic.* Edited by Edwin H. Cady. The Routledge Critics Series. London: Routledge and Kegan Paul.

242 I WORKS CITED

————. 1975. *Years of My Youth and Three Essays.* Introduction and notes by David H. Nordloh. Vol. 29 of *A Selected Edition of the Works of W. D. Howells.* Bloomington: Indiana Univ. Press.

————. 1976. *A Hazard of New Fortunes.* Introduction by Carter Everett and notes to the text by David J. Nordloh et al. Vol. 16 of *A Selected Edition of W. D Howells.* Bloomington: Indiana Univ. Press.

————. 1977. *A Modern Instance.* Introduction and notes by George N. Bennett, with text established by David J. Nordloh and David KIeinman. Vol. 10 of *A Selected Edition of W. D. Howells.* Bloomington: Indiana Univ. Press.

————. 1978. *The Minister's Charge or The Apprenticeship of Lemuel Barker.* Introduction and notes by Howard M. Munford, with text established by David H. Nordloh and David Kleinman. Vol. 14 of *A Selected Edition of the Works of W. D. Howells.* Bloomington: Indiana Univ. Press.

"How the Popular Harold Frederic Works." 1896. *Literary Digest* 13 (25 July): 397.

Hyde, H. Montgomery. 1962. *The Trials of Oscar Wilde.* New York: Dover.

"Inquest on Mr. H. Frederic, The." 1898. *Times* (London), 9 Nov., 2.

"Inquest on Mr. Harold Frederic, The." 1898. *Croydon Advertiser and Surrey County Reporter,* 12 Nov., 2.

Irving, Washington. 1983. *History Tales and Sketches: Letters of Jonathan Oldstyle Gent. Salmagundi A History of New York The Sketch Book of Geoffrey Crayon Gent.* Library of America. Cambridge: Press Syndicate of Univ. of Cambridge.

Jacobson, Marcia. 1983. *Henry James and the Mass Market.* Tuscaloosa: Univ. of Alabama Press.

James, Henry. 1981. *Selected Literary Criticism.* Edited by Morris Shapira. Cambridge: Cambridge Univ. Press.

————. 1983. *Novels 1871–1880.* Selected with notes by William T. Stafford. Library of America. Cambridge: Press Syndicate of the Univ. of Cambridge.

————. 1984. *The Tales of Henry James.* 3 vols. Edited by Maqbool Aziz. Oxford: Clarendon Press.

————. 1987. *The Complete Notebooks of Henry James.* Edited by Leon Edel and Lyall H. Powers. Oxford: Oxford Univ. Press.

————. 1988. *The Golden Bowl.* 1985. Reprint, London: Penguin Books.

James, Henry, and Edith Wharton. 1900. *Henry James and Edith Wharton Letters: 1900–1915.* Edited by Lyall H. Powers. New York: Charles Scribner's Sons.

Johnson, Allen, and Dumas Malone, eds. 1960. *Dictionary of American Biography.* Vol. 4. 1931. Reprint, with revisions, New York: Charles Scribner's Sons.

Johnson, George W. 1962. "Harold Frederic's Young Goodman Ware: The Ambiguities of a Realistic Romance." *Modern Fiction Studies* 8 (Winter): 361–74.

Judd, Alan. 1990. *Ford Madox Ford.* London: Collins.

Kantor, J. R. K. 1967. "Autobiography and Journalism: Sources for Harold Frederic's Fiction." *Serif* 4 (Dec.): 19–27.

Kazin, Alfred. 1943. *On Native Grounds: An Interpretation of Modern American Prose Literature.* London: Jonathan Cape.

Koppelman, Susan, ed. 1994. *Two Friends: And Other Nineteenth-Century Lesbian Stories by American Women Writers.* Harmondsworth: Meridian Books.

"Late Mr. Harold Frederic, The." 1898. *Croydon Guardian and Surrey County-Gazette,* 19 Nov., 3; 3 Dec., 3; 17 Dec., 3.

"Late Mr. Harold Frederic, The." 1898. *Times* (London), 17 Nov., 11.

Lee, Brian. 1987. *American Fiction 1865–1940*. London: Longman.

Lewis, Sinclair. 1927. *Elmer Gantry*. London: Jonathan Cape.

———. 1947. *Babbitt*. London: Jonathan Cape.

———. 1950. *Main Street*. New York: Harcourt, Brace and World.

Lindberg, Gary. 1982. *The Confidence Man in American Literature*. Oxford: Oxford Univ. Press.

"Locrine." 1887. *New York Evening Sun*, 17 Nov., 2–3.

Luedtke, Luther S. 1975. "Harold Frederic's Satanic Soulsby: Interpretation and Sources." *Nineteenth Century Fiction* 30: 82–104.

Lyon, Kate. 1898. "Lorraine's Last Voyage." *New York Ledger*, 28 Sept., 9–11.

Lyons, F. S. L. 1977. *Charles Stewart Parnell*. London: Collins.

McCarthy, Justin. 1899. *Reminiscences*. 2 vols. London: Chatto and Windus.

McCarthy, Mary. 1980. *Ideas and the Novel*. London: Weidenfeld and Nicolson.

McGann, Jerome. 1993. *Black Riders: The Visible Language of Modernism*. Princeton: Princeton Univ. Press.

McWilliams, Carey. 1933. "Harold Frederic: A Country Boy of Genius." *Univ. of California Chronicle* 35: 21–34.

Melville, Herman. 1992. *Moby-Dick*. Harmondsworth, Eng.: Penguin Books.

Miller, Jane Eldridge. 1994. *Rebel Women: Feminism, Modernism and the Edwardian Novel*. London: Virago.

Milne, Gordon. 1980. *Stephen Crane at Brede: An Anglo-American Literary Circle of the 1890's*. Washington, D. C.: Univ. Press of America.

Mitchell, Edward P. 1924. *Memoirs of an Editor*. New York: Scribner's.

Morey, Ann-Janine. 1992. *Religion and Sexuality in American Literature*. Cambridge Studies in American Literature and Culture. Cambridge: Cambridge Univ. Press.

Mott, Frank Luther. 1957. *A History of American Magazines: 1885–1905*. Vol. 4. Cambridge, Mass.: Belknap Press of Harvard Univ. Press.

———. 1962. *American Journalism: A History: 1690–1960*. 1941. Third ed. New York: Macmillan.

"Mr. Harold Frederic's Death." 1898. *Croydon Advertiser and Surrey County Reporter*, 22 Oct., 8; 29 Oct., 3; Nov., 3; 26 Nov., 2;3 Dec., 2; 10 Dec., 2.

Myers, Robert M. 1995. *Reluctant Expatriate: The Life of Harold Frederic*. Contributions to the Study of World Literature, 59. Westport, Conn.: Greenwood Press.

Naman, Anne Aresty. 1980. *The Jew in the Victorian Novel: Some Relationships Between Prejudice and Art*. New York: A.M.S. Press.

Nevins, Allan. 1932. *Grover Cleveland: A Study in Courage*. New York: Dodd, Mead.

"Newspaper Work Abroad." 1898. *New York Times*, 23 Jan., 9.

Norman, Henry. 1898. "France and England." *New York Times*, 6 Nov., 19.

Norris, Frank. 1964. *The Literary Criticism of Frank Norris*. Edited by Donald Pizer. Austin: Univ. of Texas Press.

———. 1986. *The Octopus: A Story of California*. New York: Penguin Books.

"Not Alarmed by the Cholera." 1884. *New York Times*, 15 Nov., 8.

Nowell-Smith, Simon. 1968. *International Copyright Law and the Publisher in the Reign of Queen Victoria*. Oxford: Clarendon Press.

"Obituary." 1898. *Times* (London), 22 Oct., 7.

O'Connor, T. P. 1886. *The Parnell Movement with a Sketch of Irish Parties from 1843*. London: Kegan Paul, Trench.

O'Connor, Mrs. T. P. 1910. [Elizabeth Paschal]. *I Myself*. London: Methuen.

O'Donnell, Thomas F. 1967. "Harold Frederic (1856–1898)." *American Literary Realism 1870–1910* 1 (Fall): 39–44.

———. 1968. "The Baxter Marginalia." *Frederic Herald* 1, no. 3 (Jan.): 5.

———. comp. 1969. *The Merill Checklist of Harold Frederic.* Charles E. Merrill Checklists, edited by Matthew J. Bruccoli and Joseph Katz. Columbus, Ohio: Charles E. Merrill.

O'Donnell, Thomas F., and Hoyt C. Franchere. 1961. *Harold Frederic.* New York: Twayne.

O'Donnell, Thomas F., Stanton Garner, and Robert H. Woodward, eds. 1975. *A Bibliography of Writings by and About Harold Frederic.* Boston: G. K. Hall.

Oehlschlaeger, Fritz. 1986. "Passion, Authority and Faith in The *Damnation of Theron Ware.*" *American Literature* 58 (May): 238–55.

Omar Khayyam Club Dinner, The." 1896. *Critic* 753 (25 July): 60.

"Origin of the Epidemic." 1884. *New York Times,* 1 Aug, 3.

"Our Marseilles Dispatch." 1884. *New York Times,* 29 July, 4.

Parrington, Vernon Louis. 1930. *Main Currents in American Thought: An Interpretation of American Literature from the Beginnings to 1920.* Vol. 3. New York: Harcourt, Brace.

Pennell, E. R., and J. Pennell. 1911. *The Life of James McNeill Whistler.* 1908. Reprint (with revisions), London: William Heinemann; Philadelphia: J. B. Lippincott.

Pizer. Donald, and Earl N. Harbert, eds. 1982. *Dictionary of Literary Biography: American Realists and Naturalists.* Detroit, Mich.: Gale Research.

Plunkett, Horace. 1904. *Ireland in the New Century.* London: John Murray.

Polk, Noel. 1979. *The Literary Manuscripts of Harold Frederic: A Catalogue.* New York: Garland.

Pula, James S., ed. 1994. *Ethnic Utica.* Utica: Ethnic Heritage Studies Center, Utica College.

"Punish the Imposters." 1898. *New York Times,* 25 Nov., 4.

"Quarantine Curiosities." 1884. *New York Times,* 4 Aug., 4.

"Queen's Bench Division: Brenon v. Frederic." 1892. *Times* (London), 6 May, 13.

Raleigh, John Henry. 1958. "The Damnation of Theron Ware." *American Literature* 30 (May): 210–27.

"Report from Marseilles, A." 1884. *New York Times,* 10 Aug., 8.

Richards, Grant. 1932. *Memoirs of a Misspent Youth 1872–1896.* London: William Heinemann.

Richardson, Margaret. 1983. *Architects of the Arts and Crafts Movement.* London: Trefoil Books.

Rideing, W. H. 1909. "Stories of a Famous London Drawing-Room." *McClure's Magazine* 33 (Aug.), 388–98.

Rowell, George. 1981. *Theatre in the Age of Irving.* Oxford: Basil Blackwell.

Sage, Howard. 1975. "Harold Frederic Newsman-Novelist: A Study of the Influence of Frederic's Journalistic Career Upon His Fiction." Ph.D. diss., New York Univ.

Schults, Raymond L. 1972. *Crusader in Babylon: W. T. Stead and the Pall Mall Gazette.* Lincoln: Univ. of Nebraska Press.

Sherard, Robert. 1897. "Harold Frederic." *Idler* (London) 12 (Nov.), 531–40.

Showalter, Elaine. 1991. *Sexual Anarchy: Gender and Culture at the Fin de Siècle.* London: Bloomsbury.

Sinclair, Upton. 1984. *The Jungle*. Reprint, Middlesex, Eng.: Penguin Books.

"Sirdar's Return, The." 1898. *New York Times*, 30 Oct., 19.

Smith, Henry Nash. 1967. "The Morals of Power: Business Enterprise as a Theme in Mid Nineteenth-Century American Fiction." In *Essays on American Literature in Honor of Jay B. Hubbell*, edited by Clarence Gohdes, 90–107. Durham, N. C.: Duke Univ. Press.

Spangler, George. 1989 "The Idea of Degeneration in American Fiction, 1880–1940." *English Studies* 70 (Oct.): 407–35.

Spencer, Benjamin T. 1957. *The Quest for Nationality: An American Literary Campaign*. Syracuse, N. Y.: Syracuse Univ. Press.

Stallman, R. W. 1968. *Stephen Crane: A Biography*. New York: George Braziller.

Stanley, Henry Morton. 1982. *Early Travels and Adventures in America*. London: Univ. of Nebraska Press.

Stein, Allen F. 1972 *"Evasions of an American Adam: Structure and Theme in The Damnation of Theron Ware."* *American Literary Realism 1870–1910*. 5 (Winter): 23–36.

Stevenson, Robert Louis. 1987. *The Strange Case of Dr. Jekyll and Mr. Hyde and Other Stories*. Edited by Jenni Calder. 1979. Reprint, Middlesex, Eng.: Penguin Books.

Stokes, John. 1989. *In the Nineties*. Chicago: Univ. of Chicago Press; Hemel Hempstead: Harvester Wheatsheaf.

Stokes, John, Michael R. Booth, and Susan Bassnett. 1988. *Bernhardt, Terry, Duse: The Actress in Her Time*. Cambridge: Cambridge Univ. Press.

Swanberg, W. A. 1962. *Citizen Hearst: A Biography of William Randolph Hearst*. London: Longman's.

Swinburne, Charles Algernon. 1962. *The Swinburne Letters*. 6 vols. Edited by Cecil Y. Lang. New Haven: Yale Univ. Press; Oxford: Oxford Univ. Press.

"Swinburne's 'Locrine': A Splendid Tragedy from the English Poet" 1887. *New York Times*, 17 Nov., 1.

"Swinburne's New Tragedy." 1887. *New York Times*, 17 Nov., 4.

Thomas, Donald. 1969. *A Long Time Burning: The History of Literary Censorship in England*. London: Routledge and Kegan Paul.

Thurber, James. 1953. *The Thurber Carnival*. Middlesex, Eng.: Penguin Books.

"Times's Cholera Dispatch, The." 1884. *New York Times*, 31 July, 4.

"Topics of the Day." 1898. *Daily Graphic* (London), 9 Nov., 7

"Topics of the Times." 1898. *New York Times*, 29 Oct., 6; 11 Nov., 6; 7 Dec., 6.

Trachtenberg, Alan. 1965. *Brooklyn Bridge: Fact and Symbol*. Oxford: Oxford Univ. Press.

Tsuzuki, Chushiki. 1980. *Edward Carpenter 1844–1929: Prophet of Human Fellowship*. Cambridge: Cambridge Univ. Press.

Twain, Mark. 1892. *The American Claimant*. London: Chatto and Windus.

———. 1903. *Sketches New and Old*. Vol 19 of *The Writings of Mark Twain*. New York: Harper and Bros.

———. 1910. *Mark Twain's Speeches*. New York: Harper & Bros.

———. 1950. *The Adventures of Tom Sawyer and The Adventures of Huckleberry Finn*. New York: Modern Library.

———. 1960. *Autobiography*. Edited by Charles Neider. London: Chatto and Windus.

Twain, Mark, and W. D. Howells. 1960. *Mark Twain-Howells Letters: The Correspondence of Samuel L. Clemens and William Dean Howells, 1872–1910.* 2 vols. Edited by Henry Nash Smith and William M. Gibson. Cambridge, Mass.: Belknap Press of Harvard Univ. Press.

Twain, Mark, and C. D. Warner. 1967. *The Gilded Age.* Edited by Herbert Van Thal. London: Cassell.

"Unchristian Folly." 1898. *Daily Graphic,* 9 Nov., 7

Untitled 1887. *New York Times,* 17 Nov., 4; 21 Nov., 4.

Untitled. 1898. *Times* (London), 15 Dec. 1898, 9 and 14.

Untitled. 1899. *Times* (London), 18 Mar., 12.

Van Der Beets, Richard. 1969 "The Ending of *The Damnation of Theron Ware.*" *American Literature* 11: 358–59.

Veeder, William. 1988. "Collated Fractions of the Manuscript of *Dr. Jekyll and Mr. Hyde.*" In *Dr. Jekyll and Mr. Hyde After One Hundred Years,* edited by William Veeder and Gordon Hirsch, 14–56. Chicago: Univ. of Chicago Press.

Veeder, William. 1988. "The Texts in Question." In *Dr. Jekyll and Mr. Hyde After One Hundred Years,* edited by William Veeder and Gordon Hirsch, 3–13. Chicago: Univ. of Chicago Press.

Veeder, William, and Gordon Hirsch, eds. 1988. *Dr. Jekyll and Mr. Hyde After One Hundred Years.* Chicago: Univ. of Chicago Press.

"Verdict Against the Scientists." 1898. *New York Times,* 9 Nov., 7.

Walcutt, Charles Child. 1939. "Harold Frederic and American Naturalism'. *American Literature.* 11: 11–22.

Walkowitz, Judith. 1994. *City of Dreadful Delight: Narratives of Sexual Danger in Late-Victorian London.* 1992. Reprint, London: Virago Press.

Warren, Arthur. 1898. "Harold Frederic: The Reminiscences of a Colleague." *New York Times,* 23 Oct., 19.

Watson, Aaron. N.d. *A Newspaperman's Memories.* London: Hutchinson.

———. 1907. *The Savage Club: A Medley of History and Reminiscence.* London: T. Fisher Unwin.

Weatherford, Richard M., ed. 1973. *Stephen Crane: The Critical Heritage.* The Critical Heritage Series. London: Routledge and Kegan Paul.

"We Get There Just the Same." 1887. *New York Evening Sun,* 17 Nov., 4.

Weintraub, Stanley. 1979. *The London Yankees: Portraits of American Writers and Artists in England 1894–1914.* New York: Harcourt, Brace, Jovanovich.

Weisberger, Bernard A. 1961. *The American Newspaperman.* Chicago History of American Civilization. Chicago: Univ. of Chicago Press.

Welland, Dennis. 1978. *Mark Twain in England.* London: Chatto and Windus.

Wells, H. G. 1972. *Tono-Bungay.* London: Pan Books.

Welsh, Alexander. 1987. *From Copyright to Copperfield: The Identity of Dickens.* Cambridge, Mass: Harvard Univ. Press.

Wharton, Edith. 1965. *The Custom of the Country.* The Constable Edith Wharton. London: Constable.

———. 1986. *The Reef.* New York: Collier Books.

Whistler [James Abbott McNeill]. 1890. *The Gentle Art of Making Enemies.* London: William Heinemann.

Whitman, Walt. 1938. *Walt Whitman: Complete Poetry and Selected Prose and Letters.* Edited by Emory Holloway. London: The Nonesuch Press.

Wilde, Oscar. 1982. *The Critical Writings of Oscar Wilde.* Edited by Richard Ellman. Chicago: Univ. of Chicago Press.

————. 1992. *The Importance of Being Earnest and Related Writings.* Edited by Joseph Bristow. Routledge English Texts. London: Routledge.

Wilson, Edmund. 1966. Introduction to *Harold Frederic's Stories of New York State,* edited by Thomas F. O'Donnell. Syracuse, N. Y.: Syracuse Univ. Press.

————. 1970. "Two Neglected American Novelists, II: Harold Frederic, the Expanding Upstater." *New Yorker* 46 (6 June), 112–34.

————. 1972. *Upstate: Records and Recollections of Northern New York.* London: Macmillan.

Wolfe, Tom, and E. W. Johnson, eds. 1990. *The New Journalism.* 1975. Reprint, London: Picador.

Woodmansee, Martha, and Peter Jaszi, eds. 1994. *The Construction of Authorship: Textual Appropriation in Law and Literature.* Durham, N.C.: Duke Univ. Press.

Woodward, Robert H. 1960. "Harold Frederic: A Bibliography." In *Studies in Bibliography,* edited by Fredson Bowers, 13: 247–57. Charlottesville, Va.: Bibliographical Society of the Univ. of Virginia.

————. 1967. "Frederic's Grave." *Frederic Herald* 1, no. 2 (Sept.): 5.

————. 1968a. "Frederic's Collection of Reviews: Supplement to the Checklist of Contemporary Reviews of Frederic's Writings." *American Literary Realism 1870– 1910* 1 (Spring): 84–89.

————. 1968b. "Harold Frederic (1856–1898): A Critical Bibliography of Secondary Comment." *American Literary Realism 1870–1910* 1 (Spring): 1–70.

————. 1972. "A Selection of Harold Frederic's Early Literary Criticism." *American Literary Realism 1870–1910* 5 (Winter): 1–22.

————. 1982. "Harold Frederic." *Dictionary of Literary Biography: American Realists and Naturalists,* edited by Donald Pizer and Earl N. Herbert, 12:173–83. Detroit, Mich.: A Bruccoli Clark Book.

Woodward, Robert H., and Stanton B. Garner. 1968. "Frederic's Short Fiction: A Checklist." *American Literary Realism 1870–1910* 1 (Spring): 73–76.

Ziff, Larzer. 1966. *The American 1890's: Life and Times of a Lost Generation.* New York: Viking Press.

Zweig, Paul. 1985. *Walt Whitman: The Making of the Poet.* Harmondsworth, Eng.: Viking.

Index

Page numbers in *italics* indicate illustrations.

Adams, Brooks, 76
Adams, Henry, 38, 76; *Democracy*, 147; *The Education of Henry Adams*, 60–61; reading by, 60–61, 64; schooling of, 31, 61n. 4; Spangler on, 189
Albany Argus (newspaper), 92, 96n. 17
Albany Evening Journal: career with, 37–38, 94–95, 179–80; "The Editor and the School-Ma'am" and, 142; proposed purchase of, 98; resignation from, 88, 96; *Seth's Brother's Wife* and, 93
Albee, Edward, 18
Alcott, Louisa May, 80, 159
Aldrich, Thomas Bailey, 77
Alger, Horatio, 16, 34, 192
"Altered Man, An." *See* Frederic, Harold
Altoona (Pennsylvania) Tribune, 116–17
American Cyclopaedia, 214
"American in London, An." *See* Frederic, Harold
American Publishers' Copyright League, 71
Ames, Fisher, 75
Ammons, Elizabeth, 74n. 18
Anderson, David, 111
Anderson, Mary, 137
Anderson, Sherwood, 145, 148
Anesko, Michael, 69
Apgar, Edgar Kelsey, 37n. 55, 96, 147
Appleton, E. D., 108n. 32
Archer, William, 8
Argus (newspaper), 92, 96n. 17
Arkell, W. J., 96
Arthur, T. S., 83
Asbury, Francis, 29n. 37
Associated Press, 99

Atherton, Gertrude, 18n. 20, 36n. 51, 129n. 3, 183–84
Atlantic Monthly, 76, 141
Atwell, 88
Auden, W. H., 18n. 20
Auerbach, Nina, 12 1n. 43
Authors' Copyright League, 71–72
Azarius, Brother (Patrick Mullany), 35–36

Bacon, Francis, 86n. 1
Bailey, Elijah Prentiss, 92nn. 9, 10
Baldwin, James, 130
Baltimore Herald, 90
Balzac, Honoré de, 83
Barnum, Phineas T., 94n. 13
Barr, Robert, 7, 41, 42, 43
Barrie, J. M., 8, 40n. 56, 138, 164n. 48
Barry, John, 50, 203
Barrymore, Maurice, 149
Baxter, Harold Frederic, 229nn. 1, 2
Baxter, Joseph, 23, 24, 29n. 37
Beardsley, Aubrey, 104
Becke, George Lewis ("Louis"), 124, 193n. 20, 199–200, 201–2
Beecher, Henry Ward, 95
Beer, Thomas, 28n. 35, 40n. 56
Beerbohm, Max, 167
Belloc, Hillaire, 106n. 31
Bennett, Arnold, 168, 185
Bennett, Henry Sanford, 42
Bennett, James Gordon, 102n. 26
Berne Convention (1887), 70, 71
Bernhardt, Sarah, 210n. 9
Berryman, John, 18n. 20, 42n. 60